VOLUME II.

SOCIAL AND POLITICAL THINKERS OF THE 19TH CENTURY

LONDON AGENTS
SIMPKIN MARSHALL LTD

STUDIES IN THE ENGLISH SOCIAL AND POLITICAL THINKERS OF THE NINETEENTH CENTURY

BY THE REV.

ROBERT H. MURRAY, Litt.D.

VOLUME II.

Herbert Spencer to Ramsay MacDonald

CAMBRIDGE
W. HEFFER & SONS LTD.
1929

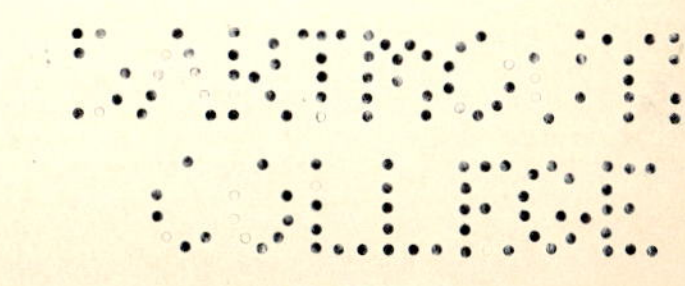

To the Most Rev. Cosmo Gordon Lang,
D.D., D.C.L., LL.D., D.Litt.
Lord Archbishop of Canterbury.

PRINTED IN ENGLAND

Contents

Chapter I.

HERBERT SPENCER AND EVOLUTIONARY POLITICS

THE first chapter of our first volume opens with a consideration of Malthus and the principle of population, and the first chapter of our second volume opens with a consideration of Darwin and the principle of evolution. It is obvious that Darwin presents us with the generalised form of the problem elucidated in part by his predecessor in thought who was in due course to stimulate him in producing his *Origin of Species* in 1859. For this date marks an epoch in political science nearly as much as in biological science. Before Darwin's crowning discovery men were accustomed to the idea of a fixed form of government around which their minds might centre: after this discovery such an idea tended to vanish from political thought. There is scarcely anything common in subject-matter between More's *Utopia,* Bacon's *New Atlantis,* Campanella's *City of the Sun,* Morelly's *Basilade,* Babeuf's *Society of Equals,* and Cabet's *Voyage to Icaria.* What is common is that the authors of these Utopias contemplate a fixed form of society: their views are as static as Darwin's are dynamic. They are all seemingly able to portray the future, and the singular feature is that it closely approximates to the present in which they live. For thinking men Darwinism very definitely ended all Utopias in which the conditions were fixed. The stationary state of Mill except perhaps in a country like China is seen to be a dream as far-fetched as More's.

Darwin used to say that no one could be a good observer unless he was an activer theoriser, a circumstance that explains the failures—as well as the successes—of scientists. "I am a firm believer," so he stated, "that without speculation there is no good and original observation." As the facts accumulated under his never-ceasing industry, Darwin in 1838 read his Malthus, and the *Essay on the Principle of Population* performed not the least of its services to mankind when it enabled Darwin to render the principles Malthus applied to men applicable to plants and animals as well. Without this *Essay* we might not have had the *Origin of Species* in 1859. The caution and the self-criticism of Darwin demanded the clearest evidence, rejecting the most welcome support if it be not flawless. With accuracy of statement went his sincerity of opinion. Yet all can seek truth and show sincerity without necessarily attaining correctness; for that, a power of logical reasoning, though no virtue, is a most necessary talent; it was a faculty that Darwin and his co-discoverer, Wallace, valued highly in themselves. Love of one's subject comes first of course, and no one can doubt the love of Darwin for geology and biology. Only because love must be first do we place truth second. Perhaps truth indeed is one facet of love; for love's self-effacement leads to that objective treatment, freed from sentiment and prejudice, which forms the very foundation of science. First of the virtues, for the man of science as for all men else, is love. Love of his fellow-creatures has led many an investigator through suffering and privation, even to his death. But without a burning love of his subject, be it the life of men, or of animals, or of stones, no man of science has achieved greatness. For the true lover the object of his affection is all, himself nothing: self-suppression is the hall-mark of the great discoverer. There are memorials to Newton and to Darwin in their own Cambridge Colleges, Trinity and Christ's respectively. It is appropriate that a plaque modelled by T. Woolner, made by Josiah Wedgwood and Sons, is on Darwin's rooms in Christ's College. A singularly beautiful statue of Newton by Roubiliac was given to Trinity College by the Master, Dr. Robert Smith, in 1750, and is now in the ante-chapel. Wordsworth, in his *Prelude*, detected in Newton's "silent face," as depicted in this work of art,

> The marble index of a mind for ever
> Voyaging through strange seas of thought alone.

The scientist in the front rank requires the power of such a voyage every whit as real as that of Darwin in the *Beagle*.

He must be able to live a lonely life with his idea, content to see men ignore it when it is put before them, content to believe with Kepler that if God can wait six thousand years for one to contemplate His works, the discoverer too can wait. Loneliness is the fate of genius.

The solitary is by no means a figure confined to religion: he is the type of all whose labours endure. Love of one's subject, the desire of truth, the power to lead a lonely life—these are the qualities of genius. But let us not forget hope, the hope that tramples on failure, "is baffled to fight better," and through mists of doubt presses forward to the goal. Hope is the virtue of youth; but the truly great man possesses perpetual youth, in mind if not in body: ever ready for new ideas, ever looking at the heights. Do we always realise that Darwin's volumes on evolution were practically published after he was fifty? "The substance of the things hoped for" is faith, and this too is a necessary virtue of the man of science. Faith assures him that what he is doing is worth while; faith gives him that singleness of purpose without which no great task was ever accomplished; faith endows him with that patience and industry which Darwin claimed as his chief qualities. On faith in the unity and meaning of creation depends that breadth of view without which few men make discoveries of fundamental importance; and surely it is "the evidence of things not seen" which kindles in the natural philosopher the fire of imagination—that "Phantasie" which the great physiologist Johannes Müller acknowledged to be "*ein unentbehrliches Gut*."

Darwin's *Autobiography* contains a vivid history of the process by which he was able to revivify "the oldest of all the philosophies—that of evolution." In 1838, thanks to Malthus, he had grasped the idea of natural selection. In 1842 he first allowed himself to write out its progress in thirty-five pages. In 1844 he enlarged this sketch into one of 230 pages. Struggle, selection, sexual selection, and variation—all were in his mind, though he attached much more weight to the influence of external conditions and to the inheritance of acquired habits than he did later. Must man be included with other animals in his quest for the origin of species? Yes. So far back as 1837 or 1838 he collected facts on this point, and they convinced him of the "Descent of Man" from an animal, though the book with this title was not published till 1871. Early in 1859, acting on the advice of Sir Charles Lyell, he began to write out his views on the origin of species on a scale three or four times as extensive as he did in 1856. By 1856 he had sent his friend Hooker his manuscript. Swinging away from any sympathy with the theories of Buffon and Lamarck, he reached an extreme position on the work of natural selection. In the July of that year he gave a brief sketch of his theory in a letter to Asa Gray, the distinguished American naturalist, mentioning the cardinal conceptions of the *Origin of Species*. The formation of species he thought almost wholly due to the selection of "chance" variations. Neither the "blind fortuity" of Empedocles nor the "progressive principle" of Aristotle is in his mind. What he means by "chance" variations is that they occur under unknown laws. At the very time that Darwin was slowly coming to his conclusions Wallace was coming to his, and on July 1st, 1858, their two papers were read together. The world of science, on the publication of the *Origin of Species*, began to undergo a profound transformation that has affected every department of it. The situation reminds one of the campanile of St. Mark's at Venice in July, 1902. The guardian of the tower wanted a few inches more elbow room in his little kitchen and took away a sort of lintel in order to enlarge the passage. Next day there was a crack in the wall above, and the week after the whole campanile sat down upon itself. Nothing was changed; the same bricks and mortar were there; only the situation was different. Darwin's *magnum opus* rendered the whole scientific situation wholly different. The idea of natural selection had been conceived by Wells in 1813, by Patrick Matthew in 1831, and by Wallace in 1858. It is remarkable that Wells and Herbert Spencer, as well as Wallace and Darwin, based their ideas on the Malthusian principle.

There is an infinite variability in wild and domestic animals. There appears to be hardly any limit to the almost infinite plasticity and modifiability of domestic animals. "It would seem," said a great sheep-breeder, speaking of sheep, "as if farmers had chalked upon a wall a form perfect in itself, and then proceeded to give it existence." Granting individual variability, then, how do species arise in nature? And how are all the exquisite adaptations of part to whole, and of whole to environment, gradually initiated, improved, and perfected? Here the book of Malthus comes to our assistance. For it teaches that here and now the world is over-populated. It is not going to be over-populated, but is actually at this moment over-populated. Species perpetually outruns subsistence. Linnaeus reckoned that if the annual plant had two seeds, each of which produced two seedlings in the succeeding season, and so on continually, in twenty years their progeny would amount to a million plants. The roe of a cod contains nearly ten million eggs. If each of these produced a young fish, which arrived at maturity, the whole sea must immediately become a solid mass of codfish. There is, then, a struggle for existence between members of the same species—not between members of different species—and this struggle is never-ending. This struggle is between cod and cod, tiger and tiger, snake and snake. *Homo homini lupus*, so runs the old proverb. *Lupus lupo lupus*, so runs the proverb Darwin might have coined for his purpose.

The three men Darwin looked to for judgment on his work were Lyell, Hooker, and Huxley. That is, from the angle of geology, botany, and zoology, three men of mark were on the side of the evolutionary hypothesis launched upon the world. All of them had their reservations, but they cordially accepted the main idea. Hooker did not disguise his opinion that he thought it had been pressed too far, holding that Darwin had ignored the view of the mutability of species held by G. Saint-Hilaire and Lamarck. Huxley pointed out, for instance, that the logical foundation of the *Origin* was insecure so long as the experiments in selective breeding had not produced varieties, which were more or less infertile, and he thought that insecurity remained. In his Romanes lecture, given in 1892, Huxley held that natural selection failed to explain the origin of our moral and ethical nature. Lyell shrank from accepting the Darwinian teaching, for he foresaw its inevitable extension to the descent of man, and that was repugnant to his feelings. Ultimately, he ceased to shrink, and Darwin thought this one of the noblest acts he knew. For Lyell "to have maintained in the position of a master one side of the question for thirty years, and then deliberately give it up, is a fact to which I much doubt whether the records of science offer a parallel."

Sir Richard Owen was a naturalist who occupied such a foremost position in science that he had been called the British Cuvier, and he could not see his way to accept evolution. Darwin's special doctrine of natural selection he never appreciated. He attacked it with acerbity in an anonymous article in the *Edinburgh Review* for April, 1860. Darwin believed him to have inspired the hostile notice given to his book by Samuel Wilberforce, Bishop of Oxford, in the *Quarterly Review* of the same date. There is also reason to think that Owen proved the source of inspiration of the speech delivered by Wilberforce at the meeting of the British Association at Oxford in 1860.

The 1860 meeting of the British Association has attained a high degree of notoriety. There was another meeting of this Association at Oxford in 1894, which is sometimes forgotten. The President then was Lord Salisbury, who proceeded to attack, in the presence of Huxley, conceptions of the evolution theory. With delicate irony he spoke of the "comforting word, evolution," passing to Weismannism. Lord Salisbury quoted Lord Kelvin against Darwin, implying that the diametrically opposed views so frequently expressed nowadays threw the whole process of evolution in doubt. This of course irritated Huxley, who naturally considered Lord Kelvin a non-expert witness on a biological question. When the President had finished his address, Lord Kelvin proposed a vote of thanks, and he did so with genuine conviction. For he saw grave difficulties from a physico-mathematical point of view in reconciling the Darwinian hypothesis of evolution in biology with the physical data he had in his mind. Huxley contented himself with a formal speech. The triumph of 1860 was not destined to be repeated, for Lamarckism *inter alia* was at last coming into its own. If the shade of Sir Richard Owen or of Samuel

Wilberforce could have been present, how he would have chuckled at the retribution falling on his former antagonist!

Huxley enjoyed the rare good fortune of reviewing the *Origin of Species* for *The Times*, and a notice in the leading newspaper of 1860 rendered incalculable service to the new contribution to thought. Still, writing in 1887, he observes, "There is not the slightest doubt that, if a General Council of the Church scientific had been held at that time, we should have been condemned by an overwhelming majority." The severe criticism passed by the *Quarterly Review* of July, 1860, rendered a notable disservice to the reception of the evolution theory. In the *Life and Letters of Charles Darwin*, there is a letter written by Hooker which we quote: "Huxley has sent me the proof of his contribution to the *Life*. I do not think it too severe. The *Quarterly* then held the highest place amongst first-class Reviews and was most bound to be fair and judicious, but proved unjust and malicious and ignorant. It went indefinitely beyond 'severity' and into scurrility, and for all Huxley says he cites abundant proof. It is not for us, who repeat *ad nauseam* our contempt for the persecutors of Galileo and the sneerers of Franklin, to conceal the fact that our own great discoverers met the same fate at the hands of the highest in the land of Literature and Science, as represented by its most exalted organ, the *Quarterly Review*."

It is one of the ironies of the situation that in their views Darwin and Wallace did not continue to see eye to eye. The longer Wallace worked practically, the more he perceived difficulties in the way. In his *World of Life* he states three of the most formidable of these. The first is that the slight beginnings of new organs would be useless, and could not therefore be preserved and increased by natural selection—to which it is answered that the usual method of evolution is to make apparent novelties by the transformation or specialisation of old-established structures. The second difficulty is that new adaptations imply a number of concurrent variations—to which it is answered that time is long and variability great, and that coincident variations are demonstrably numerous in connection with both difficulties. Professors Baldwin, Lloyd Morgan, and Osborn have suggested that adaptive individual modifiability may serve as a life-saving screen till hereditary germinal variations in the same direction have grown strong. The third difficulty is in the excessive development of characters, such as decorations and weapons beyond the limits of utility, and the answer, we glean, is found in Weismann's ingenious hypothesis of germinal selections.

Huxley and Hooker took the field with enthusiasm when Darwin extended his theory to the descent of man. From Wallace he received no support in this matter. Wallace admitted everything in regard to the morphological descent of man, yet maintained, in a mystic manner, that something else, something spiritual, must have been added to that inherited from his spiritual ancestors. Though he urged that natural selection accounted for the evolution of man's bodily frame from the simian stock, yet from this point of view some extraneous power had inspired him with his mentality, and with a future purpose in view had provided the mere savage with a brain disproportionate to his requirements, whether compared with civilised man or with the brutes.

Darwin had plainly discovered laws of evolution in biological science, but laws are by no means plain to historians in the past. They were pragmatists to a man, and this pragmatical view of history does not lend itself to the discovery of laws of any kind. The novel with a purpose seldom reaches the high standard of the novel written solely for the insight into character possessed by the writer, and this remark applies to history. History written with a purpose simply hides whatever laws might swim into the ken of the writer. At the Renaissance the historians read their Herodotus and their Thucydides, and they read them simply for the better understanding of the politics of their own time. The seventeenth century begins to witness a change when it divides history into ancient, mediaeval, and modern. That is to say, there were real divisions in history and with the recognition of these divisions there grew up the idea that the laws of the ancient period were hardly applicable to the mediaeval, or the laws of the mediaeval to those of the modern. The eighteenth century man came to hold that while history may repeat itself, it does so with a difference, and this difference is always sufficient to allow the observer to see that this repetition is not at all the simple affair the pragmatical historian had believed. With the eighteenth century we note the appearance of such philosophical historians as Vico and Voltaire, Montesquieu and Gibbon, and they all stand for natural causes as an explanation of the annals of our race.

The pragmatical historian did not disappear in the nineteenth century, and indeed it is safe to hazard the prediction that he never will disappear. He has always been with us in the past, and it seems likely that he will continue to abide with us in any future we can discern. Still, the historians who count in the nineteenth century profess to be watching for causes, courses, and consequences. Such is their formal creed, and, despite departures from it, they practise what they profess to hold. Hegel conceived the successive periods of history as corresponding to the ascending phases or ideas in the self-evolution of his Absolute Being. A philosopher before an historian, yet Hegel succeeded in impressing the conception of historical development on the mind of the thoughtful. He did not shake himself quite free from the notion of a judgment of value, a trace of the pragmatism of his day. He influenced Ranke, and yet, in spite of this influence, Ranke boldly announced in 1824 that his sole concern was to show how things actually happened. It was an announcement fraught with momentous consequences, for it meant *inter alia* that history must secure freedom to proclaim truth, regardless of consequences. Savigny made this teaching his own when he founded the "historical school" of law, the school which discerned the growth of law out of custom, precedent, and a hundred other fashions as well as out of judicial decisions and parliamentary statutes. In a word, in the company of Burke and Coleridge, he insisted that society is an organism and that all its institutions are as closely interconnected as those of an organism. It was a great thought greatly developed, and the works of Ranke and Savigny are of first-rate importance in the growth of evolutionary politics.

What Ranke and Savigny had been outlining in Germany,

Condorcet and Comte had been outlining in France. Condorcet's *Sketch of a Historical Picture of the Progress of the Human Mind* suggests vistas to its readers. His aim is to show "the successive changes in human society, the influence which each instant exerts on the succeeding instant, and thus, in its successive modifications, the advance of the human species towards truth or happiness." Obviously, he writes with a purpose quite as much as any novelist, and yet he did suggest to his readers the possibility of a law-pervaded department of human activity. His key to the past is progress, and this progress is plainly discernible in the advance of knowledge. Unlike Savigny, he thrust to the one side the preponderant part taken by institutions in social development. Comte's Laws of the Three Stages helped the diffusion of the idea of this development. He fell back on the two main ideas of Condorcet. One was that the collective behaviour of the masses was a more important element in development than the great man. The other was that, as in nature, so in history, there are general laws, necessary and constant, which condition development. In the unfolding of these two ideas we meet what Comte regarded as the social-psychological point of view. To determine the social-psychological laws which control development constitutes the task of the sociologist and the historian.

It is quite obvious that Darwin determines some of the laws which control development. True, after the manner of the Cambridge scientist, he carefully confines himself to his own special work. If he refers to anything outside his sphere, his reference is always cautious and guarded. Will the higher civilised races eliminate the lower throughout the world? Yes, this is the prospect lying before man. In his *Life and Letters* he points out how "a struggle for existence consequent on his rapid multiplication has advanced man to his present position; and, if he is to advance still higher, it is to be feared that he must remain subject to a severe struggle. Otherwise he would sink into indolence, and the more gifted men would not be more successful in the battle of life than the less gifted." Here of course we are face to face with the old objection Aristotle urged against Plato's communism, that man needs a stimulus to exertion and industry. Nor does Darwin in the least ignore other factors in the contest. "Important as the struggle for existence has been," so he writes, "and even still is, yet as far as the highest part of man's nature is concerned there are other agencies more important. For the moral qualities are advanced, either directly or indirectly, much more through the effects of habit, the reasoning powers, instruction, religion, etc., than through natural selection; though to this latter agency may be safely attributed the social instincts which afforded the basis for the development of the moral sense."

To Darwin there is no connexion between the doctrine of natural selection and Socialism. The survival of the fittest means competition of the strictest kind. Nor is it altogether surprising to find that the *Origin of Species* turned Hooker into "a jolly old Tory." The mention of Toryism suggests to Darwin the peerage, and he takes occasion to say that "primogeniture is dreadfully opposed to selection: suppose the first-born bull was necessarily made by each farmer the begetter of his stock!" Still, the peers can choose "beautiful and charming women out of the lower ranks," and so they deviously derive some benefit from the principle. Accidents like the marriage of a peer to an actress take place. Despite Condorcet and Comte, then, we cannot arrive at general laws accounting for historical development. The great man—and the small man—persists in altering the destiny of the world. Chance and coincidence also play their part. Even in the geological world it is not strictly true that nature never makes a leap. On the earth she has her earthquakes as well as her still slow processes, her Etnas as well as her Jungfraus. In times when vast forces are called into being, the eruption of a volcano may accomplish in a week what the silent processes of nature may not accomplish in an age.

Ranke and Savigny had outlined historical and legal development long before Darwin, and, after Darwin, Lamprecht had followed in their steps and in Marx's. Marx and Lamprecht turned their attention to economic history where perhaps the problem set by the appearance of the genius interferes least in the whole domain of history, though the appearance of so many great English inventors from 1760 to 1785 suggests that even in economic history we can never quite arrive at general laws independent of the accidental arrival of the inventor. The watcher on the hill, surveying the past, knows in part the meaning of a change in policy in the history of a nation, the value of a treaty; while from those who at the time plan in the plain is often hidden the issue of the policy or the treaty or the significance of the rôle men assume. Conflicting courses lie before the national leaders, and, so far as we can see, the laws Lamprecht confidently enunciates do not enable us to determine why they choose this course instead of that. He reduces—or rather attempts to reduce—history to general concepts. It is a task eminently well worth trying, but the point is, does he succeed? He argues that events show a psychical character, and that these events give rise to a phase of civilisation. This given phase of civilisation forms "a collective psychical condition" controlling the period, "a diapason which penetrates all psychical phenomena and thereby all historical events of the time." Lamprecht does not hesitate to work out a series of such phases, "ages of changing psychical diapason," and his object is to exhibit these diapasons in other social developments. Of course if he can do so, he establishes his point that these diapasons are the rule, not the exception. On principles partly Comte's and partly H. Spencer's, he shows to his own satisfaction that these ages succeed one another in a definite order, which he elaborately exhibits. The principle he perceives in these ages is that collective psychical development begins with the homogeneity of all the individual members of a society, and, through heightened psychical activity, advances in the form of a continually increasing differentiation of the individual. Lamprecht maintains that no idea can disappear without leaving behind it an effect or effects, and that all psychical life, whether in a person or in a society, means change, the acquisition of new mental contents. The new is commonly expressed in terms of the old, and must come to terms with the old, leading to a synthesis which determines the character of the new age. Accordingly, Lamprecht defines the ages of civilisation as the "highest concepts for subsuming without exception all psychical phenomena of the development of human societies, that is, of all historical events." Granted that such concepts can be determined, it is easy for the German historian to announce that there is a special historical science which he calls "historical ethnology," and this is substantially Comte's social dynamics. But can we subsume those highest concepts without exception? Chance, accident, and the presence of the great man alike forbid such a calm subsumption? The truth is that no matter how loudly we proclaim that history is a science, and that there are discoverable laws in it or in political science, we are confronted by all sorts of exceptions, and those exceptions go far to nullify the operation of laws either in history or in political science.

The evolutionary beatitude is, Blessed are the strong, for they shall prey on the weak. To this beatitude there are such manifest exceptions as that the strong protect the weak when ill. The mother protects her suffering child, the husband his delicate wife. What is true of the individual is also true of the nation. In the contest for the survival of the fittest, Sparta succeeded and Athens failed, and yet we owe immeasurably more to the failure than to the success. The struggle for existence tends to support the view that this is on the whole the best of possible worlds. For the fit appear in all their fitness while the unfit disappear with all their unfitness. We can if we like add another evolutionary beatitude, Blessed is the *status quo*, for all remain in it who deserve to be in it. Away with all forms of equality, for does not evolution sanctify inequality? In the biological world there are organisms of varying values, and why should there not be organisms of varying values in the political or the sociological world? Liberty, fraternity, and equality belong to a world which knew not what Darwin was to reveal, and in the light of the doctrines announced in 1859 this trinity possesses little validity. Socialism denies everlasting economic competition on which biology bestows its blessing. Therefore away with Socialism! Herbert Spencer accordingly tells us of "the beneficent working of the survival of the fittest" and of "the beneficent private war which makes one man strive to climb on the shoulders of another." Yet

Tarde, like Brunetière, boldly disputes the application of evolution to society, holding that the development of species and the development of society by no means trace growth to the same plan. He lays considerable stress on the share taken by inventions, which by virtue of the laws of imitation—to him of paramount place and power—modify through individual to individual, through neighbourhood to neighbourhood, the psychical diapason.

If the existence of sociological or political laws is disputable, and this is fairly evident, it is at the same time clear that evolution lends its aid in throwing light on the past. The work it performs for us is not that of which Condorcet and Comte and Lamprecht dreamt, but it is rather that of which Ranke and Savigny dreamt. It supplements history and political science, and the dreams of Comte and Lamprecht fall to this modest dimension. It is open to a man like Sir Francis Galton, a cousin of Darwin, to urge that the human race might gain an indefinite improvement by breeding from the best and restricting the offspring of the worst. There is something to be said for eugenics for a fraction of one per cent. of the population, but what about the remaining 99 per cent.? It is no doubt possible to view the peerage, as Galton does, "as a disastrous institution owing to its destructive effects on our valuable races." For the eldest son of a peer marries a wealthy heiress in order to maintain his social position, and as such an heiress is often sterile, the family disappears. As primogeniture prevents the younger sons marrying women of their own rank, the younger sons tend to remain unmarried. Yet it is possible to look on primogeniture from another angle. For it may be contended, with much truth, that primogeniture encouraged the younger sons to emigrate, and thereby to assist in the foundation of our empire. If ever there is a Parthenon for the founders of our empire, surely there ought to be a statue erected to the legislator who passed the law of primogeniture. Nor must we overlook the point that there are no class divisions in our country such as marked the history of continental countries, and this is largely due to the working of the law of primogeniture. The younger son of a peer was with us a commoner, and his interests lay with the commoners. A peer could not very well despise commoners when all his sons save the eldest belonged to that class. The easy transition from one class to another served to minimise the distinctions of birth. Macaulay lays stress on the result of this wise policy. "It (i.e. the nobility) had none of the invidious character of a caste," we read. "It was constantly receiving members from the people and constantly sending down members to mingle with the people. . . The yeoman was not inclined to murmur at dignities to which his own children might rise. The grandee was not inclined to insult a class into which his own children must descend." In France and indeed other continental countries, the nobility formed a caste regardless of any interest or concern for the rest of the nation. Tocqueville draws an unforgettable picture of how the continuance of the economical privileges of the French nobility stirred up national hatred for them, and the contrast with England is poignant.

If it is by no means easy to assess the effects of the peerage or primogeniture, it is not a whit easier to assess the effects of such customs as the celibacy of priests or military conscription. Galton, Broca, and Vacher de Lapouge condemn such customs, showing with a wealth of knowledge that they assist in the sterilisation or the elimination of the eminently fit. This inevitably tends towards a condition of equality which is deplorable. For this equality prevents the aristocracy of the blond dolichocephales from holding the position and assuming the rôle which naturally belongs to it. Nietzsche sympathised with this argument. Equality of this sort gravitated towards the increase of panmixia, and with this panmixia the species and society must inevitably deteriorate. To Marx, as to Nietzsche, the source of all progress lies in struggle. The researches of Galton and Hansen, however, demonstrate that the aristocracy of land and the aristocracy of business both tend to become effete, and we thus arrive at the comforting conclusion that the democratic movement, by breaking down class barriers, helps —not hinders—the extremely difficult task of human selection.

The question of clerical celibacy is by no means easy to

solve, as Galton supposes. It is of course obvious that as priests were forbidden to marry—though Lea's *Sacerdotal Celibacy* proves how impossible it was to enforce this prohibition,—there was an undoubted elimination of the offspring of the fit. None will deny that this elimination tended to the consequent coarsening of society. On the other hand, the fit received remained in the seclusion of their monastery cut off from the alarms of a warlike world. They were learned themselves, and they preserved the torch of learning alight in Europe when it seemed in danger of utter extinction. Can any biologist or sociologist enter on the creditor side the services of celibacy of the clergy to the cause of sound learning and then enter on the debtor side the elimination of their offspring, and, striking a balance, say where the net gain lies? We, for our part, confess our total disability in determining such a delicate process.

If it is not at all easy to assess the merits and the demerits of clerical celibacy, it is not a whit easier to assess those of military conscription. It possesses untold disadvantages, and we should be the very last to deny them. Yet there is the moral and educational value of military discipline. There is truth in Shakespeare's position that war is "the great correcter of enormous times." De Maistre urged that "*la guerre est divine par ses conséquences d'un ordre surnaturel ; tant générales, que particulières.*" In 1880 Moltke wrote his famous letter to Bluntschli in London: "Eternal peace is a dream, and not even a beautiful dream, and war is part of God's world-order. In war are developed the noblest virtues of mankind: courage and sacrifice, fidelity and the willingness to sacrifice life itself. Without war the world would be swallowed up in materialism."

A defeat in war has led nation after nation to a clearer realisation of its duty to some of its members hitherto neglected. The Crimean War led to the emancipation of the Russian serfs. The Seven Weeks' War led Austria to tear up her Concordat and liberalise her government. The Civil War in America led to the emancipation of the negro. The Franco-German War led to the removal of the impurities of the Second Empire. The unification of Germany and Italy were won on the battlefields. Nor can we deny that the World War led to the democratisation of Germany fraught with consequences hidden in the womb of time.

There is another side to the picture. The roll of honour of the World War contains name after name renowned in the history of our country; and families of proved worth have perished as though they had never been. War is far from being the biological necessity that Moltke dreamt. Darwin regarded war as an insignificant part of natural selection. He was too cautious not to state that he used the term struggle for existence in a "metaphorical sense," and that the dominant factors in the struggle for existence, as he understood it, were natural suitability to the organic and inorganic environment and the capacity for adaptation to circumstances. One species flourishes while a less efficient species living alongside it languishes, yet they may never come into actual contact and there is nothing in the least approaching human warfare.

The instances of the thylacine or Tasmanian wolf, the fiercest of the marsupials, and the dingo, a later and higher animal of the dog family, and of the black and the brown rat may be cited, for these two instances prove that there is no foundation for the view that one species exterminates another. The dingo made no war on the thylacine. The former was better able to adapt itself to finding food and in rearing young, and in evincing greater resisting power to climate and disease, and the outcome was that the dingo took the place of the thylacine. The black rat wages no war on the brown rat. The black rat is smaller, but more active and a better climber, than the brown, which is larger but less active, a burrower rather than a climber. The outcome is that the black rat is the rat of the barn and the granary, the brown rat the rat of the sewer and the drain. Each flourishes in the environment suited to him. In fact, the struggle for existence simply means that one species is more favoured by circumstances than another species; but it does not mean that one species wages war on another after the fashion of the human species. For this view there is no foundation whatsoever in the facts of the biological world.

Vacher de Lapouge considers that in modern times, though wars are fewer in number, the total of victims remains still about the same, with the result that the stream of bloodshed throughout the ages remains unaffected. He attempted to estimate the victims of war for each civilised country during half a century, and found that the total amounted to nine and a half millions, while, by including the Napoleonic and other wars of the beginning of the nineteenth century, he considered that the total would be doubled. Put in another grim form, according to Lapouge, the wars of a century spilt 120,000,000 gallons of blood, enough to fill three million forty-gallon casks, or to create a perpetual fountain sending up a jet of 150 gallons per hour, a fountain which has been flowing unceasingly since the dawn of history. Lapouge, be it noted, wrote before the World War. Nor must we ignore the diminished number of births due to the fact that possible fathers were in the fighting line.

The loss due to war is not one that this generation is likely to forget. Apart from the sacrifice of human lives military conscription entails other drawbacks. It certainly breaks the habits of industrial life at the very age when it is of high importance that they should be formed. Deferred marriage with the immorality that this means, the loosening of domestic ties, the growth of military ideals on the side that leads to violence and bloodshed, the fact that human brains spend much of their efforts in devising more and more deadly instruments of destruction—these are among the horrors war inflicts on the race. Nor can we leave out of our calculations the deeply prejudicial results that conscription inflicts on the finer and more subtle natures. It debases them just as it debases less refined natures. Men come to think that as they are being prepared to fight against the enemies of their country, perhaps they may turn their arms against the enemies of their class in their own country. This is certainly an argument employed by the Syndicalists who accept M. Georges Sorel as their guide. War to him is as beneficial a part of the world's order as it was to Moltke. For Sorel the strike is a phenomenon of war, and nowadays the only promising kind of war, provided that it embodies the proletarian violence of class struggle, "*une chose très belle et très heroïque,"* capable of saving the world from barbarism in the same way, so Sorel conceives, as war saved the world from barbarism in antiquity.

The chief apostle of evolutionary politics is Herbert Spencer (1820–1903). His family, of whom he gives a very complete account in his dull *Autobiography,* were chiefly notable for strong individualism in thought and action, with the natural consequence that they were radicals in politics and dissenters in religion. As J. S. Mill's father constantly stimulated the reasoning powers of his son, so Spencer's father stimulated those of his son. He persistently asked Herbert the cause of this and the cause of that, and allowed the boy to see that he valued the answers he received in reply to such questions This means that the lad formed judgments for himself upon everything, that he argued every point of difference, and that he refused to listen to authority in any form whatsoever. In the days to come there was to be a wide general agreement between the ideas of Mill, Bain, and Spencer, but three more contrasted systems of education of three boys could not readily be imagined. Mill's was such that he narrowly escaped being a learned prig. Bain's father, like Mill's, was a Calvinist, and he held before his son the prospect that he was travelling along the road to hell. Bain was nurtured on such books as M'Gowan's *Dialogues of Devils,* which contained a fierce attack upon Priestley and the Unitarians, the imagination being assisted by a picture of Priestley in hell. A student of child psychology may meditate on the three systems of education of startling diversity which produced men of such eminence as Mill, Bain, and Spencer. Or are we to assume the position adopted by Sir Leslie Stephen that when we say that a school or a system produced an able man we really mean it failed to extinguish him?

At an age when Mill was working at the classics, Spencer was reading novels in bed, and they are possibly the only books he ever read from cover to cover. His emotional nature had never been developed. He deeply enjoyed music, though it is the exception that proves the rule. What he enjoyed most of all was beautiful melody. Beethoven was his favourite composer, and he was never weary of listening to his music. He exhibited little appreciation of sculpture or painting, and confessed that Ruskin's *Stones of Venice* had "disgusted" him. The past appealed to him as slightly as it did to Bentham. Neither Rome nor Florence moved him a whit more than his own country. In truth, the present fascinated him so profoundly that he could not spare time for the past.

His mind was more active than his body, and thoughts on evolution were never far from it. The perusal of Lyell's *Principles of Geology* had, curiously enough, turned him into a Lamarckian. In an essay on the theory of population, written in 1852, he came within sight of one of the great doctrines of Darwin. "From the beginning," he lays down, "pressure of population has been the proximate cause of progress." He proceeds to point out that "the effect of pressure of population, in increasing the ability to maintain life, and decreasing the ability to multiply, is not a uniform effect, but an average one. . . . All mankind in turn subject themselves more or less to the discipline described; they either may or may not advance under it; but, in the nature of things, only those who *do* advance under it eventually survive. . . . For as those prematurely carried off must, in the average of cases, be those in whom the power of self-preservation is the least, it unavoidably follows that those left behind to continue the race are those in whom the power of self-preservation is the greatest—are the select of their generation."

Spencer here recognises the eliminative and selective effect of the struggle in mankind. Why was he "blind to the fact," as he afterwards owned, "that here was a universally operative factor in the development of species"? In his *Autobiography* he assigns two reasons for his blindness. One was his Lamarckian prepossession that the inheritance of functionally-produced modifications sufficed to explain the facts of evolution. The other was that he "knew little or nothing about the phenomena of variation," and that he "had failed to recognise the universal tendency to vary."

Early in his career his interest in evolution had been awakened, yet his interest in politics had been aroused earlier. When twenty-two he paid a visit to his uncle, the Rev. T. Spencer, who exercised a far-reaching effect on his mind. His uncle was deeply interested in social questions, and discussions took place which introduced the nephew to a new region of thought, and introduced him at a time when the spirit—as well as the face—of politics was undergoing a grave change. In the forties Benthamism still stood for the removal of government restrictions on the liberty of the subject. The Whigs retained a measure of belief in governmental interference, but the Liberals, who were gradually being differentiated from the Whigs, were resolutely casting such a belief to the one side. The uncle was a Liberal thoroughly imbued with the new attitude, and he of course placed his view before his nephew at an impressionable age —if ever the nephew was impressionable. He had been strongly individualistic and self-sufficient, ignorant of the past and intolerant of the claims of authority in the present, and was not unprepared for the teaching he received. The Manchester School, adorned by such determined individualists as Bright and Cobden, was in the heyday of its power. Spencer entered heartily into its adoption of *laissez-faire*. An individualist by upbringing, he remained one to the end of his long and influential life.

It is sometimes urged that great men are a product of their times, a position difficult to defend. It is much truer to adopt the view that men in a low first or a high second rank are a product of their times. If ever a man was such a product, it was Spencer. His uncle was also a product of his age, and he directed the attention of his nephew to politics with the result that he wrote a series of letters to *The Nonconformist* newspaper, embodying their common views in 1842. A series of twelve "Letters on the Proper Sphere of Government" appeared, advocating a thorough-going individualism. The State is nothing but "a national institution for preventing one man from infringing upon the rights of another." It is merely a police State with no provision for purposes of war, no restrictions on commerce, no poor laws, no national Church or national education, no sanitary administration. Alexander the Great asked Diogenes what was his greatest desire on earth, and the swift reply came that Alexander should step aside out of the sunlight. Similarly, Spencer simply desired that the State should step aside out of the sunlight of private enterprise.

These twelve letters control the whole course of Spencerian political philosophy. As he was in the beginning of 1842, so he remained to the end of his life in 1903 an uncompromising individualist. Had these letters never been written he informs us that *Social Statics*, which originated from them, would not even have been thought of. Had there been no *Social Statics*, those lines of inquiry which led to the *Principles of Psychology* would have remained unexplored. And without that study of life in general, initiated by the writing of these works, leading presently to the study of the relations between its phenomena and those of the inorganic world, there would have been no *System of Synthetic Philosophy*. In *Social Statics*, which appeared in 1850, the principles of the Spencer family are philosophised for the benefit of the public. The Corn Laws had been abolished when the author was reading—in so far as he read at all—and thinking out this his first book, and who could doubt that *laissez-faire*, in this case had wrought untold good to the people? Joined to this belief in *laissez-faire*, there was the naive belief that the laws of Political Economy were not statements in the indicative mood but in the imperative. In fact, the young author drew no distinction between a law of physical science and one of Political Economy. Ricardo seemingly drew no such distinction, and why should he? A law of Political Economy was nothing short of an ordinance of nature which resembled the laws of the Medes and Persians. Here indeed he exhibited his undoubted descent in the true Benthamite lineage. John Locke had embraced the doctrine of natural right, which travelled to America, making its appearance in the Declaration of Independence, and then to France, also making its appearance in the Declaration of Rights. In form, Bentham attacked the natural right theory, though in substance he adopted it. In turn Spencer also adopted it. He does not hesitate for a moment to declare his adhesion to the view that all men are naturally equal, that there is "the law of equal freedom," that his aim is "the liberty of each, limited alone by the like liberty of all." The last is the first law; and indeed "we may almost say that it is the sole law" on which scientific morality and the organisation of society depend. Or, as he states it later in the glory of italics, "*Every man has freedom to do all that he wills, provided he infringes not the equal freedom of any other man*," a view to which Mill was to subscribe nine years later.

Government is necessary for the present, but it is a necessary evil, being "essentially immoral." It is necessary because man, compelled by the increase of population to live in the social state, retains the predatory instincts of his primitive life, and accordingly sometimes tramples on the rights of others. Government is, according to our optimist, a passing phase. Progress is tending in all cases to less government. Take an instance. "As amongst the Bushmen we find a state antecedent to government, so may there be one in which it shall have become extinct." Nothing can hinder such extinction, because the progress of civilisation means the adaptation of man to his new conditions. Man possesses indefinite adaptability, and clearly "humanity must in the end become completely adapted to its conditions." In his loftiest moments Mill was never more optimistic, and though Spencer was only thirty when the *Social Statics* appeared, yet it is the message to which he offered his unfaltering adhesion.

Man must press forward, and must continue to press forward. For progress is a necessity. In spite of Rousseau, civilisation is not artificial: it is natural. The spirit of Condorcet comes to our optimist by way of Comte, though his argument is critical of Comte's teaching. We are bidden to contrast the houseless savages with the Newtons and the Shakespeares. Between these extremes there are countless degrees of differences, rising from the lower to the higher. Evil, like government, tends to disappear. For evil results from the non-adaptation of the organism to its conditions, good from the adaptation. How can evil persist? On true evolutionary principles, evil must disappear in time, and this holds good in the mental sphere as well as in the physical. The drunkard and the debauchee are as weak physically as they are morally, and they are on the high road to extinction through their vices. Struma, tubercle, and nervous disease are all lending a hand towards the pruning off such rotten branches from the tree of life. According to Spencer, "Always towards perfection is the mighty movement—towards a complete development and a more unmixed good." We must "never forget that the law is adaptation to circumstances, be they what they may. . . . Inconvenience, suffering, and death are the penalties attached by nature to ignorance as well as incompetence—are also the means of remedying these. And whoso thinks she can mend matters by dissociating ignorance and its penalties lays claim to more than divine benevolence." In fact, it almost seems as if *laissez-faire* is a divine as well as a human institution.

There is a certain complacency on the part of the mid-Victorians which stirs those of a later generation to active wrath. In the face of the revelation of the atrocities of the Industrial Revolution, brought home to the novel-reading public by the Disraelis and the Kingsleys, they ask, How could anyone assume a complacent tone? It is abundantly clear that Spencer did, and it is also clear that he did so in entire honesty. Evolution was a force which he seemed somehow to have personally discovered before anyone else. Nor did his discovery simply mean that he had found out its existence. He really seems to have entertained the belief that his discovery almost amounted to an act of creation. He had, as it were, called evolution into being, and by this call he had hastened the coming of perfectibility. The economists assisted him in cherishing this belief, for they indicated that *laissez-faire* was also to hasten the coming of perfectibility—though by another route. Nature was working by evolution and man was working by *laissez-faire*. The one improved the physically strong while the other killed off the morally weak. Evolution and *laissez-faire* were accordingly two of the most important forces working for the ultimate perfection of the race. We are to picture them as two invisible hands hovering over the garden of life and plucking up the weeds.

In the shape of the twelve *Letters* of 1842 or the *Social Statics* of 1850, the main thesis seems far away from the thought of our generation. If their author was over estimated in his own generation, he is certainly under-estimated in ours. He was a typical product of his age, and his reputation sank when it passed away. In 1884, in *The Man versus The State* we meet with the same individualism we met in 1842 and 1850. Historically and philosophically, however, the free individual Spencer pictured never existed in the past. The annals of primitive man record no pre-social unit with his natural rights. The astonishing thing is that Spencer himself wrote a special essay on "the social organism" in 1861, which powerfully assisted in popularising this phrase, and yet this conception never gained admittance to the inner cell of his political thought. Here he is indeed the very reverse of Burke who employed the idea of the social organism though he refused to employ this phrase, while Spencer employed this phrase and yet refused to employ the idea lying behind it. All of us may not assign to the State the position assigned to it by Hegel and Fichte and the powerful school they founded, but which of us will admit that it is simply a police State? We stoutly deny that it is, in Huxley's phrase, anarchy plus the policeman. Men are essentially social. The State is an organism composed of such men, and it possesses a general will, conceptions Spencer steadfastly refused to countenance. To read the *Social Statics* requires an effort on the part of our generation. It means passing from the corporate notion of our days to the atomistic individualism of the Victorian age. Nor have we overstressed the place of this book in Spencerian thought. For in 1879, when interrupted in the regular course of his publications to write *The Data of Ethics*, he announces that he had begun to fear that health might not permit him to reach *The Principles of Ethics*, the last part of his *Synthetic Philosophy*. He is accordingly anxious to state that "This last part of the task it is to which I regard all the preceding parts as subsidiary. Written as far back as 1842, my first essay, consisting of letters on *The Proper Sphere of Government*, vaguely indicated what I conceived to be certain general principles of right and wrong in political conduct; and from that time onwards my ultimate purpose, lying behind all proximate purposes, has been that of finding for the principles of right and wrong in conduct at large a scientific basis."

If the *Social Statics* proved a centre of its author's thought, it also proved a centre of his life. Its publication led to his meeting G. H. Lewes and Marian Evans, known to all the world as George Eliot. Between him and her there sprang up a warm friendship, and it was at his suggestion that she commenced to write her novels. Naturally an indolent man, his indolence was increased because of his fear of his hereditary tendency to a nervous breakdown. He liked society; provided that it meant intercourse congenial to him, and George Eliot's society was certainly congenial. He described her in a letter to a friend as "the most admirable woman, mentally, I ever met." As he held marriage to be one of the most desirable consummations in life, we ask, Why did he not marry her? For she undoubtedly liked him. His *Autobiography* affords a clue, for in it he calmly states: "Physical beauty is a *sine qua non* with me; as was once unhappily proved where the intellectual traits and the emotional traits were of the highest." That is one explanation, yet there may well be another. His passion for systematising and his genius for generalising exacted a price, and part of that price was a loss of spontaneity. He loved Beethoven, but did he keenly feel the passionate cry from the depths of the human heart in the Seventh Symphony? Did an aspect of life of the deepest significance yield its inner meaning to a philosopher who approached it as he approached an experiment with his foot-rule and his statistical scales? Had his emotional instincts been stronger he probably would have married George Eliot. Nor was his loss merely personal. Had his emotional instincts been stronger, they would have coloured his thought, imparting to it that quality that might have set the world aflame. Saint-Simon was surely right when on his deathbed he laid down, "*Souvenez-vous, pour faire quelque chose de grand, il faut être passioné.*"

The growth of Spencer's thought was slow, culminating late in life. Nor did he ever force the solution of a problem. In his *Autobiography* he records: "On one occasion George Eliot expressed her surprise that the author of *Social*

Statics had no lines in his forehead, to which he answered, "I suppose it is because I am never puzzled." This called forth the exclamation: "'O! that's the most arrogant thing I ever heard uttered.' To which I rejoined: 'Not at all, when you know what I mean.' And then I proceeded to explain that my mode of thinking did not involve that concentrated effort which is commonly accompanied by wrinkling the brows." The pedigree of a thought did not interest him, and this also assisted in the preservation of his unwrinkled forehead, Plato and Kant he could scarcely bear to read. He wrote his *First Principles* and his *Psychology* almost as if he had never had a predecessor in either subject. He wrote his *Education* unaware that in *Émile* Rousseau had given a great contribution to this subject. When he wrote his *Social Statics* he barely knew that Comte was a French philosophical writer. He was always an independent thinker, and yet we cannot help thinking that a virtue in some men turned to a vice in him. His early education led him to criticise all and sundry, and this critical habit prevented true appreciation of any author with whom he was in the least likely to disagree. It is easier to criticise than to construct, and Spencer might have learnt much from the remark of Comte if he had found time to read him—that one only destroys when one replaces.

Though he never read the philosophical classics, he published in 1855 his *Principles of Psychology*, which he brought into line with the plan of his *Synthetic Philosophy* in his *Psychology*, published in a first volume in 1870 and in a second in 1872. He assumed in his 1855 work the evolution standpoint, and as it was published four years before Darwin's *Origin of Species* it won scanty recognition. Before he could set himself to discover what could be known, he had to determine how knowledge originated. He accepted as his fundamental data personal identity and objective existence. Then he passed from the conception of the cosmos as a mere collection of classified particulars to the conception of the cosmos as a necessary unit, and he effected this transition by coming to the conclusion that space, time, matter, and motion are built up or abstracted from experiences of forces. Force persists. This means that the sum total of matter and motion, by which force manifests itself to us, can neither increase nor diminish. If force came into existence and passed out of existence the universe would be chaos, not the cosmos it is. This persistence of force is also known as the conservation of energy, the great principle Joule had already discovered. In his book Spencer conceives life as a correspondence between co-ordinated internal actions and connected external actions, and from this angle he shows how mind slowly evolves out of life. He traces back the intuitions of the individual to racial experience, thus widening the old experience philosophy of Hume and Mill. He attacks idealism and defends realism, in the course of which he lays down what he calls The Universal Postulate, insisting that the test of the truth of any proposition lies in our inability to conceive its negation.

George Eliot began *Romola* as a young woman, and finished it as an old woman. Spencer began his *Principles of Psychology* as a healthy man, and he finished it as an unhealthy man. The continuous strain of thought it entailed shattered his nervous system so completely that he was never the same man. For eighteen months he was unable to work, and he was never able after to study more than three hours a day. After this terrible breakdown he never again secured a sound night's rest, and his labours were henceforth conducted under as severe physical drawbacks as Darwin's.

After Spencer had recovered to some extent from the mental prostration induced by writing his *Principles of Psychology*, he met with the formula in which von Baer sums up the development through which every plant and animal passes—the change from homogeneity to heterogeneity. At once he grasped the suggestiveness of this formula, and proceeded to extend it to cover the development not only of animals, but of every order of existence that develops. At last he reached the famous formula of the *First Principles* that "Evolution is an integration of matter and concomitant dissipation of motion, during which the matter passes from a relatively indefinite, incoherent homegeneity to a relatively definite, coherent heterogeneity; and during which the retained motion undergoes a parallel transformation."

The *First Principles* was published in 1862, and from 1860 to 1896 Spencer was engaged in the erection of a gigantic structure he called his *Synthetic Philosophy*. For forty years Spencer, uncheered by popular sympathy and dogged by ill-health, persisted in his heavy labours. In early manhood he set himself the task of constructing a philosophy of the universe and man. In old age he had the satisfaction of seeing his labours completed. As he viewed the stately edifice, now in ruins, he viewed it as his emancipation from the fulfilment of the deep purpose of his life. Gibbon is not the only worker to conclude his life's labour in such calm detachment that he may meditate upon the last sentence among the acacias in a starlit garden at Lausanne. Yet we most of us, said Goethe, begin life by conceiving magnificent buildings which we intend to erect, but we are satisfied at the close of life if we have cleâred away a small portion of the ground.

The crown of permanent success fell to Gibbon, but has it fallen to Spencer? His easy fluency, his strong confidence, and his dogmatic Agnosticism attracted his generation, but do they not repel ours? His scanty reading and his imperfect knowledge of physical facts have revealed wide gaps in the structure he raised. Nor are we sure of the foundations thereof. The man who gathers facts for himself is fairly well acquainted with their limitations. The man who has facts gathered for him—and this was Spencer's position—is not likely to be acquainted with their limitations. The lamentable result is that sometimes he has misunderstood his facts, and sometimes he has misinterpreted them, and this misunderstanding and misinterpretation have damaged the whole building to a serious degree. The generations come and the generations go, and Plato among the ancient philosophers and Kant among the moderns are as eagerly read to-day as they always have been, but who reads Spencer to-day? His *Education* is of course read, but it is simply a bye-product of his philosophy. Is his philosophy read? No doubt every writer suffers a period of neglect, especially if, like Spencer, he has been over-estimated. Is it not that he is suffering from the inevitable reaction? It is much more that this. Men are dissatisfied with the explanations afforded by his *Synthetic Philosophy*. They say plainly that they are explanations that do not explain. He became an oracle to his coterie and his answers are oracular. When you come to the end of a book and endeavour to put down what solution to a problem you have discovered from his pages, you are often quite taken aback to note how little you have gained from them. It was possible to have the many-sided Leonardo da Vinci in 1700, the many-sided Bacon in 1600, the many-sided Leibniz in 1700, the many-sided Goethe in 1800, and even the many-sided Henri Poincaré—many-sided in science—in 1900, but was it really possible from 1860 to 1896 for one man to take in the whole of ever-expanding nature for his province? Be that as it may, critics so fair-minded as Professors Ward and Bowne speak their mind quite freely on the worthlessness of the *Synthetic Philosophy*. No one can read Ward's *Naturalism and Agnosticism* without seeing that he regards the *Synthetic Philosophy* as a stupendous house of cards. Professor Bowne deems it "a compound of bad science, bad logic, and bad metaphysics."

With his expansion of Von Baer's formula in his mind, Spencer examined the evolution of phenomena of all sorts, and found that in every instance it applied. The fundamental principle is the persistence of energy. Natural objects change, adopt new forms, transform themselves, die out in word, develop, simply for the reason that energy in nature never dies. Progress consists in the passage of natural objects from a homogeneous to a heterogeneous structure. The law of all progress is the same—the evolution of the simple into the complex by successive differentiations. If we ask why progress should always take this direction—from the homogeneous to the heterogeneous—the answer is two-fold. In the first place, if a body is in a homogeneous condition, it is unstable. It is impossible, for instance, to keep a pair of scales balanced. One scale will descend and the other ascend, thus assuming a heterogeneous relation. In the second place, every active force produces more than one change, and every cause produces more than one effect. The multiplicity of resultant effects naturally converts homogeneity into heterogeneity. A violent collision shatters a homogeneous body into a mass of heterogeneous fragments. It does more than this, for the homogeneous momentum is spent in a group of momenta heterogeneous in both amount and direction. A process like this holds good of all existences whatsoever. For our own convenience we may divide phenomena into biological, astronomical, physical, psychological, sociological, what we will, but the process is one and the law is one. Evolution of the parts goes along with evolution of the whole. Evolution is more than a principle: it is a fact to be admitted by all men.

In the growth of the world, in the genesis of science, in the growth of the individual organism, and in the growth of the social organism, Spencer proceeded from 1860 to 1896 to illustrate the actual working of the fact of evolution. Take the hypothesis of a nebular origin of the solar system. In the beginning—so geologists tell us—our globe was a mass of matter in a state of fusion, and was, therefore, of homogeneous structure and of a tolerably homogeneous temperature. Then came the successive changes into heterogeneity, into mountains, continents, seas, igneous rocks, sedimentary strata, metallic veins. The law holds equally good of organism. Fishes are the most homogeneous in their structure, and are one of the earliest productions on the globe. Reptiles came later, and are more heterogeneous. Mammals and birds, which come later still, are much more heterogeneous. Contrast the European with the Papuan or, if you like, with the Anglo-American variety or with the Anglo-Australian variety. Contrast not men but their social organism. Take the comparatively homogeneous organism of the savage and take the heterogeneous one of the civilised man. The division of labour implies advancing integration with the latter much more than with the former. This division of labour also indicates increasing heterogeneity with the civilised man. In a primitive community the tribesmen follow similar occupations with the result that homogeneity reigns supreme. In a European community men follow different occupations with the result that heterogeneity reigns supreme. Or, take languages. From the parent stem of Aryan have arisen Sanskrit, Armenian, Greek, Teutonic, Slavonic, and all the rest of them. From these main groups have arisen in turn differentiations which continue to form new tongues. From Sanskrit come the modern vernaculars of Northern and Western India; from Slavonic comes Bohemian, Polish, and Russian. That is, from the homogeneous Aryan proceed the heterogeneous languages of modern Europe and India.

The law of evolution with Spencer applies to every description of phenomena, and his system breaks down unless he can so apply it. All forms of existence, however diverse, pass through the series of transformations which his philosophy sets before us. Assuming for the moment that all forms of existence pass through this series, is it not possible that some new set of facts might emerge which would not conform to the law of evolution? Spencer perceived this difficulty, and found a way out of it by the stress he laid on the persistence of force. Matter was indestructible and uncreatable. We may change its form, but the total quantity of matter remains unaltered by this change. Nor can we change the quantity of energy. We may change heat to motion, we may change motion to light, and we may change light back to heat, but the sum total of energy in existence remains unchanged. Given the persistence of force, he deduced the instability of the homogeneous. Given the persistence of force, he deduced the multiplication of effects, for each part of the aggregate reacts differently to the force. Given the persistence of force, he deduced segregation. That is, in an aggregate consisting of unlike units the action of an incident force would tend to segregate or bring together those units which resembled one another, and therefore to make definite the lines of demarcation between the non-resembling portions of the aggregate. The instability of the homogeneous, the multiplication of effects, and segregation are shown to be corollaries following from the persistence of force. And from them follows the law of evolution deductively proved, as it has been inductively shown to be a fact.

Persistence of force is a sort of open sesame, and doors of difficulty fly open before it. But do they? In the revised edition of the *Principles of Biology*[1] of 1898 its author

[1] It first appeared in 1864.

confesses: "Life in its essence cannot be conceived in physico-chemical terms. The processes which go on in living things are incomprehensible as results of any physical action known to us." Consciousness, he is forced to admit, "cannot be identified with waves of molecular motion propagated through nerves and nerve-centres: a unit of feeling has nothing in common with a unit of motion." Can we bridge the gulf between matter and mind? In the last resort Spencer simply asserts that we are here in presence of an insoluble problem. Matter and mind are symbols of realities which cannot be rendered into thought, manifestations of the unknowable. Yet this does not meet the difficulty that Spencer asserts that all phenomenal existences are but specialised forms of matter and motion in the course of their ceaseless distribution. The law of evolution holds good with matter, but it does not hold good with mind, and here we have the Achilles heel of the Spencerian position. He cannot apply his evolutionary system all round. There is a chasm between conscious life and unconscious life which he fails to bridge. The chasm is more deep, or at all events felt more deep, in ethics than in biological or psychological science. The criticism of Professors Höffding and Ward seems unanswerable. In his *Outlines of Psychology* the former insists that "The supposition that a causal relation may exist between the mental and the material is contrary to the doctrine of the 'persistence of energy.' For at the point where the material nerve-process should be converted into mental activity a sum of physical energy would disappear without the loss being made good by a corresponding sum of physical energy." The latter also insists that "So far from accounting for all the phenomena of evolution, the doctrine of the persistence of energy will not account for a single one. The celestial, organic, social, and other phenomena which make up what Mr. Spencer calls cosmic evolution are so many series of qualitative changes. But the conservation of energy is not a law of change, still less a law of qualities. It does not initiate events, and furnishes absolutely no clue to qualitative diversity. It is entirely a quantitative law. When the energy is transformed, there is a precise equivalence between the new form and the old; but of the circumstances determining transformation and of the possible kinds of transformation the principle tells nothing. If energy is transferred, then the system during work loses precisely what some other part of the universe gains; but again the principle tells us nothing of the conditions of such transference."

Following upon *The Principles of Biology* came *The Study of Sociology*, which appeared in 1873, and the three volumes of *The Principles of Sociology* in 1876. In the first part of the latter work Spencer elaborated the theory of the genesis of religious ideas which finds them in the "ghost-theory." Primitive man, always uncritical, would tend to confuse his dreams with reality. Seeming in his sleep to be transported through a variety of scenes and places, and yet informed by his friends that his body all the while has been lying motionless, there would come to him the notion of a second self—of a soul, which has experiences not shared by the body Confirmatory of this belief in a second self is the explanation it afforded of his image reflected in still waters and of his shadow from which he could never escape. The independence of the body and soul being thus established, there naturally grew up the belief that the death of the body need not entail that of the soul. Accordingly when a noted warrior died, his soul still affected the welfare of his tribe, and demanded propitiation. Where this body was buried, there must be a hole in the ground, allowing the soul to come in and go out. Sometimes the people were afraid of the deceased chief, and an enormous mound would be erected over his grave in order to confine his soul securely. Food and drink would be supplied for his use. To the ancestor worship thus commenced, Spencer traced the origin of religious systems and ceremonial observances.

In an explanation like this the fallacy of a single cause requires to be borne in mind. Religious systems are by no means so uniform as the ghost-theory would seem to suggest. The difference between the cosmic philosophy of the Buddhists, the polytheism and nature-worship of the Vedic poets, the Egyptians, and the Greeks, and the ethical monotheism of the Jew calls for a recognition of modifying causes which Spencer refused to give. It is hard to credit that the most refined spiritual conceptions, the most philosophical theology, and the most earnest and unselfish religious activity all come originally from the primitive belief in a ghost. *The Study of Sociology* analysed the various liabilities to perversion of judgment which dog the path of the student of social affairs. Among the *idola theatri* we suggest that Spencer overlooked his own biased attitude to religion.

He analysed the leading traits of the different social institutions—political, ecclesiastical, industrial, and the like, and his general result was to divide them into two main groups, those which were predominantly military and those which were predominantly industrial. With the former was to be found associated an ethically low type of character on the part of individuals, while with the latter was found to be associated an ethically high type of character. Freedom characterised the latter group, tyranny and subservience the former. Generalisations of this crude character betrayed in the most unmistakable fashion that Spencer belonged to that school of thought of which Bright and Cobden were also members.

If there is a chasm between conscious life and unconscious life, between the organic and the inorganic, there is also a chasm between the laws of sociology, as Spencer finds them, and the facts of life. He will not listen to the power wielded by the man of genius whom he seeks to reduce to the environment out of which he emerges. In chemistry the mixture of two atoms of hydrogen with one of oxygen invariably produces water, and the form of the instruments of the mixture matter not. Is this true of history or sociology, as Spencer would have us believe? In history and in sociology the method of the mixture of the atoms is more significant than the elements brought into contact. Even in chemistry oil and water do not mix. Take the sixteenth century. What misery the world would have been saved had Luther and Erasmus been as sympathetic towards each other as Luther and Melanchthon were! The characters of Luther and Erasmus could neither be assimilated nor amalgamated. Would the Reformation have been so successful had not five such men as Luther, Zwingli, Calvin, Cranmer, and Knox, simultaneously appeared?

Frederick the Great, who was not exactly a recluse working out the sociological laws of the universe, gives the point of view of a man of affairs when he insists that "the older one becomes the more clearly one sees that King Hazard fashions three-fourths of the events in this miserable world." Voltaire is never tired of dwelling on the small springs on which the greater events of history turn. Burke reminds us of the case of "a common soldier, a child, a girl at the door of an inn" who "changed the face of fortune and almost of nature." Was Gibbon right in his belief that if Charles Martel had been defeated at Tours the creed of Islam would have overspread the large part of Europe? If Mohammed had been killed in one of the first battles he fought, would a great monotheistic creed have arisen in Arabia? What turn would events have taken if Alexander, the son of Philip of Macedon, had been as incompetent as Commodus, the son of Marcus Aurelius? In the spring of 323 B.C., the control of the framework of civilisation from the Adriatic to the Panjab rested upon the single will of Alexander. He was snatched away, and the union, perhaps premature, of East and West passed away with him. Spencer might, however, urge that those are examples all taken from a military type of society. Let us come, then, to a later period which shares more of the industrial type.

The industrial type of society begins to appear in the sixteenth century, for it synchronises with the Reformation. What form would French art have assumed had not Charles VIII set out on his expedition to Italy, thereby making France feel the influence of Giotto, the founder of modern painting? It is easy to speak of the inevitable working out of cause and effect, as Spencer does, but is the solution quite so simple? Had Frederick the Great never lived, would Prussia have begun the war of 1740, which started the country on the career which made the World War possible? In 1878, had the bullet of Nobiling cut short the days of Wilhelm I and given his son the throne ten years before 1888, the history of Germany would have been fundamentally altered. Indeed, had Frederick the Noble lived in all probability the devastation wrought from 1914 to 1918 would never have occurred. There has been a destroying revolution in Russia since March, 1917. There would have been a preserving revolution had Alexander I been succeeded by a ruler like himself in 1825 and not by Nicholas I. The personality of Alexander I would have effected as epoch-making a transformation as either Luther or Bismarck. Be the laws of sociology what they may, the power of personality is patent in altering, modifying, or transforming them. In the world of ghosts Spencer is willing to admit the influence of the chief, while in the world of life he is unwilling. There is a fear of the chief when he is in the other world, but is there no fear of him in this one?

Individualist as he is, Spencer more than any other thinker is responsible for the popularisation of the conception of the social organism. The comparison is as old as Plato and Aristotle, but Spencer fills in the outlines they left with masses of details. The point of view of Bentham and the Mills had been mechanical, and Spencer changed politics from the mechanical to the biological. Society is an organism, subject to well-defined laws of development, not a mere machine to be cunningly manipulated in the interests of the superior few. As an organism society is subject to the laws of growth. It has an economic root, and all political structures as well as ethical ideas are determined—not from the outside by legislation—but by the economic conditions at each particular stage. Civilisation is, in fact, a great process of adjustment whereby man's nature, physical, intellectual, and moral, develops in response to a social and industrial environment of ever-increasing complexity.

Spencer briefly expressed the conception of the social organism in his *Social Statics*, and he elaborated it in an essay in the *Westminster Review* which appeared in January, 1860. There he likened government to the central nervous system, agriculture and industry to the alimentary canal, transport and exchange to the vascular system of an animal, and pointed out that like an individual organism a society grows, becomes more complex, shows increasing interrelations, division of labour, and mutual dependence among its parts, and has a life immense in length, when compared with the life of its component parts. He indicated in his

Principles of Sociology four chief parallelisms between a society and an individual organism:

(1) Starting as small aggregates both grow in size.

(2) As they grow their initial relative simplicity is replaced by increasing complexity of structure.

(3) With increasing differentiation there comes about an increasing mutual dependence of the component parts, until the life and normal functioning of each becomes dependent on the life of the whole.

(4) The life of the whole becomes independent with a far more prolonged nature than the life of the component parts.

Genetic history of course makes much of society as an organism, and the conception has been influential in a thousand ways, often in ways of which the advocates of causes are unconscious. The advocates of pluralism in the State, for instance, owe not a little to it. For if the State is an organism, it is plain that there may be many subsidiary organisms within it. In fact, the metaphor can be carried to such an extreme that many men recoil from it. Spencer himself was well aware of the limitations of his metaphor, and he is careful to indicate four contrasts between a society and an individual organism:

(1) Societies have no specific forms.

(2) The units of an organism are physically continuous, but the units of a society are dispersed persons.

(3) The elements of the organism are mostly fixed in their relative positions; while units of a society are capable of moving from place to place.

(4) In the body of an animal only a special tissue is endowed with feeling; in a society all the members are so endowed. The social nervous system is happily wider than the government.

Society is indeed an organism, but it is an organism which exists in the thoughts and feelings of its members to a degree which Spencer was not prepared to allow. His own emotional nature was seldom actively aroused while his intellectual nature was constantly so aroused with the outcome that his philosophy allows but little scope for the emotions. Chance and coincidence, personality and genius, are not reducible to sheer cause and effect, and these he also conveniently ignored. T. H. Huxley once met him in the Athenaeum. Wearing a lugubrious expression Spencer remarked, "Oh, Huxley, there has been a tragedy in my house this morning." Without waiting to hear its nature, Huxley at once retorted, "Oh, I know what has happened. A beautiful scientific theory killed by one nasty inconvenient fact." The real tragedy is that Spencer persisted in expressing opinions that ignored the "one nasty inconvenient fact."

The last writing of Spencer that concerns us is *The Principles of Ethics* which he issued in 1879. Its first part was "The Data of Ethics" and its fourth "Justice." The contrast between empiricism and rationalism has run through the whole history of moral philosophy, but the special form the contrast has assumed has, of course, varied with the different generations. On the one side the changes have been rung on such systems as the Cambridge Platonism of Cudworth and Clarke; the moral sense or conscience of Hutcheson and Butler; and Kantianism. On the other side the changes have been rung of the purely selfish system or hedonism of Hobbes and Mandeville; Utilitarianism in its earlier form with Hartley, Paley, and Bentham; Utilitarianism in its later form with Austin, J. S. Mill, and Sidgwick; Evolutionary Ethics with Herbert Spencer and Sir Leslie Stephen.

Hitherto morality had been intimately and invariably associated with religion. Spencer divorces them, for he sheds his early Theism. There must, however, be a basis for morality, and he found the only one left to him, a basis in the theory of evolution. Accordingly, he propounds an evolutionary basis, in which he shows that all the generally recognised rules of morality might be deduced from the general doctrine of organic evolution, as he had set it forth in the *Principles of Biology*, of *Psychology*, and of *Sociology*. Spencer considered *The Principles of Ethics* to be the fine flower of his philosophy; and the most important part of it he held to be that in which he treated of "Justice." In this part was laid down in fully developed form that doctrine of the limitation of State-functions which had been the subject of his twelve *Letters*. It had never ceased to interest him, and he exhibited in "Justice" the same sturdy individualism he had exhibited in his earliest writings.

Spencer differs from the early Utilitarians as he shifts from their view of a mechanical conception of life to his own of a biological. He is at one with them in thinking that the end of life is happiness. The early Utilitarians recognised that some lines of action conduce to happiness, but they did not determine how and why they did so. This is the task to which he addresses himself. Conscience to him is not *a priori* or intuitive fact. It is rather the outcome of a slow development throughout the history of the human race and of animate life, and is thus *a posteriori* from the point of view of this racial experience on which he lays considerable stress. He defines justice as the freedom of every man to do what he wills, provided he infringes not the equal freedom of any other man. It is a definition akin to the Platonic one that justice consists in every man minding his own business and not interfering with that of his fellows. The sentiment of justice may be *a priori* to the individual, but it is *a posteriori* to the race. Impartiality and freedom are the two elements in justice on which he lays stress. He applies his ideas to topic after topic. He disposes of the argument that the ancestors of the present holders of land, for instance, obtained it by force or fraud, and that therefore their descendants may be dispossessed of it without compensation. He points out that though private ownership undoubtedly originated mainly in conquest, the landless of to-day are quite as much descendants of the original conquerors as the landed, and the landed, no less than the landless, are the descendants of those whose lands were originally conquered. Can we suppose for a single moment that the ownership of land has continued ever since in one exclusive caste? Besides, the community has a right to the land, not in its present highly-cultivated condition, but in its natural uncultivated condition. Improvements of that condition are just subjects of private ownership, and they are vested in the present possessors of the land. Consequently resumption without compensation would be a gross act of injustice. Finally, the owners of the land have spent vast sums on it and have also contributed vast sums to the poor, and compensation is also due on this account.

Spencer admits that a complete ethical justification for private property cannot be given, but he asks, Can it be given for communism? All men are not equal, and no law of justice can declare that unequal persons shall receive equal shares. Aristotle's law of distributive justice remains ethically sound, and the main difficulty is that the material to be distributed seems to be as insufficient as Malthus deemed it to be.

Our philosopher has no faith in the efficacy of State interference. It has done harm in the past, and can do nothing but harm in the present. What does it produce but the slackening of the national fibre and the destruction of national economy? He firmly holds to the principle of freedom—free trade, free competition, free contract. The Socialist, he writes, in his zeal for equality and fraternity has forgotten the first member of the triad, liberty, and would substitute for the tyranny against which he declaims another tyranny not less unjust and not less disastrous.

The Principles of Ethics is Utilitarian, but Utilitarian with a difference. Empirical ethics has progressed through three stages. First, there was egoism, pure and simple, or hedonism, if you will; then Utilitarianism of the older sort; and finally evolutional ethics. All three systems accept pleasure or happiness as the test, though they increasingly tend to sublimate the test. All are exposed to the difficulty of constructing a moral pathometer which will exhibit the helpful pleasures and the harmful pains. All have to accept the hedonistic paradox that to gain pleasure, the sole end of life, the best way is not to aim at it but at something else. To get happiness you must forget it. It comes to the emotional, imaginative natures as surely—more surely—than it comes to the logical and ratiocinative ones. Be that as it may, the Utilitarianism of Hartley, Paley, and Bentham is dead and buried beyond any hope of resurrection in a grave dug by Austin, J. S. Mill, and Sidgwick as well as by Stephen and Spencer himself.

To the outward and visible signs of success Spencer was wholly indifferent. He refused to accept the honours that were pressed on him towards the close of his career. Honorary degrees from the universities were uncoveted by him, and he regularly declined those offered to him. Neither encouraged by private approval nor discouraged by public disapproval, he heroically pursued his way from 1860 to 1896. The transparent sincerity of the man is as obvious as his utter devotion to truth. The success of his book on *Education* did not seem to move him, and the financial return it brought him also left him unmoved. Much as he wrote about helpful pleasures, it does not seem as if he shared them. The truth is that he had struggled so long and so persistently against neglect that in the end this neglect hardened his nature. The fight against adversity and disappointment toughens the character and disciplines the mind, but there is a price to be paid, and this price is inability to enjoy the rewards of success—when they at last appear. Without callousness to public opinion, Spencer could not have carried out this thirty-six years' task, and yet this very callousness prevented his enjoyment of public appreciation when at length it came. The story of Spencer is not in this respect unique. Thackeray voices the same feeling. "When I was a boy," remarked the novelist, "I wanted toffee, but I had not a shilling. Now I have the shilling, but I don't want the toffee."

The originality of Spencer's mind is obvious to all, but with this excess of originality there accompanied it a serious deficiency of receptivity. This appears in the notorious fashion in which he neglected the study of the writings of those who thought on the very subjects on which he himself was thinking. No doubt it arose in part from his habitual indolence. He was ever an impatient reader. "I never could read books the cardinal principles of which I rejected." A book of this class, if he began it, he threw down the moment he discovered that its leading ideas were uncongenial to his philosophy. It is of course a highly dangerous plan, for it means that the man who pursues it is not aware that there are many aspects of thought with which he is entirely unfamiliar. Men instinctively recognise this, and it is one reason why they rule out the claims of his *Synthetic Philosophy* to be a coherent, complete, fully reasoned-out system. It is incomplete and not fully reasoned out, though, to be sure, no one could deny that it is apparently coherent. In spite of the sweep of his system, its author possessed a highly specialised mind, carrying with it all the disadvantages—as well as the advantages—of extreme specialisation.

Facts clustered around his principles as iron filings around a magnet. An isolated fact he could not bear: it must fall into its due place alongside the principle bearing on the class of facts to which it belonged. It was a prime necessity of his mind that it must fit a fact into a class. Sir F. Galton bears his testimony: "The power of Spencer's mind that I most admired was that of widely founded generalisations. Whenever doubt was hinted as to the sufficiency of his grounds for making them, he was always ready to pour out a string of examples that seemed to have been, if not in his theatre of consciousness when he spoke, at all events in an ante-chamber, whence they could be summoned at will." One of George Eliot's witticisms poked fun at his aptitude for generalisations. He had been explaining his disbelief in the critical powers of the salmon, and his aim in making flies of "the best average representation of an insect buzzing on the surface of the water." "Yes," came her reply, "you have such a passion for generalising that you even fish with a generalisation." He fished for salmon most ardently, and he fished no less ardently for the idea which would co-ordinate the facts in his mind.

Fortunate in many ways, he was fortunate in the time when his *Synthetic Philosophy* appeared. It coincided with Darwin's discovery and the public mind was in a measure prepared for the labour of a man who employed the term evolution before Darwin and the very phrase the survival of the fittest before him. Optimism was an outstanding quality of his thought as it was also of Mill's, but before his death in 1903 confidence on the part of the public in this optimism was steadily abating. Men saw defects in the industrial organisation as keenly as Spencer had perceived them in the military organisation he decried. Nor were men so sure as he that the military organisation had entirely passed away. In 1903 Wilhelm II had been fifteen years on the throne, and his speeches were not precisely of the industrial order. The philosopher's own country had lost much of its belief in Spencerian freedom—free trade, free competition, and free contract. Men saw that while causes, courses, and consequences were potent, so too were great men who might divert these causes, courses, and consequences. Men came to think that there was more in the great man theory than Spencer allowed, and that after all Carlyle might be much nearer the truth. Originality was Spencer's, but was receptivity? A great man communicates truth, but does he not also receive truth? A story will throw light on the answer. In order to avoid any excitement Spencer carried with him a pair of ear-pads connected by a spring passing round the back of his head. Sir Ray Lankester relates how, when he was quite a young man, Spencer asked him to call to see him at the Athenaeum with a view to giving him information on biological matters. On arrival Spencer expounded to Sir Ray his own theories on the matter in question. As soon as Sir Ray began, however, to point out one or two of the difficulties, Spencer hastily closed the conversation by fitting on his ear-pads, stating that his medical advisers would not allow him to enter into a discussion. This action was parabolic. By his ear-stoppers Spencer cut himself off from the world, and at the same time the world cut itself from him.

An eclectic by nature, Spencer picked up facts here and there, and fitted them into what looked like a coherent whole. The coherence was only in appearance. In spite of his powers of generalisation the facts remained a medley. The fusion of them around principles was mechanical. Time has revealed the seams and the fissures in an artificial system of thought. There is the chasm between conscious life and unconscious, and there is the chasm between the organic and the inorganic. The mixture of absolute and relative ethics, the strengthening of the weaknesses of empiricism by the doctrine of heredity—these stones in the structure have not worn well. Under the rude action of time they are visibly crumbling away. Evolution is no longer the magic word it used to be. We want to know what evolution implies and what is the succession of creative acts which the word conceals rather than explains. Besides, he marked off a tract of life as the unknown and the unknowable, and this is the very tract we are most anxious to explore. The path to it may lie in activity, in intuition, in impulse, in the élan of life, in what you will, but it represents something towards which the thoughtful are turning, even if they are turning in vain. They may be engaged in a search as bootless as the philosopher's stone, but they will not abandon their quest at the bidding of one who tells them that it is fruitless. They exhibit little interest in, or sympathy with, one who tells them that it is all an illusion. In truth, the world has turned away from the Spencerian problems or approaches them from another angle. We do not know how better to describe the relation of Spencer's writings on science, physical or political, than by comparing them to a ruined palace which stands on the shore of Posilippo. The building was designed on a stately plan, but was never finished. It is beautiful in its desolation, and venerable in its neglect. The blue sea plashes night and day upon its foundations, and the hill above is studded with smiling villas; but the lady for whose pleasure it was destined never gladdened it with her presence. Thus the Spencerian system was planned, in the magnificence of its author's hopes, on a scale too vast for real completion. It survives, the mighty monument of a splendid failure. The thoughts of the ages find an echo there, and the imagination is kindled by the majesty of its proportions. But science has chosen her habitation elsewhere.

REFERENCES

AMMON, O. *Die natürliche Auslese beim Menschen.* (Jena, 1893.)

AMMON, O. *Die Gesellschaftsordnung u. ihre näturlichen Grundlagen. Entwurf einer Sozialanthropologie.* (Jena, 1896.)

ANONYMOUS (by Two.) *Home Life with Herbert Spencer.* (Bristol, 1906.)

BARKER, E. *Political Thought from Spencer to To-day.* (London, 1915.)

BEARE, J. I. *Organic Morality; or, the Ethics of Herbert Spencer.* (*Dublin,* 1889.)

BOUTROUX, E. *Religion according to Herbert Spencer.* (Edinburgh, 1907.)

BOWNE, E. P. *The Philosophy of Herbert Spencer: being an examination of the "First Principles" of his System.* (New York, 1876.)

COKER, F. W. *Organismic Theories of the State.* (Columbia, 1910.)

DUNCAN, D. *The Life and Letters of H. Spencer.* (London, 1908.)

DURKHEIM, E. *De la Division du Travail social.* (Paris, 1893.)

ELLIOT, H. *Herbert Spencer.* (London, 1917.)

FISCHER, E. L. *Ueber das Gesetz der Entwickelung auf psychisch-ethischen Grundlage mit Rücksicht auf Ch. Darwin, H. Spencer, u. Th. Buckle.* (Berlin, 1875.)

FISKE, J. *Outlines of Cosmic Philosophy, based on the Doctrine of Evolution.* (London, 1874.)

GAUPP, O. L. *Herbert Spencer.* (Stuttgart, 1897.)

GROSSE, E. *Spencer's Lehre von der Unerkennbaren.* (Leipzig, 1890.)

GUTHRIE, M. *On Mr. Spencer's Formula of Evolution as an exhaustive statement of the changes of the universe.* (London, 1879.)

GUTHRIE, M. *On Mr. Spencer's Unification of Knowledge.* (London, 1882.)

GUYAU, M. *La Morale Anglaise Contemporaine.* (Paris, 1900.)

HANSEN, G. *Die drei Bevölkerungsstufen.* (München, 1889.)

HÖFFDING, H. *History of Modern Philosophy.* (London, 1900.)

HUXLEY, L. *Life and Letters of T. H. Huxley.* (London, 1900.)

JAMES, W. *Memories and Studies.* (London, 1911.)

LAMPRECHT, K. *Die kulturhistorische Methode.* (Berlin, 1900.)

LAPOUGE, V. de. *Les Sélections sociales.* (Paris, 1896.)

LE DANTEC, F. *Les Luttes entre Sociétés humaines et leurs phases successives.* (Paris, 1893.)

MACKINTOSH, R. *From Comte to Benjamin Kidd.* (London, 1899.)

MACPHERSON, H. *Herbert Spencer: the Man and his Work.* (London, 1904.)

MAITLAND, F. W. *Collected Papers.* Vol. I. (Cambridge, 1911.)

MAJEWSKI, E. de. *La Science et de la Civilisation.* (Paris, 1908.)

MARTINEAU, J. *Essays.* (London, 1879.)

MICHELET, C. L. *Spencer's System der Philosophie. Spencer's Lehre von dem Unerkennbaren.* (Leipzig, 1891.)

MIKHAILOVSKY, N. K. *Qu'est-ce le Progrès ? examen des idées of de M. Herbert Spencer.* (Paris, 1897.)

MURRAY, R. H. *Science and Scientists in the Nineteenth Century.* (London, 1925.)

PEARSON, K. *The Grammar of Science.* (London, 1900.)

RITCHIE, D. G. *Darwinism and Politics.* (London, 1889.)

RITCHIE, D. G. *The Principles of State Interference.* (London, 1891.)

ROBERTSON, J. M. *Modern Humanists.* (London, 1895.)

ROBERTY, E. de. *Comte et Spencer.* (Paris, 1894.)

ROYCE, J. *Herbert Spencer: An Estimate and a Review.* (London, 1904.)

SCHULTZE, F. *Kant u. Darwin.* (Jena, 1875.)

SEWARD, A. C., Ed. *Darwin and Modern Science.* (Cambridge, 1909.)

Sidgwick, H. *Lectures on the Ethics of T. H. Green, Mr. Herbert Spencer, and J. Martineau.* (London, 1902.)

Sidgwick, H. *The Philosophy of Kant and other Lectures.* (London, 1905.)

Sorley, W. R. *The Ethics of Naturalism.* (London, 1905.)

Spencer, H. *An Autobiography.* (London, 1904.)

Tarde, G. *La logique sociale.* (Paris, 1904.)

Thomson, J. A. *Herbert Spencer.* (London, 1906.)

Ward, J. *Naturalism and Agnosticism.* (London, 1915.)

Woltmann, L. *Die Darwinische Theorie u. der Sozialismus.* (Düsseldorf, 1899.)

Chapter II.

SIR HENRY MAINE AND THE COMPARATIVE HISTORICAL METHOD

WHILE it was reserved for Herbert Spencer to apply the method of evolution from a scientific point of view, it was reserved for Sir Henry Maine to apply it from a legal one. This is all the more remarkable, as the training of the former had been in scientific pursuits, and that of the latter in classical. It is difficult to know how far Maine was consciously influenced by Darwin, for his biography, written by Sir M. E. Grant Duff, sheds no light on this important matter. It seems quite likely that Maine's own genius enabled him instinctively to divine the far-reaching truth that there were stages in the world of institutions, as there were in the world of science, and that each stage sprang out of the preceding one. Two of the legal luminaries of the last fifty years are Sir Henry Maine and F. W. Maitland, and it is regrettable that the biographies of both men are inadequate. Sir M. E. Grant Duff's is the merest sketch, and in it he does not seem to think that he is called on to explore the relations between the *Origin of Species* and the genesis of *Ancient Law*, though the former was published in 1859 and the latter in 1861. Perhaps Mr. Fisher felt handicapped by the fact that he was writing the life of his brother-in-law. His book attains the high level of all his books, but oh! that it were longer and that it possessed more of the witty letters Maitland used to scatter with so lavish a hand.

Sir Henry James Sumner Maine (1822–88) was a native of Kelso. He spent his earliest years in Jersey, but family difficulties arose and his mother, a clever and accomplished woman, brought him up. In 1829 his godfather, Dr. Sumner, then Bishop of Chester, and later Archbishop of Canterbury, procured for the lad a nomination to Christ's Hospital, and at that school he showed promise destined to speedy performance. As an exhibitioner of Christ's Hospital he proceeded to Pembroke College, Cambridge. The next year he was elected Foundation Scholar of his College. In 1842 he won the Chancellor's Medal for English verse, the Camden medal for Latin hexameters, and the Browne medal for a Latin ode. In 1843 he won two more Browne medals—one for Latin ode and the other for a Greek and a Latin epigram, becoming also Craven University Scholar. For these prizes there was keen rivalry between him and W. G. Clark, afterwards public orator, and their rivalry was long remembered. In the classical tripos of 1844 Maine was Senior Classic and Clark second. The regulations of the forties obliged candidates for the Chancellor's Senior Classical Medal to take honours in mathematics, regulations that vexed the soul of Macaulay. Maine, who was senior optime, gained the Senior Classical Medal, while Clark was again second. The victor's spirit was always willing but his body was weak. The reading for these distinctions overtaxed his strength. Like Spencer, he was never a strong man afterwards, but, again like Spencer, he accomplished an amazing amount of work. Still, he found time to become a member of the famous "Apostles' Club," consisting of a body of the most promising undergraduates who met for discussion. Tom Taylor and Henry Fitzmaurice Hallam were among his friends and contemporaries, and he contributed a memorial of the latter to the *Remains*. Men noted his weak health, but they also noted his sensitive nervous energy, manifesting itself in brilliancy of intellect and imagination.

As no fellowship was vacant at Pembroke, Maine accepted in 1845 an invitation from Trinity Hall to become tutor there. As he was not in holy orders, he could not hold the Fellowship usually associated with the tutorship. A pupil, Mr. Bristed, records: "He had the greatest dexterity in impressing his knowledge upon others, made explanations that came to the point at once and could not be misunderstood, corrected mistakes in a way that one was not apt to forget, supplied you with endless variety of happy expressions for composition and dodges in translation." In 1847 he resigned his tutorship on his becoming Regius

Professor of civil law at the early age of twenty-five, holding this chair till 1854. In 1847 he married his cousin, Jane Maine, and was called to the bar in 1850. Although he retained his rooms in college and discharged his professorial duties, he lived chiefly in London. From the beginning of his married life he had written a little for periodicals. He was contributing to the *Morning Chronicle* in 1851, an organ of the Peelites, edited by a remarkable man, J. D. Cook, who gathered around him in the *Saturday Review* such writers as Lord Salisbury, Sir James Stephen, Sir William Harcourt, Sir Richard Owen, Goldwin Smith, Walter Bagehot, T. C. Sandars, and George Venables. A Liberal-Conservative, Maine's sympathies were evident in his writings on French and American questions. He disliked Napoleon III with all the fervour of the fifties, and he also disliked Disraeli. His leaning to moderate Liberalism extended to foreign as well as to home politics.

In 1852 the Inns of Courts founded five readerships, and instituted a sytem of examinations. Maine became the first reader on Roman law and jurisprudence. He was an able lecturer with the marked advantage of a voice "like a silver bell." His manner was as effective as his voice. He introduced his students to the *Institutes* of Gaius, and he also introduced them to the conceptions soon to become famous in his *Ancient Law*. He practised for a very short time at the Common Law Bar, belonging to the Norfolk circuit, but changed over to the Equity branch. His ill health continued, interfering during those critical early years when a practice was being built up.

Cook started the *Saturday Review* in 1855, and with the writers he succeeded in attracting he made it one of the most formidable organs of public opinion in the fifties. The *Edinburgh Review* and the *Quarterly Review* still continued their influence, but the fading power of the Benthamites was evident in the dwindling circulation of the *Westminster Review*. With contributors as able as Lord Salisbury and Goldwin Smith, yet Maine ranked among the ablest. Cook used to say that Maine and one other writer were the only two men he had ever known who wrote as well from the first as they ever wrote afterwards. He wrote on all sorts of subjects suggested by Cook, sometimes reviewing books, but more often contributing leading articles. Among the latter, like Mill, he wrote in 1857 against the impending extinction of the East India Company.

To the *Cambridge Essays* in 1856 he contributed a characteristic paper on *Roman Law and Legal Education.* There he urges the value of Roman Jurisprudence as a key to the grasp of International Law. He pleads for what he was to plead all his life, the historical study of law in general and of International Law in particular—"if we fail to comprehend, first, the influence of certain theories of the Roman jurisconsults on the mind of Hugo Grotius, and next, the influence of the great book of Grotius on International Jurisprudence—we lose at once all chance of comprehending that body of rules which alone protects the European Commonwealth from permanent anarchy, we blind ourselves to the principles by conforming to which it coheres, we can understand neither its strength nor its weakness, nor can we separate those arrangements which can safely be modified from those which cannot be touched without shaking the whole fabric to pieces." Maitland was to dream of a day when "it will seem a wonderful thing that men once thought they could write the history of mediaeval England without using the Year Books." In 1856 it is just as wonderful to Maine that anyone should think of interpreting International Law without using its year books which wear the form of the thoughts of such masters as Grotius. If Maitland insists that English law *is* English history, Maine insists that International law *is* European history. Blackstone had dimly grasped this truth, but Maine with his brilliant style and his incisive thought was to render it familiar to all who cared intelligently for the meaning of the past. His *Ancient Law,* which appeared in 1861, came as a reviving breeze over the stagnant waters of legal thought. For the dry analysis of Austin the magic of Maine substituted the warmth his intellect and his imagination kindled. We move in his book in an ample region where wide prospects open on all sides. Sir Frederick Pollock, with considered judgment, records: "For the present we may at least say, looking to our own science of law, that the impulse given by Maine to its intelligent study in England and America can hardly be overrated. Within living memory the Common Law was treated merely as a dogmatic and technical system. Historical explanation, beyond the dates and facts which were manifestly necessary, was regarded as at best an idle ornament, and all singularities and anomalies had to be taken as they stood, either without any reason or (perhaps oftener) with a bad one. . . . A certain amount of awakening was no doubt affected by the analytical school, as Maine taught us to call it. . . . But the scientific study of legal phenomena such as we really find them had no place among us. . . . Maine not only showed that this was a possible study, but showed that it was not less interesting and fruitful than any in the whole range of the moral sciences. At one master-stroke he forged a new and lasting bond between law, history and anthropology. Jurisprudence itself has become a study of the living growth of human society through all its stages, and it is no longer possible for law to be dealt with as a collection of rules imposed on societies as it were by accident, nor for the resemblances and differences of the laws of different societies to be regarded as casual."

The influence of the publication of the *Ancient Law* on the private fortune of its author was decisive. At the end of 1861 Sir Charles Wood, afterwards Lord Halifax, offered him the appointment of Legal Member of the Council in India, which Macaulay had held. On consulting high medical authority, Maine "learned that if he went to Calcutta, his life would not be worth three months'" purchase. Bitterly disappointed, he declined this appointment, and William Ritchie took his place. He died in a few months, and Lord Halifax renewed his offer to Maine, which he this time accepted. He left for India in 1862, and in the event the climate proved to be thoroughly congenial to him, and he returned in 1869 a stronger man than he had left.

Maine served the last year of Lord Elgin's viceroyalty, the whole of Lord Lawrence's, and the first years of Lord Mayo's. His health stood in the way of his taking an active share in the details of bills, and in drafting them he depended largely on Whitley Stokes, his pupil and one of his successors. His ability was partly shown in seeing what legislation was needed and partly in supporting the man who had to bear the burden of responsibility for all decisions. Sir Alfred Lyall, an experienced Indian official, writes: "In the very sympathetic notice of Sir Henry Maine, which appeared in the *Saturday Review*, it is mentioned that he could read a thick volume in such a way as to appropriate what concerned him in it, while an ordinary man read a hundred pages. In just such a swift and penetrating spirit he seems to have read India, the sacred literature, the ponderous histories, the innumerable volumes of official records, and the heavy bundles of papers that came before him as a member of the Government." In his *Asiatic Studies* Sir Alfred Lyall gives striking instances of Maine's penetration of the Indian spirit. He found in Rajputana the precise practices which Maine had suggested as a possible explanation of some scattered facts which he had noticed in his reading. Buckle's *History of Civilisation* approached Indian problems in a far different spirit, suggesting that in the scenery of India and in the food the inhabitants ate there was a sufficient explanation of the phenomena prevailing there. The premises and the processes of Buckle are as wrong as those of Maine are right. His attitude to the past differs by worlds from that of Spencer, for Maine manufactured the phrase that "except the blind forces of Nature, nothing moves in this world which is not Greek in origin."

On his return from India in 1869 he was appointed to the Corpus professorship of Jurisprudence just founded at Oxford. His first course of lectures was published in 1871 as *Village Communities*. It was founded partly on the facts he had observed while a legislator in India, partly on conversation with Lord Lawrence, while Sir George Campbell checked the conclusions, and partly on the researches of Nasse and von Maurer. In this book he insisted on the value of knowledge of India and of Roman law, for he was faithful to his first legal love. To him India is "the great repository of verifiable phenomena of ancient usage and ancient juridical thought." Roman law, "viewed in the whole course of its development, . . . connects these ancient usages and this ancient juridical thought (of India) with the legal ideas of our own day." Nor does he omit to point out the abiding truth of De Tocqueville's remark that the conquest and government of India are really *the* achievements in the history of a people which it is the fashion to consider unromantic. From an eastern angle Maine afforded sidelights on the philosophy which he found decaying on his return home. What the Hindus think of equality among men is best gathered from a story he tells. A Brahmin lawyer in great practice was seeking to establish himself in the good graces of an Anglo-India functionary by enlarging on the value of Bentham's Utilitarianism, in so far as it placed the standard of law and morals in the greatest happiness of the greatest number. The Englishman expressed surprise that the principle should receive such approval in India. "No doubt," rejoined the high-caste Hindu, after a glance around the room to assure himself that nobody was within earshot, "no doubt, it is one difficulty that, according to my religion, a Brahmin is entitled to exactly five-and-twenty times as much happiness as anybody else!"

In May, 1871, Maine was gazetted a K.C.S.I., and the Duke of Argyll appointed him to a seat on the Indian Council. He interested himself in the judicial department, but he also cared for such matters as the selection and training of candidates for the Indian civil service. His prescience was abundantly seen in his opposition to the Ilbert Act which under Lord Ripon's Government proposed to give native magistrates jurisdiction over Europeans under certain circumstances. In 1882 the overwhelming consensus of official opinion was in its favour. Maine hoisted the first danger signal. He called to mind the bitter controversy which raged over "The Black Act" in Lord William Bentinck's time, and privately warned Lord Hartington who was then Secretary of State for India. Lord Hartington put the letter in his great coat pocket, went to Newmarket, and forgot all about it with the result that Maine's warning never reached Lord Ripon. In 1875 Maine published another set of lectures on the *Early*

History of Institutions, in which he interpreted the Brehon Laws of Ireland, employing Indian parallels. He studied primitive Aryan institutions on the banks of the Shannon as well as on those of the Ganges. The following year a third edition of the *Village Communities* was required, and to it Maine added his old paper on *Roman Law and Legal Education* and his Rede lecture *On the Effects of Observation of India on Modern European Thought.*

Maine returned to Cambridge as master of Trinity Hall in 1877, retaining his membership of the India Council but not of course the Oxford chair. In 1883 he published his *Dissertations on Early Law and Custom,* the last of the series he had begun in 1861. Max Müller's translations of the sacred Books of the East deeply influenced its author. Membership of learned Societies at home and abroad fell increasingly to him. At different periods of his career he declined the Chief Justiceship of Bengal, the permanent Under-Secretaryship for the Home Office, the permanent Under-Secretaryship for Foreign Affairs, and the Principal Clerkship of the House of Commons. In 1879 he expressed his warm approval of the proposed codification of law in India. He endorsed the dictum of Macaulay: "Our principle is simply this: Uniformity when you can have it, diversity when you must, but in all cases certainty."

He had written four essays in the *Quarterly Review* on the prospects of popular government, the nature of democracy, the age of progress, and the constitution of the United States, and these he sent forth in 1885 under the title of *Popular Government.* In the preface he informs his readers that it had long been his desire to apply the historical method to the political institutions of men as he had in his *Ancient Law,* and indeed as he had done in all his writings. Just, however, as he had found the path of his legal investigations obstructed by baseless theories about a law and state of nature antecedent to all laws of which history makes mention, so he found the path of his political investigations obstructed by other equally fantastic assumptions about a series of political institutions of which history makes no mention, but which a number of writers, with Rousseau at their head, have imagined to have existed in a period antecedent to history. The political institutions of this far-off time were conceived by those writers to have been of a highly popular character. Maine's object in writing this work was to examine the phenomena of popular governments in so far as they had been registered by those who had observed them, putting out of sight all theories about a state of things with regard to which it was simply impossible to know anything whatever. Lord Morley and E. L. Godkin, the editor of the American newspaper, *The Nation,* answered this sustained attack on democracy. In a private letter of 1885 he mentioned Morley's remarks, saying: "If there were an ideal Toryism I should probably be a Tory; but I should not find it easy to say which party I should wish to win now. The truth is, India and the India Office make one judge public men by standards which have little to do with public opinion." There is always the tendency on the part of the bureaucratic to turn Conservative, spelt either with a capital C or without one. To his American critic Maine replied, and his closing words are: "Mr. Godkin seems to think that the only evidence worth mentioning for the duration of democracy is that furnished by the United States, and I think so too. He thinks, at least he gives reason for thinking, that the prospects of scientific thought in democratic societies are very gloomy, and that also is my opinion. We have reached these results by different routes, but the results do not greatly differ."

On the 1887 Jubilee he contributed a masterly paper on India to Humphry Ward's *Reign of Queen Victoria.* That year he succeeded Sir William Harcourt as Whewell Professor of International Law at Cambridge. On this subject before he sailed for India he had written a book, but the manuscript had been lost. Whewell had laid down the condition that the Professor should suggest measures tending towards the extinction of war. Maine emphasised the forces arrayed against this consummation, the enormously increased armies, far greater in peace than they ever were even in the height of the Napoleonic struggle, the vast amount of intellect which now spends itself on the perfecting of warlike mechanism, the huge expenditure of capital which a single naval battle would cause, and the like. Still, there is progress. War was originally the rule, peace the exception. Prisoners were once massacred with the utmost barbarity, which has disappeared. The lecturer died in 1888, thus not surviving to witness the horrors of the World War. Slavery was once a humanitarian reform, an improvement on the massacre of the captive. Very slowly and gradually wars had been becoming less hideous, when the theological quarrels of the sixteenth century stimulated human passion to a desperate degree. The horrors of the wars of religion exercised their due effect on Grotius, leading him to produce his masterpiece. From Grotius to Vattel jurists built up the system we now know as International Law. In laying the foundations of their system they employed Roman law. The portion of it they found most useful for their purpose was the Jus Gentium originally created by the *praetor peregrinus*. He selected the rules of law common to Rome and to the different Italian communities which surrounded Rome. Then the Stoics identified this Jus Gentium with the Law of Nature, the law lying behind every other law and controlling every other law. Practically, it was the sum of the principles of conduct which man in society was imagined by the foremost minds in Rome to obey simply because he was man. These lectures were the last effort of the tired body, and on February, 1888, he passed away at Cannes. Sir Henry Maine was a close counterpart of the Roman public servant who could both think and act—scholar and man of action. The very trend of his mind agreed with this resemblance, for he had that shade of antique melancholy which sprang from a conviction of the worth of this fleeting life, not from discontent with it.

Maine was a firm believer in strong government, and a man who went to India soon after the Mutiny was likely to have this belief stamped upon his mind. Like many of the believers in strong government, he was distinctly pessimistic as to its ultimate results. Most men bury themselves in the work of the day and concern themselves neither with the past nor the present. He did not belong to these, but he did belong to that company who are borne along by sure and enthusiastic faith in the work of the British Empire. No one had more deeply the Virgilian feeling of "the sense of tears in mortal things." Sometimes he felt what Lyall expressed in his *Asiatic Studies*. There we read that "It may be that Asia has always been too deep a quicksand for Europe to build upon it any lasting edifice of morals, politics, or religion; that the material conditions forbid any lasting improvement; that the British legions, like the Roman, will tramp across the Asiatic stage and disappear; and that the clouds of confusion and superstition will roll up again. Then, after all, the only abiding and immovable figure in the midst of the phantasmagoria will be that of the Hindu ascetic and sceptic, looking on at the incessant transformation of men into gods and gods into men."

To many a man in the Victorian age the writings of Mill formed an epoch in his mental career, and to many a man so did the writings of Maine. He covers the history of society back to its dim beginnings in his own illuminating fashion. His standpoint is broadly philosophic, his style dignified. You are borne along the current of time, with this lucid and just spirit by your side upholding and instructing you. Beside you is the patriarchal system, the village community, the feudal system, the aristocracy, the monarchy, the democracy, the clash of races, the rise and fall of social systems, the conflict of nascent nationalities. Serene you float above them all, and ever as the panorama unrolls itself, the weighty measured unemotional voice whispers the true meaning of the scene in your ear.

Maine applied the comparative historical method as it had never been applied before, and this in part accounts for the resounding success of his evolutionary ideas. He sets before us the early and simple form of past political societies down to their latest and most complex developments, and he also sets before us his study of contemporary societies. We glean that mankind all over the world is at different stages in its institutional history, and that there is scarcely any stage in the past that does not exist somewhere in the present. No one can expect to note the influence of the conception of evolution in our domain at once. It takes time to work out the consequences of such a revolutionary idea. The amazing matter, however, is that we do notice it at once. For in 1861 Maine published his *Ancient Law: its Connection with the Early History of Society and its relation to Modern Ideas*. In his introduction to his translation of it M. Courcelle Seneuil remarks that the only French work he can compare with it is the *Cité Antique* of Fustel de Coulanges. At first sight the comparison seems well founded, but if Maine swept the past with a telescope Fustel de Coulanges swept it with a microscope. He boasted of being the only Frenchman who had studied every Latin text from the sixth century B.C. to the tenth century A.D., a feat Maine was incapable of performing. Nor could he have employed the tone of Fustel de Coulanges who announced one day to an enthusiastic audience, "Do not applaud me, it is not I that speak to you but history that speaks by my mouth." Maine was far too broad-minded to believe in a single cause, and in the *Cité Antique* its author offered religion as the complete interpretation of Roman civilisation.

In the *Ancient Law* nothing is more remarkable than the pleasure its author evidently took in tracing back the genealogy and kinship of law and custom, in detecting the meaning and evolution of forms, in showing the archaic descent of a rule that seemed essentially modern, in exposing the recent origin of an usage that pretended to antiquity, and in proving that the latest reform might be sometimes no more than a revival of primitive practice. The sub-title of the volume is never forgotten in the illuminating pages Maine gives us. The investigation of ancient law is, however, beset with difficulties due to the theories of men which are no more than "a series of guesses," the guesses of the Roman lawyers and their modern descendants. From Hobbes to Blackstone, men maintained that positive law originated in the social contract, but that its chief contents as regards property, contract, and the like, came from the law of nature. Maine thinks that this law proved of grave service to the Romans in their task of improving their jurisprudence. It was a good model, but it was also a vague and confused one. Applied in the eighteenth century in France under the spell of Rousseau it wrought untold anarchy. Nor is the method of an analytical jurist like Austin much better. He resolves every command into the command of a sovereign. Customs provides no real exception, for what the sovereign permits he commands. Has Austin contemplated a state of society other than that of an advanced community like that of England in 1832? If he had contemplated a primitive community he would have found no such sovereign as that demanded by the *Province of Jurisprudence Determined.* Maine indeed suggests a relationship between Austin and Bentham akin to that between Adam Smith and Ricardo. The utilitarians, like the economists, have in their mind all the time a country like England, and the position of such a country in jurisprudence or Political Economy was wholly exceptional. Was Political Economy really a science applicable to old communities as to new? Was it not rather an analysis of the higher business applicable only to a metropolis like London? Was not jurisprudence in a like plight? Was not the Austinian analysis at bottom an analysis of the conditions the jurist found in England in 1832? So Maine is disposed to argue, and it is plain how much truth lies in his argument.

The analytic method is as much required as the historical method, for we do not belong to the school of thought which can praise Maine only at the expense of Austin. History without analysis is often mere curiosity, and analysis without history is blind. It is noteworthy from a passage in his introduction that Austin had anticipated Maine's inquiry into the history of the growth of the law of nature, and had independently arrived at the same conclusions as those which are contained in Maine's difficult chapters on the subject. On the other hand, though Maine does not recognise the necessity of analysis as expressly as Austin recognises the necesssity of history, it is obvious that the precise definitions furnished by the inquiries of Bentham and Austin supplied a starting point for all his inquiries. At the same time, Austin's belief in history receives but scanty support in his two massive volumes.

From the ninth century to the eighteenth the conception

of a social contract exercised the profoundest influence on the political conduct of men. Two men dealt it a resounding blow from which it never really recovered. One was Vico and the other Montesquieu. Vico's *Scienza Nuova,* which appeared in 1725, was ignored in his own day. Well might Michelet, his translator, say that Vico wrote not for his own age, but for that which was to dawn half a century after his death; not for the eighteenth century, but for the nineteenth. It was his work, as well as Montesquieu's, to set forth the complex of moral and religious beliefs, modified by political and physical, intellectual and social causes, in the life of the State. Instead of the abstract we have the concrete unfolded in all its complexity. Such an unfolding left little space or place for the social contract conception, and it gradually disappeared into the background of thought. But in the main we must be content to attribute the change to one of those silent and mysterious movements of thought of which we only feel the effects without being able to trace them to a cause. Both Lecky, in his *History of Rationalism,* and Sir Leslie Stephen, in his *English Thought in the Eighteenth Century,* remark how modes of thought pass away—and the latter adds, how superstitions revive—without direct proof or disproof. Beliefs draw their nourishment from the atmosphere of thought, just as truly as plants draw theirs from the oxygen around them. And this doubtless is the element of truth in the common saying that certain ideas are "in the air." The mental conditions are favourable, and the ideas spring up and seed and multiply, like plants in a suitable soil and climate.

With the disappearance of the contract conception there was also a transformation, for men will not willingly part with an old conception. Natural right has a long pedigree behind it. Vico is as certain of this as any sixteenth century writer. He is, however, not so certain that the law of nature has been rightly interpreted. To him the *Diritto natural delle Genti* is not stationary, but progressive: it is a law varying with the stage of growth reached by a given community or nation, not a law the same always, everywhere, and for all. History, he argued, had suffered from the habit of ignoring psychological differences, by the failure to recapture the ancient point of view. Belief in progress he adopts, though he adopts it as a spiral movement.

Vico, like Montesquieu, shows on a grand scale that customs, laws, and institutions must be judged as historical phenomena with successive stages in their evolution. Adopting the comparative method, Vico estimates these phenomena not according to an abstract or absolute standard but as concrete realities related to given times and places. He investigates their determining causes and conditions, the whole social organism to which they belong, and the whole social medium in which they subsist. Once thinkers like Vico and Montesquieu adopt the comparative method, the rise of the historical school, the development of historical method, the idea of continuity, and the rapid advance of historical science, are bound to follow. Comparative Mythology and Comparative Law are ushered in as well as a comparative view of the State. In fact, the State has a past as well as a present, and this past exercises paramount sway over the present.

In his *Esprit des Lois*, perhaps the greatest book of the whole eighteenth century, Montesquieu proclaims that "all knowledge is knowledge of relations." It is the view of Vico, but alas! though Montesquieu had the *Scienza Nuova* on his shelves, he never read it. How much there was in common between the two is evident in the eighty-sixth of the *Persian Letters*. There Montesquieu announces: "I have often set myself to think which of all the different forms of government is the most conformable to reason, and it seems to me that the most perfect government is that which guides men in the manner most in accordance with their own natural tendencies and indications." That is, perfection is no longer abstract, but concrete, relative. Behind Maine lie the writings of Vico and Montesquieu.

Maine boldly employs the comparative historical method. In his *Ancient Law* he suggests—though he certainly never says—that when he has succeeded in giving the history of a system or a theory, he has finished with it. For example, he says that "the Law of Nature has never maintained its footing for an instant before the historical method." Though he scrupulously confines himself to facts, and is far too cautious to commit himself to any express conclusion which does not strictly fall within the limits of his inquiry, he appears to feel that he has refuted the theory, or rather all the successive theories, of the Law of Nature by tracing their genealogy. What he says in substance is this. There is no such thing as Natural Law, because you would not have thought of it had it not been for the theories of Rousseau; who adapted to his own purposes the language current among the lawyers of his day; who inherited their views from earlier lawyers; who, to serve a temporary purpose, twisted certain theories of Roman Law; which theories had at an earlier period been compounded out of the notions of certain Greek philosophers and certain doctrines about an older *jus gentium*, which meant something altogether different from what you understand by Natural Law.

All this may be perfectly true without proving the conclusion. A rational conviction of an important truth may be founded on very bad reasons. The common case of reasonable suspicion proves this. A man may suspect another of a crime and believe another to be guilty merely on account of the expression of his face or the tone of his voice, and this suspicion may turn out to be well founded. An advocate of the Law of Nature may say to Maine. It may be perfectly true that I should never have thought as I do, unless Rousseau, Grotius, the lawyers of the fourteenth century, the jurisconsults of Justinian, and the philosophers of Greece had thought certain things before me, but I can nevertheless give very good reasons for the faith that is in me. I assert that Nature imposes upon men certain laws capable of distinct enunciation, and attended by distinct penalties. For example, the Law of Nature forbids murder; and if there were no laws at all, murder would still incur natural penalties in the shape of disapprobation and vengeance. The manner in which I came by this opinion has nothing whatever to do with its truth. It is noticeable that this is practically the line taken by Herbert Spencer in his advocacy of Natural Law and the soundness of the historical method.

Maine admits that our laws have been improved from a sense of equity, which is part of Natural Law. Nor does he hesitate to tell us that "the greatest function of the law of nature was discharged in giving birth to modern international law," which is based on three postulates. Firstly, there is a law of nature. Secondly, this law of nature is binding on States *inter se*. Thirdly, sovereigns are related to each other like the members of a group of Roman proprietors, to whom certain doctrines of natural law apply. Rousseauism is so baneful to Maine that he persists in thinking that "the theory of natural law is still the greatest enemy of the historical method." Yet it seems to us that the sense of justice, for instance, is instinctive. As the result of heredity, we are born with a predisposition to it. It appears in children with their appeal to "mine" and "thine." No doubt Rousseau grossly abused natural right, but does his abuse of it remove the use of it? We trow not. With Natural Law we can employ alongside it the teaching of history, notably the history of law and institutions, considerations of general utility, the reforms suggested by it to undergo in a slow procession their transmutation into reality, and in this slow process we can pay regard to prescription. With all these checks, which Rousseau disregarded, Natural Law bestows rights to possessors of property after a certain time, and deprives original owners of them, the most important class of case in which abstract justice and natural right have to yield to the exigencies of utility. In fact, Natural Law furnishes the stoutest defence of the rights of property we can advance.

We learn that the earliest form of society was the patriarchal family, which expanded here into the tribe and there into the village community, while a union of tribes or village communities formed a nation. Law, in this early form, was nothing else than the command of the patriarch. The first appearance of civil laws, laws proper, is in the Themistes, the awards of the patriarchal sovereign, ruling over a number of families. Like decisions given in similar cases gave rise to custom, and custom to code, like the Code of Manu, the Decemviral Code or Law of the Twelve Tables of the Romans. By degrees the patriarchs were replaced by chiefs or kings, and the chiefs or kings by narrow aristocracies. These aristocracies became the exclusive depositaries first of the Themistes and in course of time of rules of law. As other parts of the nation gained power, the aristocracies were forced to publish the laws which they had formerly kept secret, and thus we have the origin of codes. Behind the code in dim antiquity we perceive the figure of the patriarch. The evolution of law is lucid, graceful, and simple, so Maine suggests, though Maitland, to be sure, believes that this evolution from the patriarch's command to the code is neither lucid, nor graceful, nor simple. He is unkind enough to regard Maine's patriarch as conspicuously modern. "He may be a savage, but he is in full evening dress."

There is a gulf between the needs of the community and the state of the law, and this gulf has been bridged by legal fictions, equity, and legislation. By fictions he means any assumptions which conceal or affect to conceal the fact that a rule of law has undergone alteration, its letter remaining unchanged, its operation being modified. These fictions are the earliest and one of the most useful of all contrivances for stretching the old rules to meet new facts, and are the only means which will effect that object in times not yet ripe for equity, or for the more difficult task of legislation. In process of time fictions are to a great extent replaced by equity. A theory grows up differing in details in different nations, according to circumstances, but always involving the conception of some broader and more reasonable system of justice than that which actually exists. This is administered side by side with the customs and the legal fictions, and involves a considerable discretion on the part of the judge, be he the praetor of Rome or the Lord Chancellor of England. Though Maine refuses to admit it, surely here is an instance of the operation of Natural Law. In time equity hardens into a technical body of law. The only remedy for this lies in legislation.

The two main topics of law are property and contract, and Maine gives an account of both. Obviously property and contract will depend on the primitive social organisation, and he seeks to determine what it was. He gives us two inconsistent accounts of this early society. In one it comes from the patriarchal family as described in the Book of Genesis, and in the other it is the Roman family still under the *patria potestas*. He identifies the patriarchal group with the Roman family. Here we have the first political society with the command of the patriarch as the first form of law. This identification of the patriarchal family with the Roman is as defective as his assumption of the universality of the *patria potestas*. Nor is this an end of his vacillation. He hovers between the conception of family groups on the Roman model and that of the tribe or clan ruled by customs, but directed by a chief.

The advance made by Maine is clearest if we employ his own method. Turn to his origin of property and compare it with that given by Paley in his *Moral Philosophy*. He dismissed the whole matter in a page and a quarter. He says that in the earliest form of society men lived alone; and that the earliest kind of property consisted of the product of personal labour; and that the earliest wills were those by which men bequeathed to others the things which they had made or collected with their own hands. Upon this purely arbitrary foundation he founds a large part of his doctrine respecting wills, and especially his distinction between the testamentary power which exists by what he calls the law of nature, and that which exists by positive institutions merely.

Dissatisfied with the *a priori* notions of men like Paley, our author seeks, like Ranke, to penetrate to what actually happened. The tribe comes from the expansion of the family, the single pair. Property once belonged to it collectively, and private property springs from "the gradual disentanglement of the separate rights of individuals from the blended rights of the community." Then he proceeds to give an account of four examples of this transition—the Highland clan, the Slav, the Hindu, and the Russian village community. In his *Early History of Institutions* he adds a second origin of property, ownership by the chief who from the first had a separate portion of land assigned to him, a beginning of private property. The rest belongs to the tribe or the village community. This common property was divided into equal portions, assigned to separate households; and these portions were changed by rotation to secure greater equality, or it was periodically redivided. By degrees the memory of the common ancestry fades away, and the community had the new orientation of being not so much an assembly of blood relations as a body of co-villagers. With this orientation each household clings with increasing tenacity to the land allotted to it. The redivisions become rarer and rarer and at last cease. The heath and the waste land remain common, but the rest of the tribal land has passed into private hands.

With the coming of private property there arrives the notion that you can alienate it, and there came into existence three modes of alienation. One plan was to classify property into higher and lower, and of this the Roman *Res Mancipi* articles which require mancipation, and *Res Nec Mancipi*, those which do not, affords an example. The English division of property into real and personal affords another. The lower kind can be conveyed with less formality, the *Res Nec Mancipi* and our personal property. As the advantages of the lower appear, the tendency is for the higher to be assimilated to it. The second plan was to mark off property into classes according to its source. One source might be alienated more freely than another. For instance the son in Roman law might dispose of his private acquisitions, the booty he won on active service for instance, as he pleased. The father in Hindu law might alienate what he had specially acquired. The third plan was to allow the usucapio of the Romans, the prescription of the moderns. If possession began *bona fide* and if the possessor acquired his title in one of the legally recognised modes, then undisturbed possession for a certain number of years, varying with the kind of property, bestowed the property upon him, curing any defect in the original title. Justinian decreed that the possession of land for ten years and of moveables for three transferred ownership from the original owner to the possessor. After a civil war or a revolution the use of prescription is of enormous value. The outcome of this evolution Maine expresses in his well-known formula that progressive societies "pass from status to contract," or from the condition in which each one's position is settled legally and socially at his birth, to that in which each one forms it for himself by contractual relations freely made.

In similar fashion Maine accounts for the rise of bequest and of contract. It is easy, in the light of our increased knowledge, to criticise the *Ancient Law*. We can show that stipulation arises in a quarter quite different from that suspected by Maine. We can see that he overrated the antiquity of the Roman law and that he gave too systematic a shape to the Twelve Tables. We can discern the extent to which he ignored the fashion in which the Civil Law continued to influence mediaeval jurists and churchmen, and we can discern the need there is for restoring the Law of Nature to its true place. In fact, there are spots in the sun, though Maine is great enough to survive the spots and much else. Where the evidence in 1861 failed him, he occasionally exercised his powers of divination, and this on the whole enhances the place he has won for himself. Before his day there were Paley, Bentham, and Austin, and if we place his writings alongside theirs, there can be little doubt that Maine emerges triumphantly from the test. His *Ancient Law* shows, by convincing proofs, that the primitive institutions of the Highlander and the Slav, the Hindu and the Russian were in all essential respects the same, and that they had a community of usages, ideas, and beliefs; it indicates clearly that the first stages of all on the path of progress were markedly alike; and it makes plain that the grave differences of condition and fortune now seen among them are in the main due to external circumstances. Anthropologists distinguish three European stocks, the Nordic, the Alpine, and the Mediterranean, and if we include Asia they can tell us of others. Maine is more anxious to point out that all races, the Highlander and the Hindu, the Slav and the Russian, belong to one human family. The general relation, not the particular, is always what arrests the attention of our author.

Nominally in his *Early History of Institutions* Maine is investigating the old Brehon Law of Ireland: really he is considering it in connexion with the general problems of history and comparative jurisprudence. In the infancy of all Aryan races law, in its present sense, has no existence; and ancient law was tribal usage occasionally declared by revered authority. The heroic king of the Greek clan, the headman of the Hindu village, the elders of the Teutonic township, the Druid priests of the Celtic sept, administered justice in various ways; and their "sentences" simply fell in with the customs in force among the surrounding community. Maine investigates two famous Brehon tracts, the Senchus Mor or Great Book of the Law, compiled by nine "pillars of Erin," under the superintendence and with the special sanction of St. Patrick, and the Book of Aicill, containing the wisdom of two Brehon judges. The Senchus Mor announces that "poets and priests" of old spoke "the Law of Nature" to the men of Erin. The Brehon tracts share the style and the character of the Brahminical writings, though we do not find the suttee. Christianity was the cause of this; for according to the Senchus Mor the "bright word of blessing" came to amend the "Law of Nature." The ancient law of Ireland was probably a mass of Aryan usage, owing little, if anything, to the government and legislation of the nascent society, developed, in long past ages, under priestly influence, and becoming at last the special craft and appanage of a learned profession of laymen. The Brehon Tracts, like the Brahminical Codes, have but the faintest ideas of courts of justice, and of positive institutions of any kind; as, in the case of the most venerable Aryan customs, their conception of the mode of doing right is by arbitration and a consensual process. For a caste, that was the depositary of the law, would expound it as a revelation from on high, would dislike to commit it to human tribunals, and would trust to its own enormous power to secure obedience and respect for it.

The Irish tribe or sept bears plain marks of society founded on a real or traditional relationship of blood; and in this respect it exhibits a strong likeness to those bodies which formed in Greece, in Rome, in India, and among Teutonic people, the seeds and beginnings of Aryan life. Yet in the sept we can perceive the growth of progress upon the very pattern of other branches of the Aryan stock; and the institution of separate property in land, one of the first conditions of civilisation, though still fettered by strange restrictions, emerges in Ireland, as in other countries, out of archaic collective ownership. The old structure of Celtic society affords proof of the ill-discerned process known as the general feudalisation of Europe; and indicates that that immense change, to which we owe much of the life of the West, may have been due, in some measure at least, to instincts common among Aryan races. From the Brehon tracts we can dimly gather that the revolution through which sovereignty, the ascendancy of certain dominant orders, and the subjection of the great mass of the people, replaced gradually, in so many countries, the old patriarchal Aryan community, was in operation in Ireland, though it was as yet only in its first development. In Celtic Ireland, as elsewhere, certain tribes emerge, attaining supremacy and gradually expanding into what we may call empire; whole tribes have been plainly reduced to vassalage, and are in a degraded and serflike condition; and in many of the dominant tribes, and even among the inferior units, we behold the chief extending his power, gaining a firmer hold on the land and the people, surrounding himself with bands of retainers—in a word, growing into a half-feudal Lord or Sovereign.

The sept was evidently a distinct organic group in the main connected by the ties of blood and claiming descent from a common ancestor; yet certainly containing other elements, introduced by adoption and like processes. In this respect, it showed much affinity with the Roman gens and the Hellenic house; and it was singularly like the Hindu joint family, united in kindred, worship, and estate, and one of the earliest nomads of Aryan life. The sept, however, had for ages settled on the land; the heads of households of which it was formed, and possibly even individuals in it, had acquired rights of independent ownership; and this drew a broad line of distinction between it and the joint family in which the possession was always in common; and assimilated it to a great extent to the Hindu village community and the Germanic mark, in which separate property in land is or was recognised. Still, except perhaps in the case of the chief, the representative of the common ancestor, the idea of individual claims to land was viewed by the sept as an innovation, and encountered older hostile ideas. Large portions of the territory of the sept was held collectively in the primitive fashion; and as the tradition of a common ownership survives in the Indian village community, and appears in the shifting severalties of the mark, so in the sept a notion prevailed that all the members had some joint right in the land; and this was maintained, as to part of the land, by a process of distribution, known as gavelkind, and perhaps by a veto of alienation, except with the assent of the whole community. In this last respect the sept and the Hindu joint family had one striking feature in common. The veto of the sept on alienation implied that the land was, in a sense, the common property of the entire sept; but this notion did not extend, or extended only in a low degree, to what we may call the clansman's peculium to what he had acquired by his own industry. A like rule exists in the Hindu joint family.

Maine examines the question whether the inchoate feudalisation of Ireland may not throw light on the more advanced changes of a similar kind in other countries, and illustrate the growth of mediaeval feudalism. He finds that the Brehon tracts contain indications of a pregnant sort as to the origin and position of the noble orders; they even explain some of the means probably through which feudalism enlarged its power; and all this certainly affords us a fresh clue to the mysteries of an historical maze in which every hint of a path is worth attention. How, then, did nobility arise in Europe, and what were the characteristic marks of it? One account of the matter ascribes it wholly to the barbarian conquests of the Roman Empire, and to the peculiar institutions of the victorious invaders as they settled upon its subject provinces. According to this view, the barbarian leaders parcelled out the territories which had fallen to their swords, among subordinate chiefs and retainers, who gradually became an hereditary caste, supreme over conquered and hostile races; and nobility is derived from these dominant orders, at least in the main and most ancient source, its true type being august descent, and ascendancy over masses of vassals. This description assuredly contains much truth, and accurately represents the most striking features of feudalism as it appeared on the continent; but modern research has clearly shown that it does not cover the field of inquiry. We have now the strongest reason to believe that the origin of nobility must be sought in causes of a more general kind, and that it runs up to the very first beginnings of primitive society in Aryan races. The honour given to the heads of houses, which everywhere formed the primary mould of the Aryan community, in its diverse aspects, was undoubtedly one great source of nobility; this was the patent, so to speak, of the Roman patrician, of the Greek eupatrid, of the Teutonic warrior; and it is impossible to doubt that it took its share in the development of nobility in feudal Europe, though other influences were more prominent.

The noble orders which grew up were not isolated hereditary castes; in the case of several Aryan races, they became true leaders, sometimes elective. If they were venerated for their ancient lineage, they were also remarkable for their possessions; wealth as well as birth determined their rank; and very frequently the acquisition of wealth gave its owner a right to obtain their privileges, and, in turn, to become noble. Now it is noteworthy that the Brehon tracts confirm this view of the earliest growth of nobility, and corroborate, in this respect, the testimony gleaned from the annals of Greece, of Rome, and of the German people. The Irish chief was usually of noble birth, but he was not seldom the choice of the tribe; he was the head of the tribe but still one with it; he was rich in the riches of primitive times and riches were required to maintain his position; and most curious of all, the possession of wealth enabled men even of low estate, in the old arrangements of Irish society, to attain the dignity and high place of the chief. The ancient law, expounded by the Brehons, therefore, lends new weight to deep theories of the beginnings of nobility among Aryan people, and of some of the earliest forms of it; and it increases our distrust of the purely feudal view of the origin of nobility in modern Europe. It also throws additional light on the early existence of a kind of nobility which grew up in the later stage of feudalism, and has had a very remarkable history. Royal power in the mediaeval monarchies became another parent of noble privilege, and has so continued down to our day. The notion that the Crown is the fountain of honour has long taken root in law and opinion, though it would have seemed strange to that proud order which had among its devices, "*ante mare undae,*" "*Roi je ne puis, Rohan je suis.*" The first creations of royal nobility had probably for their objects the household and personal following of the feudal sovereigns; and Maine reminds us of what a large part these functionaries have played in history. Nevertheless, the origin of the household was lowly; and great as the power and rank became of the nobility which grew out of it, the companions were serfs and dependents.

The aggrandisement of the companions was caused by their share in the warlike spoils of the monarch; we find, in fact, large benefices conferred on them; and thus the development of this order was, though a tardy, a potent feudal influence. Maine reveals that the very same class, in its essential features, reappears in old Celtic society. The Irish chieftain has his companions resembling those of the Teutonic king, and apparently of the same servile condition; nor is it improbable, had Ireland been permitted to grow in her own way, that these would ultimately have become a real nobility, the feudal supporters of the supreme ruler. The Brehon tracts give us an account of more than one of the various processes by which Ireland was in part feudalised, and thus illustrate the whole subject. One of the principal modes by which the feudal lord augmented his power was the usage through which men of humble estate commended themselves to a greater superior, and, in consideration of benefits of different kinds, became his vassals, and did him homage. The benefits so conferred were protection from outrage and oppression of class; but they were also sometimes advances of horses and cows, the equivalent of money; and commendation often grew out of the ordinary relations of debtor and creditor, a fact that reminds us of the immense influence of the Roman patricians and the Athenian eupatrids who kept the poorer citizens in debt. The tribal arrangements of Celtic Ireland disclose customs extremely like commendation and its result vassalage, and reflect much light on these growths of feudalism. The Irish chiefs were rich in the flocks and herds that formed the wealth of antiquity, and were usually the owners of great droves of cattle—the spoils, doubtless, of wars and raids—too numerous even for their large domains. Many clansmen, therefore, stood in need of these animals; and the chief often made loans and grants of cattle to tribal or alien clansmen, who in turn became dependent on him, and were subjected to homage and rendered service This was commendation and vassalage in all essential points; and it is noteworthy that the subjection of the clansmen to the chief was in proportion to the amount of stock received, that is to the hold of the chief upon him. Maine describes this process fully, and marks the distinctions drawn between the free, the Saer-stock tenant, and the servile, the Daer-stock tenant. Any large addition to the flocks and herds of the Saer-stock tenant, made by the chief, reduced him to the position of a Daer-stock one.

The sept always contained servile and degraded classes; and these in their relation with the chief were known as Fuidhir tenants. They were the remains of the conquered and broken septs, and they were in a state of ignoble serfdom. They were the thralls and villeins of ancient Ireland, the victims of the "cuttings," the "cosherings," the "coyne and livery" indignantly denounced by Edmund Spenser the poet and his contemporary Sir John Davies, the lawyer. The Tudor poet and the Tudor lawyer described customs which they plainly regarded as barbarous, entirely unaware of the fact that these customs had existed in the civilised States of Europe. Spenser tells us how, on the death of a chief, the sept was wont to assemble, and "to choose in the stead of the lord deceased, not the eldest son, but the next in blood," provided he were "the eldest and worthiest"; and tanistry, as this mode of inheritance was called, was abolished as a "lewd practice." Nevertheless, this primitive form of succession was but a variation of primogeniture. It is not difficult to connect tanistry with primogeniture. The beginnings of society, in Aryan races, almost always show us some one house pre-eminent among the heads of the houses, which form the gens, the village, or the tribe. Its representative is supreme in the surrounding community no doubt because he is supposed to be the nearest in kinship to the common ancestor from whom the whole settlement in theory sprang. This personage is the heroic chief or king, and his august title is transmitted in his line, for the most part from father to the elder son, so long as the tradition of descent is strong, or perhaps so long as the community is not exposed to war, or other disturbing causes. By degrees, however, as the tradition weakens, as the gens, the village, or the tribe expands, and takes in foreign elements, a new principle of succession appears, especially as military or other needs require the leader to be strong and skilful, and election, not the claims of descent, decides, at least within certain limits, the devolution of the old ancestral dignity. The rights of the revered house of the hereditary ruler are still respected; the community, when it makes a choice, selects from the race which it is taught to honour, and frequently makes no choice at all, and the title is transmitted by the ancient method. The history of the descent of the crown in several countries of modern Europe shows phenomena very similar to these, and they explain the nature of Tanist succession, and how primogeniture is related to it. It is far from improbable that, in remote ages, Irish chieftaincies passed from father to son, and that primogeniture was the general rule observed. The changes, however, which, in the course of time, must have taken place in the tribe or sept, dissolving as they did, more or less, the ties of blood within these units, and, above all, the continual want, in a country torn by strife and disorder, of capacity and mature age in the chief, introduced the mode of election; and the "eldest and worthiest" of the blood of the chief would be chosen instead of the next heir, for this would be the fittest choice for the office.

It is a striking proof of the prejudice that marked their views of Ireland that the Tudor politicians did not perceive how something extremely like the custom of tanistry, which seemed to them so barbarous and rude, had existed in civilised States in Europe. The succession to the Holy Roman Empire was elective, and yet it had always had a tendency to run in the line of certain families, and it did become the inheritance of the House of Austria. So, too, in France and in England, the title to the crown passed, as a general rule from father to son; but it had been subjected, more than once, to what we may call an elective process; and the notion that the dignity must not deviate from the strict hereditary descent was by no means fixed in opinion, though it was accepted as the prevailing principle. The very order of things which they saw around might have taught Spenser and Davies that there was nothing shocking in the mode of transmitting Irish chieftaincies; it had something in common with the conditions which gave Charles V and his descendants power, much with the reigns of the Houses of York and Lancaster, much with several Tudor settlements of the crown. Maine's verdict is: "I do not think that the disaffirmation of the legality of Tanistry, and the substitution for it of the rule of Primogeniture, can justly be reckoned among the misdeeds or crimes of the English in Ireland. . . . Probably Sir John Davis does not speak too harshly of it when he charges it with 'making all possessions uncertain, bringing confusion, barbarism, and incivility.' The decision against the Irish Gavelkind was far less justifiable. Even if the institution was exactly what Davis supposed it to be, there was injustice in suddenly disappointing the expectations of the distant kindred who formed the sept of the last holder; but it is probable that several modes of succession are conformed under the name of Gavelkind, and that in many cases a number of children were unjustifiably deprived of their inheritance for the advantage of one."

Maine discusses such other matters as the singular arrangement of the Irish family—known as the fivefold division—and he finds in it, and in Borough-English, an analogy to the potestas of the Roman father and the privileges of the emancipated sons. He also discusses such remedies for wrong as Distress, and he finds parallels to it in the old Roman action of *pignoris capio*, the Teutonic practice of taking nams, a well-known practice of our Common Law, and the sitting in dharna of Brahminical law.

The *Early History of Institutions* connects at point after point the Irish race with its Aryan kindred. The Brehon tracts present a striking likeness to the Brahminical codes in form and in structure; and they demonstrate, with Maine's interpretation, that the Celtic tribes had a social organisation and a social life, nay, primitive usages, ideas, and tendencies which unite them to the foremost Western nations, and to the civilisation of the Indian peninsula. They prove too that Ireland and a large part of Europe moved from a common point along the path of progress, and went for a time the same way; and they throw clear and instructive light on important phases in European history. With this guidance before us Maine regards the Irish race as a people retarded in development; but he willingly accords them a place in the famous group of mankind which includes the Roman, the Gaul, and the Teuton among its European members, and relates it to the original Aryan race from which they all are descended.

The more he employs the comparative historical method, the more Maine perceives the advantages of it, and the disadvantages of the analytical method of Austin. The concluding two chapters of his *Early History of Institutions* are devoted to an account of the conception of sovereignty, and in them he subjects the Austinian analysis to a hostile criticism. He reminds us of Austin's four tests for discovering the seat of sovereignty in independent States. Firstly, the sovereign is a *determinate* human superior. He is not necessarily a single person, but the sovereign must possess physical power. No doubt power has been in the hands of a number of people not determinate, but Austin would call such a state of things anarchy. Secondly, the bulk of the society must obey the sovereign. In 1715 the Jacobites disobeyed the commands of the sovereign, yet, in spite of this, the majority of the people obeyed, and the sovereign remained in possession of his rights. Thirdly, the sovereign must receive the habitual obedience of the bulk of the community. In Roman Catholic countries some of the inhabitants receive commands from the Pope which they obey. This obedience is occasional, not habitual. Lastly, the sovereign is immune from the control of every other human superior. The Indian Viceroy sounds as if he were a sovereign, yet he renders obedience to the Cabinet which appointed him.

Maine is anxious to show that Austin really revived the ideas of Hobbes, giving them at the same time a fuller examination. In his able book on *The High Court of Parliament* Mr. McIlwain emphasises this point, explaining that Austin's theory is based on the dismembered state of the seventeenth century which of course gave rise to Hobbes's *Leviathan* and his *De Cive*. Mr. McIlwain points out that Austin's view is as unhistorical as the original compact he despised. "It is a mistake," urged T. H. Green, "to think of the state as an aggregation of individuals under a sovereign," and this mistake Austin commits.

The assertions of analytical jurists like Bentham and Austin then receive critical attention, and Maine finds that the leading one is the possession of irresistible force on the part of the sovereign or the sovereign body. Practically, they throw to the one side all the characteristics and attributes of the Government and Society except this one of force. Maine then proceeds to show that it is the whole historical antecedents of each society which controls the power of using the social force. The Austinian analysis simply says there is a sovereign who may possess the authority of the King of Persia, of the Athenian Demos, of the later Roman Emperors, of the Russian Czar, and of the Crown and Parliament of Great Britain. Maine insists that it is the whole enormous aggregate of opinions, sentiments, beliefs, superstitions, and prejudices, of ideas of all kinds, hereditary and acquired, some produced by institutions and some by the constitution of human nature, which determines how the sovereign of these varied types shall exercise or forbear from exercising his irresistible coercive power. Plainly, an analysis which omits so much as this is an analysis of less value than has been imagined.

Custom rules men in primitive societies where the sovereign seldom issues a conscious command. Austin is so preoccupied with 1832 that he forgets 832 A.D. and

832 B.C., when a sovereign issuing commands through legislation did not exist. Indeed primitive society allowed no room for such a functionary. Can we bring custom under the sway of Austin's sovereign if we employ the maxim that whatever the sovereign permits he commands? We may do it with Hobbes in the seventeenth century or with Austin in the nineteenth, but can we do it with the communities Maine describes in his *Ancient Law* or in his *Early History of Institutions*? Can we conceivably bring Abraham to the state when he issued commands which the analytical jurists could call true commands? Moral force the patriarch possessed, but what irresistible force of any other order could he control? Austin thinks that it smacks of the ridiculous to apply the term sovereign to a family like Abraham's, yet out of such a patriarchal family Maine holds that law originally springs. Maine takes an Indian example. Runjeet Singh ruled despotically over the Sikhs, and the slightest disobedience to his commands would have been instantly followed by death or mutilation, yet did he ever issue a command that Austin would recognise as such? He never made a law. The rules which regulated the life of his subjects were derived from immemorial usage, and these rules were administered by domestic tribunals, in families or village communities—the very groups to which Austin refused to apply his principles. Nor is Runjeet Singh an exceptional ruler: he is a type of all Oriental communities in their native condition. What now takes place in India used to take place in Europe, and in the Middle Ages we have a condition of affairs as devoid of Austinian commands as the Sikhs. Lord Bryce does not hesitate to say that Austin has given us a theory, which is so far from being that of the normal modern State, that it is applicable to only two kinds of States, those with an omnipotent legislature, of which the United Kingdom and the late South African Republic are almost the only examples, and those with an omnipotent monarch, of which Russia and Montenegro are perhaps the only instances among civilised countries. Bryce wrote in 1901 and all these examples, except our own, no longer exist.

It is evident that Maine insists on applying everything

that goes to the making of a nation in the past, its traditions and history, in order to determine how the sovereign can use his power in the present. He concludes that there are grave limitations on the system of the analytical jurists. Bentham and Austin confined their attention to the western world, and the western world comes from the Aryan world of the east. Aryan antiquity they left to the one side though it is doubtful if they were conscious that they were so leaving it. Firstly, the western world they contemplated was one where the States were formed in a manner different from the great empires of antiquity and from the modern empires and kingdoms of the East. Secondly, a new order of ideas on the subject of legislation must be conceived as having been introduced into the world through the Roman Empire. "Unless these changes had taken place, I do not believe that the system would ever have been engendered in the brain of its authors. Wherever these changes have not taken place, I do not believe the application of the system to be of value."

A. V. Dicey and D. G. Ritchie refine the Austinian analysis, distinguishing between the legal sovereign and the political sovereign. The legal sovereign is the body whose commands are enforceable in the law courts. The King in Parliament is such a legal sovereign. Dicey recognises behind this legal sovereign the political sovereign, the body in the State "the will of which is ultimately obeyed by the citizens of the State." Dicey finds this political sovereign in the electorate while Ritchie finds it in the public opinion or sentiment to which the legal sovereign must in the last resort yield obedience. According to Lord Bryce the legal sovereign is "the person (or body) to whose directions the law attributes legal force, the person in whom resides as of right the ultimate power either of laying down general rules or of issuing isolated rules or commands, whose authority is that of the law itself." The practical sovereign is "simply the strongest force in the State, whether that force has or has not any recognised legal supremacy." Mr. McIlwain holds that this distinction between the legal and the political sovereign does little but postpone the difficulty, for the distinction is strictly subsidiary to the doctrine of parliamentary sovereignty. He cogently shows that this distinction is unhistorical. It tells against the whole theory of parliamentary sovereignty as hitherto held in England. For if the King in Parliament, or the Government, is merely the agent of the community, which it undoubtedly is, it cannot be sovereign, whatever legal powers it may otherwise possess.

From criticism of the analytical jurists we pass to criticism of *Popular Government.* Here our author's attitude is quite as detached as it is in all his writings. He can link the remotest past with the immediate present through his use of the comparative historical method. Why should he stop short of his own day? If he can interpret it in the light of the past, so much the better for all of us. Such an interpretation he gives us, but it is not an interpretation that will readily fit into the party labels of Tory and Whig, of Conservative and Liberal. We all know that there is a tendency for the Liberal in office to turn Conservative when he is faced with the difficulties of administration. Maine improves upon this when he tells Demos that all unconsciously he has it in him to be a worse Tory than any of the Tories. Nor does he omit to lay stress on the circumstance that there is no necessary connection between popular government and moral or material progress. He is a thinker who can see in the unqualified rule of the majority the gravest danger of stagnation. He claims affinity with such defenders of organic development and conservative principles as Burke in a past generation and Sir J. F. Stephen in his own.

With a short history of popular government since its introduction in modern times we begin, and we reach the conclusion that history demonstrates its extremely fragile nature. Thrice the mob of Paris has overturned the Government, in 1792, in 1830, and in 1848. Thrice the army has overturned it, in 1797, in 1799, and in 1851. Thrice foreign invasion has overturned it, in 1814, in 1815, and in 1870. Nor is the example of France unique. The causes of this fragility are the modern military spirit and military organisation which have often led to the overthrow of popular government. There is also the modern growth of irreconcilable opinions, a portent more serious now than in Maine's day. Just before the World War we witnessed the revolt of women against their unenfranchised condition, of doctors who refused to work the Insurance Act, of non-conformists who refused to pay education rates, and of Sinn Feiners who refused one form of Home Rule and of Ulstermen who refused another. With the rights or the wrongs of the measures complained of, we are not here concerned. The grave matter is that this irreconcilable opinion manifested itself to such a degree that in the most law-abiding country in the world there were four determined demonstrations against statutes passed by Parliament. Nor is there any need to point out that the General Strike of May, 1926, was the gravest case of all. For it was practically a revolution raised by irreconcilable opinion. Maine notes the dangers from the mincing of the vote into such minute fragments that the voters, if left to themselves, will care but little about the ballot. The results of the successive Reform Acts of 1832, of 1867, of 1888, of 1918, and of 1928 exhibit this to a degree that the framers of these measures may receive a rude shock. The extension of the franchise provides opportunity for the party-manager with us and for the political boss in the United States. The devices of one party will be copied by another. The outcome is that all parties exhibit a growing likeness. "Their opinions and the resulting policy will less and less reflect the individual mind of any leader, but only the ideas which seem to that mind to be most likely to win favour with the greatest number of supporters." Maine foresaw that this must lead to a more and more extended franchise, ending in universal suffrage. At the same time he bids us remember that the votes of the French returned Napoleon I and Napoleon III to power and position. Bismarck too has taken up the extension of the suffrage. Nor was Disraeli the only statesman to divine the existence of a working man who is conservative spelt whether with a capital C or not.

We are asked to suppose the competition of parties, stimulated to the utmost by modern contrivances of the wire-puller, to have produced an electoral system under which every adult male has a vote and perhaps every adult female. At first the Radicals may reap benefit so far as the destruction of existing institutions are concerned. The result, to a far-sighted man, will be a mischievous kind of Conservatism which listens to no scientific conclusions that run counter to its prejudices—fatal to all that Liberalism conceives as progress. Certainly no one can complain that Maine is a party man. Let a competently instructed person turn over in his mind "the great epochs of scientific invention and social change during the last two centuries, and consider what would have occurred if universal suffrage had been established at any one of them. Universal suffrage, which to-day excludes Free Trade from the United States, would certainly have prohibited the spinning-jenny and the power-loom. It would certainly have forbidden the threshing-machine. It would have prevented the adoption of the Gregorian Calendar; and it would have restored the Stuarts. It would have proscribed the Roman Catholics with the mob which burned Lord Mansfield's house and library in 1780, and it would have proscribed the Dissenters with the mob which burned Dr. Priestley's house and library in 1791."

The cases Maine readily collects in the past compel us to thought which is all the more pertinent because we can collect cases in the present. There is a possible conflict between the ideals of democracy and those of Socialism which Dicey indicates. The ideal of democracy is government for the good of the people by the people, and in accordance with the wishes of the people. The ideal of collectivism is government for the good of the people by officials who think they know what is good for the people better than the people themselves. These experts may possess this knowledge, but the people may not care for it. Take an instance. Medical men can prove that if vaccination were rigidly enforced, small-pox would disappear. The experts have a case which is quite convincing to all who care to investigate it. The Radicals of Leicester, however, will have none of it, for they set the law imposing vaccination at defiance. Take the Mental Deficiency Act of 1913. It approved itself to the specialist and to all who studied the case of the specialist; it approved itself to both Houses of Parliament, and yet it met with strenuous opposition from extreme democrats. Malthusianism in its old form and eugenics in its new form commends itself to many thoughtful men, but do the rank and file believe in either? So far, it has been hard to convince English people that the authority of the expert ought to count. It is the ideal of the Socialist, but it is not his. His ideal is a State governed by that broad common sense he freely believes that he himself possesses.

The opposition between democracy and Socialism may also arise in another quarter. The labourer likes his allotment, and he likes it all the more if it is his own. The peasant proprietor likes his holding, for the possession of it exercises the magical effect attributed to it by Arthur Young and by J. S. Mill. The feeling of the peasant proprietor is strong in Europe. It is not too much to say that the peasant proprietors of France in 1848 rallied around Napoleon because he promised protection against the Socialists. They dislike the individualism which the possession of a peasant holding engenders. Yet men of the peasant proprietor class are common in Switzerland, in France, in the United States, and are commoner than ever under the Bolshevist *régime* in Russia. Nor can we overlook the circumstance that in our own country the working man has saved £940,000,000 and has invested £600,000,000 in business enterprises, ranging from distributive co-operation to productive co-operation in all its manifold forms. When Socialists freely denounce savings, they come into conflict with the thrifty instincts of a far larger section of the working men than is sometimes realised.

Renan laid down that "*toute civilisation est d'origine aristocratique*" and that "*toute civilisation est l'oeuvre des aristocrats*," and Maine draws attention to this, and to the fact that Strauss—and, considering his actual part in life, this is perhaps the last opinion which might have been expected from him—held that history is a sound aristocrat. So far, at any rate, human improvement has been the work of aristocracies. The short-lived Athenian democracy, under whose shelter art, science, and philosophy flourished so wonderfully, was only "an aristocracy which rose on the ruins of one much narrower. The splendour which attracted the original genius of the then civilised world to Athens was provided by the severe taxation of a thousand subject cities; and the skilled labourers who worked under Phidias, and who built the Parthenon, were slaves." Will democracy carry on the enterprises undertaken formerly by aristocracies? Basing his forecast on the history of the past, Maine considers this eminently unlikely.

After the failure of progress and after the overthrow of existing institutions, what then? Artisans and agricultural labourers will use legislation "for what they are led to believe are their own interests." They will endeavour to distribute wealth more equally. Let them try it, Maine says. After the manner of Malthus, he argues. "If the mass of mankind were to make an attempt at redividing the common stock of good things, they would resemble, not a number of claimants insisting on the fair division of a fund, but a mutinous crew, feasting on a ship's provisions, gorging themselves on the meat and intoxicating themselves with the liquors, but refusing to navigate the vessel to port. It is among the simplest of economical truths, that far the largest part of the wealth of the world is constantly perishing by consumption, and that, if it be not renewed by perpetual toil and adventure, either the human race, or the particular community making the experiment of resting without being thankful, will be extinguished or brought to the very verge of extinction." In support of the truth of this proposition Maine invokes the authority of Mill and he might have invoked the authority of Chalmers as well. Mill was also afraid of the danger of class legislation which Maine foresees. With Carlyle, Maine clearly perceives the grave infirmities of parliamentary government.

The danger in the days to come arises just as much from the disturbance of expectation as from the disturbance of wealth. Bentham observed that the Turkish government had impoverished some of the richest countries in the world far more by its action on motives than by its positive exactions. Pursuing a similar train of argument, Maine thinks that the destruction of the vast wealth under the

Roman Empire, one of the most orderly and efficient of governments, and the decline of Western Europe into the squalor and poverty of the Middle Ages, can only be accounted for on the same principle. This means that circulating capital is more important than fixed. A country devastated by war recovers quickly, and Mill supplies the reason. What the enemy destroys the inhabitants would also destroy by their consumption. The wealth the inhabitants reproduce would have needed to be reproduced, and would have been reproduced in any case. The fund which supports the life of the human race is not a fixed wages fund in any sense of the term. It is a dynamical fund, never a statical one. As Mill shows, everything which is produced is consumed; both what is saved and what is said to be spent; and the former quite as rapidly as the latter. The wealth of mankind is the result of a continuing process, everywhere complex and delicate, and nowhere of such complexity and delicacy as in the British Islands. Capital, as Irving Fisher insists, is a flow, not a fund, and Maine generalises wealth into a flow. Stocks and shares cannot possibly represent this flow in any true sense of the term. For all wealth is essentially dynamical, and not a little of it passes out of being as it comes into being.

In Maine's judgment Spencer's *Man versus the State* is an admirable volume, which shows how possible it is to revive even in our own day the fiscal tyranny which once left European populations in doubt whether it was worth while preserving life by thrift and toil. "You have only to tempt a portion of the population into temporary idleness by promising them a share in a fictitious hoard lying (as Mill puts it) in an imaginary strong-box which is supposed to contain all human wealth. You have only to take the heart out of those who would willingly labour and save, by taxing them *ad misericordiam* for the most laudable philanthropic objects. For it makes not the smallest difference to the motives of the thrifty and industrious part of mankind whether their fiscal oppressor be an Eastern despot, or a feudal baron, or a democratic legislature, and whether they are taxed for the benefit of a Corporation called Society, or for the advantage of an individual styled

King or Lord. Here then is the great question about democratic legislation, when carried to more than a moderate length. How will it affect human motives? What motives will it substitute for those now acting on men?" There are only two sets of motives by which abundant wealth can be produced. "One is economical competition, which leads to wealth and inequality with it; the other consists in the daily task, perhaps fairly and kindly allotted, but enforced by the prison or the scourge. So far as we have experience to teach us, we are driven to the conclusion that every society must adopt one or other, or it will pass through penury to starvation."

Austin and Scherer analyse the nature of democracy as a form of government, and Maine approves of this analysis. That democracy is inevitable and irresistible would, a century ago, have appeared a wild paradox. There have been more than two thousand years of history, and at its outset monarchy, aristocracy, and democracy are all discernible. Some monarchies and some aristocracies have shown themselves extremely tenacious of life. On the other hand, democracies have risen and fallen. The fathers of the American Federal Republic repeatedly betray their regret that the only government which it was possible for them to establish was one of but little stability. The view that democracy is irresistible dates from 1789, and Tocqueville's book on democracy in America is mainly responsible for the spread of this notion, yet its author looked on its approach with dread and distrust.

The test of popular acclamation is a dangerous one to be employed by the democrat, for the tyrant is just as apt to receive it as any form of democracy. The Italian republics of the Middle Ages fell before the ever-growing power and prestige of military despotic governments. "The historian of our day is apt to moralise and lament over the change, but it was everywhere in the highest degree popular, and it called forth an enthusiasm quite as genuine as that of the modern Radical for the coming Democracy. The Roman Empire, the Italian tyrannies, the English Tudor Monarchy, the French centralised Kingship, the Napoleonic despotism, were all hailed with acclamation, most of it perfectly sincere, either because anarchy had been subdued, or because petty local and domestic oppressions were kept under, or because new energy had been infused into national policy. In our own country, the popular government, born of tribal freedom, revived sooner than elsewhere; protected by the insularity of its home, it managed to live; and thus the British Constitution became the one important exception to the 'tendency of the ages,' and through its remote influence this tendency was reversed, and the movement to Democracy began again. The Commonwealth and the Protectorate were never for a moment in real favour with the nation. The true enthusiasm was reserved for the Restoration. Thus, from the reign of Augustus Caesar to the establishment of the United States, it was Democracy which was always, as a rule, on the decline, nor was the decline arrested till the American Federal Government was founded, itself the offspring of the British Constitution. At this moment, Democracy is receiving the same unqualified eulogy which was once poured on Monarchy; and though in its modern shape it is the product of a whole series of accidents, it is regarded by some as propelled in a continuous progress by an irresistible force."

Bentham entertained a high opinion of democracy, claiming for it comparative freedom from "sinister" interests. Bentham, like Austin, argued too narrowly from the circumstances of his generation. He saw that the French Revolution had stopped reform in England, and he argued that if you extended the vote you extended at the same time the opportunity for the disappearance of these interests. Every man follows his own interest as he understands it, and the part of the community which has political power will wield it for its own objects. The remedy obviously is to transfer political power to the entire community. It is impossible that they should abuse it, for the interest they will try to promote is the interest of all, and the interest of all is the proper end and object of all legislation.

The praise Bentham gives to democracy Maine shares with monarchy, particularly in its most absolute forms. The Roman Emperor cared more for the general good of the vast number of societies subject to him than the aristocratic Roman Republic had done. The popularity of the mediaeval kings, who broke up European feudalism, arose from their showing to all their vassals a far more even impartiality than could be obtained from petty feudal rulers. Nor is this the only way to meet Bentham. Maine meets him also by drawing attention to his "low view" of human nature. Maine thinks quite otherwise. "The fact is that under its most important aspect, he greatly overrated its intelligence. He wrongly supposed that the truths which he saw, clearly cut and distinct, in the dry light of his intellect, could be seen by all other men or by many of them. He did not understand that they were visible only to the Few—to the intellectual aristocracy. His delusion was the greater from his inattention to facts which lay little beyond the sphere of his vision. Knowing little of history, and caring little for it, he neglected one easy method of assuring himself of the extreme falseness of the conceptions of their interest, which a multitude of men may entertain. 'The world,' said Machiavelli, 'is made up of the vulgar.' Thus Bentham's fundamental proposition turns against himself. It is that, if you place power in men's hands, they will use it for their interest. Applying the rule to the whole of a political community, we ought to have a perfect system of government; but, taking it in connection with the fact that multitudes include too much ignorance to be capable of understanding their interest, it furnishes the principal argument against Democracy."

The critic of democracy occupies a strong position when he points out that of all forms of government, democracy is by far the most difficult. Its difficulty lies deep in human nature and the causes which determine human volition. For in spite of such phrases as the general will, the will of the people, and the like, a very large proportion of the multitude cannot have a will unless on the simplest and most definite issue. What the people really do is to accept the will of another, the party leader or the local politician, the newspaper of wide influence or the newspaper of narrow influence. Maine then examines the share taken by party and, above all, the party leader. Such a leader has altered the form of bribery. It used to take the form of corrupting the individual: it now takes the form of corrupting the class. This leader not merely corrupts the pockets of the people: he also corrupts their intellect. He puts before them vague general propositions which they loosely accept. This bad mental habit has "seriously enfeebled the French intellect. It is most injuriously affecting the mind of England, and it threatens little short of ruin to the awakening intellect of India." Mill argued that the possession of the vote exercised an elevating effect morally and an educational effect intellectually, and Maine argues that the very reverse effects are produced. In fact, he does not dissent from what Carlyle pointed out as the result of universal suffrage, "infinite amenability to beer and balderdash." No doubt Mill recognised the evils which Maine indicates, and he offered as remedies plural voting and the representation of minorities, but these two remedies appeal but faintly to Maine. He has a remedy to offer. It is to adopt some of the American securities against haste in legislation. The Americans possess a rigid constitution, for it is in writing. Ours is a flexible constitution, and the procedure for a measure affecting a parish is the same as for a measure affecting the vital interests of the State. Maine is of opinion that we should distinguish between ordinary legislation and constitutional legislation, and require for the last special legislative procedure with the object of securing caution and deliberation. The alternative is drift to "a type of government associated with terrible events,— a Single Assembly, armed with full powers over the constitution, which it may exercise at pleasure. It will be a theoretically all-powerful Convention, governed by a practically all-powerful secret Committee of Public Safety, but kept from complete submission to its authority by obstruction, for which its rulers are always seeking to find a remedy in some kind of moral guillotine."

Our age is supposed to be the age of progress, though Maine questions if it is a permanent phase. The mass of mankind hates it, and he supports his view by appealing to western peoples, and of course to the entire Mahommedan world, the coloured races of Africa, the countless myriads of Chinese, the vast majority of the millions of Hindus. Apparently, in the eastern world only the Japanese can tolerate it. The majority of mankind agree with the attitude of the punkah-puller. An English lady advised him to improve his position. "Mem sahib," he replied, when he at last succeeded in grasping her meaning, "my father pulled a punkah, my grandfather pulled a punkah, all my ancestors for four million ages pulled punkahs, and, before that, the god who founded our caste pulled a punkah over the great god Vishnu. I a punkah-wallah for ever!" The thing that hath been is that which shall be, and there is no new thing under the sun.

The civic ideal of the classical world, the monastic ideal of the early Middle Ages, the chivalrous ideal of the later Middle Ages—these are written so plainly on the pages of history that no one can ignore them. Each in turn passes away, and we are interested in the causes of the passing. The inquirer of to-day perceives the altered ideal, and he naturally desires to note the trend of events when an ideal is translated into action. In a word, he assumes that there must be progress. The idea of progress, however, is wholly modern, and was inconceivable before the sixteenth century. Maine remarks that men fail to understand how exceptional are the conditions of western society, and he insists that the progressive conception underlying them is one of recent growth.

Most of us to-day are inclined to regard progress as a matter of course. Knowledge expands, we say, and there is no reason why it should not continue to expand indefinitely. This was not the view of the Greeks, who, for the most part, conceived on the contrary the possibility of a process of deterioration, a cycle or a succession of cycles. The majority thought that there had been a Golden Age, but that was long past. Moreover, there seems to have been the feeling that the age in which they lived was distinctly dull. Beyond the Pillars of Hercules once existed Plato's Atlantis; it is now lost to the sight of men in the depths of the sea. In it innocence and happiness reached the highest possible stage; the utmost man can expect is to return,

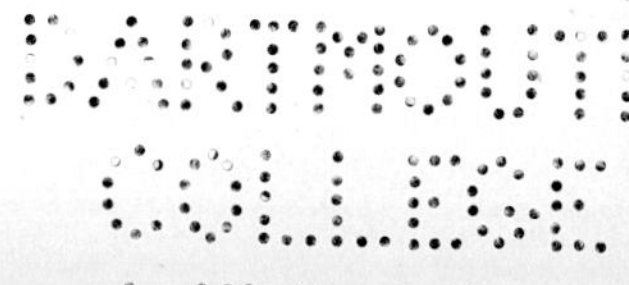

however distantly, to this stage. What George Meredith called the rapture of the forward view was denied to the Greek writers.

A look at the conflagration in which civilisation has been burning for four years renders it easy for us to hold that development includes retrogression. There are many side-currents as well as the main stream of evolution. There is no scientific reason forbidding a return of the glacial period and a spread of polar climatical conditions over the whole globe again. The man of the ancient world no doubt had reasons other than these. He inherited the natural love of mankind for old associations, and he inherited the sense of reverence. The old, simply because it was old, must be better than the new. If he was obliged to strike out a new path, he diverged as little as he could from the old and tried one. It is impossible for a country, especially a primitive one, to effect an entire break with the past. Perhaps the greatest of all breaks with the past was the French Revolution, and yet in its ideals it entertained a return to Roman republican virtue, or to the simplicity of the natural man.

The great service Copernicus rendered to mankind was the conception of the perpetual motion of this world. Motion there is in the worlds above, and incessant motion is in the worlds beneath. Petrarch is sometimes called the first modern man, and on the literary side a case may be made out for him. He was, however, as blind as Dante to the forces around him which made for political and scientific progress. What was fatal to the poem of Dante was the work of Copernicus. There was no longer possible any distinction between the heavens and the earth. True, the earth became a heavenly body, but for all time to come the substance of that heavenly body was precisely the same as that of the earthy. It was no longer possible to entertain the belief that the stars influenced the destiny of man, for their motions obeyed the same laws as that of the globe we inhabit. Four generations after Copernicus, Blaise Pascal could say, "*Le silence éternel de ces espaces m'effraie.*" The first modern man was the astronomer, the first to allow the scientific conception of Descartes. It was barely

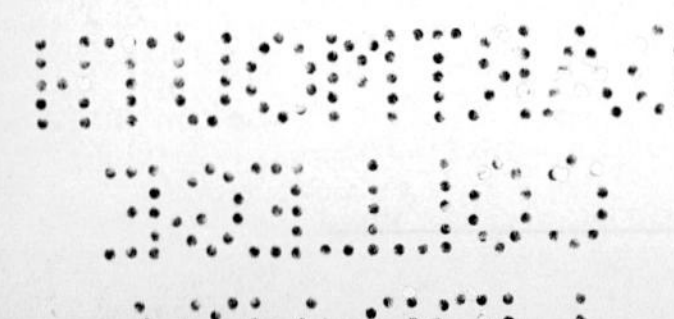

possible to conceive the idea of progress before the sixteenth century. For the doctrine of continuous change has for its basis the notion of the unity of mankind; it envisages the tribes, the cities, the nations as so many members of a great family. It assigns to each of them a providential rôle in the immeasurable career in which humanity advances. Now not only were these underlying truths unknown to the classical and mediaeval worlds; the members thereof were profoundly anti-pathetic to them. The discovery of printing, the impossibility of another Völkerwanderung, the greater ease of international relations, all combine to reject a system by which Machiavelli condemns the human race to eternal oscillations between truth and error.

All the ardour of a Mazzini inspires Condorcet's *Sketch of a Historical Picture of the Progress of the Human Mind.* From the revolutions of the past he seeks guidance for the Zeitgeist of that under which he was living. Turgot believed in evolution, while Condorcet believed in revolution. There are, in Condorcet's opinion, ten ages in the growth of civilisation. Nine of them he describes, and the tenth concerns the future. He is not fair to the past, especially to the past history of institutions. In spite of this, he holds that there are no limits to the possibilities of progress. No one can understand the future who has not a firm grasp of the past. He observes that slavery has disappeared, and he concludes that war must follow in its train. He manifests grave anxiety for the plight of the rank and file. There is to be equality of the sexes, and there are to be facilities for the multitude. Turgot is concerned to point out that, brilliant as the official society of the classical world was, the masses were barbarously treated. He rightly brings out the point that it was reserved for Christianity to render practical the Ciceronian conception of the equality of men by teaching the sons of the gentle and simple in its schools. When the lord of the manor and his serf knelt at the same altar to receive the consecrated bread, the seeds of emancipation were sown. Progress had been regarded as largely intellectual, whereas Condorcet and Turgot emphasise the fact that it is social. All schemes for the amelioration of the people go back to these two thinkers.

The belief in the current notion of the perfectibility of human nature is evident in Condorcet's view that the backward peoples will attain to the condition of France and the United States, for no people is condemned never to exercise its reason.

Bury characterises the two distinct types of theories of progress. "The one type is that of the constructive idealists and socialists, who can name all the streets and towers of 'the city of gold' which they imagine as situated just round a promontory. The development of man is a closed system; its term is known and within reach. The other type is that of those who, surveying the gradual ascent of man, believe that by the same interplay of forces which have conducted him so far, and by a further development of the liberty which he has fought to win, he will move slowly towards conditions of increasing harmony and happiness. Here the development is indefinite; its term is unknown and lies in the remote future. Individual liberty is the motive force, and the corresponding theory is liberalism; whereas the first doctrine leads to a symmetrical system in which the authority of the State is preponderant, and the individual has little more liberty than a cog in a well-oiled wheel; it is not his right to go his own way." Though Fourier, Saint Simon, and Comte attempted to ascertain the causes of progress, they signally failed. Fourier and Saint Simon dreamt of industrial socialism. It is a dream, an impressive dream, of the importance of Labour in the world. The two theories of progress still remain, and we are all familiar with them. There is no need to show that Darwinism increases the value of the second type.

Evolution discredits all attempts to assign to the future a fixed form. Is not progress confined by the limitations of the human faculty? Is the boundary to which this faculty extends capable of indefinite approach? Lave at Munich, De Broglie at Paris, and Bragg in London have been passing X-rays through crystals and getting effects by reflexion from planes of molecules in the crystals which very nearly reveal to us the individual molecule in its fixed position in the crystal. The X-rays appear to be of exceeding small wave-length—perhaps 18,600 times less than that of light—and we have already a further instrument which shows that no finality in this direction need be expected. We may realise the atom itself in some way, though we may not be able to detach and handle it. That it has a material existence seems as probable as anything we know.

The limits of research, then, are very hard to define. When we get (apparently) to the bottom of material structure, synthesis may begin, and we may build up from atoms structures that have natural properties and repeat natural things. Is it hopeless to look forward to the construction of the very complex molecule of protoplasm? and, if it can be done, will it live? In truth there is no limit to research save that imposed by our senses. Our material senses must be affected in some way by the matter that is the subject of our research. What our eye is unfitted to see may perhaps convey some sensation to smell or hearing, or may be so enlarged by our artifice that its image (which is, in the last resort, all that we ever see) shall become appreciable.

These are no idle speculations, for such a keen observer as Lord Balfour discerns progress in the modern alliance between pure science and industry. It would seem that the Labour Party regards nationalisation as a great step in progress. Socialism provides the ideal solution. The pity is that paper schemes, which inaugurate an age of bliss, have never been adjusted to the actualities of the world as it exists. The vision of the Golden Age lay in the past for the men of antiquity, and, for the most part, for the men of the Renaissance. It began to lie in the future for Descartes and the men he moulded. Science, which has altered so much, has also altered the value of the dogma of progress. Evolution will not hear of finality. "But if we accept the reasonings," inquires Bury, "on which the dogma of Progress is based, must we not carry them to their full conclusion? In escaping from the illusion of finality, is it legitimate to exempt that dogma itself? Must it not too submit to its own negation of finality? Will not that process of change, for which Progress is the optimistic name, compel 'Progress' too to fall from the commanding position in which it is now, with apparent security, enthroned? Εσσεται ἦμαρ ὅταν. . . . A day will come, in the revolution of the centuries, when a new idea will usurp its place as the directing idea of humanity. Another star, unnoticed now or invisible, will climb up the intellectual heaven, and human emotions will react to its influence, human plans respond to its guidance. It will be the criterion by which Progress and all other plans will be judged. And it too will have a successor."

Maine used to insist that, though the invasions of the barbarians smashed up the shell of the Roman Empire, yet they saved Europe from falling into the comatose condition of China. The conception of progress may one day be replaced, but the student of the past must remember what it has accomplished. He bears in mind that, when the ideas of the Renaissance filtered down to the ruled as well as to the rulers, the thoughtful saw with Montaigne that it was putting a high price on your opinions to burn a man for not holding them. The growth of the idea of progress is fundamental to a consideration of the reasons why toleration did not advance rapidly, a point to which Maine repeatedly returns. It is clear that, if truth progresses, it is not reasonable to burn men who may hold a different conception of it from that held by their judges; for the roots of persecution grow from the idea that a corporation can possess complete truth. If there is a steady movement to increasing knowledge, persecution becomes out of the question. Had this truth been grasped in the sixteenth century, how much misery might have been averted! But for the next century and a half the sword and the stake were the arguments employed. In Germany there was the Thirty Years' War, in France the Wars of Religion, and in England the scaffold for the orthodox and the unorthodox alike. The belief in some forms of progress may well be a delusion, yet, as R. L. Stevenson profoundly remarked, "the actual is not the true." What is true in fact is not necessarily true in imagination. A belief in progress wrought the silent and mysterious change which rendered the stake obsolete, and for this we should feel everlastingly grateful.

REFERENCES

BRINO, G. *Il governo popolare e la sovranità popolare secondo due ultimo pubblicazioni di E.* (or rather H. J.) *Sumner Maine e P. Ellero.* (Milano, 1887.)

BROWN, W. JETHRO. *The Austinian Theory of Law.* (London, 1906.)

BRYCE, Lord. *Studies in History and Jurisprudence.* (Oxford, 1901.)

BURY, J. B. *The Idea of Progress.* (London, 1920.)

DARETTE, M. *Mémoires de l'Académie des Sciences Morales et Politiques.* 1891.

EVANS, H. O. *Theories and Criticisms of Sir Henry Maine.* (London, 1904.)

FISHER, H. A. L. *Paul Vinogradoff. A Memoir.* (Oxford, 1927.)

FLINT, R. *The Philosophy of History.* (Edinburgh, 1874 and 1893.)

GRAHAM, W. *English Political Philosophy.* (London, 1914.)

GRANT DUFF, Sir M. E. *Sir Henry Maine.* (London, 1892.)

INGE, W. R. *Outspoken Essays.* Second Series. (London, 1922.)

MCILWAIN, C. H. *The High Court of Parliament.* (New Haven, 1910.)

MERRIAM, C. E. *History of the Theory of Sovereignty since Rousseau.* (New York, 1900.)

MURRAY, R. H. *Erasmus and Luther. Appendix, The. Conception of Progress in Classical and Renaissance Writers.* (London, 1920.)

POLLOCK, Sir F. *Oxford Lectures.* (London, 1890.)

SMITH, A. L. *Frederick William Maitland.* (Oxford, 1908.)

VANNI, I. *Egli Studi di Henry Sumner Maini e le dottrine della Filosofia del Diritto Verona,* 1892.

VINOGRADOFF, Sir P. *The Teaching of Sir Henry Maine.* (Oxford, 1904.)

ZOCCO-ROSA, A. *Discorso Commemorativo pronunziato nella Grande Aula della R. Università di Catania il* 16. (Gennaio, 1892. Catania, 1892.)

Chapter III.

RUSKIN: ROMANTICIST AND REFORMER

Herbert Spencer and Sir Henry Maine applied evolution to the sociological and the legal conceptions of the State respectively. The State was to them an organism, and their view of its functions was not widely differing. Ruskin in his teaching after that dividing year in his work, 1860, substantially assumed that the State was an organism. He is as aristocratic in his ultimate attitude to democracy as either Spencer or Maine.

Like Maine, John Ruskin (1819–1900) was of Lowland Scots family, and proud of the fact. Carlyle, Scott, and Stevenson were also Lowland Scots, a race eloquent and emotional, fiery and restrained. Not only was Ruskin Scots by descent, but the writers who directed his mental energies were also Scots—from Scott to Lord Lindsay, from Principal Forbes to Thomas Carlyle. Ruskin used to speak of himself as "a son of the Manse," but he was a son only in the third generation. His Aunt Jessie was of the ascetic temperament. "I never can be thankful enough," added her nephew in after years, "for having seen, in her, the Scottish Puritan spirit in its perfect faith and force." His mother shared this temperament, and Ruskin records, "I have seen my mother travel from sunrise on a summer's day without once leaning back in the carriage." The only toys in the nursery were a bunch of keys and a box of bricks. She imparted to her son a thorough knowledge of the Bible, a fact that conceals part of the secret of his style. Before his third birthday he repeated to his mother the whole of the 119th Psalm. He also had to learn the whole of "the fine old Scottish paraphrases." To this discipline he attributed the cultivation of his ear and his sense of style.

Father and mother gave their son unbounded affection which he returned in abundant measure. The clash of the two generations was to affect the three, but what household does it not affect? His father, a man of ample means, meant him to be a Bishop, just as Bentham's father meant him to be Lord Chancellor. Fortunately for the world, the wish of neither father was gratified, at least not in the sense meant, though Bentham left a more enduring name than most Lord Chancellors and Ruskin than most bishops. Yet Ruskin was always an overseer of souls with a diocese more extensive than any the Church of England could give him and on wider lines than even Anglicanism. The father felt the pang and the pathos of the unrealised wish, and the son also felt it. It was "an exquisite piece of tragedy altogether," owned the son on his father's death, "the loss of a father who would have sacrificed his life for his son, and yet forced his son to sacrifice his life to him, and sacrifice it in vain."

The Romantic spirit was manifest in the lad not only in the masters he acknowledged but also in those he refused to acknowledge, for we are moved by repulsion as much as by attraction. If his mother taught him religion and the Bible, his father taught him romance and Scott, Dante and Shakespeare, *Don Quixote* and Byron. He was as unconsciously influenced by Coleridge as he was consciously influenced by Carlyle. Newman and Pusey moved him, but they moved him by repulsion. It is not always an easy task to reconcile the diverse elements within us. The Hebraistic and the Hellenic elements were united within him, and yet in the clash between them, combined with their reconciliation, lies no little of the secret of the wonderful work he was to do. If art was beauty, art was also life, and therefore a call to action. He sought peace and ensued it, yet he was ever a fighter. He spent himself lavishly for others, yet practised no austere self-renunciation. St. Francis and Tolstoi made the complete surrender he refused to make. A Puritan of Puritans, he is also a great interpreter of the Catholicism of the Middle Ages. The critic of the Renaissance, he is also the man to proclaim that in Titian and Velasquez art reached perfection. The champion of the Pre-Raphaelite movement, he is not afraid to pronounce that the Pre-Raphaelites are all more or less affected by morbid conditions of intellect and temper. If art is the fine flower of life, "that in which the hand, head, and heart of man go together," he also enunciates the view that "the period in which any people reached their highest power in art is that in which they sign the warrant of their own ruin." A man who was essentially a Christian, he has "never yet met with a Christian whose heart was, as far as human judgment could pronounce, perfect and right before God, who cared about art at all." The prophet of Socialism, he yet taught that its doctrines were false and even deadly. Clearly, Ruskin was a man who entertained but little belief in that bugbear of the Englishman, consistency. He was taunted with the diverse views he put forth at different times upon the same questions. His answer was that the problems of life are mostly polygonal, and "for myself, I am never satisfied that I have handled a subject properly till I have contradicted myself at least three times."

Freedom of thought Ruskin knew, even as a lad. In a lecture given at Woolwich, he recalled an incident of his early childhood which his mother was fond of telling him. "One evening, when I was yet in my nurse's arms, I wanted to touch the tea-urn, which was boiling merrily. It was an early taste for bronzes, I suppose; but I was resolute about it. My mother bade me keep my fingers back; I insisted on putting them forward. My nurse would have taken me away from the urn, but my mother said: 'Let him touch it, Nurse.' So I touched it,—and that was my first lesson in the meaning of the word Liberty. It was the first piece of Liberty I got, and the last for some time for which I asked for."

From childhood's days Ruskin loved mountains and the sea, and he naturally loved the Lake district, ultimately making his home at Coniston. The first event in his life, so he tells us, was the sight of Friar's Crag on Derwent Water, and in after life he described this spot as "one of the three most beautiful scenes in Europe." His father wrote: "He has just gone from a hurried dinner to the sunset which he visits as regularly as a soldier does his evening parade." To him mountains were cathedrals of the earth. In *Praeterita* he tells us: "A very few years,—within the hundred,—before that, no child could have been born to care for mountains, or for the men that lived among them, in that way. Till Rousseau's time there had been no 'sentimental' love of nature; and till Scott's, no such apprehensive love of 'all sorts and conditions of men,' not in the soul merely, but in the flesh. St. Bernard of La Fontaine, looking out to Mont Blanc with his child's eyes sees above Mont Blanc the Madonna; St. Bernard of Talloires, not the lake of Annecy, but the dead between Martigny and Aosta. But for me, the Alps and their people were alike beautiful in their snow, and their humanity; and I wanted, neither for them nor myself, sight of any thrones in heaven but the rocks, or of any spirits in heaven but the clouds." The love that the mountains and the cathedrals called out of him, he called out of other people. He has done for the Alps and the cathedrals of Italy and France, for Venice and Florence, what Byron did for Greece. In his old age a child came to see William Blake. He put his hand on her head and blessed her, saying, "May God make the world as beautiful to you, my child, as it has been for me." The wish of Blake came true in Ruskin, for he made the world as beautiful to us as it had been to himself. Alone of his pleasures, the love of nature never left him. When he was showing his Turners in his bedroom to a visitor, he said, "When I die, I hope that these may be the last things my eyes will rest on in this world." His wish was gratified. He loved art, but he loved nature even more. For he held, "You will never love art well till you love what she mirrors better."

A present received on his thirteenth birthday he looked back as determining the main tenor of his life. In 1832 his father's partner in the wine trade gave the boy a copy of Rogers's *Italy* with Turner's vignettes. His life work as an interpreter of Turner dates from the hour his gaze fastened on the vignettes, and he at last succeeded in doing for Turner what Carlyle did for Cromwell. His father chose to be his own traveller for the selling of his fine sherries, and every summer drove in a leisurely fashion in a carriage with his wife and son. If there was a fine picture to be seen in any mansion by the way, he took his son to see it. The travels were extended from Britain to the Continent. At fifteen Ruskin saw the Alps from Schaffhausen for the first time, and felt that inward glow known only to the true mountain lover. No doubt he missed the discipline of a public school, but think of his gains, the storing of his imagination and his intellect while the organs were limber. The Ruskins travelled through Europe at the rate set by a great roomy carriage—not at the rate set by a motor—fitted with every device to ensure comfort, stopping towards sunset at the best of inns, where the best of rooms, the choicest of meals and wine, awaited the travellers. No wonder that Ruskin came to detest the railway and all its works. Who would not, after his experience? "I had certainly more passionate happiness," owned Ruskin in recalling his travels in 1833, "of a quality utterly indescribable to people who never felt the like, and more, in solid quantity, in those three months than most people have in all their lives." The carriage could not spoil scenery, but the railway both could and did. He never objected to main lines of railways, but he forcibly objected to branch ones, in the Lake district, for example, where the viaducts, the embankments, and the ugly buildings which—why, no one knows—are the inevitable accompaniment of the station deface the landscape.

Among his schoolfellows at a day school at Camberwell there were the sons of Colonel Matson of Woolwich. They sometimes invited Ruskin to their home, and in the Colonel, "I saw," he says, "such calm type of truth, gentleness, and simplicity as I have myself found in soldiers and sailors only, and so admirable to me that I have never been able since those Woolwich times to gather myself up against the national guilt of war, seeing that such men were made by the discipline of it." No one was to write more burning or more memorable words than his on the duty of patriotism and the sacredness of soldiership. "You have put yourselves," so he told the cadets at Woolwich, "into the hand of your country as a weapon. You have vowed to strike when she bids you, and to stay scabbarded when she bids you: all that you need answer for is that you fail not in her grasp." In *Unto this Last* he was also to say: "The consent of mankind has always, in spite of the philosophers, given precedence to the soldier. And this is right. For the soldier's trade is not slaying, but being slain. This, without well knowing its meaning, the world honours it for. The reason it honours the soldier is because he holds his life at the service of the State. Our estimate of him is based upon this ultimate fact, of which we are well assured, that put him in a fortress breach, with all the pleasures of the world behind him and only death and his duty in front of him, he will keep his face to the front; and he knows that his choice may be put to him at any moment, and has beforehand taken his part, virtually takes such part continually, does, in reality, die daily."

In January, 1837, Ruskin drove down to Oxford with his mother and entered into residence at Christ Church. On true Coleridgean lines he loved Plato far more than Aristotle, for he was a born Platonist, and his Platonism left the deepest influence on his social schemes. "I owe more of the general tone and form of my political thoughts to Aristophanes," he said, "than to any other writer, living or dead." He read the pass course with a strong and steady intelligence, and Dean Kitchin thinks that Lord Salisbury, Lord Dufferin, and Ruskin were three men on whom this course produced excellent effects. He rose with the sun, and before breakfast made notes of a few verses of the Bible, which he read in Greek and Latin as well as in English. The constant study of the Bible coloured his thought every whit as much as his style. According to Turner, "I know of no genius but the genius of hard work," and this was always the gospel of Ruskin. As a young man, as a middle-aged man, and as an old man he was an incessant worker who spared no pains. To Ruskin's father the publisher came one day exhibiting a thickly scored final revise and explaining that continuance in such practices would absorb all the author's profits. "Don't let my son know," said the old gentleman, "John must have his things as he likes them; pay him whatever would become due, apart from corrections, and send in a separate bill for them to me."

In 1843 appeared the first volume of *Modern Painters*, of which a second appeared in 1846, a third and fourth in 1856, and a fifth in 1860. "I say with pride," he wrote in 1883, in his epilogue to the second volume, "which it has become my duty to express openly, that it was left to me, and to me alone, first to discern and then to teach, so far as in this hurried century any such thing can be taught, the excellency and supremacy of five great painters, despised until I spoke of them—Turner, Tintoret, Luini, Botticelli, and Carpaccio. Despised—nay, scarcely in any true sense of the word known." Murray declined to publish it, and his ground was that the public then "cared little for Turner." Now it is perfectly plain that Ruskin did not discover Turner in the same sense as he discovered Tintoret. Turner had become a Royal Academician twenty years before Ruskin was born. He was famous and wealthy before *Modern Painters* ever appeared. What Ruskin effected for him was to rescue his art from misunderstanding. Many had praised Turner, but it was reserved for Ruskin to praise him on right lines, lines which gave the artist that keenest of joys, the joy of complete understanding. If the author did not do full justice to Claude, he certainly did justice to Claude's pensive grace, the beauty of his skies and the charm of his clouds.

Wordsworth read the first volume, and regarded its author as "a brilliant writer," a verdict with which Tennyson, Sir Henry Taylor, the Brownings, and Miss Mitford concurred. "Hitherto," wrote Charlotte Brontë, "I have only had instinct to guide me in judging of art; I feel now as if I had been walking blindfold—this book seems to give me eyes. I *do* wish I had pictures within reach by which to test the new sense. Who can read these glowing descriptions of Turner's works without longing to see them? . . . I like this author's style much; there is both energy and beauty in it. I like himself, too, because he is such a hearty admirer. He does not give himself half-measure of praise or vituperation. He eulogises, he reverences with his whole soul." "Ruskin seems to me," she wrote at a later time," one of the few genuine writers, as distinguished from book-makers of the age. His earnestness even amuses me in certain passages; for I cannot help laughing to think how the utilitarians will fume and fret over his deep, serious (and as they *will* think), fanatical reverence for Art. That pure and severe mind you ascribe to him speaks in every line. He writes like a consecrated Priest of the Abstract and the Ideal." As a seer George Eliot came to regard the author. "I venerate him," she acknowledged, "as one of the great teachers of his day. The grand doctrines of truth and sincerity in art, and the nobleness and solemnity of our human life, which he teaches with the inspiration of a Hebrew prophet, must be stirring up young minds in a promising way."

Matthew Arnold cited a passage in *Modern Painters* as marking the highest point to which the art of prose can ever hope to reach. Tennyson was asked to name the six authors in whom he found the stateliest English prose, and they proved to be Hooker, Bacon, Milton, Jeremy Taylor, De Quincey, and Ruskin. Much as the poets admired the new book, the artists were as ardent in expressing their admiration. Among them were Holman Hunt, William Morris, Burne-Jones, Leighton, and Millais. If there was an artistic message in *Modern Painters,* there was also a social message which was to be emphasised in 1860 as it was not in 1843. In the judgment of Ruskin—and who knows his mind better?—there is a development of his teaching to be found in his five most representative works, and he states explicitly in *Fors Clavigera* what it is. "*Modern Painters* taught the claim of all lower nature in the hearts of men; of the rock, and wave, and herb, as a part of their necessary spirit life; in all that I now bid you to do, to dress the earth and keep it, I am fulfilling what I then began. The *Stones of Venice* taught the laws of constructive art, and the dependence of all human work or edifice, for its beauty, on the happy life of the workman. *Unto this Last* taught the laws of that life itself, and its dependence on the Sun of Justice; the Inaugural Oxford Lectures, the necessity that it should be led, and the gracious laws of beauty and labour recognised, by the upper, no less than the lower, classes of England; and lastly, *Fors Clavigera* has declared the relation of these to each other, and the only possible conditions of peace and honour, for low and high, rich and poor, together in the holding of that first Estate, under the only Despot, God, from which, whoso falls, angel or man, is kept, not mythically nor disputably, but here in visible horror of chains under darkness to the judgment of the great day: and in keeping which service is perfect freedom, and inheritance of all that a loving Creator can give to His creatures, and an immortal Father to His children."

The second volume of *Modern Painters* awakened appreciation of the Primitives and aroused a fuller knowledge of Giotto and Tintoret. Ruskin insisted on the balanced sanity of Giotto's intellect, the broad humanity of his temper, his power of entering into the heart of a subject, and his amazing faculty of dramatic presentation. In his *History of Aesthetic* Bosanquet is as enthusiastic as Charlotte Brontë, for he records his verdict that "it is not too much to say that he, like Winckelmann, has given the mind a new organ for the appreciation of beauty."

The artist, as Plato told us long ago, has many functions. His it is to teach and enlighten the State, to make life beautiful, and to draw the soul insensibly into harmony with reason. But, among them all, none is assuredly greater than the mission which he has received from heaven to keep alive the sense of a world that is out of sight, and to show how the troubled waves of human life may dimly reflect the beauty and mystery of God. This is what Ruskin was to do. This has been the master-passion of his life, this the gleam which he has followed along earth's dark and perilous ways. Like the Knights of Arthur's Round Table he has sallied forth on a divine quest, and his feet have never faltered in the search after truth and beauty.

The Seven Lamps of Architecture appeared in 1849. These lamps were truth, beauty, power, sacrifice, obedience, labour, and memory; and to each of these ideas to be represented in stone, he devoted a chapter of ingenious enthusiasm and enthusiastic ingenuity. This book is significant in the study of architecture, and it is perhaps even more significant in national history, for its author was among the first to set forth the meaning of a great building and its relation to the autobiography of a nation. "No man of feeling," acknowledges Frederic Harrison of the peroration to *The Lamp of Sacrifice*, "who has in him the echoes of this funeral sermon, can stand before a great mediaeval cathedral without being conscious that it has gained for him a new meaning, a sublimer pathos."

Ruskin began his career by discussing morality, industry, religion, and humanity in order to lead us up to a higher sense of beauty in art. But with all the fervour of his nature Ruskin held that beauty in art must lead on to beauty in life. This view he held in 1849 or 1851 though not nearly as much as he did in 1860. The implicitness of the forties and fifties is the explicitness of the sixties. For the real truth is that he began by preaching to us a higher sense of art in order to lead us up to a nobler understanding of morality, industry, religion, and humanity. Whether he addressed Eton boys or Woolwich soldiers, whether he lectured Oxford undergraduates or Manchester working men, the condition of England was uppermost in his mind, and his chief object was the best means of securing bread and butter—and beauty—for its multitudes. In his attitude to party he stood as detached as Maine. If he were convinced that laws or institutions oppressed the poor, he was almost a Radical. If doctrines of liberty and equality were advanced, he was almost a Conservative. Fundamentally, he was a conservative. His father was a Tory of the old school, and an admirer of Disraeli. In 1852, half a century before his time, Ruskin favoured a graduated income-tax and a super-tax on large incomes, and he also favoured free trade. He advocated a system of universal suffrage combined with what came to be called Disraeli's "fancy franchises." Every man was to have his vote, but votes were to be weighed as well as counted, and he laid special stress on property and education. He urged that education should include natural history, religion, and the elements of politics, and that it should be national. In his *Latter-Day Pamphlets* Carlyle had pleaded on behalf of similar principles, and Ruskin was his faithful follower. Once

Gladstone dropped the remark to Ruskin that "Sir Walter had made Scotland." Ruskin inquired as to the meaning of the phrase, and Gladstone recounted the amazing contrast between the means of communication in Scotland before Sir Walter wrote compared with the present day, mentioning the number of coaches that were now conveying masses of happy trippers up and down the Trossachs. Ruskin's face had been deepening with horror, and at last he could bear it no longer. "But, my dear sir," he broke out, "that is not making Scotland; it is unmaking it!"

He read More's *Utopia* in 1858, and thought "What an infinitely wise—infinitely foolish—book it is! Right in all it asks—insane, in venturing to ask it, all at once—so making its own wisdom folly for evermore; and becoming perhaps the most really mischievous book ever written—except *Don Quixote*." For More satirised and Cervantes laughed at the past, and he could bear neither the satire nor the laughter. He had confessed in 1856: "I am by nature and instinct Conservative, loving old things because they are old, and hating new ones merely because they are new. If, therefore, I bring forward any doctrine of Innovation, assuredly it must be against the grain in me; and this in political matters is of infinite importance." Still, Carlyle continued to affect his thought, and *Past and Present* deeply touched him. He began to feel that if the doctrines of the political economists were not the doctrines for his master, neither were they the doctrines for him. He continued this warfare with the economists which he conducted with greater precision of attack than Carlyle, and the result was that he humanised the whole subject. Huxley had thought that evolution was a sufficient master-key to the processes of nature, but he altered his mind. In his Romanes lecture he urged that "Social progress means a checking of the cosmic process at every step, and the substitution of it for another, which may be called the ethical process, the end of which is not the survival of those who may happen to be the fittest, in respect of the whole of the conditions that exist, but of those who are ethically the fittest." As Huxley added ethics to evolution, so Ruskin added ethics to political economy, for the economy of man requires it just as much as the economy of nature.

Ruskin was never afraid to attack, and he was never afraid to defend. He took up the cause of the Pre-Raphaelites, Rossetti, Holman Hunt, Burne-Jones and Millais, and demonstrated that the same motives of sincerity impelled them and Turner. All alike were opposed to the Academical School who worked by rule-of-thumb, and the championship of Ruskin proved a turning-point in the fortunes of the Pre-Raphaelites. Men sometimes forget that he was as ready to champion lost causes as Matthew Arnold himself. They remember that he looked down on Rembrandt, despised Constable, and belittled Whistler. If his blame was unjust, so too was his praise, for he was wont to bestow it on insignificant water-colour painters who happened to attract him. Artists stood agasp to note that he appreciated Kate Greenaway and depreciated Whistler, who stood out in his day as the Impressionists stand out to-day. In spite of his defects, of his limitations if you will, in spite of his caprice and prejudice, he possesses power of illumination and grasp of general artistic ideas, but these ideas must be related to life. Art should express man's spirit, should speak to men, and should stir them by its noble appeal. This is true of the whole aesthetic aspect of life, as true of architecture as of art. There must be "in this magnificently human art of architecture, some equivalent expression for the trouble and wrath of life, for its sorrow and its mystery . . . mighty masses of shadow mingled with its surface." Accordingly he, the Puritan, constituted himself the High Priest of the Gothic Revival.

From 1851 to 1853 appeared the three volumes of *The Stones of Venice* which gave Carlyle and countless others such heartfelt joy. The change wrought by the author is evident if we turn to the letter Gibbon wrote his stepmother in 1765: "Of all the towns in Italy, I am least satisfied with Venice. Objects which are only singular without being pleasing produce a momentary surprise which soon gives way to satiety and disgust. Old, and in general, ill-built houses, ruined pictures, and stinking ditches, dignified with the pompous denomination of canals, a fine bridge spoilt by two rows of houses upon it, and a large square decorated with the worst architecture I ever saw."

The main ideas in the three volumes are as far-reaching in the social as in the artistic sphere. "The chief purpose," he wrote to Count Zorzi, "with which, twenty years ago, I undertook my task of the history of Venetian architecture, was to show the dependence of its beauty on the happiness and fancy of the workman, and to show also that no architect could claim the title to authority of magister unless he himself wrought at the head of his men, captain of manual skill, as the best knight is captain of armies." So it had been, he found, in Venice—in the days of the sound health and sound strength of the Republic. So must it be in modern States if sound health and sound strength were to return. True art, so he believed, can only be produced by artists; true freedom is the freedom of the soul. "There might be more freedom in England though her feudal lords' lightest words were worth men's lives, and though the blood of the vexed husbandman dropped in the furrows of her fields, than there is while the animation of her multitudes is sent like fuel to feed the factory smoke, and the strength of them is given daily to be wasted into the fineness of a web, or racked into the exactness of a line." The chapter containing these words, Ruskin declared in 1854, was "precisely and accurately the most important in the whole book." In the last volume of *Fors Clavigera*, written in 1877, he testified, "*The Stones of Venice* taught the laws of constructive art, and the dependence of all human work or edifice for its beauty on the happy life of the workman." Nor can we omit the moving conclusion of the chapter on *The Lamp of Sacrifice*. "All else for which the builders sacrificed has passed away—all their living interests, and aims, and achievements. . . . But of them, and their life, and toil upon the earth, one reward, one evidence, is left to us in those grey heaps of deep-wrought stone. They have taken with them to the grave their powers, their honours, and their errors; but they have left us their adoration." Clearly *The Seven Lamps of Architecture* and *The Stones of Venice* belong to the same building.

Ruskin maintained that there was a close connexion

between the good painter and the good man, a position he qualified in 1859 when he pointed out: "I do *not* say in the least that in order to be a good painter you must be a good man; but I do say that in order to be a good natural painter there must be strong elements of good in the mind, however warped by other parts of the character." Is art a function of national morality? History lends but scanty support to this view. The pictures of Perugino, Titian, and Tintoret were painted in societies corrupt to the core. Let any reader turn to the autobiography of such a sensualist as Benvenuto Cellini or let him turn to the life of Raphael. It is quite possible, from the Ruskinian angle, to produce works which might come from heaven at the very period with works which might come from hell appear. Bunyan is contemporary with Wycherley. Among the noblest buildings ever raised by man, and those which have exerted the most potent influence on after ages, we must count the Parthenon, the Pantheon at Rome, the Church of St. Sophia at Constantinople, and St. Paul's in London. Frederic Harrison points out that the Parthenon was nearly contemporary with the comedies of Aristophanes and the sophists of Athens—not with Marathon and Aeschylus. The Pantheon was nearly contemporary with the satires of Juvenal and the epigrams of Martial. St. Sophia was built by the husband of the Empress Theodora; and St. Paul's was building in the era of Charles II and James II. Were all these sublime masterpieces of architecture what Ruskin desiderated, "the production of a faithful and virtuous people"? Surely Harrison is right in drawing attention to the circumstance that they synchronise with some of the most scathing satires upon personal and social corruption that survive in Greek, Latin, Byzantine, and English literature.

The social message of *The Stones of Venice* appeals to us to-day more than the artistic, yet to the reader in the fifties the latter was the more pregnant. Catholicism, Roman and Anglican, had been associated with the Gothic Revival, and now Ruskin associated it with Protestantism. In the true spirit of the Reformation, he asserted that Gothic was for all buildings quite as much as for churches.

"It was one of the purposes of *The Stones of Venice,*" so he spoke in his inaugural *Lectures on Art* at Oxford, "to show that the lovely forms of cathedral domes and porches, of the vaults and arches of their aisles, of the canopies of their tombs, were every one of them developed in civil and domestic buildings." Nor is it amiss to hint that the Byzantinism of the Roman Catholic Cathedral at Westminster is traceable to Ruskin's vindication of St. Mark's from the charge of barbarism.

Spencer was a recluse, but never was anyone less so than Ruskin. His father's wealth left him free to pursue the manifold activities of his life, and he pursued them with all the ardour of his nature. Thought was not enough for him. He longed to do as well as to write. He was not content to talk about the happiness of the working man: he desired to contribute to it. Accordingly in 1856 he was on the staff of F. D. Maurice's Working Men's College. He taught art with the object not of helping working men to "get on" and "rise out of their class," but with the object of improving themselves by satisfying the needs of their mental and spiritual natures. To a Royal Commission of 1857 Ruskin gave his aims. "My efforts are directed not to making a carpenter an artist, but to making him happier as a carpenter." A working man asked for a subscription towards publishing a volume of his poems. "Certainly not," was the reply, "Mr. Ruskin would set poets to work, not workingmen to rhyme." For four years he was one of the main inspiring forces in the College, and then he resigned. He gave Maurice his reasons: "It is not from any failure in my interest in this class that I have ceased from personal attendance. But I ascertained beyond all question that the faculty which my own method of teaching chiefly regarded, was necessarily absent in men trained to mechanical work, that my words and thoughts respecting beautiful things were unintelligible when the eye had been accustomed to the frightfulness of modern city life." In fact, we are coming closer to the year 1860 when he more definitely altered his attitude to life. Beauty in art he witnessed, but he wanted to witness beauty in life, in the life of all.

His *Political Economy of Art* appeared in 1857. In the spirit of Spencer he compared the body politic to a farm or a household, in which the rule should be co-operation, not competition; and in this body each member should be set to the work most proper for him. His theory of government was paternal, if not semi-feudal. The State was to be a model employer, furnishing a standard to which the arts and crafts should conform. In particular, the State should more fully educate the people, and provide for the veterans of industry comfortable homes. In fact, there were to be "Soldiers of the Ploughshare as well as Soldiers of the Sword!"

Classical Political Economy in 1857 had attained the height of its power. *Laissez-faire* and the Manchester School had not fallen before the fierce invectives of Disraeli, Carlyle, and Kingsley. Ricardo and Mill still reigned supreme, if challenged. Mill's *Political Economy* had appeared in 1848, the *Das Kapital* of Marx in 1868, Jevons's *Theory of Political Economy* in 1871, Menger's *Grundsätz der Volkswirtschaftslehre* in 1871, and Cairnes's *Leading Principles* in 1874. Marshall had not begun to study economics seriously till 1867, and Ruskin was his predecessor by at least ten years.

With consummate art Sir Edward T. Cook begins the second volume of his fine biography of Ruskin with the year 1860, the year when the art critic seemed to assume the new rôle of social seer. There is the temptation to regard the year 1860 as possessing the same significance in Ruskin's life as the year 1850 in Carlyle's but it is a temptation that must be resisted. Sir Edward attended in 1877 a lecture of Ruskin when he was Slade Professor of Art at Oxford, and he gives us an account of it. The subject of the course to which the lecture belonged had been first announced as landscape painting; but it never much mattered what Ruskin's lectures were called, and the course was in fact an informal commentary at large upon his books and teaching. From 1845 to 1860, he said, he had gone on writing with more or less public applause; and then in 1860 people saw a change came over him, of which they highly disapproved. For fifteen years precisely his writings had been thought praiseworthy; and for fifteen years precisely, thought the reverse. "These volumes on my left" (turning them round and pushing them from him) "are the volumes of *Modern Painters* which were praised; this volume on my right is the one which changed praise into blame. I got a bound copy of the fifth volume of *Modern Painters* at St. Martin's in the summer of 1860, and in the valley of Chamouni I gave up my art-work and wrote this little book" (taking it up in his hand)—"the beginning of the days of reprobation. But it is written in a better style; it is the central work of my life; and it contained at once the substance of all that I have had since to say." The little book was *Unto this Last*, the 1860 volume.

The stages in the evolution of Ruskin's thought are plain. He set out as a critic of painting, coming to the conclusion that art, if really fine, must be the representation of realities of beauty and must be pursued in the spirit of delight. He proceeded as a critic of architecture, finding it to be the reflection of national character, and the secret of Gothic lying in the happy life of the worker. He advanced to the study of economics, perceiving in the stately edifice erected by Ricardo and Mill foundations shaking at their base. How could the organism called society flourish when unregulated competition existed? There was no true body, for was it not given over to material and mechanical ideas? How could these ideas co-exist with happy art or happy workers? He confessed, "I simply cannot paint, nor read, nor look at minerals, nor do anything else that I like . . . because of the misery that I know of." He had taught in the Working Men's College, "as a byework to quiet my conscience, that I might be happy in what I supposed to be my own proper life of art-teaching." He was utterly unable so to quiet his conscience. Social evils, he sorrowfully owned, were not to be cured by individual remedies. At each stage in the growth of his mind he had been called mad. He was mad in the estimation of the dilettanti when he defended Turner. He was mad in the opinion of the architects when he lauded Gothic. He was mad in the judgment of the economists when he tried to humanise their science. "He has a bee in his bonnet," observed a friend to H. J. S. Smith the great mathematician. "A bee! a whole hive of them! But how beautifully they hum!" was Smith's answer.

The forerunner of Ruskin was not Ricardo but Blake. To Blake Gothic was the only architecture which lived. As Ruskin said that little else but art was moral, so Blake said that no one but an artist can be a Christian. Blake's central thought is reaffirmed by Ruskin, only that the one speaks in terms of morality, the other of religion. "To *subdue* the passions, which is thought so often to be the sum of duty respecting them, is possible only to a proud dullness; but to *excite* them rightly, and make them strong for good, is the work of the unselfish imagination." The writer of *Unto this Last* worked in the spirit of Blake's lines:—

I will not cease from mental fight,
  Nor shall my sword sleep in my hand,
Till we have built Jerusalem
  In England's green and pleasant land.

We hasten to add that if Blake gave voice to the need for reform, Ruskin gave it form. Movements such as those for the preservation of commons, the protection of footpaths, the limitations of rural advertisements, the consecration of land to a National Trust, and access to mountains are decidedly traceable to the successor of Blake. Nor does he fail to advocate the necessity for fair rents, fixity of tenure, and compensation for improvements. For property "belongs to whom proper"; "The land to those who can use it." He upholds free trade, but objects to the price of labour being fixed by competition; he is in favour of gratuitous and compulsory education; he wishes to see the aged poor pensioned by the State, the unemployed supplied with work, and the incurably lazy and vicious placed in government workshops or colonies. A deep-seated distrust of democracy runs through all his teaching. The people, he is convinced, cannot help themselves; and it is to the goodwill and intelligence of the governing classes that we must look for any permanent reform of the social order. While he perceives and condemns the failure of our upper classes in the past, with Coleridge and Carlyle he firmly believes that true progress can only be attained by a moral appeal to the heart and intelligence of individual members, the heroes if you will. He advocates honest production, just distribution, and wise consumption, the last a matter particularly overlooked by the classical economists. In his zeal for his three great reforms we may smile, if we please, at his diatribes against machinery and railways: we may, if we like, call his dreams Utopian. Yet if to-day, as a nation, we think less of gain and more of justice and benevolence, if we realise our responsibilities and apply ethics to social questions, it is largely owing to the man who was denounced as mad in the sixties. His protest was delivered with less noise and fury than that of his master Carlyle, but it was the more precise and definite in its character, and has proved more fertile in lasting benefit to the public weal.

In an Oxford lecture of 1877 there is a parable. Ruskin was expatiating, as was his wont, on the vandalism of the modern world. On an easel beside him was a water-colour drawing of Leicester by Turner. "The old stone bridge is picturesque," he said, "isn't it? But of course you want something more 'imposing' nowadays. So you shall have it." And taking his paint-box and brush he rapidly sketched in on the glass what is known in modern specifications as a "handsome iron structure." "Then," he continued, "you will want, of course, some tall factory chimneys, and I will give them to you galore." This he proceeded to do in like fashion. "The blue sky of heaven was pretty, but you cannot have everything, you know." And he painted clouds of black smoke over Turner's sky. "Your 'improvements'," he went on, "are marvellous 'triumphs of modern industry,' I know; but somehow they do not seem to produce nobler men and women, and no modern town is complete, you will admit, without a gaol and a lunatic asylum to crown it. So here they are for you." By this time not an inch of the Turner drawing was left visible under the "improvements" painted upon the glass. "But for my part," said Ruskin, taking his sponge, and with one pass of the hand wiping away those modern improvements against which he had inveighed in so many volumes— "for my part, I prefer the old." Yes, he preferred the old, but the old was to be informed by the spirit of *Unto this Last.* He was content to move slowly, yet surely. "Man's fruit of justice ripens slow." Law lags behind public opinion, but Ruskin was among the forces that perceptibly quickened public opinion. The moral impulse in the man mastered the audience that listened to his voice, and in the end it mastered the audience that read his writings.

The generation of the sixties was wayward and perverse, and refused to listen to the voice of the prophet. His father and his friends could not grasp the inwardness of the message he delivered so vehemently to the political economists. Rage at the waywardness and the perverseness of a stubborn generation consumed him, and in a letter of 1862 he gives vent to it. His friends had been counselling him to moderate the force of his expressions, but, like Carlyle, he felt utterly unable to do so. "Those expressions," he replied, "may do me harm, or do me good; what is that to me? They are the only true, right, or possible expressions. The Science of Political Economy *is* a Lie,—wholly and to the very root (as hitherto taught). It is also the Damnedest, —that is to say, the most utterly and to the lowest pit condemned of God and his Angels—that the Devil, or Betrayer of Man, has yet invented, except his (the Devil's) theory of Sanctification. To this 'science,' and to this alone (the professed and organised pursuit of Money) is owing *All* the evil of modern days. I say All. The Monastic theory is at an end. It is now the Money theory which corrupts the Church, corrupts the household life, destroys honour, beauty, and life throughout the universe. It is *the* Death incarnate of Modernism, and the so-called science of its pursuit is the most cretinous, speechless, paralysing plague that has yet touched the brain of mankind." So he wrote in 1862, and so he thought in 1860.

None of Ruskin's historical researches pleased him so much as his discovery of an early inscription on the Church of St. Giacomo di Rialto. "There are none of the rewarding accidents of my life," he acknowledged, "in which I take so much pride." Ruskin attached this inscription, in a note, to a new edition of *Unto this Last,* and it runs thus, "Around this temple let the merchant's law be just, his weights true, and his contracts guileless." It is another form of his plea for honest production, just distribution, and wise consumption. As in *The Political Economy of Art,* so in *Unto this Last* he urges that society is an organism. The circulation of wealth in a nation resembles that of blood in the natural body, and he presses this analogy down to minute particulars.

True work meant the production of the means of life; every one ought to take some share in it, according to his powers; some working with the head, some with the hands; but all alike acknowledging idleness and slavery to be immoral. As in *The Crown of Wild Olives,* he holds that justice demands that equal energy expended should bring equal reward. Was it just that incomes should be equalised? By no means, for some are sure to be more diligent and saving than others. Some work involves a great preliminary expenditure of energy in qualifying the worker as contrasted with the unskilled labourer. "*There is no wealth but life.* Life, including all its powers of love, of joy, and of admiration. That country is the richest which nourishes the greatest number of noble and happy human beings; that man is richest who, having perfected the functions of his own life to the utmost, has also the widest influence, both personal and by means of his possessions, over the lives of others." The emphasis passes from beauty to truth, from wealth to welfare. The needs of the body stand paramount. "Government and Co-operation are in all things the Laws of Life; Anarchy and Competition the Laws of Death."

Our author pleads for wise consumption, for fair distribution, and for a more thoughtful direction of labour, and he continues his plea: "And if, on due and honest thought over these things, it seems that the kind of existence to which men are now summoned by every plea of pity and claim of right, may, for some time at least, not be a luxurious one; —consider whether, even supposing it guiltless, luxury would be desired by any of us, if we saw clearly at our sides the suffering which accompanies it in the world.

Luxury is indeed possible in the future—innocent and exquisite; luxury for all, and by the help of all; but luxury at present can only be enjoyed by the ignorant; the cruelest man living could not sit at his feast, unless he sat blindfold. Raise the veil boldly; face the light; and if, as yet, the light of the eye can only be seen through tears, and the light of the body through sackcloth, go thou forth weeping, bearing precious seed, until the time come, and the kingdom, when Christ's gift of bread, and bequest of peace, shall be 'Unto this last as unto thee'; and when, for earth's severed multitudes of the wicked and the weary, there shall be holier reconciliation than that of the narrow home, and calm economy, where the Wicked cease—not from trouble—but from troubling—and the Weary are at rest."

The political economists assumed that their maxims were laws like those of the Medes and Persians, and Ruskin boldly called this assumption in question. The law of supply and demand incurred his particular aversion. He gave reasons for his aversion when he declared that "In a community regulated only by laws of demand and supply, but protected from open violence, the persons who become rich are, generally speaking, industrious, resolute, proud, covetous, prompt, methodical, sensible, unimaginative, insensitive, and ignorant. The persons who remain poor are the entirely foolish, the entirely wise, the idle, the reckless, the humble, the thoughtful, the dull, the imaginative, the sensitive, the well-informed, the improvident, the irregularly and impulsively wicked, the clumsy knave, the open thief, and the entirely merciful, just, and godly person."

Owen had advocated the wisdom of high wages, and he had justified his wisdom by his results. Ruskin followed, all unknowingly, in Owen's track, reaching a far wider audience in the end. The toiler was no mere machine: he is, if a machine, one whose motive-power is a soul, and on this aspect of the toiler he concentrated his attention. Nor is it wrong to trace to *Unto this Last* the growing recognition of the soul in co-operation, co-partnership, profit sharing, bonuses, progressive wages, and the like. The chapter on *The Roots of Honour* placed all the stress on social service, not on profits for employer of wages for employed, as the industrial motive.

Ruskin's books on art met with a ready sale. The 1862 edition of *Unto this Last* consisted of a thousand copies, and ten years later it was still not exhausted. For a generation it was an unspent force. In the seventies Ruskin re-issued it on his own account, and the rate of sale for the following thirty years was two thousand a year. In 1906 there was a large number of Labour Members, and a journalist asked them what work influenced them most, and *Unto this Last* appeared most frequently on their lists. In his preface the author stated in seven propositions "the worst of the political creed" to which he wished his principles to lead, and this no doubt influenced the Labour Members. The reforms he indicated were:

(1) National Schools for the young to be established at Government cost and under Government discipline over the whole country.

(2) Every child to be taught, further, some trade or calling.

(3) In connexion with these technical classes, Government workshops to be established, at which, without any attempt at establishing a monopoly, "good and exemplary work should be done, and pure and true substance sold."

(4) Any person out of employment to be set forthwith to work at the nearest Government workshop.

(5) Such work to be paid for at a fixed rate in each employment.

(6) Those who would work if they could, to be taught. Those who could work if they would, to be set to penal work.

(7) For the old and destitute comfort and home to be provided.

The mad man of 1860 is the sane man of to-day, for with the exception of the third all the others, in whole or in part, have been adopted. The third too sees recognition in the position the State assumes as a model employer and we see it in the extension of the anti-adulteration laws. Elementary and technical education, the first and second points, have long ago been adopted. The establishment of a Labour Department with all that it means, the occasional establishment of municipal relief works, and the operation of the dole are all steps towards the fourth point. The setting up in certain industries of Wages Boards and the increasing adoption, by the central and municipal authorities, of the principle of fair wages or Trade Union wages realise the fifth. The first part of the sixth is also realised, but is the second part? Old Age Pensions have done much towards the last point. In fact, in the sixties these seven propositions were immoderate whereas to-day they are moderate. The distance we have travelled from the immoderation of the sixties to the moderation of the twenties is a measure of the power Ruskin wields over all of us, a power all the greater since it has passed into the life of the nation.

The assault on Political Economy was renewed in 1862 in *Munera Pulveris.* In it he subjected to an able analysis the conception of wealth, a conception which takes "dust for deity," leading men to "gather dust for treasure." Fierce opposition sprang up, but Ruskin was greatly cheered by an encouraging letter from Carlyle who received an equally encouraging letter from Erskine of Linlathen. Carlyle wrote in 1862: "I have read, a month ago, your First (article) in *Fraser,* and ever since have had a wish to say to it and to you, *Euge macte nova virtute.* I approved in every particular; calm, definite, clear; rising into the sphere of Plato (our almost best), wh^{h}. in exchange for the sphere of MacCulloch, Mill & Co. is a mighty improvement. Since that, I have seen the little green book, too; reprint of your *Cornhill* operations,—about $\frac{2}{3}$ of wh^{h}. was read to me (*known* only from what the contradict^{n}. of sinners had told me of it);—in every part of wh^{h}. I find a high and a noble sort of truth, not one doctrine that I can intrinsically dissent from, or count other than salutary in the extreme, and pressingly needed in England." Erskine was "thankful for any unveiling of the so-called science of political economy, according to which, avowed selfishness is the Rule of the World. It is indeed most important preaching—to preach that there is not one God for religion and another God for human fellowship—and another God for buying and selling—that pestilent polytheism has been largely and confidently preached in our time, and blessed are those who can detect its mendacities, and help to disenchant the brethren of their power."

The encouragement of Carlyle gave fresh stimulus to the endeavours of Ruskin to win social justice. With Owen he realised that this was more far-reaching than any electoral reform which was absorbing the efforts of both the political parties in 1867. He had met Thomas Dixon, of Sunderland, a corkcutter by trade, a man with "the ingenuous simplicity of a child and the tender sympathetic heart of a woman." He was a working-man after his heart, and intercourse with him suggested that it was well worth while to develop the thoughts in *Unto this Last* and *Munera Pulveris*. He wrote letters to Dixon, and these he gathered into a volume in 1867 which he entitled *Time and Tide by Weare and Tyne: Twenty-five Letters to a Working Man of Sunderland on the Laws of Work*. In it he denied that Political Economy was entitled to the adjective: to him it was mercantile economy. Its very basis contemplated man as an isolated factor in the commonwealth, whereas he insisted that he was a corporative factor. The economic man contemplated by Ricardo was a being whose sole motive was gain, one who bought in the cheapest market and sold in the dearest. In order to arrive at such a conception, it was vital to strip this man of his love of religion and of his love of country. He was, in fact, a mere outline of a man. Ruskin pours forth his soul in a comparison of classical Political Economy to "a science of gymnastics which assumed that men had no skeletons." On the strength of this comparison "It might be shown . . . that it would be advantageous to roll the students up into pellets, flatten them into cakes, or stretch them into cables; and that when these results were effected, the reinsertion of the skeleton would be attended with various inconveniences to their constitution. The reasoning might be admirable, the conclusions true, and the science deficient only in applicability. Modern political economy stands on a precisely similar basis. Assuming, not that the human being has no skeleton, but that it is all skeleton, it founds an ossifiant theory of progress on this negation of a soul; and having shown the utmost that may be made of bones, and constructed of interesting geometrical figures with death's-head and humeri, successfully proves the inconvenience of the reappearance of a soul among these corpuscular structures."

We should be slow to maintain that the character and the consistency of Ruskin's writings are an article of the faith, and yet as we turn to *The Stones of Venice, Unto this Last, Time and Tide,* and the Inaugural Oxford Lectures we note this sameness of character and consistency of purpose. *The Stones of Venice* laid down "the dependence of all human work, or edifice, for its beauty, on the happy life of the workman." In *Unto this Last* he laid down "the laws of that life itself, and its dependence on the Sun of Justice." In *Time and Tide* he laid down the laws of work which make up life. In Oxford he continued his teaching in preaching the necessity that such life "should be led, and the gracious laws of beauty and labour recognised, by the upper, no less than the lower, classes of England"; and, finally, "it is simply one part of the practical work I have to do in Art-teaching," he said in *Fors Clavigera,* "to bring somewhere (the conditions of fine art) into existence." No doubt there is an evolution in this thought, though we are more impressed by its character and consistency throughout.

In his writings he is always anxious to bring out the Pauline truth that no man liveth to himself. If the workman is an individualist and if the employer is also one, where is the goodwill which means so much to the success of a business? Your Adam Bede works for wages, but he also works for pride in his labour. Take this away, and how long will a business last? The relations of a colonel to his men are not based on the elimination of the social affections. Why, he asks, does the soldier receive more honour than the manufacturer or the merchant? Because the latter acts in the spirit of the political economist. When in Durham Westcott was stopped by a manufacturer who asked him, "Why, my lord, are we business men not ranked with professional men?" Swift came the answer, "When a merchant will die for his workman as a doctor will for his patient, then you will be held in the same honour."

It is an answer that would have delighted Ruskin. For one of the firmest articles in his creed was that the riches of the State will be greatest where there are Captains of Industry working under a code of unselfish honour. Of course he knew quite well that there were such Captains, but were there enough of them to transform the relation of employer and employed not into the cash-nexus which Carlyle decried but into social service? It is significant that the title of the first chapter in *Unto this Last* is *The Roots of Honour*.

The individual is not at bottom a unit: he is a member of society. He creates wealth, but he does not create it wholly for himself: he cannot do so. Yet wealth is not the main matter, which is rather the persons who make it. He pleads: "Since the essence of wealth consists in power over men, will it not follow that the nobler and the more in number the persons are over whom it has power, the greater the wealth? Perhaps it may even appear, after some consideration, that the persons themselves *are* the wealth—that these pieces of gold with which we are in the habit of guiding them, are, in fact, nothing more than a kind of Byzantine harness or trappings, very glittering and beautiful in barbaric sight, wherewith we bridle the creatures; but that if these same living creatures could be guided without the fretting and jingling of the Byzants in their mouths and ears, they might themselves be more valuable than their bridles. In fact, it may be discovered that the true veins of wealth are purple—and not in Rock, but in Flesh—perhaps even that the final outcome and consummation of all wealth is in the producing as many as possible of full-breathed, bright-eyed, and happy-hearted human creatures. . . . In some far-away and yet undreamt-of hour, I can even imagine that England may cast all thoughts of possessive wealth back to the barbaric nations among whom they first arose; and that, while the sands of the Indus and adamant of Golconda may yet stiffen the housings of the charger, and flash from the turban of the slave, she, as a Christian mother, may at last attain to the virtues and the treasures of a Heathen one, and be able to lead forth her Sons, saying, 'These are *my* Jewels'."

What is wealth? Does Political Economy define one of its fundamental terms? Ruskin finds, to his surprise, that it does not define it. This he had urged in *Unto this Last,* and he urged it in *Munera Pulveris,* and in his urgings in the latter he writes: "The most reputed essay on the subject which has appeared in modern times, after opening with the statement that 'writers on political economy profess to teach, or to investigate, the nature of wealth,' thus follows up the declaration of its thesis—'Every one has a notion, sufficiently correct for common purposes, of what is meant by wealth'. . . . 'It is no part of the design of this treatise to aim at metaphysical nicety of definition.' . . . And Mr. Mill contentedly proceeded, as if a chemist should proceed to investigate the laws of chemistry without endeavouring to ascertain the nature of fire or water, because every one had a notion of them, 'sufficiently correct for common purposes.'

"Metaphysical nicety, we assuredly do not need; but physical nicety, and logical accuracy, with respect to a physical subject, we as assuredly do. Suppose the subject of inquiry, instead of being House-law (Oikonomia) had been Star-law (Astronomia), and that, ignoring distinction between stars fixed and wandering, as here between wealth radiant and wealth reflective, the writer had begun thus: 'Every one has a notion, sufficiently correct for common purposes, of what is meant by stars. Metaphysical nicety in the definition of a star is not the object of this treatise';—the essay so opened might yet have been far more true in its final statements, and a thousand-fold more serviceable to the navigator, than any treatise on wealth, which founds its conclusions on the popular conception of wealth, can ever become to the economist."

The fault he finds in Mill he does not commit himself. He offers us his own definitions—wealth, "things in themselves valuable"; money, "documentary claims to such things"; riches, "the relation of one person's possessions to another"; value, "the life-giving power of a thing," which involves usefulness and the capacity to use it; cost, "the quantity of labour required to produce a thing"; and price, "the quantity of labour which the possessor of a thing will take in exchange for it." He disowns Ricardo, and yet what is there more essentially Ricardian than his definitions of cost and price? Consciously we feel certain he had not imbibed these notions from Ricardo, but subconsciously they came all the same from him.

Ruskin was to meet the Duke of Argyll in the future. The Duke found things very well as they are, and Ruskin found them very ill. He eagerly desired to remould "this sorry scheme of things nearer to the heart's desire." With an air of triumph the Duke concluded, "You seem to want a very different world, Mr. Ruskin." "Yea, verily a new heaven and a new earth, and the former things passed away." Yet there was nothing of the "leveller" about the reformer. Indeed he attacked Gladstone as assuming this rôle. He said to the Liberal leader, "You see *you* think one man is as good as another, and all men equally competent to judge aright on political questions; whereas I am a believer in an aristocracy." And straight came the answer from Gladstone, "Oh dear, no! I am nothing of the sort. I am a firm believer in the aristocratic principle—the rule of the best. I am an out-and-out *inequalitarian*," a confession which Ruskin greeted with intense delight, clapping his hands triumphantly. Order and reverence, authority and obedience, these watchwords of Conservatism, are ever on his lips, these ideas ever present in his mind. Radical and revolutionary doctrines, as he interprets them, conflict with these watchwords, and accordingly he denounces such doctrines. With Carlyle he scornfully repudiates liberty and equality as the very negation of order and government. In the fifth letter in *Fors Clavigera* he asks for: "No liberty, but instant obedience to known law and appointed persons; no equality, but recognition of every betterness and reprobation of every worseness." When Eyre put down the revolt of the negroes in Jamaica in 1865 with a strong hand, he was prosecuted. He found friends in Carlyle, Ruskin, Kingsley, and Tennyson, and enemies in Mill, Huxley, Thomas Hughes, Herbert Spencer, and Goldwin Smith.

If Plato desired to see the philosopher act as king, in his spirit Ruskin in *Time and Tide* pleads for his king, the captain of industry, who is to fulfil in the industrial age what the baron fulfilled in feudalism. The employer of labour could be a captain, a king, in our day, the leader and the helper of his fellow-men. For surely the function of commerce was not to prey upon society but to serve society. Once more the ideas of Coleridge were awake in Ruskin. For Ruskin, like Coleridge, advocated the preservation of class distinctions and the fixing of the status of all. Is he, then, against equality, equality of opportunity? Decidedly not. The land, the capital, the power to use the land and the capital, go to him who can use them to the advantage or the weal of all. Special aptitude in all, high or low, must be sought for and employed on behalf of the community. "If indeed no effort is made to discover, in the course of their early training, for what services the youth of a nation are individually qualified; nor any care taken to place those who have unquestionably proved their fitness for certain functions, in the offices they could best fulfil—then to call the confused wreck of social order and life, brought about by malicious confusion and competition, an arrangement of Providence, is quite one of the most insolent and wicked ways in which it is possible to take the name of God in vain." Such is the plain teaching of *Time and Tide*.

There is, then, to be equality of opportunity, nevertheless there are "unconquerable differences in the clay of the human creature." There are differences, some due no doubt to class yet others due to ability, and he lends his support to class differences which he attributes to a natural as well as to a social reason. There is Platonism in all his writings, and it is as evident in *Time and Tide* as in any other part of them. If the upper classes possess rights, they equally certainly possess duties, and Ruskin is most anxious to set forth their duties. *Noblesse oblige* is an idea never out of his mind, and he presses it on the landlord, the employer, and the bishop respectively. Society required reconstruction, but the reconstruction must be on Platonic principles—assigning to each man his due place, and requiring from each man the fulfilment of his duties. "In heaven," according to Plato, "there is laid up a pattern of such a city: and he who desires may behold it, and beholding, govern himself accordingly. But whether there really is, or will be, such an one, is of no importance to him, for he will act according to the laws of that city and no other." So Ruskin acted, and he found that his acts at home brought him into touch with Maurice and the Christian Socialists and abroad with the Roman Catholic Socialist party and the State-assisted industrial societies which Schultze-Delitzsch favoured. The Golden Age for Ruskin was not coming to-day or to-morrow, but it surely was coming, and it was his part to hasten its advent.

We all know that our author persuaded his undergraduate hearers at Oxford to embrace the gospel of labour, and men laughed in 1874 at the amateur diggers on the Hincksey road. Among them were Arnold Toynbee and Alfred Milner, beautiful and devoted spirits who served their generation faithfully, Toynbee for a short time and Milner for a long one. They felt in their lives the principle of *noblesse oblige*, and the world, forgetful as it is, will not lightly forget their splendid lives. "I tell you," so Ruskin announced at the close of one of his lectures, "that neither sound art, policy, nor religion can exist in England until, neglecting, if it must be, your own pleasure-gardens, you resolve that the streets which are the habitations of the poor, and the fields which are the playgrounds of their children, shall be again restored to the rule of the spirits, whosoever they are, in earth and heaven, that ordain and reward, with constant and conscious felicity, all that is decent and orderly, beautiful and pure." These words fell on appreciative ears, and to them we can trace the Universities' Settlements and Public School Settlements in London and other cities.

It is easy—and profitless—for the economist who is merely a man of thought to criticise Ruskinian teaching which is based on feeling for the under dog. If East and West are never to meet, according to Rudyard Kipling, till the judgment seat, it almost seems as if the man of thought and the man of feeling were in a similar predicament. Yet Ruskin brought his due contribution to the man of thought. He taught him that man is a being who belongs to an organism, and that there is more in society than a fortuitous collection of its members together. If Political Economy is to treat of man in society, it must be more than merely mercantile: it must be really political. What Spencer and Maine had essayed in one fashion, he essayed in another. If their thought is evolutionary, so is his. If they look forward to anything but the present framework of society, his outlook is not unlike. We made progress in the past, and if the Platonic—and the Ruskinian—conception of society prevails, there is every reason to think that this progress will continue.

There are spots in the sun, and we shall be the last to contend that the classical economists were wrong and it was reserved for Ruskin to set them right. True, the times were out of joint, and he is quite as determined as Hamlet to set them aright. If he effected advance when he humanised Political Economy and when he insisted, with Huxley, on the due place of the ethical motive, he surely went astray when he denounced the whole process of lending capital as unproductive, when he denounced usury in general and Bishop Fraser in particular for upholding the lawfulness of interest, and when he asserted that there should be no profit in the loan of capital. It is quite easy to pick holes in what he taught—if we forget the mighty power he exercised over civic and national politics. A friend criticised Marlborough before Bolingbroke who was no friend of the greatest general we ever possessed. Bolingbroke's reply was, "He was so great a man that I forget his errors." Ruskin is an influence, and as such we endeavour to estimate him.

The weal of all is the motive uppermost in the mind of our romanticist and reformer. It is not in his nature—even if it were in his power occasionally—to adjust his outlook to the very varying one of the Conservative or the Liberal. In 1869 he wrote a letter on his lecture at Woolwich on the future of England: "That there are two great parties in the state—the Radical and Conservative—that I have thought over their respective wishes, and that they have two opposite watchwords, which are both right—and only right *together*—namely:—Radical, 'Every man his chance.'

Tory, 'Every man in his rank.' I shall ask leave of my audience to make myself a Thorough Radical for the first half-hour, and to change into a Thorough Tory in the second." The extension of the franchise, from his angle, meant but little, and in 1881 he said, "So far from wishing to give votes to women, I would fain take them away from most men," and he would take them away on Platonic grounds.

Ruskin was a candidate in 1880 for the Lord Rectorship of Glasgow University. The Conservative Club supported him against John Bright. He warned the undergraduates at the outset that though he was "the staunchest Conservative in the British Islands," yet he held advanced opinions on land and rent which no Conservative Club would sanction. As the contest proceeded, he was increasingly asked to declare himself more definitely, and he did. He wrote: "What in the devil's name have *you* to do with either Mr. D'Israeli or Mr. Gladstone? You are students at the University, and have no more business with politics than you have with rat-catching. Had you ever read ten words of mine with understanding you would have known that I care no more either for Mr. D'Israeli or Mr. Gladstone than for two old bagpipes with the drones going by steam, but that I hate all Liberalism as I do Beelzebub, and that, with Carlyle, I stand, we two alone now in England, for God and the Queen."

Plato and Aristotle believed in slavery because the produce of the slave left the citizen free to devote his time to the problems of the City State, and both Carlyle and Ruskin were imbued with this spirit which they conceived could not emanate from the mass of mankind. The great man, the hero, call him what you will, must retain the leadership of men. Give each man his place in society, and then let him discharge his duty in his place. In an ideal government the clergy and the civil officers shall unite to rule, each supporting and correcting the other, "the clergy hallowing all worldly policy by their influence, and the magistracy repressing all religious enthusiasm by their practical wisdom."

Ruskin's autobiography appears in *Fors Clavigera*, and

it is as discursive as his lectures at Oxford. In January, 1871, he commenced the series of monthly letters called *Fors Clavigera,* and in these letters he pours out his impatience with the past and his patience in believing that a new heaven will surely come. Not a little of *Fors* was written under stress of deep emotion. His first marriage had been a failure, and on its dissolution his wife had married Millais. He met Rose La Touche as a mere child, and grew to love her with all the passion of his lonely nature. She accepted him, and the disparity in age suggested a three years' probation. He was as content to wait as Jacob of old, and the years seemed to him but a few days for the love he bore her. Difficulties came. She was an Irish girl with an Evangelical outlook on religion, and the lapse of her lover from orthodoxy distressed her sensitive nature. Her mind was tortured by doubts and despairs, which stand out in her *Clouds and Light.* One of the pieces reveal her attitude:—

I would look back upon my life to-night,
  Whose years have scarcely numbered twenty-two;
I would recall the darkness and the light,
  The hours of pain God's angels led me through;
Out of His love He orders all things right,
  I, slow of heart, would feel that this is true.

I, in those years, have learnt that life is sad,
  Sad to heart-breaking did we walk alone.
I, who have lost much which I never had,
  Yet which in ignorance I held mine own,
Would leave the clouded past, its good and bad,
  Within His hands to whom all things are known.

Ruskin's deep love for her was to realise all the pangs of hope deferred, and alas! doomed to disappointment. His heart ached to have her at his side. "*You,*" he once wrote to Susan Beevor, "expect to see your Margaret again, and you will be happy with her in heaven. I wanted my Rosie *here.* In heaven I mean to go and talk to Pythagoras and Socrates and Valerius Publicola. I shan't care a bit for Rosie there, she needn't think it. What will grey eyes and red cheeks be good for *there*!" An interval of unclouded happiness came before the end, but the storms of life were too much for the frail body, and she passed away in May,

1875. His heart was buried in her grave. Sir E. Cook tells us: "Ruskin's love-letters to Rose are not in existence. Communicative, expansive, un-reticent though Ruskin was, his literary executors felt that these letters, though perhaps the most beautiful things he ever wrote, were too sacred for publicity. A letter from Rose to him which he specially valued he used to carry in his breast-pocket between plates of gold. After her death, he kept them all—his to her, and hers to him—in a rosewood box. On a day in autumn, Mrs. Severn and Professor Norton took them to the woodland garden, above Brantwood, and gave them to the flames. A wind was blowing, and one letter fluttered away from the pyre. It was written from Brantwood, when Ruskin was first settling in his new home, and in it he wonders whether Rosie will ever give him the happiness of welcoming her there. But she never came to Brantwood. The garden, lake, and shore which became so dear to Ruskin were left without any memory of her presence, though often, as it seemed to him, graced by her spirit." Like Shakespeare and Milton, Burke and Cervantes, and so many of the greatest, Ruskin's only ultimate descendants are his books.

The storm and stress through which Ruskin was passing is evident in *Fors*. In *Praeterita* he says, "I wonder mightily what sort of creature I should have turned out, if instead of the distracting and useless pain, I had the joy of approved love, and the untellable, incalculable motive of its sympathy and praise. It seems to me that such things are not allowed in this world. The men capable of the highest imaginative passion are always tossed on fiery waves by it." To his ineffable pain he himself had been long tossed on these fiery waves, and yet has it not proved to be to the deep pleasure of the world? For we can only give what we feel, and because Ruskin had been stirred to the depths of his nature by his passion for Rose La Touche he gave more to the world than otherwise he could have given. Mill sorrowed for the loss of his wife, and out of his sorrow there came that emotional blend with reason which profoundly moved his readers. On the other hand, because Spencer never felt deeply he was unable to communicate any deep feeling to others. The Icelandic proverb is true. "What a happy world it is, and how happy it is for the sorrow in it." Sorrow with his shovel mines the heart. But he is surely a cunning workman. He deepens the channels whereby happiness may enter, and hollows out new chambers for joy to abide in, when he is gone.

The influence of Carlyle is plain in the pages of *Fors Clavigera*, and in it he notably follows the exhortations of *Past and Present*. If he follows them, he follows them with a difference. The master's work was generally destructive, seldom constructive. The disciple's was both destructive and constructive. The work of destruction is visible in the criticism of the nineteenth century which colours the whole book. Material progress had been acclaimed by the Victorians, and Ruskin asks, What is it really worth? The submarine cable had been acclaimed as a triumph of mechanical skill, but Ruskin asks, What messages does it convey? Similarly, the extension of the railway system had been acclaimed. Ruskin demands, Is it any real advantage that "every fool in Buxton can be at Bakewell in half-an-hour, and every fool in Bakewell in Buxton"?

On the constructive side the old remedies of trade guilds, a State Church, and a paternal government are urged, and urged with a vehemence which betrays signs of the emotional crisis through which he had been passing. The tyranny of capital, we gather, is the old sin of usury. Why does not Bishop Fraser denounce it? The commercialist spirit is rampant. Why does not his clergy denounce it? *Past and Present* had shown what Church and State did execute in the Middle Ages. Why do not Church and State execute something—or somebody—now?

The spirit of construction is present in *Fors Clavigera*: so too is the spirit of destruction. Carlyle was pleased, and in 1871 he wrote:—

'Dear Ruskin,

This 'Fors Clavigera' Letter 5th, which I have just finished reading, is incomparable; a quasi-sacred consolation to me, which almost brings tears into my eyes! Every word of it is as spoken, not out of my poor heart only, but out of the eternal skies; words winged with Empyrean wisdom, piercing as lightning,—and which I really do not remember to have heard the like of. *Continue*, while you have utterance in you, to give them voice. They will find and force entrance into human hearts, *whatever* the 'angle of incidence' may be; that is to say, whether, for the degraded and inhuman Blockheadism we, so-called 'men' have mostly now become, you come in upon them at the broadside, at the top, or even at the bottom Euge, Euge—Yours ever,

T. CARLYLE."

Fors Clavigera bore witness to constructive work when it recorded the doings of the St. George's Guild. It was composed of holy and humble men of heart who were to reclaim land for food production. Floods were to be averted and fens to be drained. The landlords were to be "men of independent fortune, devoting gifts and ingenuity to the service of the Guild, and owing their lordship to the fact that they could work as much better than their labourers as a good knight than his soldiers." The labourers were to be "young people bred on old estates"; the commandants over them, "veteran soldiers"; for Ruskin had "observed constantly in historical readings the beneficence of strict military order in peace, and the justice, sense, and kindness of good officers acting unrestrictedly in civil capacities." Rents were to be fixed, and for the most part they would return to the land in the shape of improvements. The Master was to govern the Guild with supreme and dictatorial powers. Under him were the Marshals, officers over great districts. Next to them came the Landlords. Under them came the Comites Ministrantes, Companions of the Guild who spent themselves in public service. Under them came the Comites Militantes, Companions of the rank and file, working as land-agents, tenant farmers, hired labourers, or tradesmen. Last of all came the Comites Consilii, companions pledged to St. George's Vow and giving tenths of their income to the Guild, but living their own lives and not resident on St. George's lands. Dress in all classes would be determined by the rank in which each lived. There would be no idle rich, no oppressed poor. Luxury would be realised, but it would be luxury for all. Landladies would wear beautiful clothes, and peasant women would carry their wealth in gold and silver ornaments for their hair. There would be model schools and museums on every estate, and each cottage would have its Shepherd's library and pictures, selected for it by the Master. In fact, the Golden Age was to return, and under St. George's Guild our country would once more become the Merrie England it had long ceased to be.

Such was the dream. An Owen might have put some of it into operation in a New Coniston, but Ruskin's gifts did not allow him to turn the ideal into the real. The scheme dwindled into a few Companions with some cottages in Wales, twenty acres of partly cleared woodland in Worcestershire, a few bleak acres in Yorkshire, and a single museum. Rose La Touche had passed away in 1875, and as the dream of his own happiness faded away, he also began to perceive that the prospects of his Guild were also fading away. His reason for a time gave way, and at this we do not greatly wonder. The sense of failure and of disappointed hopes, privately and publicly, weighed heavily upon him. What made him mad, he used to say in late years, was not his work, but the feeling that nothing came of it. Moses is not the only man to stand on Mount Pisgah to see the promised land with his eyes and to feel that he is not destined to cross over to possess it. The days of allotments, afforestation, small holdings, industrial villages, and garden cities was not as yet, but who shall say how much the vision of St. George's Guild contributed to their realisation? Browning is right. There shall never be one lost good. There is pathos in the story of his courtship of Rose La Touche. There is also pathos in the feeling that he was never to know how deeply his message had taken root in the land he loved with such devotion. He has lifted the art and the architecture of England to a higher level. He has opened our eyes to the divine loveliness of the world of nature, and has taught us anew that beauty leads up to God. The wreath of the village tailor bore the words, "There was a man sent from God, and his name was John." He has spoken to us, as George Eliot testified, with the inspiration of the old Hebrew prophets, and his burning words have quickened the national conscience to a new sense of duty and justice to all. His *Sursum corda* has not been uttered in vain.

Tolstoi regarded Ruskin as the greatest Englishman of his time, and there is a singular parallelism between the two men. They were prophets with a message for the nineteenth century, and, like the prophets of old, their message was an agony to them. The Puritanism of their character is evident to all, though there is an asceticism in Tolstoi never to be found in Ruskin. They lived to a great age, and ended in the gloom of hopes shattered in private and in public. Their writings are full of details, which if related by anyone else would seem tedious or absurd, but which as they tell them, have an inexplicable significance working upon our minds like the great passions and events of tragic poetry and by a process which, if it is slower, is surer. They are constantly moved to emotion by the details of life, and this emotion is never sentimental. Neither Tolstoi nor Ruskin forces it for the purposes of his art; he does not affect any preternatural sensibility or sagacity. Neither attempts to conceal his prejudices; and though they may interrupt the narrative for a time, they do not pervert it. Both were at times prone to colour their verdict on books by their opinion of authors. Both acted on the maxim "*Nulla dies sine linea,*" and recorded in common-place books not only events and conversations, but also resolutions and prayers. Both used to crystallise reflection by pithy and pointed sentences. Both boasted considerable self-confidence in matters where they were not always more competent than those to whom they honestly dictated. The Philistines could quarrel with each on the ground of eccentricity. Each owned no immunity from crotchets, and their teaching has thereby lost the full strength of its appeal. There are in Tolstoi's *War and Peace* and *Anna Karenin* a dislike of doctors and philosophers, and an absurd, though fashionable, theory of Napoleon's career. But these are not more prominent than the prejudices to be found in the works of other great writers, as, for instance, Milton; and with Tolstoi and Ruskin they are, on the whole, harmless because they are isolated and do not affect the judgments pronounced on the great mass of mankind or their sympathy with them.

The message of the two writers came home to men partly

through its truth and partly through the circumstance that they were consummate artists in language. Tolstoi hated and despised art, and Ruskin experienced its repulsion as well as its attraction, realising to the full the opposition between art and Puritanism which is one of the permanent antinomies of life. Swinburne has said that there is no possible truce between art and Puritanism; and Tolstoi's later life seems to prove that he is right. For Tolstoi was the greatest of modern Puritans, and by his Puritan standard he condemned *War and Peace* and *Anna Karenin*. Yet both men maintained that art ought not to be a thing apart: it was an essential factor in the life of all. Their writings are voluminous because, like all prophets, they delivered their message because necessity was laid on them. Both came to think little of literature in comparison with preaching. They alike advocated the gospel of labour by their example as well as by their precept. They seem to have experienced life with the calm of a philosopher as well as with the sensibility of a poet. Their knowledge of all kinds of affairs is immense, and they never display it as if they had acquired it for the purposes of their art. Their sense of brotherhood impelled them to reject commercial competition and profit-seeking as destructive of the true spirit of the workman. They inevitably leant to the country and its freer life rather than to the town with its machine-made civilisation. The cry, Back to Nature, is common to both, and both were, consciously and unconsciously, deeply stirred by the influence of Rousseau.

Tolstoi and Ruskin conceived that it was the duty of man to do the best he can, though Ruskin feels that it is scarcely our lot to try to do what we cannot. There is a moral obligation on all moral teachers to discover the best that man can do, not to set impossibilities before him, and to tell him that, if he does not follow them, he is damned. For impossibilities, because they are impossibilities, are wrong. Our problem is not to discover what we ought to do if we were different, but what we ought to do, being what we are. There is no end to the beings we can imagine different from ourselves; but they do not exist, and therefore we cannot assume that they would be better than we are if they did exist. With them we have to assume a whole reality that is not; and that reality, since it is a figment of our minds, would probably be inferior to the reality that is. For there is this to be said in favour of reality: that we have nothing to compare it with. Our phantasies are always incomplete, because they are phantasies; and reality is complete. We cannot compare their incompleteness with its completeness. So the beings we imagine different from ourselves are incomplete. The Bolshevists perhaps have tried to be the beings that Tolstoi imagined; but they remain in reality as it is, and they cannot, in that reality, perform the impossibilities that he demanded of them.

The resemblances between Tolstoi and Ruskin are striking, but so too are the differences. Tolstoi never saw that government and all institutions are not impositions but growths, except where one nation conquers and tyrannises over another. Ruskin saw this. There may be, and always is, evil in government and institutions; but it is not the evil only of a few governors; it is not the result of a conspiracy; it is the evil of a whole society expressing itself in institutions or in the working of them. The Russian Government was corrupt because corruption is a vice of the Russians, not because it was government. In Russia the natural man is corrupt, not merely the unnatural rulers; and so it is with the vices of government everywhere, as Ruskin noted. Where they persist, it is because the people consent to them, not because government in itself is evil. The evil remains when the government is removed.

As you read Tolstoi and Ruskin you feel that life is not to be judged by its pleasures or pains, nor by any ordinary standard of failure or success. It has some unseen goal, and men are moved by some unknown force towards it, and by inexplicable passions when they think of it. Though the Russian and the Scotsman cannot tell us what this goal is or the force that draws us towards it, yet each writer is constantly and steadily aware of both. It is the peculiarity of their genius that they combine this mystical consciousness of what life desires to be with a vast curiosity and knowledge of what it is. Mystics are apt to be impatient of the routine of life, of everything in which the purpose of life, as they conceive it, is not clear and strong. Yet Tolstoi and Ruskin have sought for that purpose with a scientific ardour and patience, not only in their own mind or in the noblest works of God and actions of men, but also in all that men do when they seem to be the slaves of circumstance and of their own habits, errors, and appetites. The great tragic poets show us the glory of life triumphing even in death. Tolstoi and Ruskin do what is even harder and more comforting. They show us the glory of life triumphing in the midst of its own failures and squalor and wearisome routine. If they bring knowledge to the world, they also bring the world to knowledge.

Men grow and change with experience, and the greatest never cease growing and changing. But with all growth there is some decay and loss. We know truths when we are young that we lose in middle age; for the change of experience, as it forces new truths upon the mind, obliterates old ones from it. And the keener this experience the more complete is this process. Did any men that ever lived experience more keenly than Tolstoi and Ruskin? We know from the story of their lives that the events of the mind were to them like battles; and they always threw the whole force of their will and intellect into them. For a long time they seem to have lived almost blindly, turning eagerly from one experience to another, trying one kind of life after another like a child in its make-believe. Yet it was never make-believe for them, for there was in them the unconscious principle which made them determined to experience all things before they came to their own conclusion upon life. And so each of their experiences possessed a cumulative power, and they profited by them all. As with the greatest so with the least of men—each goes his own narrow way, however vociferous of applause or of contempt the phantom spectators of this world may be; however urgent the viewless witnesses of another. A man takes up his candle, and in its clear but baffling light must push his way through the darkness of life's corridor past every hindrance, stopping his ears as best he can against fear and the conflicting voices, towards the glimmer of the window at the far end, only to stand at last confronting in the dark glass, against the deeper darkness of the night without, his own weary and haunted face; bravely aware that even the candle that has been his guide and comrade must be extinguished before he can see beyond—so, out of their courage and sacrifice, stand the figures of Tolstoi and Ruskin.

REFERENCES

BARDOUX, K. *Le Mouvement idéaliste et social dans la Littérature anglaise au XIXe Siècle. John Ruskin.* (Paris, 1900.)

BENSON, A. C. *Ruskin: A Study in Personality.* (London, 1911.)

BOSANQUET, B. *The History of Aesthetic.* (London, 1892.)

BROICHER, C. *John Ruskin u. sein Werk.* (Leipzig, 1907.)

BRUNHES, J. *Ruskin et la Bible.* (Paris, 1901.)

BURNE-JONES, Lady. *Memorials of Edward Burne-Jones.* (London, 1904.)

CHEVRILLON, A. *Nouvelles Etudes Anglaises.* (Paris, 1910.)

COLLINGWOOD, W. G. *The Life and Work of John Ruskin.* (London, 1900.)

COOK, Sir E. T. *Studies in Ruskin.* (Orpington, 1890.)

COOK, Sir E. T. *The Life of Ruskin.* (London, 1911.)

COOK, Sir E. T. *Literary Recreations.* (London, 1918.)

FROUDE, J. A. *Carlyle. History of his Life in London* (1834–81). (London, 1884.)

GEDDES, P. *John Ruskin, Economist.* (Edinburgh, 1884.)

HARRISON, F. *Tennyson, Ruskin, Mill, and other Literary Estimates.* (London, 1899.)

HARRISON, F. *John Ruskin.* (London, 1902.)

HERKNER, H. *Ruskin, als Sozialreformer.* (Berlin, 1900.)

HOBSON, J. A. *John Ruskin, Social Reformer.* (London, 1898.)

HUNT, HOLMAN. *The Pre-Raphaelite Brotherhood.* (London, 1905.)

KITCHIN, G. W. *Ruskin in Oxford and other Studies.* (London, 1904.)

MACKAIL, J. W. *Life of William Morris.* (London, 1899.)

MAITLAND, F. W. *Life and Letters of Leslie Stephen.* (London, 1906.)

MAUROIS, A. *Etudes anglais* (*Ruskin and Wilde*). (Paris, 1927.)

MAUROIS, A. *Quatre études anglais, de Ruskin à Wilde.* (Paris, 1927.)

MEYNELL, Mrs. *John Ruskin.* (London, 1900.)

MILSAND, J. *L'esthétique anglais.* (Paris, 1864.)

RITCHIE, Mrs. *Records of Tennyson, Ruskin, and Browning.* (London, 1892.)

ROBERTSON, J. M. *Modern Humanists.* (London, 1895.)

SIZERANNE, R. de la. *Ruskin et la Religion de la Beauté.* (Paris, 1897.)

SMART, W. *John Ruskin. His Life and Works.* (Manchester, 1880.)

SPIELMANN, M. H. *John Ruskin.* (London, 1900.)

WALSTON, Sir C. *The Work of Ruskin.* (London, 1894.)

WHITEHOUSE, J. H., Ed. *Ruskin Centenary Addresses.* (Oxford, 1919.)

WHITEHOUSE, J. H., Ed. *Ruskin the Prophet, and other Centenary Studies.* (London, 1920.)

WILLIAMS-ELLIS, A. *The Tragedy of John Ruskin.* (London, 1928.)

Chapter IV.

MATTHEW ARNOLD THE POET-CRITIC

Thomas Arnold is known to all the world through Dean Stanley's penetrating biography and through Thomas Hughes's *Tom Brown's School Days*. Mr. Lytton Strachey has immortalised the bands and the gown and the "slightly puzzled look" of the headmaster. He has sketched the career of the teacher with inimitable irony, and yet does he explain how the curious being he describes moved his generation? A man's influence is not so lightly divorced from his personality as Mr. Strachey imagines.

The root interest in all the Arnolds lies in religion which was destined to wear in the second and third generations widely differing forms. Mrs. Humphry Ward was a granddaughter, and her *Robert Elsmere* differs from *The Case of Richard Meynell* almost as much as Thomas Arnold differed from his sons Matthew and Thomas. Thomas Arnold, senior, and Matthew were schoolmasters in different fashions. In the father the theologian and the historian ascended the pulpit, in the son the poet and the critic. Perhaps the son did not exhibit the solemnity and the energy of the father. Nor was the message they delivered precisely the same, though if we allow for the Zeitgeist we wonder if the difference between what the father spoke to his age is so very different from what the son spoke to his. In their earnestness, in their goodness, and in their essential Puritanism there is no marked difference. They displayed a perception of beauty rare everywhere, though of course less so since Ruskin's day. They loved nature and they loved travel. They were full of as strong sympathy for all that was lovely and of good report in our modern social movements and of as strong antipathy to all that was unlovely and of evil report. No doubt the son showed more sweetness and light, more Hellenic intelligence, the father more fire and strength, more Hebraic zeal. The son cared more for the weal of the middle classes: witness his attacks on them delivered in the spirit of "faithful are the wounds of a friend." The father cared more for the weal of the working classes: witness his attitude of horror to the outcome of the Industrial Revolution. With ruffled—and unruffled—courage they faced difficulty after difficulty hindering the delivery of the message laid on them to convey to their countrymen. They did valiant battle in the cause they felt to be right with their whole heart and soul, and the father, if not the son, would have cheerfully gone to the stake for the opinions he advanced with such fearlessness.

Thomas Arnold and Matthew stood aloof from the Oxford Movement which the former viewed with undisguised hostility. They insisted on the value of the connexion between Church and State, which, in divers fashions, meant so much to them. It is the function of Church and State, though from a different point of view, to be instruments and organs of this ideal. So thought the father and so thought the son. There may not, there must not, be any separation between them; the State needs for its moral ends the religion of the Gospel, and the Church can exercise its educating influence over the nation only within the constituted forms and regulations of the State, the Christian State. Father and son showed their countrymen the possibility of reading the Bible with honest human eyes freed from the discolouring glasses of dogmatic presuppositions. The latitudinarianism of Thomas Arnold gave as dire offence to his generation as that of Matthew gave to his. Pfleiderer regards the father as the pioneer of free theology in England, and the son in this respect undoubtedly continued the labour of his father.

The complete confidence that Thomas Arnold and Matthew showed in themselves is very remarkable, and it goes far to explain the power they wielded over their respective generations. Both were men of ideals rather than men of ideas. If the father shines most as a teacher, the son shines most as an interpreter. Both were amateurs, in the best sense of the term: the father was an amateur in history, the son in theology. Yet Matthew Arnold is in thorough agreement with Adolf Deissmann of our generation when he pleads in his generation that the letters of St. Paul should be read like the papyri unearthed in Egypt by Grenfell and Hunt. Josiah Wedgwood used to wander through his pottery, demolishing with his cane all the creations which revealed the slightest flaw. So Thomas Arnold and Matthew wandered through the literary and historical, the theological and political, creations of their respective generations, demolishing with their powerful pens the faulty creations they encountered.

As educationalists father and son believed with keen conviction in the classics as the groundwork of a liberal education, though of course the classics were not to be taught in a wooden and mechanical fashion. Both were humanists in the Renaissance meaning of the term when education meant the drawing forth the whole powers of a boy or a man. To the father in his school at Rugby the boy is a moral being and the school a human society, and the teaching is to train the intelligence and inform the mind and, above all, to touch the springs of character. To the son as an inspector of schools or as a publicist the citizen is a moral being and his country a human society, and the teaching is to train the intelligence and inform the mind and, above all, to touch the springs of character. Trust the boy, was the watchword of the one. Trust the citizen, was the watchword of the other. Liberalism in politics is common to both, though their Liberalism was almost as moderate as that of Ruskin himself. In truth, Matthew Arnold and his father were prophets every whit as much as Tolstoi or Ruskin, men whose missions were to interpret the higher possibilities, responsibilities, and duties of the life of the school and the life of the city respectively.

Father and son grasped truth which subtler men missed through their sheer honesty and singleness of heart and mind, through their sheer impatience and imprudence. They evinced a deep-seated belief in a power that makes for righteousness, and with it they also evinced a sincere appreciation of piety. The son recognised the beauties of Bishop Wilson's *Sacra Privata* and St. Thomas à Kempis's *Imitatio Christi* just as warmly as his father. Both were absolutely convinced that the world cannot live on physical science only, important as it undoubtedly is, and that it needs other knowledge besides that of inductive science, and that as a condition thereof it must have religion. True, the religion of the son—or rather the theology—differed seriously from that of the father, though we require to bear in mind the two very different generations in which their lot was cast. If Matthew Arnold had professed the theology of his father, it would have been cant. Henry Drummond was once asked to define cant, and he did so. "There is a religion for a young man and there is a religion for an old man. If the young man professes the religion of the old man, that's cant." If the son professes the theology of the father, that's also cant. The theology of Thomas Arnold and his son differed: their religion was closely alike. Their enthusiasm for reform in Church and State does not assume a popular form. With both the first question is, How of your own temper? Is it serene, under complete control? How of your judgment? Is it capable of right decision? Is there no lurking desire or bias which hampers its concision and precision? Lying behind all the questions which Thomas and Matthew Arnold raise, we feel conscious of the Weltschmerz, the world pain, which broods over their writings, and is apparent in the deepest mind of both. They feel this Weltschmerz not cautiously and conservatively but acutely and even audaciously. Right stoically they bore their own pain and their own disappointment, but they were no Stoics where the pain of the world was concerned. We cannot think better or more truly of the two men than Matthew Arnold has himself taught us to think of the high-hearted Emperor, Marcus Aurelius, with whose inner life he has so much in common. "We see him just, wise, self-governed, tender, thankful, blameless, yet with all this agitated, stretching out his hands to something beyond—

> Tendentesque manus ripae ulterioris amore.

Matthew Arnold (1822–88) was the eldest son of his father, Thomas Arnold, senior. Thomas Arnold, the father of Mrs. Humphry Ward, was a younger brother of Matthew. As he quaintly called himself, Matthew was his "papa's continuator." He was not only the son of his father, but he was also the godson of his father's friend, the author of *The Christian Year*. Matthew migrated with his family to Rugby in 1828 on his father's appointment as headmaster of the school. His mother was a woman of remarkable character and of no less remarkable intellect, with whom

Matthew kept up to the day of her death both a sympathetic and affectionate correspondence. In 1830 he returned to his birthplace, Laleham, near Staines, where he was the pupil of his paternal uncle, the Rev. John Buckland. His father was a Wykehamist who entertained a high belief in his old school, and accordingly he sent Matthew to Winchester in August, 1836. Dr. Arnold thought "a period at Winchester would do his boys no harm"; and he sent "Mat" and "Tom" to be under Dr. Moberley. In that transparently sincere narrative, *Passages in a Wandering Life,* Tom affords us glimpses of his brother's boyhood. "Mat," he says—and it is quite in keeping with this after life—"always talked freely," and once, when at breakfast with the headmaster, spoke, in the presence of another bigger and stronger boy, of his form-work as being rather easy. The result was that Dr. Moberley increased its amount, and the sequel to this was that the other boy and his companions naturally "took it out" of Mat after school. At the same time, he distinguished himself by gaining the Queen's Medal—it was the year of her accession—for a recitation, and he chose Byron, his favourite poet, the favourite of most youthful poets of that time. As a boy at Winchester he used to visit Keble at Hursley.

In August, 1837, Matthew was removed from Winchester to Rugby, where he lived in his father's house, and lived at the most strenuous and stimulating school of the day. According to Dean Stanley, Arnold was "the elder brother and playfellow of his children." Matthew, devoted as he was to his father, rather viewed him in the light of a good man intent upon the salvation of others. In *Rugby Chapel* the son so regards his father:

> If, in the paths of the world,
> Stones might have wounded thy feet,
> Toil or dejection have tried
> Thy spirit, of that we saw
> Nothing; To us thou were still
> Cheerful, and helpful, and firm.
> Therefore to thee it was given
> Many to save with thyself;
> And, at the end of thy day,
> O faithful shepherd! to come,
> Bringing thy sheep in thy hand.

Arnold remained attached to his father, and when he passed away in 1842 this devotion by no means ceased. For just as in the days of her widowhood Queen Victoria tried everything by what Prince Albert would have thought, so Matthew dwelt upon what his father would have thought of things if he had been alive. His father read but one poem of his, *Alaric at Rome,* which he recited in Rugby School in June, 1840. The motto from *Childe Harold* prepared the reader for its Byronic character.

In 1840 he won an open scholarship at Balliol, and in 1841 a school exhibition. Oxford was then in the throes of the Oxford Movement which influenced Mark Pattison and J. A. Froude deeply, and left Arnold and Kingsley unmoved. Tennyson's set at Trinity, Cambridge, is ever memorable in *In Memoriam,* and yet the Balliol set of Arnold's day is not unworthy of comparison. Among them were E. M. Goulburn, Stafford Northcote, A. H. Clough, Frederick Temple, J. D. Coleridge, James Riddell, Edwin Palmer, Theodore Walrond, F. T. Palgrave, William Sellar, Henry Smith, and Alexander Grant. The bidding prayer asks for "persons qualified to serve God in Church and State," and surely they were to be found on this bead-roll. Of Dr. Arnold's old pupils at Balliol, Stanley had become a Fellow of University and Clough a Fellow of Oriel. Among Arnold's inner circle of friends were J. D. Coleridge, afterwards Lord Chief Justice of England, and J. C. Shairp, afterwards Principal of the United College, St. Andrew's. The vignette portrait of Arnold by the latter is well known:

> So full of power, yet blithe and debonnair,
> Rallying his friends with pleasant banter gay,
> Or, half a dream, chaunting with jaunty air
> Great words of Goethe, catch of Béranger:
> We see the banter sparkle in his prose,
> But knew not then the undertone that flows,
> So calmly sad, thro' all his stately lay.

One who knew him well wrote of him: "His perfect self-possession, the sallies of his ready wit, the humorous turn which he could give to any subject he handled, his gaiety, exuberance, versatility, audacity, and unfailing command of words, made him one of the most popular and successful undergraduates that Oxford has ever known." His brother Tom, who went up to Oxford in the autumn of 1841, gives a similar account, and we remember that for the next three years the brothers were together. "During these years," writes Tom, "my brother was cultivating his poetic gift carefully, but his exuberant versatile nature claimed other satisfactions. His keen bantering talk made him something of a social lion among Oxford men; he even began to dress fashionably. Goethe displaced Byron in his political allegiance; the transcendental spells of Emerson wove themselves around him; the charm of an exquisite style made him and long kept him a votary of George Sand."

Oxford left indelible traces on the mental nature of Newman and Gladstone, of Thomas Arnold and Matthew. To the latter she was ever dear as the "home of lost causes, and forsaken beliefs, and unpopular names, and impossible loyalties." His was the Oxford of William Turner's paintings and Ingram's views. No mean suburbs interposed between him and the country all around the city of the dreaming spires, and his passion for it finds free expression in *The Scholar Gypsy* and in *Thyrsis*. In 1885 he wrote: "I got out to Hinksey and up to the hill within sight of the Cumnor firs. I cannot describe the effect which this landscape always has upon me: the hillside with its valleys, and Oxford in the great Thames valley below." Until the nineteenth century Oxford had produced few poets, but in the last half of the century she is really rich. As Tennyson won the chancellor's medal for English verse with *Timbuctoo*, so Arnold won the Newdigate with a poem on Cromwell. He belonged to "The Decade," a small debating society, where, as Coleridge tells us, they "fought to the stumps of their intellects." A poet, a debater, a social personage, Arnold neglected the schools. Like his friend Clough, he took in 1844 but a second class at the final examination for Classical Honours. The next year he more than redeemed his failure by winning a Fellowship of Oriel, where just thirty years before his father had been a Fellow. Among his colleagues at Oriel were Church and Burgon, Fraser and Buckle, Earle and Clough.

Arnold returned to Rugby, and taught classics to the fifth

form. His father's successor was Tait and Tait's successor was, after Benson, to be Temple. The last two became Archbishops of Canterbury, and who can say what fate held in store for Thomas Arnold had he lived? He was forty-six only when he died. Many years afterwards, at a dinner given at Balliol, Matthew Arnold, with characteristic irony and urbanity, contrasted Tait and himself as types of the Balliol man who had succeeded and the Balliol man who had failed in life. Be that as it may, Arnold began at Rugby his long connection with education, which only ceased in 1886, two years before his death. He loved nature, whether at Rugby or Laleham, and loved her with a devotion akin to Wordsworth's. In 1848 he wrote to his mother: "It was nearly dark when I left the Weybridge Station, but I could make out the wide sheet of the grey Thames gleaming through the general dusk as I came out on Chertsey Bridge. I never go along that shelving gravelly road up towards Laleham without interest, from Chertsey Lock to the turn where the drunken man lay. To-day, after Morning church, I went up to Pentonhook, and passed the stream with the old volume, width, shine, rapid fulness, 'kempshott' and swans, unchanged and unequalled, to my partial and remembering eyes at least." Though a poor shot he liked shooting. "Need I say that I am passionately fond of the Colchian bird," he writes in one of his letters.

Much can be said on behalf of patronage, at least when bestowed by a man so discerning as Lord Lansdowne. He had introduced Macaulay to the House of Commons, and he also introduced Arnold to public life. In 1847 he was Lord President of the Council, and he appointed Arnold his private secretary. The effects of the year 1848, the year of revolutions, is apparent in the first of Arnold's sonnets, addressed *To the Hungarian Nation*. In England he sees the riots of March, 1848, and is convinced that "the hour of the hereditary peerage and eldest sonship and immense properties has struck," and thinks that a five years' continuance of these institutions is "long enough, certainly, for patience, already at death's door, to have to die in." He pities "the armies of the homeless and unfed," though he resents the "hot, dizzy trash which people are talking" about the Revolution.

England is "not liveable-in," yet will a Government of the Chartists usher in the millennium? Abroad he is as convinced in 1848 as he was all his life that "the French are the most civilised of European peoples," a view which his high opinion of Renan and Sainte-Beuve steadily strengthened. The fall of the French monarchy is likely to produce social changes with us, for "no one looks on, seeing his neighbour mending, without asking himself if he cannot mend in the same way." He notes "a wave of more than American vulgarity, moral, intellectual, and social, preparing to break over us." The thoughts of a young man are long thoughts, and these are the thoughts of Matthew Arnold at twenty-five. The first interest of Tennyson is England while Arnold's and Browning's is the whole world, though Arnold was more European than Browning.

Browning is convinced that apparent failure is never more than apparent: his optimism sustains him amid the difficulties and the disappointments of the world. Arnold feels the sense of a thwarting destiny. He follows nature as Wordsworth follows her, and he loves, as the Lake poet loves, her; yet he never feels the calm hopefulness that Wordsworth feels. In a note to Fitzgerald's translation of Omar Khayyám a Persian tale is quoted. "A thirsty traveller dips his hand into a spring of water to drink from. By-and-by comes another who draws up and drinks from an earthen bowl, and then departs, leaving his bowl behind him. The first traveller takes it up for another draught, but is surprised to find that the same water which had tasted sweet from his own hand, tastes bitter from the earthen bowl. But a voice—from heaven, I think—tells him that the clay from which the bowl is made was once *man*; and, into whatever shape renewed, can never lose the bitter flavour of mortality." Such seems to be the attitude of Arnold. Nature tastes of human destiny; and in that destiny there is something akin to bitterness or at least melancholy.

Tennyson was to sing to men that nature sacrifices the individual to the type, and that an unfriendly environment can strangle the type. Does Arnold, except perhaps in the sonnet *In Harmony with Nature*, ever complain of her? There is no denunciation of her laws, which he is prepared to accept without question. We have no rights against her, though we have duties towards her and mankind. In Bacon's spirit, we learn that if we conquer nature, we do so by obeying her.

> We mortals are no kings
> For each of whom to sway
> A new-made world up-springs,
> Meant merely for his play;
> No, we are strangers here; the world is from old.

He felt as few felt the Zeitgeist. When men tell the bead-roll of Mill's disciples, they uncommonly omit his name, yet it deserves inclusion. Arnold stood far away enough from the French Revolution of 1789, though too close to that of 1848, to look back upon it and its effects critically. It had shattered the old world of privilege and inequality, and what sort of new world had come into being? The year 1789 had indeed shattered the old world hopelessly. On the other hand, he did not stand far enough away to see what was to be the nature of the new world which must arise from its ruins. He was

> Standing between two worlds, one dead,
> The other powerless to be born.

Where was the power that promised to make all things new? What delayed its coming? Arnold looked around him for any force capable of reconstructing society. The age just past had been powerful in destruction, powerless in construction and creation. Macaulay was at ease in Zion because of the material progress of the age. Browning was convinced that "God's in His heaven," and therefore "all's right with the world." Arnold was unable to share the optimism of either the historian or the poet. The old order has changed, but it has not, in spite of Tennyson, given place to the new. Here lies the secret of Arnold's melancholy, his loneliness.

His first volume of poems was *The Strayed Reveller, and other Poems* (1849). Among the other pieces were that great poem *The Forsaken Merman*, *Mycerinus*, *To a Gipsy Child*, *Resignation*, and the sonnets *To a Friend*, praising Homer, Epictetus, and Sophocles, and *Shakespeare*. His first volume was a very remarkable one, and yet the public was not in the least conscious of its appearance, and the discouraged author soon withdrew it from circulation.

In 1851 Lord Lansdowne appointed Arnold inspector of primary schools, a post he was to retain for thirty-five years. This appointment made possible his marriage to the girl he loved passionately, Frances Lucy Wightman. A devoted son, he was a devoted husband and father, and his letters certainly prove that the sweetness and light he diffused abroad he also diffused in his own family circle. The idol of his friends, he was also the idol of his family. He found his work sufficiently laborious, though we do well to remember that another Wordsworthian, F. W. H. Myers, deliberately chose to become an inspector on the ground that it afforded him the maximum of free time for private research and writing. Myers, however, was appointed in 1872, and the intervening twenty-one years since Arnold's appointment had rendered the post distinctly less onerous. This is plain from the fact that Myers was able to take a house at Cambridge while Arnold could do nothing of the kind. In his first general report for the year 1852 we learn that his district included Lincoln, Nottingham, Derby, Stafford, Salop, Hereford, Worcester, Warwick, Leicester, Rutland and Northants., Gloucester, Monmouth, all South Wales, most of North Wales, and some schools in the East and West Ridings. Of course this amazing range is due to the fact that he inspected the schools of dissenters exclusively, for to 1870 the Anglican and Roman Catholic schools were excluded. Nor must we ignore the fact that for almost twenty years of his life the people he met most often were nonconformists. In fact, he was obliged to frequent Salem Chapel, not Barchester Towers. On his resignation in 1886 he feelingly said: "Though I am a schoolmaster's son, I confess that school-teaching or school-inspecting is not the line of life I should naturally have chosen. I adopted it in order to marry a lady who is here to-night, and who feels your kindness as warmly and gratefully as I do. My wife and I had a wandering life of it at first. There were but three lay-inspectors for all England. My district went right across from Pembroke Dock to Great Yarmouth. We had no home. One of our children was born in a lodging at Derby, with a workhouse, if I recollect aright, behind and a penitentiary in front. But the *irksomeness* of my new duties was what I felt most, and during the first year or so it was sometimes insupportable."

Once the feeling of irksomeness disappeared, he threw himself into his duties with chastened hopefulness. In January, 1879, he wrote, "I think I am gradually making an impression about public secondary education." The rate of progress was at a glacier's pace. "This reform interests me," he acknowledges, "as the first practicable of those great democratic reforms to which we must, I believe, one day come. And they call me a bad Liberal, or no Liberal at all!" In August, 1879, his mood is sober, for he feels obliged to own: "I more and more learn the extreme slowness of things, and that though we are all disposed to think that everything will change in our lifetime it will not. Perhaps we shall end our days in the tail of a return current of popular religion, both ritual and dogmatic. Still, the change, for being slower than we expected, is none the less sure." Compare this with a letter he wrote to his sister in 1851: "The aimless and unsettled, but also open and liberal state of our youth we *must* perhaps all leave, and take refuge in our morality and character; but, with most of us, it is a melancholy passage, from which we emerge shorn of so many beams that we are almost tempted to quarrel with the law of nature which imposes it on us. I feel this in my own case, and in no respect more strongly than in my relations to all of you. I am by nature so very different from you, the worldly element enters so much more largely into my composition, that, as I become *formed*, there seems to grow a gulf between us which tends to widen till we can hardly hold any intercourse across it. But, as Thomas à Kempis recommended, *frequenter tibi ipsi violentiam fac* . . . so I intend not to give myself the rein in following my natural tendency, but to make war against it till it ceases to isolate me from you, and leaves me with the power to discern and adopt the good which you have and I have not." In his daily round through school after school he confessed that he met men and women with duties and responsibilities, private and public, at least as irksome as his own, and he freely owned that their example helped him to check and control his natural tendency.

Arnold was a man widely read in literature both modern and ancient. He had the Bible as perfectly at his fingers' ends as Ruskin himself. Throughout his life his "unapproachable favourites" were Sophocles and Homer, while Hesiod was "a Greek friend to whom he turned with excellent effect." He was familiar with English literature and with all that was best in Italian, French, and German, elevating Goethe to a lofty rank. His *Note-Books* attest the width of his interests and the comfort they afforded him. The study of classics and modern literature formed the basis of the educational system he advocated, at any rate for the public schools. Science and mathematics were also to be studied, but he did not hesitate to avow his opinion that "for the majority of mankind a little of mathematics goes a very long way." What did it profit a boy to know that "when a taper burns, the wax is converted into carbonic acid and water"? What did he not lose when he had not read the last book of the *Iliad*, or the sixth book of the *Aeneid*, or the *Agamemnon*? He listened with impatience to the teachers who deduced our descent from "a hairy quadruped furnished with a tail and pointed ears, probably arboreal in his habits." If a lad was really scientific in his bent, by all means let him learn science; but for the majority of boys he plainly believed that the classics and literature were likely to confer more lasting benefit on them. His mind comes out in a letter he wrote in 1868: "An admirable English mathematician told me that he should never recover the loss of the two years which after his degree he wasted without fit instruction at an English University, when he ought to have been under superior instruction, for which the present University course in England makes no provision. I dare say he *will* recover it, for a man of genius counts no worthy effort too hard; but who can estimate the loss to the mental training and intellectual habits of the country, from the absence—so complete that it needs genius to be sensible of it, and costs genius an effort to repair it—of all regular public provision for the scientific study and teaching of any branch of knowledge."

In October, 1852, appeared *Empedocles on Etna, and other Poems*, by "A," and its reception was as cold as that of its predecessor. Arnold withdrew it from circulation before fifty copies had been sold. Among the other poems were some of his best verse, including much of *Switzerland* and *Faded Leaves, A Summer Night, Stanzas in Memory of the Author of "Obermann,"* and *Memorial Verses.* In 1853 came the first series of his *Poems* and two years later the second series. *New Poems* also appeared in 1867, and with their appearance he ceased to write poetry. True, to the end of his life he wrote occasional verse, but with the exception of *Westminster Abbey* they did not add much to his reputation. His 1849 and his 1852 volumes met with a reception that saddens the heart, but with the later ones he stepped into the proud position of being second only to one, Tennyson. Gauss's motto in mathematics, *pauca sed matura,* was his in poetry.

If solitude is required for the travail of the soul, assuredly it is required for the expression of the muse. How could Arnold have solitude in the midst of the bustle and confusion of his incessant journeys across half England? No doubt Scott and Southey secured it, but look at the price they paid! If they are exceptions, they are the exceptions that prove the rule. Besides, he was so much irritated by the dissenters he met that tranquillity of mind was rarely possible to him. His pessimism did not allow him to indulge in that direct energy and that passionate fervour conspicuous in Tennyson. Nor did his interests lie in the present to the same extent as those of his great contemporary. He had constant recourse to antiquity for subject and method. He exalted Achilles, Prometheus, Clytemnestra, and Dido as eternally interesting, asserting that the famous poems of the nineteenth century "left the reader cold in comparison with the effect produced upon him by the latter books of the *Iliad*, by the *Oresteia*, or by the episode of Dido." In the preface to the poems of 1853 Arnold insists that poets must seek their inspiration in the past, for action is the only theme of poetry, and it is in the past alone that action is found.

Art is objective; when this is forgotten, as it is by modern poets, all work is hopelessly vitiated. The choice of a good subject is indispensable, for without a worthy theme success is unattainable. That is to say, he establishes the rules of classic composition as the Medean laws of poetry for all times and all conditions; he ignores the differences between ancient Hellas and modern England, takes the classics for his masters, and, in deference to their decisions, consistently excludes *Empedocles on Etna* from his republished poems.

His conduct is magnificent, but is it war? The public thought it was not. Unmoved by the attitude of his readers—or rather of his want of readers—he solved the moral, as he solved the aesthetic, problem confronting him in the same fashion. He insisted that for the moral problem he required calm, patience, endurance, acceptance of fate, submission to the omnipotence of unrelenting law, and this is but to state the aesthetic problem in terms of the moral one. He was in not a few respects a Stoic, and Stoicism is a creed that requires attention.

The world has never been an easy place in which one discharges one's duty, yet there are times of special stress, and it is remarkable that if we glance at such seasons of stress as the Renaissance, the Reformation, the French Revolution, and the middle of the nineteenth century we find Stoicism re-emerging. These were all times when the religious sanctions of morality no longer exercised unquestioned authority. Stoicism then makes its due appeal to the autonomy of conscience, its peremptory command to live by law and to follow nature, and its exalted sense of duty. In what Renan calls its *frénésie de renoncement*, its resolute protest against self-indulgence and self-seeking, it endeavours to counteract the corroding effects of modern scepticism and cynicism in private and public life. True, in some of its aspects, it reflects the hopelessness and world-weariness which sees in modern progress only "an endless advance by endless effort, and, if need be, by endless pain." The same pessimistic tendency sees in evolution nothing but a long series of cycles of death and revival, of endless mutations inconstant progression. *Tout lasse, tout casse, tout passe, tout se refait.* Yet, in strange contradiction with this, there is the unalterable conviction too of a perfection in nature, of harmonious development according to law, and of a wistful outlook towards a distant goal.

At the Renaissance Montaigne reads Plutarch "since he speaks French" (i.e. in Amyot's translation), and sees in Seneca a kindred soul, "*ondoyant et divers*" like himself; and he speaks of the works of these writers as "the prime and cream of Philosophy." At the Reformation, as Lord Acton reminds us, Erasmus esteemed Seneca more highly than any Christian divine, saying of him, "If you read him as a heathen, he wrote like a Christian; if you read him like a Christian, he wrote like a heathen." Seneca was the favourite reading of Zwingli and Calvin, and indeed the first work of the latter is an edition of the *De Clementia.* We all know that Leibniz accuses Spinoza of having revived Stoicism in his ethics. From Stoicism Rousseau and "The Saints of the Encyclopaedia" learnt their own glorification of nature; and from it the leaders of the French Revolution derive their stern severity in applying its principles to political life. In the *Prelude* Wordsworth speaks like a Stoic of "The calm existence that is mine When I am worthy of myself!" thus exhibiting the continuity of its influence.

In its modern form Stoicism has become, to use Amiel's expression, "the last resource of doubt," the evangel of those who have lost their faith in the supernatural. There is nothing of the *libido moriendi* of the old Stoicism. There is no fear of final extinction, yet some would say with Eléonore de Condé, "It is not for us to desert the garrison." On these grounds Carlyle declined to commit suicide. J. Addington Symonds, speaking of the need of a deep firm faith to escape from the misery of scepticism, writes: "In these difficulties I fall back on a kind of stoical mysticism—on the prayer of Cleanthes, the proem of Goethe's '*Gott und die Welt,*' the phrase of Faust, '*Entbehren sollst du, sollst entbehren,*' the almost brutal optimism of Walt Whitman's 'I cry to the Cosmos, Though thou slay me, yet will I trust in thee.' Can a religion be constructed out of these elements? Not a tangible one, perhaps; nothing communicable to another heart. But a religious mood of mind may be engendered for the purpose of living not ignobly." Symonds who died with a little volume of prayers, originally given him by his mother, by his side, had placed on his tombstone the epitaph, consisting of his own translation of the following lines from the hymn of Cleanthes:

Lead Thou me, God, Law, Reason, Motion, Life!
All names for Thee alike are vain and hollow.
Lead me, for I will follow without strife,
Or if I strive, still must I blindly follow!

A French writer living in the time of the Terror tells us that before that event he was repelled by the gloomy tone of Seneca's writings, but that he began to read him with much relish, as affording comfort during the worst days of revolutionary tyranny. In the same way F. W. H. Myers, in his essay on the disenchantment of France, written in 1888, quotes a passage from Bourget in which the latter refers to the class of savants whose stoical candour and personal virtue are beyond doubt, yet who express the utter hopelessness of science in its inability to answer the questionings of the mind, or to satisfy the cravings of the heart. He also points to Renan as a remarkable example of disenchanted optimism which can scarcely be distinguished from the pessimism of the ideologists, who, in the presence of the irresistible and irresponsible forces of nature, uncontrolled by a higher power, despair of finding a solution of the mystery of the universe. A few hours before his death Renan said to his wife: "Be calm and resigned; we undergo the laws of nature of which we are a manifestation. We perish, we disappear, but heaven and earth remain, and the march of time goes on for ever." Sainte-Beuve, Arnold's ideal critic, says of himself that on attaining what he had hoped in life, and as it approached its termination, "I sought to arrange my existence with quietness and dignity." His aim is to cultivate "a good healthy solidity," and with steady dutifulness to perform the necessary functions of existence, to face the facts of life fairly and fully.

Men seek for composure and ethical fortitude amid the restlessness of our existence. So seeks Arnold, and he expresses his quest in the following lines written in Kensington Gardens:

Calm soul of all things! make it mine
  To feel, amid the city's jar,
That there abides a peace of thine
  Man did not make, and cannot mar.

The will to neither strive nor cry,
  The power to feel with others, give
Calm, calm me more! nor let me die
  Before I have begun to live.

The paramount idea dominating him is the high sense of duty, an idea which the Stoics introduced into European ethics. Duty, the "stern daughter of the voice of God," is that which the modern poet of nature appeals to in order to calm "the weary strife of frail humanity." This duty is not imposed by authority from without, but is the following-up of the rational impulse of the mind in harmony with the cosmic order. It means the unreserved acknowledgment of the sovereignty of conscience. For self-subjection is a means to an end, and that end the attainment of moral freedom. Happiness consists in virtuous activity. Here modern Stoicism differs from ancient. Marcus Aurelius tendered the advice: "Spend your brief moment then according to nature's law, and serenely greet the journey's end, as the olive falls when it is ripe, blessing the branch that bear it, and giving thanks to the tree which gave it life." The Stoicism of our day demands a deeper sense of human solidarity and altruistic duty as distinguished from public beneficence. It asks for a higher conception of the dignity of labour, due to the change in the moral and social atmosphere wrought by Christianity. Stoic benevolence and Christian philanthropy join forces by an adaptation of Seneca's principle to modern needs, "*Homo sacra res homini*." Stoicism and Christianity endeavour to realise the ideal of Zeno who dreamt of a commonwealth where all shall be as one fold under one shepherd, "where men should not be separated by cities, states, and laws, but all should be considered as fellow-citizens, partakers of one life, and the whole world, like a united flock, should be governed by one common law."

The modern Stoic lays deep stress on self-development, but it is self-development for social ends, and this is quite clear in the teaching of Arnold. The individual is a member of the social organism, so he would have held in common with Spencer, Maine, and Ruskin. He would have emphasised just as much as Ruskin that we live for others in order that we may live in others. The service of man stands out paramount. Yet surely A. Sabatier is right to ask the question, What does Christian law become without the sentiment of love, without the impulse of mercy, but a sort of moral Stoicism rigid and severe? Stoicism lacks the emotional motive which Christianity supplies, thereby melting and mellowing its harsher features. What F. W. H. Myers says of Stoicism in his essay on Marcus Aurelius is true still, that it "prescribed the curbing and checking of those natural emotions which Christianity at once guided and intensified by her new ideal." Arnold himself has shown that the peculiar charm pervading the meditations of the Stoic Emperor consists in their being "suffused and softened by something of this very sentiment whence Christian morality draws its best power."

Stoic Arnold was and to his Stoicism we owe his devotion to duty and to the weal of others. This is as manifest in his poetry as in his prose. In his poetry there is hint after hint of his life of the soul, *The Buried Life,* which gives its name to one poem and makes its presence felt in so many others—the life which we enter into too seldom, without which

> Each will have one anguish—his own soul
> which perishes of cold.

His poetry, then, told something; but it was not till after his sudden death when his daughter published his *Note Books.* that all who care may read his secret. There is a sonnet among his poems called *Austerity of Poetry.* It tells the story of Jacopone da Todi's bride, suddenly killed in all her springtime of beauty and splendour, and found to have worn, under the silks and satins, next her skin, a robe of sackcloth:

> Such, poets, is your bride, the Muse! young, gay,
> Radiant, adorned outside; a hidden ground
> Of thought and of austerity within.

Such was Arnold himself as revealed in his *Note Books.* In them, like other men, he recorded his engagements, and in them, unlike other men, he also recorded texts and sayings which he wished to think about and remember. It is characteristic of him, of the "outside" of him which always remained "young, gay, radiant," that, as his daughter tells us, he "used to say, half jokingly, that if anyone would ever take the trouble to collect all the extracts from various writers which he had copied in his notebooks, there would be found a volume of priceless worth." For the most part they relate to the inner life of the poet, the sonnet's "hidden ground of thought and of austerity within." The man of letters is evident in quotations of maxims of efficiency from Turgot, of equality from Georges Sand, and of the saying of Goethe, often repeated: "The act of producing is itself a pleasure and its own reward." The man of religion, to our surprise, is far more evident that the man of letters, and this not occasionally but throughout the notebooks.

In the notebooks there is the coincidence that he had written in the space given to the Sunday on which he died April 15th, 1888, the text from Ecclesiasticus: "Weep bitterly over the dead, as he is worthy, and then comfort thyself: drive heaviness away: thou shalt not do him good, but hurt thyself." For the Sunday after his burial he had quoted another significant text from Ecclesiasticus: "When the dead is at rest, let his remembrance rest; and be comforted for him when his spirit is departed from him." The thought of death, then, was with him, as it was with many Stoics.

What was far more often in his thoughts than death was life and the difficulty of living it well and wisely for himself and for others. He quotes repeatedly from the Bible, and his quotations are some of the texts making most demand upon man. With Schopenhauer he implicitly compares and contrasts Stoicism with Christianity. Schopenhauer compares it with the teaching of Christ, "that noble figure, containing the greatest poetic truth and depth of meaning, standing before us in perfect virtue, holiness, and loftiness, though at the same time under conditions of the highest form of suffering." True, religion is morality touched with emotion, but must not the emotion be founded on a person? So Arnold seems to think in his *Note Books*, if not in his other writings. In the notes in 1878, for instance, we find nearly half of them are taken from the Bible or the

Imitatio Christi, and some of the rest from such writers as Epictetus, Marcus Aurelius, and Bishop Wilson.

There are sayings or ethical maxims from the Psalms or Proverbs, but the bulk of the quotations are not of this order. Some texts he repeats year after year, or several times a year, and among them are these. "If any man will come after Me let him deny himself and take up his cross daily and follow Me. How shall we that we are dead to sin live any longer therein? Know ye not that so many of us as were baptized into Jesus Christ, were baptized into His death?"

And the former of these two, perhaps the most often repeated of any, is headed *The Secret*. So he chooses time after time from the *Imitatio Christi* such texts as: "The more each of us dies to himself, the more he begins to live to God. . . . If we were more dead to ourselves and less involved in things of earth, we should be better able to taste things that are divine. . . . There is no other way to life and to true internal peace except the way of the Holy Cross and of daily dying."

It is clear that Arnold did not find it easy to live the Stoic life—who indeed does?—and that Christianity, conscious or unconscious, came to his assistance. On Good Friday he naturally examines himself even more severely. His note for Good Friday, 1868, is "By means of death for the redemption of the transgressors." Above it he placed this prayer from the *Imitatio Christi*: "Would that but for one day we could live well in this world!" He had not fled from the world, and he wanted to live well in it, and to live well meant the practice of Stoicism, but it meant a Stoicism suffused and softened by Christian morality.

The moral feelings of the poet as well as his intellectual instincts incline him to the classical school. From his father he had inherited his moral ardour and sterling honesty, the lofty didactic impulse which breathes an earnest, serious air through all his poetry and indeed through all his writings. In his views of life, of death, of necessity, of fate, of equanimity, of the relations of man with nature, he was in sympathy with the classical world rather than with modern conditions of existence. The Middle Ages attracted him, for he thought that Tennyson had not done justice to them. In a letter to Sir M. E. Grant Duff, to whom he wrote some of his best letters, he acknowledges that "One is from time to time seized and irresistibly carried along by a temptation to handle political or religious or social matters directly; but, after yielding to such a temptation, I always feel myself recoiling again and disposed to touch them only so far as they can be touched through poetry." Under the influence of his Stoic Christianity he increasingly yielded to the temptation, and the recoil became gradually less.

He thought Tennyson "deficient in intellectual power." He thought that he himself had perhaps "less poetical sentiment than Tennyson, less intellectual vigour and abundance than Browning, but more of a fusion of the two than either," and, above all, that he "had more regularly applied that fusion to the main line of modern development." The main line of development in the first half of the Victorian age was certainly not to be found in Arnold, and was equally certainly to be found in Tennyson. No poet of that age was more sympathetic to the new outlook created by evolution than Tennyson, and it is not too much to say that Arnold held himself studiously aloof from science and all that it meant to the mid-Victorians. He never perceived that the epoch-making book of 1859–61 was not *Essays and Reviews,* not even Renan's *Vie de Jésus,* but Darwin's *Origin of Species.* Officially, as an inspector of schools, Arnold recognised the due place of science, but privately it occupied but a lowly position in his thoughts. His *Note Books* betray the existence of religion, but they do not betray the existence of science or record any contemplation of its mysteries. Indeed he thought Lord Salisbury a dangerous young man because he advocated the larger introduction of Natural Science into Oxford.

A Cambridge man, Henry Sidgwick felt to the full the changes made in the conception of the universe by a son of his own University, Darwin. Sidgwick records his view of *In Memoriam,* of "its unparalleled combination of intensity of feeling with comprehension of view in dealing with the deepest needs and perplexities of humanity." He proceeds to inform us: "In the sixties I should say that these deeper issues were somewhat obscured by the discussions on Christian dogma, and Inspiration of Scripture, etc. One may recall Browning's reference to this period—

> The *Essays and Reviews* debate
> Begins to tell on the public mind,
> And Colenso's words have weight.

During those years we were absorbed in struggling for freedom of thought in the trammels of an historical religion; and perhaps what we sympathised with most in *In Memoriam* at this time, apart from the personal feeling, was the defence of 'honest doubt,' and, generally, the forward movement of the thought. Well, the years pass; the struggle with what Carlyle used to call 'Hebrew Old Clothes' is over. Freedom is won, and to what does Freedom bring us? It brings us face to face with atheistic science; the faith in God and Immortality, which we had been struggling to clear from superstition, suddenly seems to be 'in the air'; and, in seeking for a firm basis for this faith, we find ourselves in the midst of the 'fight with death' which *In Memoriam* so powerfully presents."

The "march of mind," the "steamship and the railway and the thoughts that shake mankind," the "happy sails that bear the Press," the "parliament of man, the federation of the world"—these are to be found in *Locksley Hall, The Princess,* and the lines on the opening of the 1851 Exhibition, and Arnold passes them all by. Tennyson strikes the note of Imperialism in a fashion that came home more to men's hearts than any attempt of Carlyle had ever done. If Arnold mentions the dominions overseas, it is to speak of them as more the children of the Philistines than his own folk at home. The extension of the franchise, the emancipation of woman, the universal application of our parliamentary system, free trade, a free press, and a free Church in a free State, nationality, the unification of the State—these are the burning topics of the day, and they are the very topics that Arnold summarily dismisses. The reaction against Liberalism was in full swing in the seventies, and Arnold shared it, but so too did Tennyson, Ruskin, and Dickens.

There are affinities between the poet's position and that of

Disraeli. Both of them were phrase-makers, and their phrases caught the ear of the public. The resemblance between them, however, cut much more deeply than that. As Disraeli offered opposition to the Manchester school, so did Arnold. As Disraeli offered opposition to the merely material and mechanical advance of England, so did Arnold. It finds expression in the famous apostrophe to England as "the weary Titan" in the lines on *Heine's Grave*. There is a passage in *Sybil* on the stock utilitarian argument of "cheaper silk stockings" which is echoed in *Culture and Anarchy*. The ideas of both on "*pouvoir sans savoir*," "natural rights," the proper position of the middle classes are the same. Arnold's attitude to our aristocracy and the lofty place he assigns to our monarchy are also the same as the statesman's. Both bewail the ignorance of their countrymen. If Disraeli compares our golden youth with the Greeks who read no books and lived chiefly in the open air, Arnold compares them with "young barbarians all at play." To Arnold "the world of ideas is the possible, the future," and Disraeli went further and called ideas "divine." The need in our midst of a "root" for such ideas Arnold ascribes to "the want of flexibility of our race." Disraeli and Arnold were sound Europeans, if not cosmopolitans, though the latter leaned to the creed of Young England, as interpreted by the former, more than is commonly realised, and indeed much more so than Tennyson. Arnold and Disraeli recognise as characteristic of the community British justice, British honesty, British good humour. Yet Arnold is not afraid to touch incidentally in his Irish essays, what Disraeli emphasised throughout our foreign relations and our Irish ones as well, on one of our grave shortcomings, our failure to put ourselves in the place of alien races. The Englishman on the whole lacks imagination, the power to visualise things unseen, and what he does not see he does not feel. Why, then, should others feel it? Under such a circumstance, he thanks God that he is not even as this foreigner:

For it's greatly to his credit,
And he himself has said it,
That, in spite of all temptations
To belong to other nations,
He remains an Englishman.

The quality of insularity is the last one we can attach to Arnold. His travels abroad gave him perhaps too high an impression of the worth of the foreigner as compared with his own countrymen. In 1858 he "thinks there cannot be a moment's doubt" that the French will beat the Prussians even far more completely than they are beating the Austrians. Lord Cowley, our ambassador at Paris, "entirely shared" his conviction that "the French will always beat any number of Germans who come into the field against them, and never be beaten by any one but the English."

Arnold secured the first outstanding recognition of his poetry in his election by Convocation to the Professorship of Poetry at Oxford in 1857. He spoke to men with the conviction that he occupied a chair which proved for him to be a real *cathedra*. He had a pulpit and naturally he preached from it. He had published *The Strayed Reveller, Empedocles*, and the first and the second series of his *Poems*, and he was torn in two directions. Was he to deliver his message for the future in poetry or prose? Was he to be a critic of literature or was he to be a critic of politics and religion? His classical interests and his Stoicism were pulling him in opposite directions. It is at least significant of the struggle that his first book, after his election to the chair of poetry, was on *England and the Italian Question*, which saw the light in 1859. It was published seven years before Prussia waged war with Austria and eleven years before she waged war with France, and in it Arnold records his impressions: "Prussia is a great power only in name . . . Prussia, with neither territory nor population enough for her support as a great military power, can only have a large efficient army at the expense of having her finances in ruin. She sensibly chooses to have her finances in prosperity. But her army, therefore, is a shadow. In her regular forces she has not a man who has served three full years. The majority of her landwehr are respectable married citizens, fathers of families. To require such troops to repel a charge of Zouaves would be as reasonable as to make this demand of the Marylebone Vestry. French military men know this perfectly well. They speak with great respect of the Austrian army. '*C'est une belle armée*,' they say of the Austrian army, '*mais elle est malheureuse*'; of the Prussian army they say, '*C'est une garde nationale.*'" The motto on the title-page of this pamphlet is from the Vulgate, *Sed nondum est finis.*—"But the end is not yet." The end was not in 1866 or in 1871 or even in 1919, and this pamphlet did contain the prophecy that Alsace must always be French.

Classical interests prevailed when he published in 1861 his three lectures *On Translating Homer,* and in them he lays down luminously the general principles of translation. He overrates Clough as much as he underrates Pope whom he dismisses with Bentley's scornful remark. The test to which he subjects a translation is to offer it to men who know Greek and appreciate poetry, and he suggests such men as Dr. Hawtrey of Eton, Dr. Thompson of Trinity, and Mr. Jowett of Balliol. Arnold believed as passionately as Tennyson or Gladstone, Lang or Bury, in the unity of Homer, which Jebb finds incredible. The newer generation of critics, however, are finding this unity quite credible. It certainly is a case where one is prepared to trust a poet like Tennyson rather than any critic, however eminent.

The two great series of *Essays in Criticism* appeared in 1865 and in 1868, and it is to these two volumes that their author owes his real recognition with a wide audience. Between 1830 and 1860 there was a fine critical school in France which included such men as Michelet and his friend Quinet, Gautier and Villemain, Merimée and Nisard, and, above all, Sainte-Beuve. In England there had been Dryden's *Essay on Dramatic Poesy,* Johnson's *Lives of the Poets,* and, best of all, Coleridge's *Biographia Literaria,* not to speak of the work of Hazlitt and Lamb. At last a worthy successor to them appeared, and showed an astonished generation what a great critic might accomplish for it. No doubt he still tended to overrate foreign literature as compared with our own, He ranks French and German literature before our own in 1861 when France possessed only Victor Hugo and Germany not a single writer of the calibre of Tennyson, Browning, Carlyle, Ruskin, Thackeray, Dickens and not a few others. He was even able to write in 1867 that "our only first-rate body of contemporary poetry is the German" when there was not a single poet in the front rank save Heine, and he was not a German but a Jew. Undoubtedly Arnold does not feel for a single instant that it's greatly to his credit that he remains an Englishman, for, so far as literature was concerned, he might have been a Frenchman or a Prussian.

The preface to the first series contains the moving address to Oxford: "Beautiful city! so venerable, so lovely, so unravaged by the fierce intellectual life of our century, so serene!" As Mark Pattison showed, the Oxford of 1865 was not so free from intellectual strife as in Arnold's undergraduate days. He asks the question to which he had his own answer ready: "And yet, steeped in sentiment, as she lies, spreading her gardens to the moonlight, and whispering from her towers the last enchantments of the Middle Ages, who will deny that Oxford, by her ineffable charm, keeps ever calling us nearer to the true goal of all of us, to the ideal, to perfection,—to beauty, in a word, which is only truth seen from another side?—nearer, perhaps, than all the science of Tübingen."

Had Maurice and Eugénie de Guérin and Amiel been English, we should not have heard so much about them in the *Essays in Criticism*. In his essay on Heine Arnold first uses the word Philistine, which assumes so active a rôle in his philosophy. He praises Burke whose good fortune it has been to be as much praised by posterity as he was in his own day. The bent of Burke's conservatism is compatible with a hatred of injustice so strong that it has been his mission to bring equal comfort to Liberals as to Tories. Arnold gives us a spirited summary of the *Tractatus Theologico-Politicus*, Spinoza's treatise on Church and State. The sympathy with Marcus Aurelius betrays at every turn the Stoicism that marked our critic. The Emperor remains, in Arnold's eyes, "the especial friend and comforter of all clear-headed and scrupulous, yet pure-hearted and upward-striving men, in those ages most especially that walk by sight, not by faith, and yet have no open vision; he cannot give such souls, perhaps, all they yearn for, but he gives them much; and what he gives them they can receive." The essayist brings out not a little of the persistent influence of Stoicism and its undiminished fascination for the noble-minded of any creed or no creed, in almost every age or country of the civilised world.

With the stress that modern Stoicism lays on duty and especially on *noblesse oblige,* Arnold found himself in increasing sympathy. When Browning asked him why he wrote no more poetry, he replied that he could not afford it. This may have been a reason, but there were deeper ones. He met Disraeli, and he referred to Disraeli's abandonment of literature for politics. "Yes," replied the statesman, "one does not settle these things for one's self, and politics and literature are both very attractive; still, in the one, one's work lasts, and in the other it doesn't." He went on to say that he had given up literature because he was not one of those people who can do two things at once, but that he admired most the men like Cicero, who could. Arnold, like Disraeli, could not do two things at once, and he turned from poetry to politics. Arnold once said of Goethe:

> He took the suffering human race,
> He read each wound, each weakness clear,
> And struck his finger on the place
> And said, *Thou ailest, here and here!*

Our political physician allotted a similar rôle to himself, and from the end of the sixties, like Ruskin at the beginning of the sixties, he prescribed for the complaints he diagnosed. To him "the citizens of a State, the members of a society, are really 'a partnership,' as Burke nobly says, 'in all science, in all art, in every virtue, in all perfection.' Towards this great final design of their connexion, they apply the aids which co-operative association can give them." His general point of view is quite plain. He is as detached from the pure party angle as Ruskin himself, though to both men politics is a science at once "noble and true." Arnold no doubt exalts it to a higher position than Ruskin can possibly do. It is the chief of all sciences, "because it deals with this question for the benefit of man not as an isolated creature, but in that state 'without which,' as Burke says, 'man could not by any possibility arrive at the perfection of which his nature is capable'—for the benefit of man in society.' Man is a member of an organism, and his main need is that the whole body of society should come to live with a life worthy to be called *human*, and corresponding to man's true aspirations and powers. This, the humanisation of man in society, is civilisation. The aim for all of us is to promote it, and to promote it is above all the aim for the true politician."

Not even Coleridge was a truer disciple of Burke than Arnold. Civilisation, he contended, is humanisation. But what is civilisation? Is it material and mechanical progress? Perish the thought! A society is civilised when its members live a humane, a moral, a cultured life. To him as to Burke the foundation of society is basically spiritual. Intellect and knowledge, conduct and beauty, social life and manners—all go towards the making of the citizen. "These are the means towards . . . civilisation; and the true politician, who wills the end, cannot but will the means also. And meanwhile, whether the politician wills them or not, there is an instinct pushing it to desire them and to tend to them, and making it dissatisfied when nothing is done for them, or when impediment and harm are offered to them; and this instinct we call the instinct of self-preservation."

Mankind is to advance to a fuller humanity, and, Englishman as he is, Arnold is willing to allow that this advance can take place on widely differing lines. In ancient times the Hebrews and the Greeks pursued their own paths, and in modern times the French, the Germans, and the Italians pursued theirs. The Hebrews advanced along the line of religion, and laid almost exclusive stress on conduct; the Greeks advanced on the parallel lines of intellect, science, and beauty. The French advanced along the line of social life and manners; the Germans advanced on the power of knowledge; and the Italians on their aesthetic faculty. Now in throwing out these ideas Arnold acted as a far-reaching influence, and through his principles he stirred up society to think that it was at least possible that its constitution was not quite so sound as its members believed. In effect, he permeated society with solvents of current conventional ideas, and these solvents transformed men's minds more than they realised. The particular remedies he proposed might in practice be as ineffectual as Ruskin's were in his day, but were they ineffectual with the rising generation?

He was as insistent as Ruskin that all our political reform was mere machinery. What was vitally wanted was social reform, the humanising of the citizen. What Ruskin was accomplishing in his fashion, Arnold was also accomplishing in his, and their ultimate aim was undoubtedly not the improvement of any kind of machinery, mechanical or electoral, but the improvement of man himself.

For the aristocracy of other countries his appreciation was strictly bounded, but for that of his own country it was unbounded. He mixed with it all his life from the days when he served Lord Lansdowne as private secretary, and from what he wrote in 1859 he never departed. "I desire to speak of it with the most unbounded respect. It is the most popular of aristocracies; it has avoided faults which have ruined other aristocracies equally splendid. While the aristocracy of France was destroying its estates by its extravagance, and itself by its impertinence, the aristocracy of England was founding English agriculture, and commanding respect by a personal dignity which made even its pride forgiven. Historical and political England, the England of which we are all so proud, is of its making." Such a boast is true, for the landlords of the south and east wrought that revolution in agriculture in the eighteenth century which is comparable, in some respects, to the revolution in industry the manufacturers of the north and west wrought. It is significant, too, to note that in his admiration of the share taken by our aristocracy he is in the line of succession to Coleridge, Disraeli, and Ruskin.

His opinion of the middle class was as low as his opinion of the aristocracy was high. He used to declare that his feeling towards his brethren of the middle class was that of St. Paul towards his brethren of Israel: "My heart's prayer for them is that they may be saved," but admittedly the process was a difficult one. Strait was the gate and narrow was the way for them. In 1882 he declared his views with the utmost plainness. "Suppose we take the figure we know so well, the earnest and non-conforming Liberal of our Middle Classes, as his school and his civilisation have made him. He is for Disestablishment: he is for Temperance; he has an eye to his Wife's Sister; he is a member of the local caucus; he is learning to go up to Birmingham every year to the feast of Mr. Chamberlain. His inadequacy is but too visible."

The contrast between the aristocracy and the middle class is plain, and he draws it. "The lower class see before them the aristocratic class, and its civilisation, such as it is, even infinitely more out of their reach than out of that of the middle class; while the life of the middle class, with its unlovely types of religion, thought, beauty, manners, has naturally, in general, no great attraction for them either. And so, too, they are thrown back upon themselves; upon their beer, their gin, and their fun." It is a tragedy which appals him every whit as much as it appalled Ruskin. Was the enfranchisement of the artizan the chief step to progress? Arnold was as far-sighted as Disraeli in foreseeing that the hope of Liberalism was not likely to be realised by any Reform Bill, for he discerned the existence of the conservative working man. A Liberal of this type—and it was far from an uncommon one—forgot those elements which went to the humanising of the voter, and this to Arnold was the vital matter. His Stoicism is continually cropping up.

Society possesses spiritual foundations—if it is likely to last. He believes in a national Church, the Church of England, and he believes in national schools. He affirmed that religion was the sweetest and the strongest element in the world, and he affirmed with Burke that without it there could be no perfect culture, no complete civilisation. "The Sadducees," he confessed with sorrow, "are our friends the philosophical Liberals, who believe neither in angel nor spirit but in Mr. Herbert Spencer." In his lectures on the Epistle to the Romans Bishop Gore acknowledges: "Life in Christ Jesus, Christ living in me—there can be no question that these beautiful phrases which, if St. John's witness be true, represent the teaching of Christ Himself, express also what was most central in St. Paul's idea of Christianity. It was the great merit of Matthew Arnold's *St. Paul and Protestantism* that it recalled the fact to notice in ordinary educated circles. Recent scientific study of St. Paul has gone in the same direction." In his *Last Essays on Church and Religion* Arnold owns: "I know of no other Establishment so reasonable. Churches are characterised, I have said, by their great men. Show me any other great Church of which a chief actor and luminary has a sentence like this sentence, *splendide verax*, of Butler's:—'Things are what they are, and the consequences of them will be what they will be; why then should we wish to be deceived?' To take in and digest such a sentence as that is an education in moral and intellectual activity. And, after all, intensely Butlerian as the sentence is, yet Butler came to it because he is English, because at the bottom of his nature lay such a fund of integrity."

The message of *Culture and Anarchy*, his greatest prose work, appeared in 1869. In the preface its author refers to the "undesirable provincialism of the English Puritans and Protestant Nonconformists." In place of it he preaches his favourite doctrine of "sweetness and light," a phrase he borrows from Swift. Swift used it of the bees because they make honey and wax. Arnold transferred it to the operation of culture which would, if it could, "make reason and the will of God prevail." He contrasted with it the motto of the "Nonconformist" newspaper: "The Dissidence of Dissent and the Protestantism of the Protestant religion."

Where culture is present there is liberty: where it is absent there is license, the license of anarchy. There is unity at home, and there is the prospect of unity abroad. Through culture the humanised citizen becomes an implicit member of a world community. Long before the war Eduard Zeller, the German historian, expressed the opinion: "It is questions of power and advantage, it is prejudices and ambitions, which divide the peoples; what unites them is the culture of ideal interests, morality, art, science, education. In this domain they can unfold all their powers without hostile collision; here they have all common aims, while the widest scope is left for their individual genius in conceiving and executing them." Long before Zeller, Arnold delivered the same message. Long before Arnold, Wordsworth delivered this message. Indeed Wordsworth and Arnold approach, from opposite sides, the ideal of law and liberty which answers to the deepest instincts of our mind. The pillar of Wordsworth's politics is order, the pillar of Arnold's is liberty; Wordsworth's order is not despotism but the spontaneous activity of the hive; and Arnold's liberty is not anarchy but self-discipline, the self-discipline of the Stoic. Conceive national greatness in terms of power or territory or wealth, and how can the conception of a commonwealth of nations ever emerge? Another nation is a possible rival with power to be transferred, territory to be taken, wealth to be acquired. Conceive, as Arnold implores us to conceive, national greatness in terms of culture, mental and moral, and is not the whole situation transformed? The commonwealth of culture is possible, nay probable. Another nation is a possible rival with culture to be absorbed, with enlightenment to be received, and received all the more eagerly because the national standpoint will give it a milieu not our own. Nations, in truth, are no longer rivals, but complementary each to the other in the many-sided pattern woven by the whole of humanity. The love of each man for his country is as Mazzini insisted, transformed. For patriotism, to the Italian seer, is only the most definite expression of a man's love for all the nations of the world. As Edith Cavell acknowledged, patriotism is not enough. Something more is needed. It is the sense that all nations belong to a community where the smallest of them as well as the largest can make its due contribution to the civilisation of the whole world.

Arnold rose to a lofty height in 1869 when he insisted that "there is of Culture another view, in which not solely the scientific passion, the sheer desire to see things as they are, natural and proper in an intelligent being, appears as the ground of it. There is a view in which all the love of our neighbour, the impulses towards action, help, and beneficence, the desire for removing human error, clearing human confusion, and diminishing human misery, the noble aspiration to leave the world better and happier than we found it—motives eminently such as are called social—come in as part of the grounds of Culture, and the main and pre-eminent part Culture is then properly described as not having its origin in curiosity, but as having its origin in the love of perfection; it is a *study of perfection.* It moves by force, not merely or primarily of the scientific passion for pure knowledge, but also of the moral and social passion for doing good. . . . There is no better motto which it can have than these words of Bishop Wilson: 'To make reason and the will of God prevail.'"

In *Friendship's Garland* Arnold urges that "what unites and separates people now is Geist," and the spread of Geist inevitably makes for conciliation, and *Culture and Anarchy* developes the same conception. In the latter we read: "The great men of culture are those who have had a passion for diffusing, for making prevail, for carrying from one end of society to the other, the best knowledge, the best ideas of their time; who have laboured to divest knowledge of all that was harsh, uncouth, difficult, abstract, professional, exclusive; to humanise it, to make it efficient outside the clique of the cultivated and learned, yet still remaining the *best* knowledge and thought of the true, and a true source, therefore, of sweetness and light."

Material and mechanical devices will never diffuse Geist. In the soulless labour of millions who work the exquisitely elaborate machinery Arnold saw an enslavement of the spirit to mechanism. If we travel from the England of the sixties to the Germany of our own day, the same protest is being made. In drama Ernst Toller and Georg Kaiser utter in the twentieth century what Arnold uttered in the nineteenth. In Kaiser's powerful play, "Gas," we have a vivid portrayal of the mechanisation of industry. "Gas" stands as the symbol of money. Machine-made industry produces money for the capitalist who uses up the men who run the plant. The hero, son of a multi-millionaire, has succeeded in manufacturing a gas more powerful than all known fuels. The whole world besieges him for it. Alack! there is a terrific explosion in which many of the hands perish. The rest strike, and there is a serious shortage of gas. The inventor bethinks himself of solution of his troubles. But is there any? The formula he employed was quite correct, and in the manufacture of the gas nothing went wrong. Suddenly the solution flashes upon him. The formula for the gas was not wrong, but the process was fundamentally wrong, for it mechanised men. "Away with the Machine, and discover Man! The millions of men mechanically used up to produce it!" Such is the message Kaiser dramatically delivers. Nor is there any difference in the drama of Toller save that perhaps it touches us more closely. For Toller takes not the manufacture of gas, but the manufacture of lace in Nottingham. Before the Industrial Revolution it was made on the domestic system which left the operatives human beings, not hands in a factory. The lace-machines came, and with their coming man began to be mechanised. He is in process of being devoured and consumed by the insatiable demands of industry. Count Keyserling, an aristocrat who has travelled around the world in search of spirituality, professes to have found it in India which as yet is not mechanised. He sums up Chicago as the city where machinery has mastered man, its creator but really its creature. According to Count Keyserling, "it is not that the machine kills man, but that it reduces all that is spiritual to material, all that is organic to mechanical, terms, by showing that without soul, cultural interests, or emotional cultivation, it is possible to live a full and busy life." Where the machine comes there is chaos. It is the message of Arnold, as it is the message of Kaiser, of Keyserling, and Toller, that this chaos must become cosmos. This chaos, however, is not hopeless and unmitigated anarchy: it is chaos that longs to be cosmos if the Arnolds of a past or a present generation stand any chance of an audience for their summons of mankind from mechanisation to spiritualisation.

In *St. Paul and Protestantism; with an Introduction on Puritanism and the Church of England* Arnold in 1870 continued his interpretative mission. His object is to prepare the way for all to the unity of a broader and more comprehensive Church than has ever yet been formed, and inevitably he manifests his dislike for those who defend existing divisions. This dislike concentrates itself around the nonconformists. He is convinced that these denominational bodies, placing their centre of coherence on Pauline dogmas, are proceeding on an assumption essentially wrong and mischievous. A vision arises before him of a time when differences in discipline, in modes of worship, and even in speculative doctrine, shall not only be tolerated in separate communities, but borne with, and even welcomed, within the limits of the same community—welcomed, because thus alone can we provide for the various requirements of the individual temperaments, and welcomed because all shall have learned that it is not always best for themselves to have their own prepossessions gratified and flattered and exaggerated. Arnold criticised theology: he never criticised religion, and his own life was fundamentally religious. He held for himself—and he held it for mankind as well—that "not to break one's connexion with the past in one's religion is one of the strongest instincts in human nature," and it was an instinct too strong for him to attempt the task. A Church Establishment is expedient for man, and it is expedient for the organism of which he is a member. With Tocqueville he discerns in the power of religion the required counterpoise to the weakness of democracy. "Men want religion," so he urges in his *Higher Schools and Universities in France* "a rule and sanctions for conduct which enlist their feelings; and the actual forms of Christianity are approximations to this. And men want it public and national, to prevent religion, the proper source of all solidity and union, from being precarious and divided. Hence the national churches," which he defended with all the passion of his soul. In his present book he pleads in the same strain: "But surely the moment we consider religion and Christianity in a large way as goodness, and a Church as a society for the promotion of goodness, all that is said about having such a society before men's eyes as a city set upon a hill, all that is said about making the Gospel more and more a witness to mankind, applies in favour of the State adopting some form of religion or other—that which seems best suited to the majority—even though it may not be perfect; and putting that forward as the national form of religion."

The maintenance of culture is a function of an Established Church on which he lays considerable stress at all times. He points out that "the fruitful men of English Puritanism and Nonconformity are men who were trained within the pale of the Establishment—Milton, Baxter, Wesley. A generation or two outside the Establishment and Puritanism produces men of national mark no longer." True, yet Arnold forgets that no other result was possible for generations as nonconformists were excluded from the two ancient universities, and the newer ones had not sprung into existence in 1870. Nor does he take into account that such prelates in the Church of England as Creighton and Tait, the greatest archbishop of the nineteenth century, came of Nonconformist parentage. The truth is that culture gravitates to the Church of England. Creighton and Tait left nonconformity because it was uncongenial to their ideals, and they joined the Church of England because it was congenial to them. Arnold was at bottom right when he insisted on the importance of Geist. The spirit of separation is due less to doctrinal differences than to a frame of mind. The ethos of a community attracts one type while it repels another.

Literature and Dogma, which appeared in 1873, continues the author's task of enlightening the public. Dogma is minimised and religion is maximised. The attractiveness of this Arnoldian solution at first sight is very strong, and it has been the refuge of many who have sought in Christian work the satisfaction they could not find in Christian thought. Cannot a man, they ask, serve his generation according to the will of God without troubling himself with so many conflicting theories? Is not the life after all the main thing? The religion we learnt at our mother's knee is unmixed with dogma—Can we not keep *that* and let dogma go? And as with the individual, so with the Church. Does not history, they ask, show what a failure dogma has been as a basis of union, how impossible it must always be to mould men's thoughts to a single type? Can there not be substituted for it something broader—a union, for instance, in Christian beneficence, a kind of co-operation in social Christianity? There is something surely attractive in this solution. Yet though it may be best for some individuals, to thinking men and to the Church in general it can give only temporary satisfaction. For the human mind is such that it *will* inquire; and neither in the individual nor in the Church could Christianity flourish for any length of time without producing a corresponding doctrine. "Religion," in the judgment of Lord Salisbury, "can no more be separated from dogma than light from the sun."

The Zeitgeist is evident in *Literature and Dogma*. We ask with its author, What is the proper place of doctrine in religion? Is it primary or secondary, essential or accidental, immutable or mutable? Can we define it, as Arnold asks us, as the theory of religion and so relegate it to that inferior position which most people give to theory as compared with practice? For in all the activities of our human life there does appear to be this twofold aspect. We find everywhere theory combined with practice and for every art a corresponding science; but as a matter of fact it is the practice which produces the theory and not the theory the practice. The pre-historic savage knew nothing of the law of specific gravity when he launched the first canoe; and men conversed with one another for ages before the need was felt for formulating the laws of language. It is the practice, then, which produces the theory; but, we hasten to add, the theory generally reacts on the practice which produced it. For there is no doubt whatever—to take the same examples—that a modern steamship could not be constructed without a theoretical knowledge of hydrostatics or a poem of Arnold composed without conscious reference to the laws of grammar.

Is it the same with religion? Does the practice come before the theory or the theory before the practice, or instead of saying sharply which comes first,—are we to admit the action of each on the other? After all the discussions which have been held on this question, the truth seems to be that there is a certain intellectual element in our religion from the very first. There are a few essentials of knowledge without which no man can become or be a Christian. But as for the great mass of doctrine, as Arnold perceived, it comes second both in point of time and importance. The order is still that of the Master, "If any man will do his will he *shall* know of the doctrine." We may even go farther and say that for the great majority—these are the people of whom our author was thinking and for whom he was writing—the place of minute and sharply defined doctrine is taken first and last by those vague and dumb impressions, the Geist, which form such a powerful factor in all departments of human life. It is, therefore, becoming more and more clearly recognised that the great question is not to lay before men a set of minute doctrines, however good, to which they must bring themselves into allegiance by whatever effort—the great matter is rather to bring men into a condition of life in which they can corroborate these doctrines from their own experience. There is certainly need of dogma: there is a Christian truth in Christianity—only instead of placing it all at the outset the greater part of it is to be placed at the end. Instead of deriving the Christian life from it, it is itself largely the product of the Christian life. In great part it is the special work of the intellect reflecting upon the life already existing, examining its foundations, its nature, and its elements. That life contains as one of its factors an intellectual element, an irreducible minimum, at least, of doctrine, is manifest; and so far we admit that doctrine is primary. Yet these ideas, really indispensable to the existence of the religious life, are relatively few in number. By far the greater part of theology consists in the work of the intellect on these primary ideas and on life in general, and, so far as this is the case, we must hold that doctrine is not primary but secondary, not essential but accidental. It may be urged that this division opens the way to all kinds of extravagance in which each man settles for himself how much it is necessary and how much is optional; but perfect identity of belief is impossible in any case and if a few fundamentals be agreed on—you may call them religious ideas if you will—the more purely abstract and theological ideas, which have little effect on the religious life, may be safely left to take care of themselves.

To Arnold if the State is to be maintained, the Church is to be maintained, and he accordingly felt the congruity—not the incongruity—of his labour in writing his *Mixed Essays* in 1879. In them he writes with keen insight on democracy and equality. In his survey of democracy he revises the views of the political economists on the dislike of State action, setting forth reasons for considering that there is no need of jealousy of such action. England had been governed by an aristocracy up to 1832, or, indeed, to 1867, and this aristocracy had governed in the grand style. Its day, however, has passed. Now "democracy is trying *to affirm its own essence*; to live, to enjoy, to possess the world, as aristocracy has tried, and successfully tried before it. Ever since Europe emerged from barbarism, ever since the condition of the common people began a little to improve, ever since their minds began to stir, this effort of democracy has been gaining strength; and the more their condition improves, the more strength this effort gains. So potent is the charm of life and expansion upon the living; the moment men are aware of them they begin to desire them, and the more they have of them the more they crave."

Once more he urges the power of social life and manners as one of the great elements in humanisation, and once more he urges that unless we have cultivated it we are incomplete. It is a promoter of equality, and indeed it is by the humanity of their manners that men are made equal. His essay on equality also takes the form of an able—if elaborate—argument against freedom of bequest, an idea enjoying the hearty support of Mill. Men object, Certainly equality will never of itself alone give us a perfect civilisation. Arnold agrees and asks, But with such inequality as ours, is not a perfect civilisation impossible? The effects of inequality have been the creation of "an upper class materialised, a middle class vulgarised, a lower class brutalised." Besides, there has arisen that intellectual estrangement between classes which he considers truly deplorable. He is anxious that the three classes should combine in order to form a strong State. The multitude alone can effect but little. Turn to his verdict on it: "It lacks principle, it lacks persistence; if to-day its good impulses prevail, they succumb to-morrow; sometimes it goes right, but is very apt to go wrong. Even a popular orator, or a popular journalist, will hardly say that the multitude may be trusted to have its judgment generally just, and its action generally virtuous. It may be better, it is better, that the body of the people, with all its faults, should act for itself, and control its own affairs, than that it should be set aside as ignorant and incapable, and have its affairs managed for it by a so-called superior class, possessing property and intelligence. Property and intelligence cannot be trusted to show a sound majority themselves; the exercise of power by the people tends to educate the people. But still, the world being what it is, we must surely expect the aims and doings of the majority of men to be at present very faulty, and this in a numerous community no less than in a small one."

Equality is desirable on the ground of civilisation, but not on the ground of natural right which he detests as heartily as Bentham himself. The great utilitarian could not write more frankly than Arnold on this subject "Peasants and workmen have no natural rights at all," so he states, "only we ought instantly to add that kings and nobles have none either. If it is the sound English doctrine that all rights are created by law and are based on expediency, and are alterable as the public advantage may require, certainly that orthodox doctrine is mine. Poverty is created and maintained by law. It would disappear in that state of private war and scramble which legal society supersedes. Legal society creates, for the common good, the right of property, and for the common good that right is by legal society limitable. That property should exist, and that it should be held with a sense of security, may be taken . . . as a settled matter of expediency." In true Stoic spirit, he concerns himself much more with duties than rights.

His *Irish Essays* of 1882 approaches the land question in the spirit of Maine. Arnold's remedy for the agrarian trouble, the root cause of the discontent in Ireland, was the institution of a Commission which should inquire into the conduct of the landlords who recognised that property carried duties no less than rights and those who recognised nothing of the sort. The latter he proposed to expropriate. With Burke he would endow all the religions of Ireland and would supply good schools. To Home Rule he offered his vehement opposition, partly because he desired cohesion instead of disintegration and partly because he disliked Gladstone. Though his *Irish Essays* nominally deal with the theme suggested by their title, Arnold discusses topic after topic which had appeared in his other writings. For instance, his denunciation of natural right is once more in evidence.

He had paid many visits in Europe, and at last in 1883 he paid a visit to the United States where he was, with true

American hospitality, warmly greeted. He gave a course of lectures which were well attended and badly delivered. He observed the people and their institutions attentively, and concluded that there was that close union between the classes he so much desiderated. Was the "human problem" solved with equal success? By this problem he meant the problem of civilisation, and of course civilisation meant "humanisation in society." In this respect he pronounced the United States defective. In some respects his verdict anticipated that of Count Keyserling. On his return home he issued his *Discourses in America* in 1885, the book, so he told George Russell, of all others by which he should most wish to be remembered. Once more he analyses the multitude, finding the majority always wrong, the remnant always right. The old Stoic element in him re-appears. If Marcus Aurelius represented the remnant in Rome, Isaiah represented the remnant of Israel, Plato the remnant of Athens. The small City-State—for the Jew regarded Jerusalem as his centre—contained this remnant, but did the huge population of the United States?

The remnant counts, and it counts because it can produce Isaiah, Plato, and Marcus Aurelius. No doubt there is a tinge of sadness and resignation in their aspirations, for all alike found duty by no means easy to fulfil. In the midst of the whirlpool of life all alike felt the need of religion. They sought for a higher ideal to lend direction and force—this is of the last importance—to the movement for self-repression and unselfish devotion to the common good. It is also true of Arnold, whose inner life, as revealed in his *Note Books*, bears ample testimony to his quest of the power of turning the ideal into the real. Not a few Stoics failed to effect this transformation, and he was determined not so to fail. The morning of his death he worshipped in Sefton Park Church, Liverpool, where John Watson, well known as the novelist, Ian Maclaren, preached. Arnold was deeply impressed by the sermon on the Cross of Christ, and remarked that he had rarely been so affected by any preacher as Watson. One of the hymns sung was:

> When I survey the wondrous Cross
> On which the Prince of Glory died.

Arnold when he came home repeated the lines, and declared the hymn to be the finest in the English language. "Yes," he went on, "the Cross remaineth, and in the straits of the soul makes its ancient appeal."

REFERENCES

BICKLEY, F. L. *Matthew Arnold and his Poetry.* (London, 1911.)
BIRRELL, A. *Res Judicatae.* (London, 1892.)
BROOKE, S. A. *Clough, Arnold, Rossetti, and Morris. A Study.* (London, 1910.)
BROWNELL, W. C. *Victorian Prose Masters.* (London, 1902.)
DAWSON, W. H. *Matthew Arnold and his Relation to the Thought of our Time.* (London, 1904.)
DIXON, W. M. *The Republic of Letters.* (London, 1898.)
FITCH, Sir J. *Thomas and Matthew Arnold.* (London, 1897.)
GALTON, A. *Two Essays upon Matthew Arnold, with some of his letters to the author.* (London, 1897.)
GRANT DUFF, Sir M. E. *Out of the Past.* Vol. I. (London, 1903.)
HUDSON, W. H. *Studies in Interpretation.* (London, 1896.)
HUTTON, R. H. *Literary Essays.* (London, 1871.)
HUTTON, R. H. *Essays on some of the modern Guides in matters of Faith.* (London, 1887.)
HUTTON, R. H. *Criticisms on Contemporary Thought and Thinkers.* Vol. I. (London, 1894.)
KELSO, A. P. *Matthew Arnold on Continental Life and Literature.* (London, 1914.)
KINGSMILL, H. *Matthew Arnold.* (London, 1928.)
LUND, T. W. M. *Matthew Arnold. The Message and Meaning of his Life.* (London, 1888.)
MERRICK, J. B. *Matthew Arnold and Goethe. English Goethe Society.* Vol. IV. (London,1828.)
PAUL, H. W. *Men and Letters.* (London, 1901.)
PAUL, H. W. *Matthew Arnold.* (London, 1902.)
RUSSELL, G. W. E. *Letters of Matthew Arnold,* 1848–88. (London, 1895.)
RUSSELL, G. W. E. *Matthew Arnold.* (London, 1904.)
SAINTSBURY, G. *Corrected Impressions.* (London, 1895.)
SAINTSBURY, G. *Matthew Arnold.* (London, 1899.)
SAINTSBURY, G. *A History of Criticism.* Vol. III. (Edinburgh, 1904.)
STEPHEN, Sir L. *Studies of a Biographer.* Vol. III. (London, 1898.)
SWINBURNE, A. C. *Essays and Studies.* (London, 1875.)
TOVEY, D. C. *Reviews and Essays on English Literature.* (London,1897.)
WALKER, H. *The Greater Victorian Poets.* (London, 1895.)
WARD, T. H. *The English Poets.* Vol. IV. (London, 1894.)
WARREN, T. H. *Essays of Poets and Poetry.* (London, 1909.)
WATSON, W. A. *Gospels of Yesterday. Drummond, Spencer, Arnold.* (London, 1888.)
WORSFOLD, W. B. *The Principles of Criticism.* (London, 1897.)

Chapter V.

SEELEY THE IMPERIALIST STATESMAN

On the surface, no men could be more unlike than Matthew Arnold and Sir John Seeley, yet underlying the superficial differences there are fundamental resemblances. Each man was a poet, though of course there is no comparison between the poetry of Arnold and that of Seeley, yet what the former was to poetry the latter was to history. Both expressed unbounded faith in the commonwealth of culture, and both set themselves resolutely to humanise civilisation. What Sainte-Beuve and Renan meant to the poet, Calderon and Goethe meant to the historian. They were moralists rather than theologians, but moralists who manifested keen interest in social questions and their solution. What Philistinism meant to Arnold secularity meant to Seeley. Each, in divers fashion, attempted to reconcile the Hellenic ideal of self-development with the Christian ideal of self-sacrifice. Their attitude to politics was detached, for though both professed to be Liberals yet their form of Liberalism was not such as to commend itself to Gladstone. Politics was to each of them religion in another form and vice versa. Their natures rendered them keenly alive to the poetry of history, realising in the pageantry of the present the politics of the past. No doubt their views in theology did not commend them to the orthodox, yet over orthodoxy each exercised a revivifying power. They believed with all their heart and with all their head in the connection of Church and State, and indeed neither man could conceive of the permanent existence of the State apart from religion. The State exists, and continues to exist, but how can it do so without the Church to sustain it? The writings of Seeley and Arnold rest upon the fundamental assumption that there is a natural religion, and that there are a hundred ways of attaining the truth about religion. The student of literature like Arnold or the student of history like Seeley is just as likely to arrive at truth in religion as any professed theologian. Both belittled dogma to an undue extent, yet if one had lived in a day when a philanthropist like Shaftesbury could speak of Seeley's *Ecce Homo* as "the most pestilential book ever vomited from the jaws of hell," one might feel that the protest of Arnold and Seeley against the orthodoxy of the sixties was seriously required. The works of both men have so become part of the spirit of the age now that we are apt to forget what manner of men our grandfathers were.

Sir John Robert Seeley (1834–95) was born in London. He was the third son of Robert Seeley, the publisher, a man of strongly marked mental and physical energy. The father belonged to the order of Clapham churchmanship, and his publications were mainly confined to books setting forth the ways and works of evangelicalism. A decided churchman, he published a volume of essays in 1834 in defence of Church Establishment, and he was one of the founders of the Church Pastoral Aid Society. With Lord Shaftesbury he exerted himself vigorously in supporting the factory bills. In 1860 he published his work on *The Greatest of the Plantagenets, Edward I*, and he successfully defended that monarch against the strictures of Hume and other historians, and he also set forth the title of our English Justinian to the rank of greatness. In not a few respects the thought of the father reminds us as much of the son as the thought of Thomas Arnold reminds us of his son Matthew. From his father Sir John inherited his habit of thinking about religion and his devotion to history.

At an extremely early age J. R. Seeley learnt to read and to read widely. He went first to school under the Rev. J. A. Barron at Stanmore. The headmaster taught reading for reading's sake, and he communicated to his pupil his own love of English literature. There the lad learnt to care for Milton and Pope, and learnt to care with what proved a lifelong devotion. On leaving Stanmore he attended the City of London School, then under Dr. Mortimer, whose pupils were winning scholarships at the Universities. Mortimer's administrative ability combined with his genial manner attracted many boys to his school, and in 1861 he had the unique distinction of seeing two of his scholars respectively senior classic and senior wrangler at Cambridge. Charles Kingsley read privately with him for ordination. A precocious boy, Seeley was encouraged to read too hard. He worked so well that he entered the sixth form when little over thirteen. His two elder brothers were in the sixth at the same time, the eldest—afterwards a fellow of Trinity College, Cambridge—being captain of the school. There are advantages in a day school, but among the grave drawbacks one certainly is that little time is spent on games. Seeley was kept so busy at home in the preparation of his lessons that his only form of exercise was the daily walk between Bloomsbury and Cheapside. His health suffered so severely that he was obliged for a time to leave school and to give up all work. The tragedy is that, like Darwin, he never recovered his health, and insomnia dogged his steps.

Seeley spent a year with the family of the Rev. F. Fitch, Vicar of Cromer. Forced to give up his classics, he resumed his reading of English literature. In later life he delighted in recalling this year of enforced idleness, for he owed, so he said, to it most of his knowledge of English literature. There is a deep truth in the saying of Töpfer that a year of downright loitering is a desirable element in a liberal education. Such an element was entirely unknown to Seeley at any other period of his life. To toil terribly was part and parcel of his character. He seldom had a margin in his life of hurried—and unceasing—thought. He had read through *Paradise Lost* four or five times before he had left school.

In 1852 he went up to Cambridge, entering the university as a scholar of Christ's College. Among his contemporaries at his own college were Calverley, Besant, Peile, Skeat, and Sendall. Able as these men undoubtedly were, he was reckoned one of the ablest. In conversation he exhibited already the analytical skill and epigrammatic expression which continued to characterise him. He had a faculty for pricking bubbles which he exercised as freely as Walter Bagehot. He spoke but seldom at the Union, but when he spoke he secured attention. He read classics with Robert Burn, and afterwards with Shilleto, but he was more engrossed with the matter of his classical authors than with their manner. Even as an undergraduate the philosophical and historical contents of his authors moved him far more than any graces of style. His ill-health continued, and he was forced to defer his degree for a year. He graduated in 1857 when his name appeared with three others, at the top of the Classical Tripos. Academic distinctions do not prove everything, as the cases of Arnold and Newman attest, but they prove something. Lord Goschen was once asked the good of first classes. "Perhaps they're not much good. Still, I should like to mention that out of twelve of my colleagues in the Cabinet, eight are first classes." The gaining of a good degree reveals to a man that he possesses powers which are above the average, and there is nothing an able young man requires so much as confidence in himself. Well as Seeley had done in the Tripos, he did better in the competition for the Chancellor's Medals when he came out senior medallist.

Christ's College elected him a fellow in 1858, and for two years he held a classical lectureship. In 1859 he published, under the pseudonym of John Robertson, a volume of poetry entitled *David and Samuel; with other poems, original and translated*. This volume contains a poem on the call of David, versifications of several psalms, and a series of sketches, chiefly monologues, of Nero, William the Silent, the Prince of Orange in 1672, and others. As Arnold was always interested in religion and poetry, so Seeley was always interested in religion and history, and when both turned to theology there is much in common in their writings. The personal and the dramatic element in the religion of both is more marked in early life than in late. It is noticeable that in his first volume Seeley selected all his subjects from the Old Testament.

In 1859 he left Cambridge in order to teach under his old headmaster, Dr. Mortimer, and for the next four years he was chief classical assistant. In 1863 he was appointed professor of Latin in University College, London, as successor to the curiously unorthodox brother of Cardinal Newman, Frank. Here he remained for six years, but the publication of *Ecce Homo* in 1865 revealed to the public that his mind had been as much engrossed by religion and politics as by the classics. *Ecce Homo* and *The Expansion of England* caught the attention of the English-speaking public, and in fact took it by storm. All the world read *Ecce Homo,* and of course it received a first-class advertisement by the persistent attacks of the orthodox. It was published anonymously because Seeley felt certain that his father would dislike it, and out of consideration for his susceptibilities Seeley kept the secret till his father was dead. *Ecce Homo* came at a time when there was a marked and vigorous investigation of things sacred. *Essays and Reviews* appeared in 1860, Colenso's work on the Pentateuch in 1862, Renan's *Vie de Jésus* in 1863, and Strauss's shorter *Leben Jesu* in 1864. In the days before the Synoptic problem had been barely broached, with the intuition of genius Seeley placed the strength of his survey of the life and work of Jesus Christ in St. Mark's Gospel, the earliest of the four. In the union of morals and politics he characteristically finds the marks of Christianity. He lays stress on the circumstance that Christ came to found a society, and he investigates the conditions of membership in Christ's kingdom. Baptism is a condition, and baptism means cleansing with fire, and fire means warmth. How can warmth cleanse? "The answer is that *moral* warmth does cleanse. No heart is pure that is not passionate; no virtue is safe that is not enthusiastic." He, just as much as Arnold, seeks for the power which enables men not merely to live, but to live well. Historical parallels appear continually, and in the hands of Seeley they teach much. John the Baptist was like the Emperor Nerva. Socrates holds his place in history by his thoughts and not by his life, Christ by His life and not by His thoughts. In sundry ways and divers fashions the author directs our attention mainly to the Christian society he seeks to analyse. This is as clear in his *Natural Religion,* published in 1882, as in his *Ecce Homo.*

Lives of Christ have thrown so much emphasis on the God-man that His mission has been left to the one side. Seeley comes in to redress the balance, and he redressed it so drastically that we do not altogether wonder at the scoffs of the scornful. Thanks to Seeley, we to-day can read the Bible in the light of the illumination he gave to it, and we see how national and political religion almost necessarily is. The State is the dominating thought in his philosophy, and he tells us that he received this thought from the Bible. For the Bible reveals the knowledge of the past, and bestows insight on its course. To Father Joseph, the confidant of Richelieu, "ordinary history is like the face of a clock; we see the hands that move and mark the time, but not the wheels and secret springs whereby it goes." Seeley saw these wheels and springs in his Bible. "But I may say in one word that my ideas," so he owns in the preface to his *Natural Religion*, "are Biblical, that they are drawn from the Bible at first-hand and that what fascinates me in the Bible is not a passage here and there, not something which only a scholar or antiquarian can detect in it, but the Bible as a whole, its great plan and unity, and principally the grand poetic anticipation I find in it of modern views concerning history."

Theologians regard Christ as a moralist who spoke with authority. In Seeley's judgment the Greek philosophers spoke as moralists and spoke with authority. To our historian what differentiates Him from all others is that He was a moralist who spoke with authority and who also founded a society. What notably characterises Christianity is this marriage of morals and politics henceforth never to be divorced by your Machiavellis or by anyone else. The older prophets had contemplated a race, the Jews, whereas Christ contemplates humanity forming a society which recognises no racial, social, and political distinctions. From the very first this society was organised, and baptism was the mode of admission to it. Seeley is careful to emphasise the story of Nicodemus as an illustration of the high place He assigned to baptism. This Christian society is bound together by an *esprit de corps*, "by a passion of the same nature as patriotism without its exclusiveness." The enthusiasm for humanity, the love of man in man, is as outstanding a feature of Seeley's thought as Arnold's.

Our philosopher turns to the pages of history as well as to the pages of the Bible, and in both he finds confirmation of his views. People who forget that religion is political as well as private "do not see that the Holy Roman Empire of the Middle Ages is to Rome just what the Christian Church is to Judaism, that it is the resurrection of a fallen nationality in an idealised shape." Then he pursues this train of thought. "Look almost where you will in the wide field of history, you find religion, whenever it works freely and mightily, either giving birth to and sustaining states, or else raising them up to a second life after their destruction. It is a great state-builder in the hands of Moses and Ulfilas and Gregory and Nicholas; in the ruder hands of Mohammed and many another tamer and guide of gross populations down to the Prophet of Utah it has the same character, the same too in the hands of the almost forgotten Numas and propagators of the Apollo-worship who laid the foundation of Roman and Greek civilisation, and of the pilgrim fathers who founded New England. In the East to this day nationality and religion are almost convertible terms; the Scotch national character first awoke in the adoption of a new religion and afterwards expressed itself more than once in national covenants; the Reformation itself may be represented as coming out of the German national consciousness, and it has been proposed to call the various forms of Protestantism by the collective name of Christianity. Lastly, in Christianity itself, in Romanism, and partly also in Mohammedanism, we see religion in the form of an aggressive or missionary nationality bringing foreign nations into a new citizenship."

Whether Seeley reads his Bible or his history, it is out of his power to avoid drawing a moral. Let your historian proceed as skilfully and as scientifically as he pleases—and Seeley is as anxious about his science as about his skill—there must be a moral to the tale unrolled before the reader. As Seeley conceives history as a science, he also conceives it as an art. It must, if it is to be of service to us mortals, anticipate the future. In his *Expansion of England* he enforces this point. There is a fatalism which leads us to take for granted Turgot's famous parallel between colonies and fruit. As the fruit drops off the tree when ripe, so our colonies will leave us when the proper time comes. God forbid, cries out Seeley. If we acquiesce in this parallel, we do so because of three misunderstandings. There is the misunderstanding of the special influences at work in the war of American Independence; there is the misunderstanding of the characteristics of modern English colonisation; and there is the misunderstanding of the fact that time has brought us into a period of "greater political magnitude and higher numbers" and swifter communications. Parallels are valuable, but we must see to it that they are real parallels, and, above all, we must not misread their inner meaning.

It is the business of the historian to interpret the past. He unrolls the story of society in its many acts and scenes, the organism casting off outworn functions and taking to itself fresh ones as needs arise. So the historian is sent to deliver us "from the bewilderment and horror which the past excites, when we open its records at random." Unless rightly guided in this fashion, the unhappy reader may come to a conclusion of the worth of history too Gibbonian for Seeley's taste. The Church, in bygone days, enabled her members to discern the secret wheels and springs by which history moves. She displayed "a grand outline of God's dealings with the human race, drawn from the Bible and the Church doctrine, a sort of map of history was possessed by all alike. Are we sufficiently aware what bewilderment must arise when this is no longer the case, when these old outlines grow unserviceable, but no new map is furnished?"

The spirit of Burke and Coleridge is alive in the man who argues that "All old philosophers knew that the fabric of the State rested ultimately upon a way of thinking, a habit of opinion, a 'discipline,' which was a thing so delicate and easily deranged that in the opinion of some of them new tunes coming into vogue might be enough to cause a revolution." So thought Plato, and so thought Seeley. The new tunes of science in general and biology in particular have come, and they have introduced everywhere a sceptical condition of mind. With Bagehot we listen to the argument that "yet if such scepticism became practical, if large communities came to regard every question in politics and law as absolutely open, their institutions would dissolve, and science, among other things, would be buried in the ruin." Religion, so the argument runs, is and always has been the basis of societies and states. "From history," so our author is convinced, "we learn that the great function of religion has been the founding and sustaining of states. At this moment we are threatened with a general dissolution of states from the decay of religion," an argument which we are destined to hear tolerably often in the immediate future.

In his *Lectures and Essays*, published in 1870, their author asks the Church to moralise the history of England. No doubt the history of the kings of Israel reveals the hand of God in history, but does not the history of the kings of England fulfil this purpose? Surely the lives of Milton or Gordon have their contribution to make towards the understanding of God's way in the past. To him religion may wear three forms. It may wear the form of devotion to an ideal of human conduct. Then it will be Christianity. It may wear the form of devotion to an ideal of physical beauty. Then it will be the religion of art. It may wear the form of devotion to the unity of nature. Then it will be science or theism. His *Natural Religion* attempts to show that even if the creeds of the Churches became wholly incredible, yet what is vital in religion will remain. Its author still testifies that science is insufficient unless science is religious, and in fact that religion is "the principle by which alone life is redeemed from secularity and animalism."

Between *Ecce Homo* and *Natural Religion* the philosophy of Goethe had come to influence Seeley powerfully. Standing aloof, like Fontenelle, from the great causes that throbbed through the world of his day, Goethe looked on not unmoved, but drew aside from the swift-flowing current. When a man stands on the summit of the Wetterhorn the meadows and houses below become unsubstantial mist. Goethe saw from a height, but—this is the tragedy of it—he saw dimly. This quality failed to impress Seeley who was a statesman engrossed in the affairs of his country. He was, however, impressed by another quality of Goethe's, and that was his seriousness. In *Goethe Reviewed after Sixty Years*, in 1893, in fact, Seeley dwells on this. "Of all imaginative writers, Goethe is perhaps the most serious; not the most solemn, nor the most passionate, nor the most earnest, but the most serious. He is absolutely bent upon grasping and expressing the truth; he has no pleasure in any imaginations, however splendid or impressive, which he cannot feel to be true; on the other hand, when he feels that he is dealing with the truth, he seems to care little, and sometimes to forget altogether, that it is not interesting." It was the work of Goethe to chasten German taste by setting up the canons of classical antiquity and by recalling literature from the clouds to the solid ground of experience. The patriotism of Seeley is undoubted, and yet he cannot help thinking that it was better for the world for Goethe to be a man of culture than to be a patriot breaking his heart because Napoleon was overrunning his country. "Culture is more than half politics," such was the maxim by which Goethe lived, and such was the maxim by which Arnold and Seeley in their day, and Kaiser and Toller in our day, would have us live.

Natural Religion never captured the world-wide audience reached by *Ecce Homo,* and the reason is quite plain. The gospel of culture, as preached by Seeley and Arnold, is devoid of personality. Seeley despised Napoleon who could have taught him the place of personality. For the French genius insists that it was not the Roman legions that conquered the Gauls, but Caesar. It was not the Carthaginians that made Rome tremble, but Hannibal. It was not the Macedonian phalanx that penetrated to India, but Alexander. It was not the French army that reached the Weser and the Inn, but Turenne. It was not the Prussians soldiers that for seven years defended Prussia against the most formidable Powers in Europe; it was Frederick the Great. Arnold and Seeley now and then forget that it is only through personality that we move men. The eloquent ending of *Ecce Homo* demonstrates this, and it demonstrates how far Seeley had travelled from Gibbon's fifteenth chapter. Turn to it. "The achievement of Christ, in founding by His single will and power a structure so durable and so universal, is like no other achievement which history records. The masterpieces of other men of action are coarse and common in comparison with it, and the masterpieces of speculation flimsy and insubstantial. When we speak of it the commonplaces of admiration fail us altogether. Shall we speak of the originality of the design, of the skill displayed in the execution? All such terms are inadequate. Originality and contriving skill operated, indeed, but, as it were, implicitly. The creative effort which produced that against which, it is said, the gates of hell shall not prevail, cannot be analysed. No architects' design were furnished for the New Jerusalem, no committee drew up rules for the Universal Commonwealth. If in the works of Nature we can trace the indications of each calculation, of a struggle with difficulties, of precaution, of ingenuity, then in Christ's work it may be that the same indications occur. But these inferior and secondary powers were not consciously exercised; they were implicitly present in the manifold yet single creative act. The inconceivable work was done in calmness; before the eyes of men it was noiselessly accomplished, attracting little attention. Who can describe that which unites men? Who has entered into the formation of speech which is the symbol of their union? He who can do these things can explain the origin of the Christian Church. For others it must be enough to say, 'the Holy Ghost fell on those that believed.' No man saw the building of the New Jerusalem, the workmen crowded together, the unfinished walls and unpaved streets: no man heard the clink of trowel and pickaxe: it *descended out of heaven from God*."

Ecce Homo remains the most remarkable of all the writings of Seeley, and it made its way into circles but little suspected as under the influence of its author. The notion of the independence of religion has done much to quiet those to whom a generation ago the very name of science was anathema; and the historical study of the Bible is allowed to-day where thirty years ago higher criticism and infidelity were convertible terms. Seeley, however, pushes this notion of independence too far. The real distinction between scientific and religious truth should not be carried to the length of complete separation; and a middle course can surely be found between the older view that the testimony of the Spirit to the Bible debars us entirely from criticism and the view of Seeley—which is that of Ritschl—that our deep conviction of its worth renders us absolutely indifferent to critical results. For if religion is to retain the dignity of embracing a general view of the world, it must come to some terms with science other than a complete separation; if its historical character is to be guarded it cannot be altogether independent of historical facts or of that criticism which discusses them.

In 1869 Seeley married Mary Agnes, eldest daughter of Arthur Phillott. While on his honeymoon he received a letter from Gladstone offering him the Regius Professorship of Modern History at Cambridge, then vacant through the resignation of Charles Kingsley. In his thirty-fifth year Seeley received the work congenial to a man of his temperament. For he was as admirable a lecturer as he was a writer, contriving to invest everything he said with the impress of his personality. An old pupil, Mr. J. R. Tanner, records his impressions of his professor. He owns: "His old pupils used to say that Seeley's lectures were, at any rate, an education in lucidity and thoroughness—virtues which they were accustomed to claim as specially characteristic of the university in which he was, for a quarter of a century, Regius Professor. . . . He would take pains to travel to the same conclusion by several roads in order to make it irresistible. Lines of argument, however different, converged inevitably upon the same point. The result was that one of the greater objects of the teacher was secured, and it became impossible for his scholars to misunderstand or to forget what he was teaching them. They left the lecture-room feeling that though other departments of knowledge might be affected by the process of the suns, the conclusions of the Regius Professor of History were established upon adamantine foundations. This note of dogmatism was in all Seeley's professorial utterances. Personally reserved and reverent, when he spoke *ex cathedra* it was with no uncertain sound. Even in its published form *The Expansion of England* begins with the words, 'It is a favourite maxim of mine,' and those who were accustomed to hear him lecture will recollect the autocratic phrase, 'according to me.' Yet this dogmatism appeared as the natural expression of an austere and dignified personality, and it was impossible that it should ever be resented. The professor had studied all the sources, and had arrived at certain results; why should he make a pretence that he did not himself believe in them?" This monarchical manner sat as well upon Seeley in the University of Cambridge as it sat upon Fustel de Coulanges in the University of Strasbourg.

Seeley did not confine himself merely to lecturing to large classes of undergraduates. He held weekly classes for the purpose of discussing political and historical questions with advanced students. At first they were real "conversational classes," though latterly they turned to a sort of monologue, in which the professor took his class through a regular course of political science which to him formed the backbone of history. According to Mr. Tanner "The subject was political science studied by way of discussion, and discussion under the reverential conditions that prevailed resolved itself into question and answer—Socrates exposing the folly of the Athenians. It was mainly an exercise in the definition and scientific use of terms. What is liberty? Various definitions of the term would be elicited from the class and subjected to analysis. The authors of them would be lured by a subtle cross-examination into themselves exposing their inconsistencies. Then the professor would take up his parable. He would first discuss the different senses in which the term had already been used in literature. . . . From an examination of inconsistent accounts the professor would proceed to the business of building up by a gradual process, and with the help of the class itself, a definition of his own. . . . It was not told us on authority as something to remember, but we assisted ourselves at the creation of it. Thus it became a possession to be enjoyed with a title analogous to the title of authorship. It took an hour to define liberty, but the leisurely process had the highest educational value."

As the income of his chair was small, and as his marriage brought his fellowship to a close, Seeley was compelled to add to his income by lecturing in London and the chief provincial towns of the north and of Scotland. These lectures added to his growing reputation, and he collected them in his *Lectures and Essays*, which he issued in 1870. The most noteworthy of these is his analysis of the fall of the Roman Empire, of Milton, and his inaugural lecture at Cambridge. Freeman coined the phrase that history is past politics and politics present history, but it is the phrase that accurately represents Seeley's mind. History was the school of statesmanship, and it was his business to make statesmen or, at any rate, to make statesmen possible. History was not for him the hero-worship it was for Carlyle, for hero-worship was a doctrine of despair of society, a sign of pessimism. If history was not the story of heroes, neither was it a series of biographies of men, however great. History was not the story of art or society, nor was it even the story of religion, though it was intimately bound up with religion. History was, in fact, the history of the State. Hence "our University must be a great seminary of politicians." For the statesman "the indispensable thing . . . is a knowledge of political economy and of history." "Politics are vulgar when they are not liberalised by history, and history fades into mere literature when it loses sight of its relation to practical politics." When the Historical Tripos was established at Cambridge he infused into it a strong political element which has persisted down to the appointment of Mr. Trevelyan to Seeley's chair. This element was so dominant that it led to a protest from Sir George Prothero who pleaded that history might be studied for its own sake. The atmosphere of Cambridge assisted Seeley's efforts, for the very Bidding Prayer, used in the University Church, asks that "there never may be wanting a supply of persons duly qualified to serve God both in Church and State, ye shall pray for a blessing on all places of religious and useful learning."

All history was at bottom political science to Seeley, and he naturally dwelt particularly on international history, the relation of State to State. In spite of his classical training he devoted most of his attention to the last three centuries, and in his lectures he steadily kept in view Great Britain as a member of the European States-system, a position which, he contended, many historians ignored. With them civil and constitutional history replaced the international attitude which Seeley invariably assumed. The World War revealed to us how much solid truth there is in this attitude which with our professor was part and parcel of his outlook. The three volumes of *The Cambridge History of British Foreign Policy* are a post-war production, and they are three volumes that Seeley would warmly have welcomed. He lectured on English foreign policy in the eighteenth century, international history from the sixteenth century, the wars of Louis XIV, and Napoleon, and in such lectures he was able to impress on the members of his class that broad-minded conception of our history which has been grievously neglected.

While still professor of Latin at the request of Oxford University Press he had begun an edition of the first decade of Livy, but all that ever saw light was the first book which appeared in 1871. In an introduction the editor shows his familiarity with German research and his admiration for German scholarship. He rejects the traditional history because of the conflicting nature of the different accounts, and he suggestively accounts for the growth of this traditional history. Fortunately for modern history, though less so for ancient, an anonymous benefactor increased the stipend of his chair, and the Cambridge University Press paid Seeley in advance for the book on the statesmanship of Stein on which he was engaged. The result was that he was able to give up his lecturing outside Cambridge and to devote himself wholly to his investigations into Prussian history. The three volumes on *The Life and Times of Stein* appeared in 1878, and with scholars, if not with the public, they at once gave their author the position of one who had made a real contribution to learning. Pertz had compiled a life of the great statesman which successfully hid his claims to greatness, claims which Seeley amply revealed till Lehmann's three volumes gave us his exhaustive—but not exhausting—biography. It is a tenable thesis that the best history of any land is generally the work of a foreigner, and the massive volumes of M. Halévy and of Seeley go far to attest its truth. Carlyle's *Frederick the*

Great would belong to the same class as those of M. Halévy and Seeley were it not so much disfigured by its hero-worship, a tendency to which Seeley never fell a victim.

Dedicated to Reinhold Pauli, and with a quotation from Goethe on the back of the title-page, *The Life and Times of Stein* is written in the spirit of Ranke, an historian whom Seeley heartily admired. The two photographs most conspicuous in his drawing-room were those of Ranke and Goethe, his chief masters among modern men. The place of the State is duly indicated amid the details of the history of Prussia from 1806 to 1822. Stein stands for the national State, Napoleon for the universal, and Seeley loves the former State as much as he loathes the latter. Dislike of the universal State is combined with detestation of Napoleon, whose genius he simply could not appreciate. Seeley abhorred his policy and he abhorred the motives behind his policy. A publicist like Bluntschli can date the modern era from the characteristically Prussian date of 1740 when Frederick the Great makes his bow on the European scene. For Seeley, however, the transformation of Prussia into a modern State dates from the epoch-making labours of Stein, whom he, following Hausser, compares to the "god-like" Turgot. In fact, there was a revolution with violence in France which had accomplished little. There was also a revolution without violence in Prussia which had accomplished much. The work of Stein stands out, and so too does the work of Fichte whose admirable *Addresses to the German People* stirred their patriotism to its very depths. The foundation of the University of Berlin, the educational tasks of the Humboldts, the austere personality of Niebuhr, and the reform of the army by Scharnhorst and Gneisenau all appear. There is no lack of insight into character, though it is plain that Seeley felt nowise attracted to the biographical aspect of his subject now or indeed at any other time. Ideas always fascinate him, and he is at his best in showing that there was a revolution in Germany from 1806 to 1813, and the root cause of this revolution lay in the opposition to Napoleon as a sheer despot. The battle of Jena inaugurates a new epoch in

European history, the epoch of nationalities. We learn that "The three principal wars of Prussia, since her great disaster (at Jena), those waged in 1813, in 1866, and in 1870, have a character of greatness such as no other wars have. They have, in a manner, reconciled the modern world to war, for they have exhibited it as a civilising agent and a kind of teacher of morals."

Seeley had pronounced history the school of statesmanship, and so it stood revealed in his biography of Stein. He put contemporary history above past history, a view which declares war on the position that to-day is not only the child of yesterday but of all the yesterdays. He valued past history, not as a storehouse of great deeds or great warnings, nor as a portrait gallery of great men, nor for its poetical and dramatic interest, but as a guide towards action in the present and judgment in the future. If not directly practical, it was apparently worthless. Naturally he included in its definition the old position of "philosophy teaching by examples," which agrees with the conception of Thucydides, though he carefully confined it to its bearing on the politics of to-day and to-morrow. The difficulty is that the professor who adopts Seeley's attitude may cross the thin line dividing the statesman from the politician. It was not a difficulty to him, though we wonder what Gladstone's feelings were when he found that the man he had appointed Regius Professor of History was opposing his Home Rule policy as stoutly as Arnold. To our professor this policy stood for the disintegration of the Empire, a perfectly tenable position, but to men in the eighties, especially if they were Liberals, it might well seem that Seeley professed not history but Conservative politics. Doubtless he would have asserted—what was perfectly true—that he approached the problem of Home Rule for Ireland purely as a man of science.

He was concerned with the explanation of historical phenomenon, and causes he must investigate. These causes, however, must be perfectly concrete. A succession of plagues, which means the failure of the human harvest, determines the downfall of the Roman Empire, and a succession of marriages the rise of the Hapsburgs.

Tocqueville assigns subtle suggestions for the fall of the French monarchy. "Well," according to Napoleon, "do you know the cause of the fall of the Bourbons? It was the battle of Rossbach." Seeley perceives the concreteness of this answer which entirely harmonises with his mode of thought. Yet he holds with Bury that history is a science, though we must not forget the remarkable confession of the latter that "I know for myself that on days when I am a determinist I look on history in one way, and on days when I am an indeterminist, in quite another." Proclaim as loudly as we please the doctrine that history is a science, yet every historian approaches its lock with his own bunch of keys. The main ward in Seeley's key was the outstanding position of the State.

Seeley had surveyed the Prussian State and he had surveyed the British State, in his lectures, but he had surveyed both from the international angle. This angle became of paramount worth when he set himself seriously to consider not merely Great Britain but the Greater Britain into which it had expanded. Obviously the Colonial Office was one thing in the days of Napoleon and Stein, and quite another in the eighties. In the former time the Mother Country told the colonies what they should do, and they for the most part obeyed. No doubt the American Colonies proved an awkward exception to this rule. It was becoming clear that the colonies were growing up into the position of daughter nations which must be consulted, and Seeley felt it incumbent upon him to examine the inner meaning of *The Expansion of England*, and he published his book in 1883. Few serious historical works have attained so speedy a success or have influenced so powerfully the destinies of our race. In fact, the only books comparable to it are the weighty writings of Admiral Mahan on Sea Power, and they approached Imperialism from one angle just as Seeley approached it from another. When Lord Rosebery offered Seeley the honour of knighthood he laid particular stress on the imperialistic strain of his works, and it was specially appropriate that the knighthood should be that of St. Michael and George, the order of our Empire. It is fitting that St. Paul's Cathedral, the parish church of the British Empire, should be the home of this order, uniting Church and State in the manner which gave Seeley such deep-seated pleasure.

The connection between the separation of the colonies from the Mother Country and the policy of *laissez-faire* is sufficiently obvious. If the cry was "Hands off business," it was easy to extend it to "Hands off the colonies." Besides, emancipation was the natural and indeed inevitable destiny of the colonies. From 1850 to 1870 such was the dominant feeling. The voice of Carlyle was the voice of a man crying in the wilderness. On the lines indicated by Cornewall Lewis, the Regius Professor of History at Oxford, Goldwin Smith, used his brilliant pen on behalf of those separatist tendencies which were in keeping with the Manchester School. Sir Charles Dilke shared the views of this School, and yet his *Greater Britain*, which described his travels around the Empire in 1866–67, was a book which played its due part in shattering separation. He dismisses with gross contempt such arguments for the retention of the colonies as that they give the Mother Country a monopoly of their trade, that they add to her strength, and that they afford an outlet for emigration. Like Cornewall Lewis and Goldwin Smith, he does not believe that they confer any prestige on England. He does, however, hold other positions in which he anticipated Seeley. He believes that there is a provinciality of mind in England, and the colonies tend to preserve his country from that insularity which he disliked quite as much as Seeley. Moreover, the union of the colonies with us brings us a step nearer to the virtual confederation of our race, a prospect as pleasant to him as it was to Seeley. There is much virtue in a good title, and the title of Dilke's book, *Greater Britain*, went some distance towards impressing his ideas on his readers. Nor must we forget that he applied his title to include the United States, believing with an American historian of our day, Mr. Beer, that its separation from England was temporary, due to temporary circumstances. In 1890 Dilke published his *Problems of Greater Britain*, and in it we see that the work of his early book was done. In the meantime Seeley had made his outstanding contribution in 1883, and Froude, by the magic of his style, had led his readers farther along the imperialistic path.

The end of the sixties marks the turn of the tide. The anti-Colonial school, headed by Bright, Cobden, and Goldwin Smith, witnessed the wane of their influence. For one thing, the weakness of the Manchester School was visible at home in the factory, and it was easy to conclude that because it was weak at home it was also weak abroad. The argument that trade follows the flag was urged repeatedly, and there is much virtue in repetition. "What I say three times is true," cried the queen in *Alice in Wonderland*, and what is said thirty times three must be true. The colonists, too, it was discovered with surprise, were attached to home, which even to those who had never left their own colony meant England. The laying of the cable across the Atlantic and the development of steam led to an ease in communication unknown before the Victorian age. Europe, moreover, was travelling towards the union of small states into larger. Cavour unified Italy in 1861 and Bismarck Germany in 1871. If there was union in Europe, why should there not be union among ourselves? The tide was flowing in this direction in the late sixties.

The Liberals were in power to 1874, and it was popularly believed that Gladstone was anxious to get rid of the colonies. In 1869 Lord Granville owned that he "would be exceedingly sorry to see England deprived of all her colonies, but England would never attempt to retain them by brute force." The next year Gladstone declared: "There ought to be nothing to preclude the hope when the growth of a colonial possession is such as to make separation from the mother country a natural and beneficial result, that that separation so far from being effected by violence and bloodshed might be the result of a peaceable and friendly transaction. Surely it is a great object to place, if possible, our colonial policy on such a footing, not for the purpose of bringing about a separation but of providing a guarantee that, if such a separation should occur, it should be in a friendly way." On the other hand, a Conservative statesman like Sir Stafford Northcote expressed in 1869 his belief that the bulk of the people were by no means in favour of dismemberment. The views of Carlyle and his disciple Ruskin were beginning to prevail, and this is attested by the agitation in 1869 and 1870 in favour of State-aided emigration of the unemployed to the Colonies. Ruskin holds up colonial expansion as a task worthier of England than materialism and mammon-worship, and his attitude unconsciously influenced not a few. Many had advocated Imperialism, but they had been men without power or position. Carlyle and Ruskin had both, and so too had Froude and W. E. Forster, the Liberal statesman. Froude appeals to Disraeli and the Conservative party, for he believed with Carlyle and Ruskin that the colonial question was one which the aristocracy is best fitted to solve. Froude, even more than Dilke, anticipates Seeley's ideas, for he urges the changes wrought by the annihilation of distance through steam and electricity, the vital necessity of considering the colonies as much integral parts of England as the English counties, and the belief that the future belongs to powers with a greater territorial extent than merely those of Western Europe. Schemes of federation begin to be propounded, and by the early seventies it is quite clear that the tide has very definitely turned.

Office lay two years ahead of Disraeli when in 1872 he bestowed his blessing on Imperialism. His speech then initiated that intimate connection between Conservatism and Imperialism which of itself was almost enough to drive his rival Gladstone even more completely into the opposite camp. In 1872 Disraeli announced that the three great objects of the Conservative party were the maintenance of English institutions, the preservation of the Empire, and social reform. On the second of these points he proclaimed that "If you look to the history of this country since the advent of Liberalism—forty years ago—you will find that there has been no effort so continuous, so subtle, supported by so much energy, and carried on with so much ability and acumen, as the attempts of Liberalism to effect the disintegration of the Empire of England. And, gentlemen, of all its efforts, this is the one which has been the nearest to success. Statesmen of the highest character, writers of the most distinguished ability, the most organised and efficient means, have been employed in this endeavour. It has been proved to all of us that we have lost money by our colonies. It has been shown with precise, with mathematical demonstration that there never was a jewel in the Crown of England that was so truly costly as the possession of India. How often has it been suggested that we should at once emancipate ourselves from this incubus! Well, that result was nearly accomplished. When those subtle views were adopted by the country under the plausible plea of granting self-government to the colonies, I confess that I myself thought that the tie was broken. Not that I for one object to self-government; I cannot conceive how our distant colonies can have their affairs administered except by self-government.

"But self-government in my opinion, when it was conceded, ought to have been conceded as part of a great policy of Imperial consolidation. It ought to have been accompanied by an Imperial tariff, by securities for the people of England for the enjoyment of the unappropriated lands which belonged to the Sovereign as their trustee, and by a military code which should have precisely defined the means and the responsibilities by which the colonies should be defended, and by which, if necessary, this country should call for aid from the colonies themselves. It ought, further, to have been accompanied by the institution of some representative council in the metropolis, which would have brought the colonies into constant and continuous relations with the Home Government. All this, however, was omitted because those who advised that policy—and I believe their convictions were sincere—looked upon the colonies of England, looked even upon the connexion with India, as a burden upon this country, viewing everything in financial aspect and totally passing by those moral and political considerations which made nations great, and by the influence of which alone men are distinguished from animals.

"Well, what has been the result of this attempt during the reign of Liberalism for the disintegration of the Empire. It has entirely failed. But how has it failed? Through the sympathy of the colonies for the Mother Country. They have decided that the Empire shall not be destroyed, and in my opinion no Minister in this country will do his duty who neglects any opportunity of reconstructing as much as possible our colonial Empire, and of responding to those distant sympathies which may become the source of incalculable strength and happiness to this land."

The statesman-novelist had spoken, but Tennyson had before him announced in his verse the glory of Imperialism, the unity of our race in its very variety. He regarded the Empire as a deep-rooted tree which sustains and nourishes its flourishing branches, while in turn the branches lend support and vitality to the stem. A patriot always, the diary of his wife attests that in 1870 he was growing interested in Imperial unity and the means of accomplishing it by federation. In 1872 in the epilogue to Queen Victoria which he added to the new edition of the *Idylls of the King* he spoke plainly his thought on the school of separatists:

And that true North,[1] whereof we lately heard,
A strain to shame us "keep you to yourselves;
So loyal is too costly! friends—your love
Is but a burden: loose the bond and go."
Is this the tone of empire? hers the faith
That made us rulers? this, indeed, her voice
And meaning, whom the roar of Hougoumont
Left mightiest of all peoples under heaven?
. . . . The loyal to their crown
Are loyal to their own far sons, who love
Our ocean-empire with her boundless homes,
For ever-broadening England, and her throne,
In our vast Orient, and one isle, one isle,
That knows not her own greatness: if she knows
And dreads it we are fall'n.

What the poet wrote in 1872 the statesman-novelist spoke in 1872, and the conjunction of the two bestowed a marked impetus on the flowing tide of Imperialism. Four years later in *Harold* Edward the Confessor dimly sees the Imperialistic vision rise before his eyes. In 1852 Tennyson had written *Hands all Round,* and he had written it in denunciation of France and a declaration of friendship with America. But in 1882 he transformed it:

To all the loyal hearts who long
To keep our English Empire whole!

[1] Canada.

To all our noble sons, the strong
New England of the Southern Pole!
To England under Indian skies.
To those dark millions of her realm!
To Canada whom we love and prize,
Whatever statesmen hold the helm,
Hands all round!
God the traitor's hope confound!
To this great name of England, drink my friends,
And all her glorious empire, round and round.

To all our statesmen so they be
True leaders of the land's desire!
To both our Houses, may these see
Beyond the borough and the shire!
We sailed wherever ship could sail.
We founded many a mighty state;
Pray God, our greatness may not fail
Thro' craven fears of being great.

The Exhibition of 1851 was meant as a contribution towards the peace of mankind. The Indian and Colonial Exhibition of 1886 was held the year before the first Jubilee of Queen Victoria, and was as imperialistic in tone as that of 1851 had been cosmopolitan. In 1851 the Manchester School had been dominant, but in 1886 there was none to do it reverence. Tennyson's feelings are again plain in the poem he wrote on Imperial unity in 1886:

Sharers of our glorious past,
Brothers, must we part at last?
Shall we not thro' good and ill
Cleave to one another still?
Britain's myriad voices call,
Sons be welded each and all,
Into one imperial whole,
One with Britain, heart and soul!
One life, one flag, one fleet, one throne!
Britons, hold your own.

The ground for *The Expansion of England* had been prepared, and it was distinctly *felix opportunitate vitae*. Its author had given it as a series of lectures in 1881–82, though according to Oscar Browning its leading idea was conceived at Pontresina in 1879. Mr. Tanner informs us that the romantic story of the growth of our empire was first told in a Cambridge lecture-room, and told in such a way as to stir the pulses of the dullest undergraduate among the audience. Seeley's conception of our empire was the conception of a poet as well as an historian. To him it was a "world-Venice":—

> The sea is in the broad, and narrow streets,
> Ebbing and flowing.

In history we may see with Ranke "*was eigentlich gewesen ist*," or with Lamprecht "*was eigentlich geworden ist*," or with C. F. Lehmann Haupt "*das Gewordenes als Werdendes verstehen*." With Seeley, as with the last historian, it was his duty to envisage the facts as a process. It grades with the Crocean doctrine of the reality of history as the reality of mind acting and always active.

There is no undue exaltation of our countrymen shown by Seeley. "When we look at Europe from a distance we shall be tempted by the ethnological fallacy, we shall attribute the political success of Englishmen exclusively to 'English political capacity,' or to the 'quiet perseverance,' the 'common-sense,' or the 'natural moderation' of the Anglo-Saxon in distinction to all other races. It is, no doubt, hard to reject the doctrine that we are better than other people when it presents itself in the form of a grand inductive law," and Seeley loved laws and generalisations. Nor is there a touch of the Jingo in the whole book. He does not for a single moment endorse the Nelsonian view that one Englishman can beat three Frenchmen and an incalculable number of browns and blacks, reds and yellows. In fact, from first page to last there is not a trace of hubris. In the magic hands of Macaulay the building of our Indian Empire by your Clives and your Warren Hastings is a romance which quickens the blood, but in the hands of Seeley our wonder is lessened though our interest in the process is correspondingly increased. He draws a sharp line between the white colonies and India, the possession of which, he declared, increases our responsibilities but not our power. Nor does he fail to point out that "Bigness is not necessarily greatness. If by remaining in the second rank of magnitude we can hold the first rank morally and intellectually, let us sacrifice mere material magnitude."

We had conquered and peopled half the world, declared

Seeley, in a fit of absence of mind, and even now we had not ceased to think of ourselves as a race inhabiting an island off the northern coasts of Europe. There was a provinciality of mind in our historians which must be altered. The key to the eighteenth century lies in the hundred years' war between France and England, and both countries fought for a prize of incalculable worth, the headship of the colonial world. The main struggle of England, so he envisaged it, from the time of Louis XIV to the time of Napoleon was for the possession of the New World. It was one of these large generalisations he loved. Unlike many who love generalisations, he worked out his with a wealth of convincing evidence. Seeley and Darwin had both been members of Christ's College, and it is singular to note the attraction generalisations possessed over the historian and the biologist, and no less singular is the meticulous attention each bestowed on these details which are vital to the driving home of any thesis with overpowering conviction. Sound requires atmosphere, and there was the atmosphere in the public mind in which the voice of *The Expansion of England* could be heard, and heard it was throughout the length and the breadth of the Empire. Within two years of its publication, eighty thousand copies were sold. In 1884 Lord Morley wrote a carping criticism of the *Expansion*, detecting danger in it. For to this Liberal Seeley appeared as one of the founders of a new school of Imperialism celebrated by poets like Henley and Kipling as well as by Tennyson, and by such Liberal statesmen as Lords Rosebery and Milner, Oxford and Haldane, Grey and Joseph Chamberlain. "Nobody expected Canadian regiments to storm the Redan side by side with the English soldiers. Nobody hopes to see Australians or New Zealanders volunteer for service out of their own country," so declared Lord Thring in 1865. "Australia has militiamen, but who supposes that they can be spared in any numbers worth considering for long campaigns, and this further loss and dislocation . . . ? Supposing for the sake of argument, that Australia were represented in the body that decided on war, though we may notice that war is often entered upon even in our own victorious days without preliminary consent from

Parliament, nobody believes that the presence of Australian representatives in the imperial assembly that voted the funds would reconcile their constituents at the other side of the globe to paying money for a war, say, for the defence of Afghanistan against Russia, or for the defence of Belgian neutrality," so declared Lord Morley in 1884. Let the battlefields of Europe and in particular the slopes of Gallipoli attest how far Australians were prepared to die in defence of Belgian neutrality. The truth is that Morley conceived, in the spirit of Manchester, that our empire was united, if it were united, by community of interest, whereas Seeley conceived it as bound together by community of race and religion.

In *The Expansion of England* he had inevitably been preoccupied with the hostility of Napoleon, and in 1885 he published his unsympathetic sketch of this amazing genius. Vandal holds that Napoleon codified the Revolution. "*Il ne crée pas le progrés, il l'enregistre et le fixe, le stabilise. En lui l'ardente matière se concrète sous forme solide, indestructible ; par lui en cette partie la Révolution se fait bronze et granit.*" This is a point of view Seeley could never reach. To him Napoleon was a man destitute of originality, whose one idea was to regain the old French Colonial Empire from England. He takes as low an estimate of Napoleon's statesmanship as Taine. The finest and the fullest survey of Napoleon's many-sided labours is to be found in Meredith's four *Odes in Contribution to the Song of French History,* and the gulf fixed between Seeley and him is unbridgeable. Seeley asks questions, and he also answers them. How far was Napoleon assisted by circumstances? How far were his ideas his own? How far did his peculiar character affect the destinies of France? He answers that Napoleon was shaped as well as favoured by circumstances; that if his armies were at first victorious, it was because they were inspired not by the personal idea of liberty which meant so much to Seeley, but by the greatness of France; that if we praise his institutions we must remember that he borrowed his despotism from the Jacobins, his Concordat and his nobility from the monarchy, his system of civil liberties from the men of 1789; and that, in a word, he was heir of the Revolution. The thesis of *The Expansion of England* is repeated. We learn that "the special and peculiar work of Napoleon is that colossal attempt to conquer England by conquering Europe" in his desire to regain the French colonies. Nor did he ever know when he came to the street called Stop. Bismarck always realised when he came to that street, but Napoleon seemed incapable of so doing. He should have held his hand at latest in 1805. Seeley points out that by the invasion of Spain and Portugal, Napoleon prepared the way for the independence of South America, and we are invited to consider this independence as the chief result of his career. *The Growth of British Policy,* which appeared in 1895, is as international a piece of work as any Seeley has given us. It was based on forty manuscript volumes of extracts copied from the Record Office and other sources, and this is but an example of the thoroughness with which he worked. In this book he carefully traces our place in the European States-system from the instability of its religious and dynastic phases to the relative stability of its commercial phase. Three great rulers accomplished this transition, and they are Elizabeth, Cromwell, and William III. The greatness of Elizabeth, lies not so much in what she did as in what she left undone, in "her wise parsimony of action." She refused to contract a foreign marriage, which might have made her realm tributary to Hapsburg or Valois; she refused to go to war with Spain for fear of kindling in a fresh blaze the embers of religious strife; she refused to ask Parliament for money; and, last of all, she refused to name her heir. Froude drew a discouraging picture of the woman: Seeley drew an encouraging one of the stateswoman, declaring "that if, in her own language, she was married to that generation of Englishmen, we may add, that she is the mother of all generations that have succeeded."

Gardiner and Seeley agree in pronouncing the policy of the Stuarts dynastic. Cromwell was the true heir of the Queen, for he pursued the same national policy. Our historian is as blind as Carlyle to the financial embarrassments which would have wrecked the Protector's policy—if he had lived longer. Seeley discerns and exposes his

Imperialism, and we are asked to consider Cromwell not as a mere parliamentarian or even as a party leader but as the man who united the British Isles, the Sulla or the Bismarck of our policy. If Elizabeth gave the falling Spanish monarchy a blow, Cromwell gave it the knock-out. Elizabeth had raised England to the position of the great Protestant power, the Stuarts had constantly lowered her from this position to which Cromwell restored her, and it was reserved for William III to complete the labours of his two great predecessors. In his brilliant analysis Seeley never for a moment ignores the share taken by religion. We are asked to note the difference between the monarchical and conservative tendencies of Lutheranism and the popular and rebellious ones of Calvinism. Nor are we allowed to gaze at William III as if the causes of the 1688 Revolution were largely English. Macaulay approaches it from this angle, whereas Seeley, with Klopp, approaches it from the angle of foreign policy. The dynastic connections of the Stuarts are all important, for it was his family connection that lent a French tinge to the policy of Charles II and to that of his brother. Had it not been for, say, their mother, they might have preferred the safety of Austrian amity which meant Romish amity as well. Seeley supplies the background to the Popish Plot of Oates, and sees it in the growth of French militarism under Louvois and the aggressions of French Roman Catholicism under Madame de Maintenon. For the figure of Oates we discern that of Louis XIV as he signs the Revocation of the Edict of Nantes in 1685. Our historian supplements these conclusions in his *Introduction to Political Science,* which Sidgwick saw through the press in 1896. There Seeley explains that the Restoration of 1660 looms larger in his eyes than the Revolution of 1688, and he proves his point conclusively. The Revolution did not establish Parliamentary Government, for the Long and Cavalier Parliaments had done so. Nor did it diminish the royal power, for the Restoration had done so. Seeley reveals the diplomatic unity of Europe as no one save Ranke has revealed it, and yet we feel with his survey of our foreign policy, as indeed we feel with Ranke's surveys of foreign policy, that too much is attributed to the designs of the diplomatist. Still, it is the glory of Seeley that he created foreign policy as a department of history. "While we have," he writes, "entered early into the conception of constitutional history, and have seen in this department first a Hallam and then a Stubbs, we have scarcely yet perceived that Constitutional History requires the History of Policy as its correlative." Such was the correlative he supplied.

His *Introduction to Political Science* is his last work, and in it we are conscious once more of the conception of the State as a great organic reality, the inspiration of the higher life which manifests itself in religion, in literature, and in a hundred other fashions. "Who can describe that which unites men? . . . Who can describe exhaustively the origin of civil society?" In his slender volume our author essays this task, and performs it suggestively. If he reviews the beginnings of the Roman State, he takes occasion to remind us that "The legends of Numa Pompilius and of Epimenides; the ancient priesthoods, more ancient commonly than purely secular institutions; many survivals, such as the Amphictyonic Confederation and the Comitia Curiata,—all these indications in Greek and Roman history, and others quite similar in the histories of other states, lead us to conclude that of states it may be said, as the poet has said of individuals, 'Heaven lies about them in their infancy'." He admits that the history of the last two centuries show that in Europe the State disentangles itself from the particular institution of the Christian religion with which it has been connected. Men speak of community of interest and community of race, but Seeley never forgets the community of religion.

The two books of Seeley's which manifest least unity, a quality generally pervading his writings, are *The Life and Times of Stein* and *The Introduction to Political Science*. *Obiter dicta* in the latter set one thinking, but it is certainly difficult to glean from it a coherent idea of political science. Seeley announces "I should like to meet the man who would venture to tell me plainly that it would have been safe to introduce toleration in the great European states earlier by a century than it was introduced; that, for instance, it might have been introduced into England under Elizabeth, or that Philip II might have introduced it into Spain, or the House of Valois into France." The reason of course is that an earlier introduction would have grievously hindered the unity of the State. Incidentally, there are two fine lectures on conceptions of liberty. The world of 1895 is revealed in the observation: "What would become of conversation among us if there were no Parliament? We should all be struck dumb. This is often explained by saying that the Englishman is a political animal, and King Louis Philippe used to say that the French would not have so many revolutions if they could learn the English habit of talking politics after dinner."

Seeley emphasises the importance of the Restoration of 1660, for he is well aware that every restoration is at bottom a revolution. This importance lies in the permanence of Parliament. He refuses, however, to date the decline of the influence of the monarch before the middle of the eighteenth century. Nor will he allow that George I and George II lose power because of the presence of Walpole unless you are prepared to argue that the monarchy declined, instead of gaining enormously in power, under Richelieu and Mazarin.

It was in keeping with the interests of Henry Sidgwick that he edited the last work of Seeley, his colleague at Cambridge. He himself was primarily a moral philosopher who followed Mill with the many qualifications suggested by his subtle mind. In 1891 his *Elements of Politics* appeared, and in 1903 posthumously his *Development of European Polity*. The two works usefully supplement each other, for the historical element present in Seeley's *Introduction* and indeed in the *Development of European Polity* is conspicuous by its absence in the *Elements of Politics*. In the last book we are continually aware that its author has a case in mind which is applicable to the argument he is unfolding, but as it is not precisely applicable he refrains from its use. In its first part he analyses the principles on which legislation should be based in a well-ordered community, and which should regulate the relations of the State with foreign powers. In the second part, which is almost of equal length with the first part, he describes the methods and instruments of government in a civilised country, detailing the duties of the legislature, the executive, and the judicature respectively. In both parts he seldom employs induction from the political experiences which history records, as Seeley was so prone to do. On the other hand, he usually employs the deductive method, though it is a deductive method not so much checked by experience as Mill's was. The opening words of *The Expansion of England* are: "It is a favourite maxim of mine that history, while it should be scientific in its method, should pursue a practical object." It is quite surprising in Sidgwick's book to note how often we meet with such sentences as "I am inclined to think," or "I am of opinion." Not that the writer was in the least egotistic, but it is the natural outcome of the fashion in which he sets down his conclusions. If Mill's *Representative Government* is apt to suggest the conditions of thought and legislation in 1861, Sidgwick's *Element of Politics* is also apt to suggest similar conditions thirty years later; yet if Darwin ever taught anything he certainly taught that there is no finality in politics.

With Mill we find that Sidgwick admits that the ultimate criterion of the goodness of law, and of the actions of government generally, is their tendency to increase the general happiness. This happiness is to include not only the human beings who are actually living but those who are to live hereafter. Happiness may be promoted by a policy of *laissez-faire* or one of paternal legislation. Apply we *laissez-faire* as rigidly as we please, yet we come to what he terms the individualistic minimum. We may try to limit the interference of the government in the ordinary affairs of life, yet such interference is inevitable in contracts, property, and the personal safety of each member of the community. Sidgwick sanctions the enforcement of contracts, the maintenance of property, the prevention of wrongdoing, and the appointment of a public prosecutor. He believes that the principle of individualism is applicable to adult males but not to children or in all cases to women. If Socialism means the substitution of common for private ownership, of governmental for private management of the instruments of production in all important departments of industry, he is opposed to it.

Sidgwick applies the Utilitarian test in foreign as in domestic politics. The achievement of the greatest happiness of the greatest number will normally be attained by a system of *laissez-faire*. According to him "the ultimate standard of right governmental conduct (is) the general happiness of all the human beings concerned, and not merely the interests of one particular State." Here we are travelling from the national to the international ideal. In practice, however, he is not slow to admit that his principle cannot be universally applied. In cases of "high-handed aggression"—we may instance Germany in Belgium in 1914—"where the assailant is clearly in the wrong I think that any powerful neighbouring State—even if its own interests are not directly threatened—ought to manifest a general readiness to co-operate in forcible suppression of the wrong. . . . Unless we suppose that the mere exercise of superior force is kept under some check by the fear of intervention of other States against palpable injustice, war between States decidedly unequal in strength will hardly retain its moral character at all. . . . And I think that co-operation to prevent wanton breaches of international peace is the best mode of preparing the way for the ultimate federation of civilised States, to which I look forward. But in the present state of civilisation it would, I think, be a mistake to try to prevent wars altogether in this way. We may hope to put down by it palpable and high-handed aggression, including perhaps the refusal to submit minor points to arbitration; but it is not applicable where there is a conflict of reasonable claims, too vague and doubtful to be clearly settled by general consent, and at the same time too serious to be submitted to arbitration."

If anyone takes the trouble—and the exquisite pleasure he will reap will be his reward—to read the biography of Henry Sidgwick, he will find a man close to our ideal of the thinker. Every sentence of his writing illustrates the familiar slowness and cautiousness in method combined with a sincerity of spirit so constant and so intense that the heart of it may almost be heard throbbing as the words are read.

Characteristic of Sidgwick, it is also, we like to think, the very quality which made him so typically English a thinker. Our love of truth is not intellectual, but moral; the virtue of the gentleman rather than that of the man of science. The typical Englishman among our men of letters is Samuel Johnson. But Johnson is not the typical English thinker, because he was not primarily a thinker at all. For the thinker all questions are open. For Johnson, however, many questions—the wisdom of the English constitution for instance, the wickedness of the Whigs—were closed. "*Quieta non movere,*" the policy of not questioning the actual system of things but making it somehow workable, may be the wisest for the majority of men. But it cannot be the method of the thinker or inquirer. And it was not the method of those who are most typical of English thought, especially Joseph Butler, the most typical of all. No one was so like Butler in the nineteenth century as Henry Sidgwick. There is of course more play of intellect in Sidgwick—a play which sometimes goes so far as real humour—and there is far less of that sorrowful earnestness as of a prophet calling to a perverse generation which is so frequent a note in Butler. But there is the same visible and audible sincerity, the same resolute and persistent will to give its fair weight to every objection and never to say one syllable more than the truth allows. Such a spirit in science, political and other, would change the tone and temper of the twentieth century, turning it into a brotherhood of men striving for the whole truth and turning aside from making this brotherhood into the sheerest of rivalry of nation with nation. The common aims and the common interests of all thinkers and scientists, whatever their nationality, ought to bind them into a commonwealth of culture.

REFERENCES

BODELSEN, C. A. *Studies in Mid-Victorian Imperialism.* (London, 1924.)

BRADLEY, F. H. *Mr. Sidgwick's Hedonism.* (London, 1877.)

DOYLE, J. A. *Essays on Various Subjects.* (London, 1911.)

GAZEAU, J. *L'Imperialisme anglais: son évolution. Carlyle, Seeley, Chamberlain.* (Paris, 1913.)

GOOCH, G. P. *History and Historians in the Nineteenth Century.* (London, 1913.)

GOOCH, G. P. *Germany and the French Revolution.* (London, 1920.)

HAYWARD, F. H. *The Ethical Philosophy of Sidgwick.* (London, 1901.)

MORLEY, Lord. *Miscellanies.* Vol. III. (London, 1892.)

REIN, A. *Sir John Robert Seeley. Eine Studie über den Historiker.* (Langensalza, 1912.)

RUGGIERO, G. DE. *La formazione dell'Impero britannico.* (Brescia, 1925.)

SIDGWICK, A., and SIDGWICK, E. M. *Henry Sidgwick.* (London, 1906.)

STEDFELD, G. F. *Ueber die naturalische Auffassung der Engländer... Eine Studie... zu dem Buche: "Ecce Homo" von einen ungennanten Verfasser.* (Berlin, 1869.)

"The Heart of the Empire." (London, 1901.) See Gooch's essay on "Imperialism."

Chapter VI.

BAGEHOT'S SEMINAL MIND

Walter Bagehot was one of the outstanding imaginative intellects of the nineteenth century. He was a man of wide culture, of fine sensibility, and of ready intellect. His criticism has been fragmentary, but it has been fruitful. The contributions he makes to thought, rich, ample, and suggestive as they are, have all the characteristics of his outwardly uneventful but inwardly eventful life. In literary criticism and in biography, in political philosophy and in political economy, he drove the shaft deep and gave us samples of the wealth of ore lying in their confines. Although he worked these mines at irregular intervals and passed rapidly from the one to the other, yet, by their leavening and quickening activity, he bestowed an amazing stimulus on thought. The reader felt entranced by the ideas unfolded before him, the subtlety of their suggestiveness, the wealth of their insight, and the far-reaching nature of this suggestiveness and insight. Bagehot was so full of views that it was a relief to him to part with some portion of them to others. After a dawn of unsurpassed promise and performance, he prematurely passed away at fifty-one, carrying with him an originality of outlook seldom equalled and never surpassed. His life had never been calm outwardly, saddened as it was by the madness of his mother to whom he was passionately attached. Nor had it been calm inwardly, for it was animated by deep-seated and never resting intellectual and imaginative forces. The strength of his character and unique individuality is evident in all his writings. His world was not our every-day working world, but one created out of his own inner consciousness. No other publicist, not even Maine or Seeley, has been an initial influence, a generative influence, on so many readers. Like Coleridge, he possessed the rare quality of fecundating thought in others, to whom his works came as a revelation. No English prose is nearer to that of Goethe in its power of sweeping the reader along, with or without his consent, till he is left wondering what it is that has seized hold of him. Beyond most, Bagehot opened to our mental gaze vast and varied fields of reflection, and invoked illuminating and thickly-crowded thoughts.

His rank is with Coleridge or Arnold, and as with them, we may draw a line between the active or practical genius and the passive or speculative. It is a distinction Bagehot had in mind when he laid down: "Certain minds, the moment we think of them, suggest to us the ideas of symmetry and proportion. Plato's name, for example, calls up at once the impression of something ordered, measured, and settled; it is the exact contrary of everything eccentric, immature, or undeveloped. The opinions of such a mind are often erroneous, and some of them may, from change of time, of intellectual data, or from chance, seem not to be quite worthy of it; but the mode in which those opinions are expressed, and (as far as we can make out) the mode in which they are framed, affect us, as we have said, with a sensation of symmetricalness. . . We may lay it down as the condition of a regular or symmetrical genius, that it should have the exact combination of powers suited to graceful and easy success in an exercise of mind great enough to task the whole intellectual nature.

On the other hand, men of irregular or unsymmetrical genius are eminent for some few peculiarities of mind, have possibly special defects on other sides of their intellectual nature, at any rate want what the scientific men of the present day would call the *definite proportion* of faculties and qualities suited to the exact work they have in hand."

Our critic is not for a single moment laying stress on an external attitude, for in the development of his thought he anticipates the point of view worked our by Jung in his *Psychological Types*. Bagehot proceeds: "Possibly it may be laid down that one of two elements is essential to a symmetrical mind. It is evident that such a mind must either apply itself to that which is theoretical or that which is practical, to the world of abstraction or to the world of objects and realities. In the former case the deductive understanding, which masters first principles, and makes deductions from them, the thin ether of the intellect—the 'mind itself by itself'—must evidently assume a great prominence. To attempt to comprehend principles without it is to try to swim without arms, or to fly without wings. Accordingly, in the mind of Plato, and in others like him, the abstract and deducing understanding fills a great place; the imagination seems a kind of eye to descry its data; the artistic instinct an arranging impulse, which sets in order its inferences and conclusions. On the other hand, if a symmetrical mind busy itself with the active side of human life, with the world of concrete men and real things, its principal quality will be a practical sagacity, which forms with ease a distinct view and just appreciation of all the mingled objects that the world presents—which allots to each its own place, and its intrinsic and appropriate rank."

Once he states principles Bagehot, unlike Sidgwick, is always anxious to apply them. To him Chaucer affords an example of the second type of regular genius, as he himself affords another, and then concludes: "Eminence in one or other of these marking faculties—either in the deductive abstract intellect or the practical sagacity—seems essential to the mental constitution of a symmetrical genius, at least in man. There are, after all, but two principal all-important spheres in human life—thought and action; and we can hardly conceive of a masculine mind symmetrically developed which did not evince its symmetry by an evident perfection in one or other of those pursuits, which did not leave the trace of its distinct reflection upon the one or other, or its large insight upon the other of them."

Shakespeare attests how difficult it is to mark off men into the type of practical seeing sagacity or of deductive practical intellect. Perhaps he has more of the former than of the latter, and perhaps we ought to say that all men of genius belong to both types, and that according as one or other type prevails, so we regard them. The practical seeing sagacity was Bagehot's and all his writings afford proof of it.

Walter Bagehot (1826–77) was born at Langport, an old-fashioned little town in the heart of Somersetshire. There he lived and there he died, and there he conducted his business as a banker. In the Middle Ages Langport was important enough to return two members to Parliament, until the burgesses petitioned Edward I to relieve them of the expense of paying their members. This economy and open indifference to patriotic pretensions pleased Bagehot, who used to boast of it to his friends as a note of true political sobriety The town then was a close corporation with a portreeve of its own, and a long sober constitutional history. The importance of Langport and its commercial prosperity are due to its being the first ford from the mouth of the river Parret. It is close to Glastonbury and Sedgemoor, and Chatham's old home, Burton Pynsent, is not far away. The great spaces of uninterrupted air and sky of the West Country always appealed to Bagehot, whose affections were closely bound up with them. Its delightful natural beauty turned his poetic longings to Wordsworth, and its innate conservatism tinged his political thought.

At Langport in 1772 Vincent Stuckey established the bank variously known at Stuckey's Bank, the Somersetshire Bank, and the Bristol and Somersetshire Bank. Thomas Watson Bagehot, Walter's father, married a niece of Vincent Stuckey, and thus became connected with this bank, becoming its vice-chairman. It was one of the earliest joint-stock banks in the country, and in time it had fourteen branches. Thirteen banks became amalgamated with it, and this meant it stood in a position of commanding importance in the West Country. Till it amalgamated with Parr's Bank in 1909, it enjoyed the privilege of issuing notes, and its note issue was, after the Bank of England, the largest in the country. Chatham was at least once driven to borrow from it. In 1909 its deposits amounted to nearly £7,000,000 and its capital to £1,751,000.

The Stuckeys and the Bagehots dominated Langport and its neighbourhood for a hundred and fifty years after the middle of the eighteenth century. Walter Bagehot used to explain his family by dwelling on the characteristics of these two families, and set out how each supplied traits wanting in the other. The Stuckey nature was shrewd and wilful, sociable and hospitable. The Bagehot nature was intellectual and cultured, dignified and retiring. Both natures blended in Walter Bagehot. His mother, Edith Stuckey, was as voracious a reader as her son was to be. The bond between mother and son was an unusually strong one, and the son in the days to come refused the office of Finance Minister to the Council of India in order to be with his mother during her attacks. There was this element of tragedy in his life which he felt intensely. "Every trouble in life is a joke compared to madness," so he used to think.

If the home was to be an anxious one, for the lad it was a home of love. Its atmosphere was steeped in religion—in a variety of outlook in religion, for his father was a spiritually-minded Unitarian and his mother a convinced Churchwoman. Burke enjoyed a similar diversity of views, and it promoted that width of outlook which was distinctly desirable on the part of one who was to be a thinker. A governess taught Walter at home till he entered Bristol College, where he remained from 1839 to 1842. On entering it he took up classics, mathematics, German and Hebrew, and his progress was as rapid as Seeley's. At Bristol lived Dr. Prichard, his mother's brother-in-law, who wrote a book on *Races of Men* which was to leave its mark on Bagehot's outlook on life. Over two hundred letters passed between the son and his father and mother while he was at school at Bristol. In these letters the father treats his son more as a younger brother, writing *inter alia* on Peel and communicating to his son his own ardour for Free Trade. Walter attended scientific lectures given by Dr. Carpenter, and at Clifton he met such men as Carpenter, Prichard, and Symonds, father of the historian of the Renaissance. The conversation of these men set the lad thinking about many subjects that never swim into the ken of the average public school boy. The races of mankind, their physical history, the additions to such subjects then being made by the traveller—these came his way before he was sixteen, and subconsciously influenced his mind. Seeds were sown in it which were destined to bear fruit in his writings.

T. W. Bagehot objected to the doctrinal tests then in force in the two ancient universities, and accordingly his son entered University College, London, in 1842. There he had the rare good fortune to meet as a fellow undergraduate Richard Holt Hutton, and the two became friends for life. In an article on Oxford reform Bagehot wrote out of his undergraduate days: "So, too, in youth, the real plastic energy is not in tutors, or lectures, or in books 'got up,' but in Wordsworth and Shelley, in the books that all read because all like; in what all talk of because all are interested; in the argumentative walk or disputatious lounge; in the impact of young thought upon young thought, of hot thought on hot thought; in mirth and refutation, in ridicule and laughter; for these are the free play of the natural mind, and these cannot be got without a college." Undergraduates are influenced by other undergraduates rather than by their professors, and Bagehot and Hutton exercised a marked power each on the other. They both delighted in discussing their subjects of study, and Hutton relates how on one occasion they "wandered up and down Regent Street for something like two hours in the vain attempt to find Oxford Street," so absorbed were they in debating "whether the so-called logical principle of identity (A is A) was entitled to rank as a law of thought or only as a postulate of language." The nature of the friendship between Bagehot and Hutton was like that between Carlyle and Mill while it lasted. Bagehot, like Carlyle, grasped truth with the intuition of genius while Hutton, like Mill, worked his way to it with thorough thought. The bond between the two men was intellectual, and when the intellectual bond was strengthened by the tie of religion, it was unbreakable. After Bagehot's death Hutton wrote in a letter to the sister-in-law of his dearest friend: "You remember that sonnet of Wordsworth's Bagehot was so fond of, beginning—

> Surprised with joy, impatient as the wind
> I turned to share my rapture—oh! with whom?

It often comes back upon me now when I have something I want to talk to him about, and I remember I shall never hear his step coming up my stairs again."

Bagehot grew up in a religious atmosphere, and his religion meant everything to him. He used to say when it was a question of abolishing religious teaching in schools: "It is one thing to have a dogmatic religion implanted in children from their babyhood, however less dogmatic their views may become as they grow up to be men and women, and quite another to bring up children without any religious creed at all. We have yet to see what a nation would be like whose men and women had never had any religious training whatever given to them as children." It was a point of view Matthew Arnold would urge, and it is a point of view by no means out-of-date. In his essay on Bishop Butler Bagehot writes: "In every step of religious argument we require the assumption, the belief, the faith, if the word is better, in an absolutely *perfect* Being; in and by whom we are, who is omnipotent as well as most holy; who moves on the face of the whole world, and ruleth all things by the word of His power. If we grant this, the difficulty of the opposition between what is here called the natural and the supernatural religion is removed; and without granting it, that difficulty is perhaps insuperable. It follows from the very idea and definition of an infinitely perfect Being, that He is within us as well as without us—ruling the clouds of the air, and the fishes of the sea, as well as the fears and thoughts of men; smiling through the smile of nature as well as warning with the pain of conscience—'*sine qualitate, bonum; sine quantitate, magnum; sine indigentia, creatorem; sine situ, praesidentem; sine habitu, omnia continentem; sine loco, ubique totum; sine tempore, sempiterum; sine ulla sui mutatione, mutabilia facientem, nihilque patientem.*' If we assume this, life is simple; without this, all is dark."

Hutton tells us that within the last two or three years of his life, Bagehot spoke on one occasion of the Trinitarian doctrine as probably the best account human reason could render of the mystery of the self-existent mind. Nor is it possible to divorce his religious from his political thought. The union of the two peeps out in many ways. His wife thought it required great grace to be a nun or a monk. To what other person in the world—except Bagehot—would it occur that one way to meet this argument was to appeal to the early Utilitarian system? He writes: "If it means simply retiring from the world and living a life of contemplation in one place, I do not think there are many things easier and pleasanter. It is completely realising the *laissez-faire* system of grappling with the evils of the world. Every one knows on a small scale how easy that is. That bodily penance is considered by most men easier than the everyday work of duty is quite evident from the history of all religions. Then Catholics would say that to live a life of prayer was difficult. But it is surely not so difficult as to live in the world a life of prayer and labour also."

Bagehot was a personal author who reveals not a little of his character to the discerning reader. Is anyone more impersonal than Shakespeare? Yet Bagehot boldly asserts that it is quite possible to know our greatest dramatist. He points out that "to a great experience one thing is essential, an experiencing nature. It is not enough to have opportunity, it is essential to feel it. Some occasions come to all men; but to many they are of little use, and to some they are none." He instances Guizot who had not this experiencing nature, and he also instances Macaulay, though how he could instance the historian, who profited so much by his stay in India, we cannot divine. He tells us that Macaulay's "mind shows no trace of change. What he is. he was; and what he was, he is. He early attained a high development; but he has not increased it since; years have come, but they have whispered little; as was said of the second Pitt, 'He never grew, he was cast.' The volume of speeches which he has published place the proof of this in every man's hand. His first speeches are as good as his last, his last scarcely richer than his first. He came into public life at an exciting season; he shared of course in that excitement, and the same excitement still quivers in his mind. He delivered marvellous rhetorical exercises on the Reform Bill when it passed; he speaks of it with rhetorical interest even now. He is still the man of '32. From that era he looks on the past."

Bagehot's own nature was essentially experiencing. He enjoyed the rare good fortune of constant intercourse with Hutton, a man whose nature was so different from his own, each in fact supplying the deficiencies of the other. Nor is it possible to dissociate the effects of his mother's illnesses on the growth of his character. In his biography his sister-in-law, Mrs. Russell Barrington, emphasises this point. She thinks that his sorrow tended to ripen all that was distinguished in his character, and stimulated, rather than suppressed, his intellectual forces. The necessity of having to face the inevitable, without loophole for hope, to acquiesce in the necessity without flinching; to learn through experience the deeper secrets of life in which mysteries are so closely interwoven with realities, was the very training which matured exceptional qualities in a finely wrought nature. Among the fruits of this experience, she believes, were a dispassionate equilibrium of judgment, a wide sympathy with, and tolerance towards, those who are maimed by any of the various evils which befall humanity; above all, a diffidence in asserting that any conclusive methods, any hard or fast theories, can rectify such evils. The intellectual interests of the young man were aroused, and so too was his emotional existence, which his constant care of his mother stirred to its very depths.

At the age of twenty-one he experienced a phase of morbidity and melancholy for which he found the exact description in a passage from Keats's Preface to *Endymion*, which runs thus: "The imagination of a boy is healthy, and the mature imagination of a man is healthy; but there is a space of life between, in which the soul is in a ferment, the character undecided, the way of life uncertain, the ambition thick-sided." What he had been taught to think and what he had taught himself he had come to feel, and his feelings turned his thoughts into vigorous activity. College regulations obliged him to study the Greek philosophers, together with Hume, Kant, J. S. Mill, and Sir William Hamilton. But he was never a man to be confined within narrow regulations. He read Shakespeare, Keats, Shelley, Wordsworth, Coleridge, Martineau, and Newman, but, above all, Wordsworth and Newman. Nor could he bear the attitude of the *Edinburgh Review* to the romanticism or the mysticism of Coleridge and Wordsworth, Scott and Shelley. Bagehot, as befits a Liberal, praises its Whig views, but the praise gradually changes to blame. "A clear, precise, discriminating intellect shrinks at once from the symbolic, the unbounded, the indefinite. *The misfortune is that mysticism is true.* There are certainly kinds of truths, borne in, as it were, instinctively on the human intellect, most influential on the character and the heart, yet hardly capable of stringent statement, difficult to limit by an elaborate definition. Their course is shadowy; the mind seems rather to have seen than to see them, more to feel after than definitely apprehend them. They commonly involve an infinite element, which, of course, cannot be stated precisely, or else a first principle —an original tendency—of our intellectual constitution, which it is impossible not to feel, and yet which it is hard to extricate in terms and words. Of this latter kind is what has been called the religion of nature, or, most exactly, perhaps, the religion of the imagination. This is an interpretation of the world. According to it the beauty of the universe has a meaning, its grandeur a soul, its sublimity an expression. As we gaze on the faces of those whom we love . . . as a charm and a thrill seem to run along the tone of a voice, to haunt the mind with a mere word; so in nature the mystical sense finds a motion in the mountain, a power in the waves, and a meaning in the long white line of the shore, and a thought in the blue of heaven, an unbounded being in the vast, void air, and

> Wakeful watchings in the pointed stars.

There is a philosophy in this which might be explained, if explaining were to our purpose. But be this as it may, it is certain that Mr. Wordsworth preached this kind of religion and that Lord Jeffrey did not believe a word of it. His cool, sharp, collected mind revolted from its mysticism; his detective intelligence was absorbed in its apparent fallaciousness; his light humour made sport with the sublimities of the preacher; his love of perspicuity was vexed by its indefiniteness; the precise philosopher was amazed by its mystic unintelligibility. Yet we do not mean that in this great literary feud either of the combatants had all the right or gained all the victory. The world has given judgment. Both Mr. Wordsworth and Lord Jeffrey have received their reward. The one had his own generation, the laughter of men, the applause of drawing-rooms, the concurrence of the crowd; the other a succeeding age, the fond enthusiasm of secret students, the lonely rapture of lonely minds. And each has received according to his kind. If all cultivated men speak differently because of the existence of Wordsworth and Coleridge, if not a thoughtful English book has appeared for forty years without some trace for good or evil of their influence, if sermon-writers subsist upon their thoughts, if 'sacred poets' thrive by translating their weaker portion into the speech of women, if, when all this is over, some sufficient part of their writing will ever be fitting food for wild musing and solitary meditation, surely this is because they possessed the inner nature—'an intense and glowing mind,' 'the vision and the faculty divine.' But if, perchance, in their weaker moments the great authors of the *Lyrical Ballads* did ever imagine that the world was to pause because of their verses, that *Peter Bell* would be popular in drawing-rooms, that *Christabel* would be perused in the City, that people of fashion would make a handbook of the *Excursion,* it was well for them to be told at once that this was not so. Nature ingeniously prepared a shrill, artificial voice, which spoke in season and out of season, enough, and more than enough, what will ever be the idea of the cities of the plain concerning those who live alone among the mountains; of the frivolous concerning the grave; of the gregarious concerning the recluse; of those who laugh concerning those who laugh not; of the common concerning the uncommon; of those who lend on usury concerning those who lend not; the notion of the world of those whom it will not reckon among the righteous. It said, 'This won't do!' And so in all time will the lovers of polished Liberalism speak concerning the intense and lonely prophet."

The private misfortune of Bagehot turned out to be of advantage to the public. Only a man who had experienced much could write as he wrote. Newman's *Parochial Sermons* he seems to have had by heart, and two of them, *The Invisible World* and the *Greatness and Littleness of Human Life,* are constantly in his thoughts. He may write about the state of the money-market or about the growth of the British constitution, yet ever

> From the soul's subterranean depths upborne,
> As from an infinitely distant land,
> Come airs and floating echoes

of eternity. Yet he shrinks from Newman, and he shrinks from him for reasons all his own. "To finish about Newman, I do not think his want of self-consciousness can be the reason for his wanting precise moral convictions. Arnold, who was not self-conscious, had very precise notions of duty. I think in Newman's case the reason is that his intellect is more subtle than his sense in discriminating: he can conceive finer shades of feeling and motive than his conscience will confidently estimate."

That there was an ascetic element in Bagehot's nature is undoubted, but it is sometimes forgotten that asceticism is quite compatible with pleasure, and indeed makes for the deeper enjoyment of pleasure. In his essay on Macaulay, he sympathises with the old English Cavalier, and there was an element of it in himself. "Talk of the ways of spreading a wholesome Conservatism throughout the country . . . as far as communicating and establishing your creed is concerned, try a little pleasure. The way to keep up old customs is to enjoy old customs; the way to be satisfied with the present state of things is to enjoy that state of things. Over the 'Cavalier' mind this world passes with a thrill of delight; there is an exultation in a daily event, zest in the 'regular thing,' joy at an old feast." Nor can we omit to mention the fact that he was as devoted to the chase as any Cavalier could be: hunting was the only sport he really cared for. In his early writings there is the elasticity of youth combined with the feeling of the fresh wind of the field, as though he had been thinking in the saddle, for he characteristically uttered the remark, "There is no time for quiet reflection like the intervals of the hunt."

Bagehot took his B.A. degree with the mathematical scholarship in 1846 in the university of London, and his M.A. degree in 1848 with the gold medal in mental and moral philosophy and political economy. Then he began to read law in the chambers, first, of Charles Hall, afterwards Vice-Chancellor Sir Charles Hall, and Quain, afterwards Mr. Justice Quain. He liked both men personally, but he did not like law with the exception of the art of special pleading. He always professed to regret the abolition of special pleas. "The only thing I ever really knew," he once wrote, "was special pleading, and the moment I had learnt that, the law reformers botched and abolished it." He was called to the bar in the summer of 1852, nevertheless he had made up his mind to abandon law and join his father in his shipowning and banking business at Langport.

Arthur Clough had become Principal of University Hall, London, and Bagehot was much in his society from 1848 to 1850. Hutton records his opinion that Clough was "the man who had, I think, a greater intellectual fascination for Walter Bagehot than any of his contemporaries." The chief element in this fascination for Bagehot was that he had as a poet rediscovered, or at least realised, as few before him, the enormous difficulty in finding truth. The subtle scepticism of Clough was obvious, yet Bagehot's faith combined with his experience of life enabled him to resist it. The influence of Arnold and Newman wrought untold harm upon Clough, so Bagehot judged. Clough was "one of Arnold's favourite pupils because he gave heed so much to Arnold's teaching; and exactly because he gave heed to it was it bad for him. He required quite another sort of teaching: to be told to take things easily; not to try to be wise overmuch; to be 'something beside critical'; to go on living quietly and obviously and see what truth would come to him. Mr. Clough had to his latest years what may be noticed in others of Arnold's disciples—a fatigued way of looking at great subjects. It seemed as if he had been put into them before his time, had seen through them, heard all which could be said about them, had been bored by them, and had come to want something else."

Arnold had flattered himself that he was a principal opponent of Newman, yet Bagehot shows how the teaching the poet had received at Rugby, by removing the "happy apathy" of the common public school boy, exposed him all the more sensitively to Newman. "The doctrinal teaching which Arnold impressed on the youth about him was one personal to Arnold himself, which arose out of the peculiarities of his own character, which can only be explained by them. As soon as an inquisitive mind was thrown into a new intellectual atmosphere, and was obliged to naturalise itself in it, to consider the creed it had learned with reference to the facts which it encountered and met, much of that creed must fade away."

Bagehot had been abroad in 1844 when he warmly admired the paintings of Rubens, The aesthetic side of his nature was not so highly developed as the intellectual, and he made a compact with his sister-in-law, Mrs. Russell Barrington, that he should give her intellectual and she give him artistic enjoyment. The very year of his death he said to her, "You must take me to hear Joachim; I think I might understand Joachim." Just before the end he also said, "You must take me to see Watts—I should like to see the outside of the person who does these things." He was in the habit of attending George Eliot's gatherings on Sunday afternoons at The Priory, St. John's Wood. He recognised the value of William Morris's art, and he had his London house furnished and decorated by his firm.

Before settling down at Langport he spent some months in Paris, and was living there at the time of the *coup d'état* in December, 1851. He wrote a set of letters for *The Inquirer* in the course of which he stoutly supported the military violence of Napoleon III, eulogised his character and that of the Roman Catholic Church, attacked the freedom of the press, and, above all, maintained that France was wholly unfit for parliamentary government. At all costs the political fabric must be kept together, and to keep it together Bagehot was willing to sacrifice progress and good government. The French are quick-witted and vivacious, the English slow-witted and stupid, and accordingly free institutions cease to flourish with the former whereas they flourish with the latter. He insists that "the first duty of society is the preservation of society. By the sound work, of old-fashioned generations, by the singular painstaking of the slumberers in churchyards, by all dull care, by stupid industry, a certain social fabric somehow exists; people contrive to go out to their work, and to find work to employ them actually until the evening; body and soul are kept together,—and this is what mankind have to show for their six thousand days of toil and trouble." You cannot improve the living by political change, so he maintains, unless you contrive to regulate change to a slow and sober pace, quiet, almost insensible, like that of the growth of grain. If you cannot do that, perhaps it is better to hold steadily to the old present ways of life, under a strong, unshaken, unquestioned government, capable of guidance and command. With him, as with Burke, politics are viewed in the light of time and place, and time and place must be related to national character. For, despite all the nonsense talked about national character, Bagehot retains unshaken his belief in it. "I need not prove to you," he goes on, "nor need I try your patience with a likeness of it: I have only to examine whether it be a fit basis for natural freedom. I fear you will laugh when I tell you what I conceive to be about the most essential mental quality for a free people whose liberty is to be progressive, permanent, and on a large scale: it is much *stupidity*."

There is nothing paradoxical in this verdict in favour of stupidity, as Bagehot explains it. The susceptibilities of his countrymen might have been wounded had he not with lively art compared their character with the Roman, "the great political people of history. Now is not a certain dullness their most visible characteristic? What is the history of their speculative mind? A blank. What their literature? A copy. They have not left a single discovery in any abstract science, not a single perfect or well-formed work of high imagination. The Greeks, the perfection of human and accomplished genius, bequeathed to mankind the ideal forms of self-idolising art; the Romans imitated and admired. The Greeks explained the laws of nature; the Romans wondered and despised. The Greeks invented a system of numerals second only to that now in use; the Romans counted to the end of their days with the clumsy apparatus which we still call by their name. The Greeks made a capital and scientific calendar; the Romans began their month when the Pontifex Maximus happened to spy out the new moon. Throughout Latin literature this is the perpetual puzzle—Why are we free and they slaves?—We praetors and they barbers? Why do the stupid people always win and the clever people always lose? I need not say that in real sound stupidity the English are unrivalled. You'll have more wit, and better wit, in an Irish street-row than would keep Westminster Hall in humour for five weeks. . . . These valuable truths are no discoveries of mine. They are familiar enough to people whose business it is to know them. Hear what a douce and aged attorney says of your peculiarly promising barrister. 'Sharp? Oh! yes, yes: he's too sharp by half. He isn't *safe,* not a minute, isn't that young man.' 'What style, sir,' asked of an East India Director some youthful aspirant for literary renown, 'is most to be preferred in the composition of official despaches?' 'My good fellow,' responded the ruler of Hindostan, 'the style *as we* like, is the Humdrum.'"

In 1852 Bagehot definitely relinquished the bar and joined the staff of Stuckey's Bank. His account of the *coup d'état* enabled him to realise the extent of the ideas welling up in his mind. For he spawned ideas and wrote on Hartley Coleridge, Shakespeare—the man, Cowper, the first Edinburgh reviewers, Shelley, Macaulay, Béranger, and the like. These articles were generally published in the *National Review,* though some appeared in the *Prospective Review.* In 1858 he gathered them into a volume, and published them with the title *Estimates of some Englishmen and Scotchmen,* and it met with as little success as M. Arnold's poetry. This is really surprising, as it contains some of the best work he ever did. Was the title against the book? We can hardly think this. Besides, the essays had already appeared in two reviews, and surely the public that first read them would care to possess them in book form. In the days to come it met with success when republished as *Literary Studies.* To the student of literature these essays reveal the presence of a creative mind, of a man who looks at authors in his own way, and communicates his views of them in a fashion impossible to mistake for that of any other man. The self-confidence he displayed in banking arose out of his intuitive power of seizing the main issues of a question.

The self-confidence he displayed in criticism arose out of the same source. Nor was he in the least eccentric in his judgments in banking or in literature. Of Lord Stanhope he wrote admirably that he had "the cautious scepticism of true common sense," and shrank from "wonderful novelties." This was his own frame of mind. His excursive imagination and his vivid humour strengthened—not weakened—his sound judgment. An original mind like his could play with paradox, but his good sense confined this play within rigid limits. Yet, as Aristotle says of Plato, he made a "new cut" into things, piercing to their very marrow. Such essays as those on Hartley Coleridge, Bishop Butler, and the first Edinburgh reviewers reveal this "new cut" into politics as well as into literature. Indeed we are by no means sure that they do not give us his ultimate creed more clearly than any of his formal writings.

The article on Butler naturally discusses religion, and yet by a transition peculiar to the author we feel that in the background of the Bishop's thought there is his attitude to the State as well as to the Church. If Bagehot reveals the man, he also reveals the stateman. If he reveals the weakness of Hartley Coleridge, he does so out of his own emotional experience, realising full well that life is ever a tragedy to those who feel. If he reveals Shakespeare as a man, he also combines with this revelation his own attitude to democracy. No one who merely knows *The English Constitution* knows to the full the attitude of its author to democracy, and in his article on Shakespeare, of all places, he elects to give it to us. He makes out the dramatist's political views, and he makes them out from the historical plays. Shakespeare, we learn, accepted, like everybody else, the constitution of his country. The Wars of the Roses had exposed the weaknesses incident to a controverted succession and a selfish aristocracy. "Yet they had not repelled, and had barely disconcerted, our conservative ancestors. They had not become Jacobins; they did not concur—and history, except in Shakespeare, hardly does justice to them—in Jack Cade's notion that the laws should come out of his mouth, or that the commonwealth was to be reformed by interlocutors" in act four, scene two of *King*

Henry VI. Bagehot proceeds: "An audience which, *bona fide*, entered into the merit of this scene, would never believe in everybody's suffrage. They would know that there is such a thing as nonsense, and when a man has once attained to that deep conception, you may be sure of him ever after. And though it would be absurd to say that Shakespeare originated this idea, or that the disbelief in simple democracy is owing to his teaching or suggestions, yet it may, nevertheless, be truly said, that he shared the peculiar knowledge of men—and also possessed the peculiar constitution of mind—which engenders this effect. The author of *Coriolanus* never believed in a mob, and did something towards preventing anybody else from doing so. But this political idea was not exactly the strongest in Shakespeare's mind. We think he had two other stronger, or as strong. First, the feeling of loyalty to the ancient polity of this country—not because it was good, but because it existed. In his time, people thought no more of the origin of monarchy than they did of the origin of the Mendip Hills. The one had always been there, and so had the other. God (such was the common notion) had made both, and one as much as the other. Everywhere, in that age, the common modes of political speech assumed the existence of certain utterly national institutions, and would have been worthless and nonsensical except on that assumption. This national habit appears as it ought to appear in our national dramatist. A great divine tells us that the Thirty-nine Articles are 'forms of thought'; inevitable conditions of the religious understanding; in politics, 'kings, lords, and commons' are, no doubt, 'forms of thought,' to the great majority of Englishmen; in these they live, and beyond these they never move. You can't reason on the removal (such is the notion) of the English Channel, nor St. George's Channel, nor can you of the English Constitution, in like manner. It is to most of us, and to the happiest of us, a thing immutable, and such, no doubt, it was to Shakespeare, which, if any one would have proved, let him refer at random to any page of the historical English plays."

The second peculiar tenet which we ascribe to his political creed, is a disbelief in the middle classes. We fear he had "no opinion of traders." Bagehot then points out in his own fashion why Shakespeare entertained so little belief in the trading class and so much belief in a tempered and qualified polity.

The love of literature is evident in his estimate of Shakespeare: so too is his love of politics. Throughout life, books brought a healing balm to him. He never smoked, and when, as a youth, a friend told him that his cigars cost him £30 a year, Bagehot exclaimed, "But imagine how many books that would buy!" Still, he hunted and his hunters cost a good deal. The hum of hunting—as well as the hum of business—sounds through all his writings. He speaks of business in the serious way a banker would, but this seriousness in his case is distinctly tempered with amusement. "An inexperiencing mind," he called Macaulay's: his own was certainly an experiencing mind drawing on everything in which he was interested—and in what was he not interested? Science was not outside his ken, and he at once grasped the political implications of Darwin's *Origin of Species*.

A banker and a shipowner, Bagehot inevitably attached a high place to property. To him it was a test of character, political and other. "If it has been inherited, it guarantees education; if acquired, it guarantees ability." He was a Liberal, but he was as detached in his Liberalism as Arnold. He confessed that he was "between sizes in politics," a confession Lord Acton was also to make. He stood as a Liberal for Bridgwater in 1866, and when he lost the election he consoled himself with the reflection that parliamentary work would not have suited him. Of this we are by no means sure, for he certainly would not have given up to any party—Liberal or other—what was meant for mankind. We question if the wear and tear of the House of Commons would have proved too much for his sensitive organisation, for the wear and tear of business did not prove too much for it.

Like Burke, he was wedded to the past, and its influence is always present in his writings. He would have allowed more changes in the constitution than our greatest political philosopher, yet his feeling was to effect change slowly and after long discussion. He would allow public opinion to ripen on all alteration. "And the reason is, that all important English institutions are the relics of a long past; that they have undergone many transformations; that like old houses which have been altered many times, they are full both of conveniences and inconveniences which at first sight would not be imagined. Very often a rash alterer would pull down the very part which makes them habitable, to cure a minor evil or improve a defective outline." Here we feel the accent of the true conservative. Conservatism wears many forms. Consider, for instance, the conservatism of Mill and Tocqueville, Cornewall Lewis and Bagehot. Mill was a conservative only so far as conservatism was forced upon a mind essentially radical and even revolutionary, imbued with a profound faith in abstract principles leading far beyond universal suffrage to Socialism. He was so forced by the danger which he foresaw to individual liberty and unfettered intellectual freedom from the ascendancy of mere numbers. Upon this point he agreed with Tocqueville, though upon nearly every other their views were as opposite as their character and experience. Tocqueville's conservatism sprang from his wide observation of Europe and America and from his bitter disappointment with France. The conservatism of Cornewall Lewis was that of a profoundly sceptical instinct, of practical cautious incredulity. Bagehot's was the conservatism of middle-class thought and business experience.

He saw that we deify the king in sentiment as we once deified him in doctrine. It is of course an illusion, but one that "has been, and still is, of incalculable benefit to the human race." The "theatrical show of society" impresses the popular imagination; and the "climax of the play is the Queen." There is an ingrained conservatism present in the bulk of the people, and with this conservatism they combine a deference to society which is of the last importance. An incident that happened to him during the Crimean War he narrated with great gusto to Hutton. "The Somersetshire view," he wrote, "of the chance of bringing the war to successful conclusion is as follows:—Countryman: 'How old, zir, be the Zar?'—Myself: 'About sixty-three.'—

Countryman: 'Well, now, I can't think however they be to take he. They do tell I that Rooshia is a very big place, and if he doo goo right into the middle of 'n, you could not take he, not nohow.' I talked till the train came (it was at a station), and endeavoured to show how the war might be finished without capturing the Czar, but I fear without effect. At last he said, 'Well, zir, I hope, *as you do say, zir*, we shall take he,' as I got into the carriage." Bagehot realised quite as much as Newman that man is more moved by a person than by a principle, and he saw the necessity of this as vividly as Seeley. The tendency to deify the king is still present, and perhaps present all the more because he is familiar to the people in a hundred ways his ancestors never were. Means of communication enable him to move all over England, his face is to be seen in the topical budget of the cinema, and the pictorial papers illustrate his doings as well as his goings. In all these ways he is a living person to his subjects as even Queen Victoria never was, and while there are many sources of the loyalty to the Crown we feel that the realisation of his personality is among them. The Jubilees of 1887 and 1897 attest the place in the affections of her subjects Queen Victoria won, and the loyalty she won has been maintained and even increased by her son and her grandson. The British Empire is held together to-day by the active principle of loyalty to a common sovereign. The pageantry of procession on the part of royalty also plays its part. "Why," Bagehot would say, "should they not give the poor the indulgence of enjoying the show?" That they enjoy the show has been repeatedly proved, and this enjoyment of the show forms a feature of modern life. Bagehot recognised the great value in aristocratic atmosphere, provided the aristocrats recognised that they had duties as well as rights. He inherited something of it in the blood of the Bagehots and the Stuckeys. Did he not possess the influence of an atmosphere in his own person? True, the "deferential" England he knew has vanished from the ken of men, but if it has vanished one way we feel by no means certain that it has not returned in another. It is an undoubted fact that the personal influence of the sovereign since the days of Queen Victoria has increased, and is increasing, and there is not the least outcry that it ought to be diminished. Compare—or rather contrast—the popularity and the prestige of Parliament in Bagehot's day and to-day. Compare—there is no necessity to contrast—the popularity and the prestige of the Crown in Bagehot's day and to-day.

Mrs. Russell Barrington gives an amusing description of Bagehot's first visit in 1857 to Claverton Manor, the home of her father, the Right Hon. James Wilson, Financial Secretary of the Treasury, and afterwards Finance Member of the Council in India. Bagehot wanted to write for the *Economist* which Wilson had founded in 1843, but his visit had an additional result. Wilson had six daughters and no son, and Bagehot instantly won the hearts of the girls by comparing their German governess to an egg. "From that moment he rose in our eyes from the status of a political economist to that of a fellow-creature. He became one of us. It was something strangely new, delightful, and nutritious that he brought into our lives." The intimacy grew, and Bagehot and Miss Wilson were married in April, 1858. Her diary, from which her sister, Mrs. Russell Barrington, constantly quotes, shows how fully Mrs. Bagehot shared her husband's friendships with the most interesting people of the day, and how true and loyal a comrade she was to him in all his occupations until his death in 1877. A sketch by Mrs. Russell Barrington shows Mrs. Bagehot at the time of her marriage as a woman of striking intelligence as well as beauty, with large expressive eyes and features of great regularity and refinement. She lived to be eighty-eight, and her husband's span of years was only fifty. What has political thought not suffered by the irreparable calamity of his early death! Yet influence of a life like his is not to be measured so much by its length in action as by its intensity in thought. Our sense of his premature loss is all the keener as we read Sir Robert Giffen's estimate: "Mentally, Bagehot was at his best when he died, and he looked forward to many years of happy toil, both in finishing the *Economic Studies* and other work beyond. So far from becoming absorbed in economic science as he grew older, though his later writings happened to be almost all economic, Bagehot to the last gave me the impression of only passing through one mental stage, which being passed through he would again leave political economy behind. To his historical and descriptive account of English political economy he was likely enough to have added a history of political ideas, or at any rate some other work of general philosophy, which had necessarily more attraction for him than the ordinary topics of political economy."

The *Estimates of some Englishmen and Scotchmen* had not been received with favour, and this of course made its author all the more gratified when M. Arnold wrote that the article on Shelley and "one or two others . . . seem to me to be of the very first quality, showing not talent only, but a concern for the *simple truth* which is rare in English literature as it is in English politics and English religion." This was what Arnold thought of them in magazine form in 1856, but the public did not share his appreciation. In 1859 Bagehot wrote on Parliamentary reform, and his article won the commendation of Robert Lowe and gave him that position in the inner circle of political life which was henceforth his. The view he adopted was that though every class should be represented in the councils of the nation, yet by unduly lowering the franchise you commit an injustice towards the class whose interests would thus be represented, owing to the enormous majority of the poorer class. The only purpose for which a vote is useful is representation. Each class, from the highest to the lowest, should possess representation, but no class should possess domination. Bright sought a guarantee that his class should be included in representation, but did he seek a guarantee that other classes, hitherto unrepresented, should be included? Bagehot did seek for the inclusion of these classes, and he was to plead in 1865 that representation was not right, and did not look right, if the labourers had no representatives in Parliament.

Lord Melbourne used habitually to ask, "Can't you let it alone?" Bagehot was sufficiently of this way of thinking to adopt a similar attitude to most questions. If the stupidity or the solidity of the English won his admiration, their energy in politics won nothing of the sort. Here he followed one who meant much to him, Sir George Cornewall

Lewis, and Sir George was distinctly sceptical of the benefits conferred by legislation. He keenly perceived that if you cure an evil by a measure, you are just as likely as not to give rise to another evil, and on striking a balance the policy of *laissez-faire* commended itself to his cautious judgment. If Bagehot brought himself to approve of the Irish Land Bill, he brought himself with hesitation. If his father-in-law was Finance Member of the India Council, yet he would not have been sorry if we could give up that vast continent we call India. True, we had other colonies, but might we not be better without them? The Duke of Wellington once criticised a peer in a speech in the House of Lords. "I regret," he remarked, "that the noble lord's education has been vastly in excess of his powers of taking advantage of it." Bagehot seemed to think that our possessions—and our legislation—were vastly in excess of our powers of taking advantage—for their benefit—of them. What we really required was leisure to take thought for our present and our future policy. Fresh possessions and fresh legislation were depriving us of this leisure. He quotes from the poetry of his friend Clough what was the motto of his own political creed:

> Old things need not be therefore true,
> O brother men, nor yet the new;
> Ah, still awhile, th' old thought retain,
> And yet consider it again.

We cannot feel sure that Bagehot was right in his attitude. The English are provincial to a degree, and their Empire renders them at least this benefit that it remedies this provinciality of outlook. They are compelled, even against their will, to look abroad, and this look abroad is of inestimable advantage to themselves and indeed to the human race. Napoleon called us a nation of shopkeepers, and so we might have become had it not been for the Government of India which successfully redeems us from this taunt. For this Government forms one of our title-deeds to the esteem of humanity.

The *National Review* came to an end in 1864, and was replaced the next year by the *Fortnightly Review* under the editorship of Lewes, with whom George Eliot lived, and of

John Morley. The historian of English rationalism in the nineteenth century, Mr. Benn, rightly attaches importance to attacks on theology in the new periodical, attacks that marked the signal change passing over thought in the seventies. The *Fortnightly Review* first appeared on May 15th, 1865, and the first chapter of Bagehot's *English Constitution* headed its list of contents. The last chapter came out in it on January 1st, 1871. In 1872 he wrote a lengthy introduction to the second edition, explaining the difficulty he experienced in endeavouring "to sketch a living Constitution—a Constitution that is in actual work and power. The difficulty is that the object is in constant change." His method of meeting it was "to keep the original sketch in all essentials as it was first written, and to describe shortly such changes either in the Constitution itself or in the Constitution compared with it, as seem material."

Among the many merits of *The English Constitution* is the outstanding one that it broke away from its legal aspect, as laid down by Blackstone, and concentrated on its actual working. Since he wrote his essay on parliamentary reform in 1859 he knew the inner circle of the leading statesmen, and this intimacy lent actuality to all that he wrote. *Le beau monde* still governed *le monde*. With the rulers of this world he was on those terms in which he either knew them or knew about them. If he did not know one of them personally, he was yet familiar with the type of man he was. Nor did he disdain any more than Lord Acton the rumours and the stories then current about the Prime Minister and his Cabinet or the leading members of the Opposition. All this intimate knowledge he had the happy knack of conveying to his readers, contriving to make them feel that they were listening to him, as Hutton might have listened, after dinner. He inspired men with that reverence for the past, that confidence in the present, and that faith in the future which characterised himself.

The accepted literary theory of the constitution was Montesquieu's with its insistence on the separation of the legislative, the executive, and the judicial powers. This accepted theory Bagehot at once swept away, for what he insisted on was the union of all three. The influence of

Montesquieu through Blackstone came to a conclusion as Bagehot demonstrated the essentially unitary nature of our constitution, and this unitary nature is carried into effect by the Cabinet which acted as a "hyphen." The work of the Prime Minister and of the Cabinet, their control of expenditure, and indeed even then of legislation, the relations of the two front benches—these and a hundred other matters were explained in such a fashion that one almost came to the conclusion that Bagehot was simply throwing additional light on what one knew already. The truth of course is that one did not know it already: he was the first to set it down. We glean that we have not a "mixed" constitution, with separation of powers, but that the United States certainly has. In fact, England is a republic with an hereditary President, the United States a monarchy with an elective King. In the background we see—though dimly—the figure of our Queen, and our author sets down the dignified and the efficient parts of the constitution. The Cabinet is of course the efficient, and the Queen the dignified, and one of the most illuminating parts of the book is that in which the share taken by the dignified parts is inimitably explained. We do well to remember that even Bagehot did not discern all that the monarch might accomplish. Prince Albert had died in 1861, and till the coming of Disraeli to power in 1874 the Queen seemed to be what she was called, the widow of Windsor. She lived in retirement, and before her letters were published it was difficult to believe that she was as active behind the scenes as she undoubtedly was. Her activity was not before Bagehot as it is before us, and he did not live to witness the Jubilees of 1887 and especially 1897, which demonstrated what a wonderful hold she possessed over the affections of her people abroad quite as much as at home. Take a story told by Mr. Le Sueur, the biographer of Rhodes. He was at Fort Usher, in the Matoppos, and one day a large number of natives, led by Babyan, came in and asked that a certain missionary who had just come to Rhodesia might be hanged. Mr. Le Sueur asked why, and was told that the missionary had described a great "'n Koos Pezulu," who was supreme over the earth, and had asked them if they knew what he meant. One immediately replied, "u' Lawli" (Lawley, the administrator). He was told he was wrong "Umlanule M. Kunoji" (Rhodes), said another; but the missionary said, "No; some one greater than Rhodes." Then Babyan, with an air of confidence, pronounced "i' Queeni" (the Queen). "No," said the missionary, "some one even greater than the Queen." "U'Yamagna" (you liar) cried Babyan, and the natives rose in a body to have the missionary hanged. Bagehot lived before the heyday of Imperialism which, so far as he saw it, he rather mistrusted. Accordingly, it is not surprising that he never discerned that our monarchy constitutes one of the strongest of all the links that bind our daughter nations to ourselves. Yet the potency of personality of the sovereign appealed to him as it never appealed to Seeley.

It is hard to realise the attitude of their subjects to such sovereigns as George IV and William IV, though we frankly confess that as we motor about England we are constantly surprised at the number of inn signs in honour of both sovereigns. No one, however, who has read the memoirs relating to their reigns can doubt of the contempt and dislike into which George IV and William IV deservedly fell. The change wrought by Queen Victoria is hardly credible to anyone familiar with the attitude of, say, *The Times* to her two predecessors. What the Queen began has been continued by Edward VII, by George V, and by the present Prince of Wales. No one can doubt that Edward VII spent himself, and that George V and his son spend themselves on behalf of their country in a manner that moves us all. The dignified parts of the constitution assume a rôle for which not even Bagehot has prepared us. True, he does explain that a family on the throne brings down the pride of sovereignty to the level of ordinary life. "We smile at the *Court Circular*; but remember how many people read the *Court Circular*! Its use is not in what it says, but in those to whom it speaks. They say that the Americans were more pleased at the Queen's letter to Mrs. Lincoln than at any act of the English Government. It was a spontaneous act of intelligible feeling in the midst of confused and tiresome business. Just so a royal family sweetens politics by the seasonable addition of nice and pretty events."

The principle of evolution fitfully appears in the *English Constitution.* In his *Physics and Politics* he was to apply this principle with so much skill and success, and yet he allowed it but slight weight in the natural selection which operates so powerfully upon the character of hereditary princes and aristocracies. Why did he draw his illustrations of the working of constitutional monarchy so exclusively from the past, especially from the examples of George III and William IV, ignoring the experience of Queen Victoria's reign? Why did he ignore the deep and, for the most part, wholesome influence exerted in European politics by Leopold I, William I and Prince Albert? We know, for instance, that one of the last letters Prince Albert altered avoided what seemed inevitable, war with the United States in 1861. Germany owes much to Bismarck, and she owes Bismarck to William I. Italy owes much to Cavour, and she owes Cavour to Victor Emmanuel. Bagehot believes that Parliament is wiser than the average sovereign, but he scarcely lays enough stress on the fact that a prince is exempt from the influence of party, whose action in a crisis of national fortune has been occasionally disastrous. Bagehot dwells almost exclusively on the unfavourable incidents of a royal education .He overlooks the direct and indirect influences which are brought to bear from the very cradle on an hereditary prince—the sense of responsibility, the consciousness of a great position, the familiarity with the gravest interests, a youth passed under the tuition of the ablest masters, which secure for the future sovereign a moral and intellectual training unequalled in its excellence. The effect of that training we see in our own royal family. A prince of fair abilities, with such a training and such a knowledge of the men with whom he is necessarily brought into contact, possesses every means of knowing, at least as well as Parliament, who are the competent and trustworthy statesmen and diplomatists, generals and admirals. His continuous experience of politics, legislation, and government, his access, notably in foreign affairs, to wider and more impartial sources of information, lend to his counsels an authority which no prudent or thoughtful Prime Minister will disregard. For the prince looks at affairs from a higher point of view, with a broader survey as a rule, and also with a calmer and more unbiassed judgment.

The King's name is even yet a great power. The law is too mere an abstraction, the names of Ministers represent too much party feeling, excite too much antagonism, to command the prompt obedience, the loyal reverence, the enthusiastic support which is rendered to the name of the sovereign. Nor can we overlook the certainty which personal sovereignty gives, the absence of a moment's possible doubt on which side is the supreme arbiter, sure to be backed by nine-tenths of the physical forces of society. The royal name possesses power over the passions of the enlightened as well as over the ignorance of the unenlightened. The omnipotence of Parliament or the Cabinet, even when, in the belief of half the nation, a parliamentary majority represents a minority of the people, is due less to traditional respect for the House of Commons, or superstitious reverence for a majority vote, such as prevails in the United States, than to the fact that resistance means rebellion, visible, unmistakable disobedience to the King. The services still feel proud to consider that they serve, in their own phrase—not the State but—"Gentlemen, the King." No one who has ever been present at the sacrament of the Mess can forget the loyalty, which goes so deep, with which the toast of the King's health is drunk every night. A hardened Canadian politician, of the real boss type, a narrow, selfish anti-Imperialist, owned of Albert, Lord Grey: "I had never heard any one give the toast of His Majesty in a way that made me think what it meant, or feel the least tremor of emotion, until I heard His Excellency say, 'The King!' This party manipulator acknowledged: "The rich tone of his voice made me feel the loyalty that was filling his heart, and it made it very affecting to drink the King's health with him." That sentiment of loyalty, which Bagehot ascribes to the ignorant alone, is as strong in the upper or middle as in the lower orders, and has a far wider, deeper influence than he allows, than perhaps it was consistent with the whole scope of his book to allow.

Much of what has been written upon the contrast between the American and English constitutions—the two great types of popular government, parliamentary, the direct and indirect election of the actual executive—was anticipated in the best chapters of the *English Constitution*. Bagehot wrote in 1865, and Maine did not publish his *Popular Government* and Dicey his *Law of the Constitution* till 1885, and Bryce his *magnum opus* on the *American Commonwealth* till 1888. All three explain the differences between flexible and rigid constitutions in the eighties, but our author had anticipated them in the sixties. Few writers so terse, compact, and clear as Bagehot, have been so completely free from the temptation of deliberate phrase-making; yet few professional phrase-makers in our time have left in the minds of their readers so many telling, forcible, and suggestive phrases; sentences in which a novel or striking thought, an impressive view of new or old truth, a principle apt to be forgotten or imperfectly appreciated, is vivified and incarnated in a few emphatic words. Of Peel we read that "no man has come so near our definition of a Constitutional Statesman—the powers of a first-rate man and the creed of a second-rate man." "Toryism is enjoyment." "He who runs may read, but it does not seem likely he will think." "The great difficulty which history records is not that of the first step, but that of the second step." "The most benumbing thing to the intellect is routine, the most bewildering is distraction; our system is a distracting routine." "A Constitutional administrator has to be always consulting others, finding out what this man or that chooses to think; learning which form of error is believed by Lord B., which by Lord C., adding up the errors of the Alphabet and seeing what portion of what he thinks he ought to do, they will all of them together allow him to do." The difficulty when you begin quoting his *obiter dicta* is to stop. His phrases remain with the reader who does well also to remember that in addition to coining them, he anticipated many a thinker of the next generation.

Bagehot's belief in democracy had been chastened by his experiences in Paris in 1851. The lesson life taught him confirmed him in this attitude. In 1859 he wrote that "every person has a right to so much political power as he can exercise without impeding any other person who would more fitly exercise such power." A "supremacy of the central group of trained and educated men" must guide the course of parliamentary government. Power was to be proportionate to capacity, for he had not been a Greek scholar for nothing. The rule of mere numbers did not in the least attract him. The ignorance of the voter, his haste, and his excitement—these were dangers he could discern, and, if these dangers were not heeded, the preface to his second edition demonstrates how much he feared the masterfulness of democracy. He was afraid that the Tory would befriend the artisan of the town and that the Liberal would befriend the labourer of the country, and that in their competition for support the Tory and the Liberal would try each of them to outbid the other. "*Vox populi* will be *Vox diaboli* if it is worked in that manner." Household suffrage seemed to him the inevitable consequence, the logical development, of the Reform Bill of 1832. It was at that point, as he considered, that the right and wrong path had diverged; that chance and destiny, rather than choice, determined at the moment the adoption of that which necessarily and logically led to sheer democracy. The practice of the old system had become thoroughly vicious, but the underlying principle was sound and safe. All classes, all interests, were represented; but accident had given, not to wealth or birth, but to a particular kind of wealth, a certain set of families, an enormously disporportionate representation. The landed interest was wronged in the utterly inadequate representation of the counties. Ireland was misrepresented; and the Scots could not be said to be represented at all. Still, every class, every great interest, had its spokesmen, exercising a direct and independent influence on the national councils. Rotten or pocket boroughs were not only nurseries of professional statesmanship, but a back door through which interests, whose direct representation was impossible, found access in Parliament. The West Indian interest, the East India Company, and the statesmen trained in its service, with their special knowledge and zealous care for the welfare of our Oriental Empire, could secure a hearing for views to which no English constituency would listen.

The working classes were represented through those numerous constituencies in which the scot and lot franchise prevailed. It was imperative that the abuses of the system should be redressed; that the new communities which had grown up since the Industrial Revolution should be directly represented; that the borough proprietors and the great families should be deprived of their excessive weight in Parliament; that the middle class should acquire a new power more adequate to its new social and political importance; and that Scotland should be really and directly represented. But in Bagehot's view, which was Burke's, universal and varied representation was of more consequence than arithmetical proportion. No class, no interest, represented in the House of Commons, was likely to be grossly wronged, none could be neglected or unheard. No class intelligent enough to understand its own grievances, to have distinct ideas and desires of its own, would have failed, under a reform retaining the principle of the old system, to command attention and secure redress. Had Pitt been able to carry out his thoroughly sincere scheme of practical reform, or had Canning and his followers sided with the Whigs upon this as upon almost every other question, reform might have anticipated revolution. It was the weakness, rather than the will, of the Whigs that compelled them to travel not only farther and faster, but in another direction, than their actual opinions and traditional inclinations would have carried them. They were compelled to present a scheme broad, simple, and extreme enough, to attract irresistible support.

When once uniformity of franchise and proportionate representation were made the basis of the electoral system, the extension of the former, the more and more accurate adjustment of the latter, became a mere question of time. The poorest class of householders in towns in 1886 are probably as intelligent and competent as were the ten-pounders of 1832. The masses might have been satisfied with the gradual enlargement of their old representation: having been once disfranchised in wholesale fashion, it was certain that they would ere long demand and ultimately secure that complete enfranchisement, by which every other class must necessarily be swamped. Minority representation, electoral districts, and single seats, are at best lame and unsatisfactory methods of engrafting on pure democracy securities and checks, which were essential and natural parts of the old representation of classes and interests When once every borough below a certain numerical standard had been extinguished, and all below another deprived of their second member, the downward extension of the principle became a logical and historical necessity.

Critics, competent and incompetent, hailed the publication of the *English Constitution.* Among the former Dicey certified in 1881 that "Bagehot has brought more knowledge of life and originality of mind to the elucidation of the theory and practice of English politics than any man since Burke. He is the only Englishman of first-rate talents who, during the last half-century, has applied the whole force of his mind to the analysis of the mass of laws, maxims, and habits which go to make up the English Constitution. In the course of a few years he will undoubtedly be recognised by all the world as the most eminent of constitutionalists. If this recognition has not yet been attained, the failure, such as it is, is due mainly to the versatility of Bagehot's interests, and to the consequent difficulty felt by ordinary students in believing that a writer who excelled in so many fields of speculation—in the sphere of criticism, of imaginative literature, and of political economy—could be so pre-eminent in one field; and to the lucidity of Bagehot's explanations, which led even those who learnt most from his pages into the delusion that what their teacher explained so easily was in itself easy to explain and hardly needed explanation."

The versatility of our author's interests is evident in the fact that the first chapter of his *Physics and Politics* appeared in the *Fortnightly Review* on November 1st, 1867, ten months after the conclusion of the *English Constitution.* Maine's *Ancient Law* had in 1861 applied evolutionary ideas to explain the growth of law, and now Bagehot applies these ideas to explain the growth of society. The formula of Darwin had been heredity and variation: the formula of Bagehot was invention and imitation. In his pregnant manner he described his book as an attempt to apply the principles of natural selection and inheritance to political society. His general view was that in early times the value of government chiefly consisted in the drill of a society into fixed habits, customs, preferences and rules of its own, so as to subdue arbitrary personal caprice, and to create a common mind and character, a common groove of thought and feeling. The conservatism of mind of the author is apparent in his *English Constitution,* and it is no less apparent in his *Physics and Politics,* and indeed here he takes rank with Bolingbroke and Burke. His conservatism was naturally more scientific than theirs, for Darwin had taught him that the only sure way to conserve a tradition is to prolong it. Nor are we sure that his conservatism does not hark back to Shakespeare himself. There is however, a conservatism that springs from simple acceptance of fact and one that springs from fear. The latter is as evident in some to-day as the former is in Bagehot. He simply—or subtly—accepted fact. Lord Eldon, for instance, was a conservative through fear. Nor does Bagehot fail to point out: "There was another cause beside fear which then inclined, and which in similar times of miscellaneous revolution will ever incline, subtle rather than creative intellects to a narrow conservatism. Such intellects require an exact creed; they want to be able clearly to distinguish themselves from those around them, to tell each man where they differ and why they differ; they cannot make assumptions; they cannot, like the merely practical man, be content with rough and obvious axioms; they require a *theory.* Such a want is difficult to satisfy in an age of confusion and tumult, when old habits are shaken, old views overthrown, ancient assumptions rudely questioned, ancient inferences utterly denied, when each man has a different view from his neighbour, when an intellectual change has set father and son at variance, when a man's own household are the special foes of his favourite and self-adopted creed. A bold and original mind breaks through these vexations, and forms for itself a theory satisfactory to its notions, and sufficient for its wants. A weak mind yields a passive obedience to those among whom it is thrown. But a mind which is searching without being creative, which is accurate and logical enough to see defects, without being combinative or inventive enough to provide remedies—which, in the old language, is discriminative rather than discursive—is wholly unable, out of the medley of new suggestions, to provide itself with an adequate belief; and it naturally falls back on the *status quo*."

Not a little of the *Physics and Politics* is occupied with the investigation of the *status quo* and the manner into which it has come into being. He sets out by telling us that in early times the quantity of government is much more than its quality, and that in point of fact it is difficult to get a government at all. What you virtually require is a rule binding men together, compelling them to execute the same things in the same way at the same time. The problem is in fact the securing of obedience. To gain that obedience what we now call Church and State combine, and the priest supports the chief and the chief the priest. The organisation to which each belongs creates what Bagehot calls a cake of custom. By means of this cake of custom, "all the actions of life are to be submitted to a single rule for a single object; that gradually created the 'hereditary drill' which science teaches to be essential, and which the early instinct of man saw to be essential too." Under this *régime* there is no room for the genius: he must conform to type or be persecuted till he does. The view of Herbert Spencer that a great man is the product of his time is untrue in our days, but if ever it was true it was so in primitive antiquity. The age then was monotonous, for otherwise even the rudiments of society could not come into being, and when in being could not persist, and persistence was necessary to existence. Once mankind at last fixed the yoke of custom upon its shoulders, society began to make faint attempts towards progress. Imitation was the order of the day.

A Socrates could not be allowed, for he was practically pulling to pieces the cake of custom on which society reposed. "The first duty of society is the preservation of society," and a Socrates threatened the very framework of society. Toleration was a vice, not a virtue. The limits of free speech are positive, for "no Government is bound to permit a controversy which will annihilate itself." Bigotry is the ruling principle, and it is rightly the ruling principle. Persecution is at bottom the effort of mankind to secure that uniformity of creed and practice, in religion and in politics, which is essential if society is to endure. Imitation is vital and invention is not vital. Once, however, imitation has been successful on a large scale, then invention is possible. Originality could not be encouraged till imitation had reduced all men to a strong custom of obedience.

The imitative instinct, the herd instinct, and the tests of verifiable progress are matters on which massive volumes have been written by Tarde and others, but the fount of their inspiration is the *Physics and Politics*. Swift drily remarked that "if you want to gain the reputation of a sensible man, you should be of the opinion of the person with whom for the time being you are conversing." In primitive times the aim of all alike was to be sensible men and women. You conformed, because the cake of custom obliged you so to do. The doctrine of imitation is true in primitive society, and it is also true in modern—though we sometimes forget that this is so. Bagehot points out that we were all frivolous under Palmerston and earnest under Gladstone. A great political leader still dictates the tone of the community. True, there is variation or invention as well as imitation, and Bagehot skilfully shows that it is as accurate to take up this position in literature as it is in society. In this fashion he explains the style of Queen Anne's age. One considerable writer, say, Steele, secures a sort of start because what he writes is just a shade more congenial to the minds around him than any other sort. What Steele writes, Addison writes. They catch hold of the public mind, and "a curious process soon assimilates other writers in appearance to them." Similarly the uniform style of the leader writers of *The Times* is explained. There is usually one writer better than all the others, and the rest of them copy him, consciously or unconsciously. For a writer is aware that there is a change in his style as he writes an article for one review as compared with another.

The examples of imitation given by Bagehot are far more convincing than those offered by Tarde in his *L'Évolution Littéraire*. Arguing against Spencer's theory of evolution in art, Tarde holds that literature always "begins with a book," and his instances are the Iliad, the Bible, and Dante. Now it would seem to us that all these books come at the end of a long process of evolution, not at the beginning. This is certainly true of the Bible and of the Iliad, no matter what view we may take about its authorship by Homer. Dante, too, is the fine flower of the Middle Ages.

Once the problem of imitation is solved, the next danger to society is that it may remain stationary and perish. On the line of imitation Bagehot showed that Rome was able to triumph over Greece and other indifferently welded, though cleverer and more reflective, communities. The Greeks of our own day suffer grievously because they know neither restraint nor reverence, neither tradition nor national discipline. Hence the dull fixed habit of acting all in one way as the English do was better than the sprightly divergences and differences of opinion among the French which make it difficult to know what they really wish, or whether they have any wish in common by which the masses are seriously affected. As Bagehot took trouble to point out, this drill may be too effective, it may go too far, and when it does we have cases of what he called "arrested civilisations." Such an arrested civilisation we have in China, where the common drill completely trampled out the disposition for cautious criticism and review of national prejudices, which ought to come sooner or later if ever there is to be an age of progress and discussion. Stimulating and suggestive as the whole book is, the author surpasses himself when he comes to discuss verifiable progress politically. Maine was to analyse this problem, but there is nothing in all his scattered hints comparable to the closing pages of the *Physics and Politics*. In his book he writes: "If anyone were asked to describe what it is which distinguishes the writings of a man of genius, who is also a great man of the world, from all other writings, I think he would use the words, 'animated moderation.' He would say that such writings are never slow, are never expansive, are never exaggerated; that they are always instinct with judgment, and yet that judgment is never a dull judgment; that they have as much spirit in them as would go to make a wild writer, and yet that every line of them is the product of a sane and sound writer. The best and almost perfect instance of this in English is Scott." Another instance is Walter Bagehot himself. That our verdict is by no means extravagant men like Maine and Bryce testify. The former wrote to him: "Thank you very sincerely for your book on *Physics and Politics*. It is practically an old friend. I do not know that I was ever more struck with anything than with the essays when they first appeared. I don't think it was your handsome allusions to me which influence me—but I am much obliged to you for them all the same." Bryce acknowledges that "Had he lived to apply his method he might have exercised almost the same kind of influence that Montesquieu exerted in the middle of the eighteenth, and Tocqueville in the earlier part of the nineteenth century; and we feel in him the power of an intellect worthy to be compared even with that of the earlier and greater of those two illustrious men."

His *Lombard Street*, which appeared in 1873, gave a description of the banking world as full of animated moderation as his *English Constitution* and his *Physics and Politics*. Bankers and bill-brokers flit across the pages of *Lombard Street*, but its author is far more immersed in the principles of banking than he is in them. In his *English Constitution* we note the place of the dignified elements of the political constitution, and we note what the monarch can and cannot do. In *Lombard Street* we note the place of the efficient elements of the business constitution, and we note what the monarch, now the head of a great business, can and cannot do. We gather that there is very little indeed that he cannot do. For Bagehot maintains that capitalists are the great generals of commerce, that they plan the present and—more important—the future of the business whose strategy they control. Nor does he confine himself to strategy: he perceives the nature of their tactics, and all this is set forth with his usual stimulus. For anyone who wishes to realise the business of the seventies there is no book comparable to it for the picture it presents.

A Chancellor of the Exchequer like Gladstone and a President of the United States like Woodrow Wilson speak warmly of Bagehot. The former gladly records the "advantage of frequent and free communication with him on all matters of finance and currency. Nor have I in all my experience known any one from whom in this important province more was to be desired, or who was more free and genial in the communication of his large knowledge and matured reflection." Woodrow Wilson freely confesses that Bagehot's writings "have all the freshness, the vivacity, the penetration of eager talk, and abound in those flashes of insight and discovery which make the speech of some gifted men seem like a series of inspirations." Bagehot meant much to the reading public, he meant much to the leading statesmen, and he meant most of all to his own friends. Let Hutton testify for the last. "Not very many perhaps, outside Bagehot's inner circle, will carry about with them that hidden pain, that burden of emptiness, inseparable from an image which has hitherto been one full of the suggestions of life and power, when that life and power are no longer to be found; for he was intimately known only to the few. But those who do will hardly find again in this world a store of intellectual sympathy of so high a stamp, so wide in its range and so full of original and fresh suggestion, and judgment to lean on so real and so sincere, or a friend so frank and constant, with so vivid and tenacious a memory for the happy associations of a common past, and so generous in recognising the independent value of divergent convictions in the less pliant present."

The followers of Bagehot are legion: Tarde with his *Lois de l'Imitation* is only one of them. There are of course anticipators, and among them we may partly reckon Buckle whose *History of Civilisation* appeared in 1857, suffering from the fact that it was two years before Darwin's *Origin of Species*. Buckle, like Kidd, was a man of large views without the detailed knowledge required in order to drive home the conviction that his large views were true. Vico and Montesquieu had endeavoured to reduce the phenomena of societies to the reign of law, and substantially this was the aim of Buckle. Crimes, suicides, and acts of forgetfulness, e.g. the omission of an address on an envelope, were shown to recur with statistical regularity. To physical causes he traced the rise of civilisation in Egypt, India,

Mexico, and Peru. To the overpowering energy and the "unmanageability" of nature was due the entire absence of civilisation in Brazil. To the absence of the combined conditions of heat and irrigation north of the twentieth parallel was due the lack of civilisation in America. To the abundance of cheap food was due the abjection of the Indian and Egyptian peoples. Bagehot speaks of "Mr. Buckle's idea that material forces have been the mainsprings of progress, and moral causes secondary, and, in comparison, not to be thought of."

Darwin explained the energy and the initiative of the colonist by the stimulating atmosphere of his new home. With him, as with Buckle, the climate was the magic reason. Is this really so? For the enterprise of the colonist has emerged under almost every condition of heat and cold, of high level and low level. The energy is at least as much due to the reason that a man of abundant activity, cramped by a narrow environment at home, found scope at last for his ability abroad. Physically, he was above average. For example, the Scots who fought in the war between North and South in the United States in the sixties were nearly two inches taller than the average at home. Mentally the Puritan, the Huguenot, who migrated because his religious or political freedom was attacked, was one of the select. The abundance of land, and the consequent feeling of hopefulness, the altered conditions demanding new solutions of old problems, the resulting initiative, adaptibility, and receptivity to new ideas, all emancipated a man from the cake of custom in the old country. Strabo is well aware that variation combined with isolation modifies the original type, though he, like Bodin, clearly anticipates Buckle in ascribing too much importance to climate.

Buckle does not take sufficiently into account the happy effects of migration. The movement of the energetic in quest of better opportunities, by bringing them into flourishing communities where they have larger families than the stay-at-home, builds up an enterprising breed. In the colonies the men marry early; and, on account of the fewness of the women, the inferior men find no mates. Galton thinks that the rapid rise of the new colonies and the fall of old civilisations are mainly due to the social agencies which in the one case promote and in the other retard the marriage of the more suitable. Out-worn traditions, narrow local sentiments, and obstinate prejudices meet and cancel one another. Races fuse and intermarry. There appear new combinations of hereditary factors. Variation is more common. The shutters of the intellect are taken down. The mind becomes alert and supple, though running excessively to material issues. Freed from the hampering net of kin and class ties, the individual emerges. A new environment is suddenly entered, freedom of opportunity is open, the cake of custom is broken, and new activities, new lines of growth, new institutions and new ideals are brought into existence. Now and then the emergence of a man takes place by his leaving the country for the city. "The air of a town makes a man free." The town is a hot-bed where seed-ideas more quickly germinate than in the country. The formation of large, dense, complex bodies of population is favourable to a belief in the rights of man as man that underlies individualism and democracy.

Climate, in spite of considerations like these, works wonders in the hands of Montesquieu, Buckle, and Treitschke. Montesquieu ascribes the immutability of religion, manners, customs and laws in India and other Oriental countries to their warm climate. Buckle ascribes the highly wrought imagination and gross superstition of the Indians to the presence of towering mountains and vast plains, which by their overpowering aspect excite the fancy and paralyse the reason, just as Treitschke similarly accounts for the absence of artistic and poetic development in Switzerland and Alpine Lands. It is much more probable that the geographical isolation of India is the cause, for on land the great sweep of high mountains restricts intercourse with the interior, and by sea the swamps of the Indus and the Ganges on the west and the marshes and lagoons on the east constitute barriers to accessibility. If migration is barely possible, a static condition of society is the inevitable outcome. Greece was as accessible as India was inaccessible, and the setting of the former made it the intellectual focus for the eastern Mediterranean.

The master like Bagehot requires disciples if his teaching is to prevail. If the pupils possess the graceful style of a Huxley, so much the better for the diffusion of his views. There is a class of scientist who aches for strife, and Huxley belonged to it. He cared for truth. No one who has read the fine biography of him by his son, Mr. Leonard Huxley, can doubt that for a single moment. Did he never care for controversy for controversy's sake? He spawned hypotheses, as Bagehot spawned them, though he never, so far as we know, originated a single discovery save the one he made as an undergraduate of nineteen. He went astray over the Bathybius hypothesis, and he went astray over the phylogeny of the horse. Now before both these mistakes were discovered, would it, we imagine, have gone well with a young man who pointed out the errors in either? A pure lover of truth, like that supreme genius, Faraday, would probably have admitted the error. We are not altogether so sure in the case of a man who loved controversy as Huxley did, for it was the very breath of his nostrils. Can you chase truth with a logical forceps?

Nothing came amiss to the destructive powers of Huxley. It might be the views of General Booth on social reform or it might be the folks who talked about the natural rights of man. He lashed them all, and right vigorously he laid on the lash. To use present-day phraseology, his controversial complexes suffered no repression. No doubt the subconscious is as much overworked as x, y, and z in algebra, and we hesitate to employ this term. Still subconsciously this attitude of Huxley towards controversy, psychologically speaking, affected his attitude towards the pursuit of truth. Instead of constructive work, his is destructive work, and it is seldom possible for the same brain to undertake these two types of creative energy. Even the *élan vital* of Bergson is not sufficient for such a task. Huxley's coinage of the word Agnosticism has always seemed to us to be a parable of the whole man in science as well as in political philosophy. Despite the opposition of Herbert Spencer, in 1871 Huxley in his article on administrative nihilism pleads with all his wonted power on behalf of the education of the people by the Government. He has few general views on the question of *laissez-faire.* He simply faces a problem like education in an empirical spirit. Is there more loss from lack of education than gain by the non-interference on the part of the State? He sees that there is loss, and accordingly he settles the matter. For his part he is unable to entertain the belief that the functions of the State may be summed up in one great negative commandment, "Thou shalt not allow any man to interfere with the liberty of any other man." Yet such a commandment constituted the burden of the teaching of his friend Herbert Spencer. Huxley's argument is that if his next-door neighbour chooses to have his drains in such a state as to create a poisonous atmosphere, which anyone breathes, he restricts the just freedom of anyone to live just as much as if he went about with a pistol threatening life. If he is to be allowed to let his children go unvaccinated, he might as well be allowed to leave strychnine lozenges about in the way of one's children; and if he brings them up untaught, he is doing his best to restrict his neighbour's freedom, by increasing the burden of taxation for the support of gaols and workhouses, which someone has to pay. He endorses Locke's view that the end of government is the good of mankind, terming it the noblest, and at the same time the briefest, known to him. Nor will he ignore any more than Bagehot the share an Established Church may take. "A Church in which, week by week, services should be devoted, not to the iteration of abstract propositions in theology, but to the setting before men's minds of an ideal of true, just, and pure living; a place in which those who are weary of the burden of daily cares, should find a moment's rest in the contemplation of the higher life which is possible for all, though attained by so few; a place in which the man of strife and of business should have time to think how small, after all, are the rewards he covets compared with peace and charity. Depend upon it, if such a Church existed no one would seek to disestablish it."

Huxley subjects the natural inequality of men to a vigorous analysis in 1890. His examination of the doctrines of Rousseau is searching, and there are few places in English where the natural inequality of man is set forth with such lucidity and such power. He does not sufficiently see that the law of nature has a long pedigree, taking it back to Canon and Roman law, nor does he seem to see the truth that there is in the law of nature a power able to set bounds to the authority of the State He is, however, quite clear that Rousseau's state of nature never existed as a fact, and he invokes ancient law and ancient religion, anthropology and archaeology to disprove it. This year he continued his investigation into natural rights and political rights, and from the historical point of view he attacks with little eagerness Quesnay and the Physiocrats in the eighteenth century and with the keenest eagerness Henry George and his views on the unearned increment derived from land in the nineteenth. In Huxley's survey of the growth of society he shows himself as much an imitationist as Bagehot himself. He exposes the *reductio ad absurdum* of natural right in land with cogency. "My free and equal fellow countrymen, there is not the slightest doubt that not only the Duke of Westminster and the Messrs. Astor, but everybody who holds land from the area of a thousand square miles to that of a tablecloth, and who, against all equity, denies that every pauper child has an equal right to it, is a ROBBER. (Loud and long-continued cheers; the audience, especially the paupers, standing up and waving their hats.) But, my friends, I am also bound to tell you that neither the pauper child nor Messrs. Astor, nor the Duke of Westminster, have any more right to the land than the first nigger you may meet, or the Esquimaux at the north end of this great continent, or the Fugeians at the south end of it. Therefore, before you proceed to use your strength in claiming your rights and take the land away from these usurping Dukes and robbing Astors, you must recollect that you will have to go shares with the four hundred and fifty odd millions of Chinamen, the hundred and fifty millions who inhabit Hindostan, the . . . (loud and long-continued hisses; the audience, especially the paupers, standing up and projecting handy movables at the orator)."

In 1890 Huxley subjected two conceptions of government to his able criticism. Was it to wear the form of anarchy? Was it to wear the form of regimentation? His survey of the answers to these two questions runs back to classical times. Once more he investigates the working of the law of nature, and in the course of his investigation he comes to the conclusion that Locke, not Hooker, is the father and founder of individualism. While Huxley is personally respectful to Herbert Spencer, he is devoid of respect for the view of the functions of the State which contemplates it as anarchy plus the policeman. No Christian could feel the parlous plight of mankind more vividly than Huxley, who writes: "I do not hesitate to express the opinion, that, if there is no hope of a large improvement of the condition of the greater part of the human family; if it is true that the increase of knowledge, the winning of a greater dominion over Nature which is its consequence, and the wealth which follows upon that dominion, are to make no difference in the extent, and the intensity of Want, with its concomitant physical and moral degradation, among the mass of the people, I should hail the advent of some kindly comet, which would sweep the whole affair away, as a desirable consummation." It is akin to a wish expressed by Mill before him and by Sidgwick after him.

The followers of Huxley felt the same consternation at his Romanes lecture of 1893 as those of Mill felt on the publication of his posthumous *Three Essays on Religion*. In the latter their author showed that religion meant much more to him than had been imagined, and in the former its author showed that ethics meant much more to him than had been imagined. The Romanes lecture dealt with evolution and ethics, and we can well imagine the surprise of the biologist to note that Huxley felt concern in the ethical ends of the universe. The lecturer shows that the conception of evolution was familiar to men in India as in Greece six centuries before our era. He is not content with the survival of the fittest, if the fittest simply mean those who are so on physical grounds. To the amazement of the evolutionist, Huxley is decidedly of opinion that "Social progress means a checking of the cosmic progress at every step and the substitution for it of another, which may be called the ethical progress; the end of which is not the survival of those who may happen to be the fittest, in respect of the whole of the conditions which obtain, but of those who are ethically the best." Huxley urges that the practice of that which is ethically best involves a course of conduct which, in all respects, is opposed to that which leads to success in the cosmic struggle for existence. Instead of ruthless self-assertion, it demands self-restraint; instead of thrusting aside all competitors, it requires that the individual shall not merely respect, but shall help his fellows. There is the community, and Huxley thinks in terms of the community. Locke may be the father of individualism, and Huxley may admire him, but he is not in the least content to adopt a creed of individualism which means the adoption of the beatitude of evolution, Blessed are the strong, for they shall prey on the weak. Rather, he holds, Blessed are the strong, for they shall help the weak. It is a fine creed, but how Huxley reconciles it with evolution is by no means plain.

The publication of B. Kidd's *Social Evolution* in 1894 attracted as much attention as the publication of H. T. Buckle's *History of Civilisation* in 1857. His thesis gave a point-blank contradiction to the thesis of Buckle. The latter traced the progress of humanity to the growth of reason, and this brutal, selfish faculty is to Kidd the evil genius of humanity. Kidd professes to find the key to social evolution in the cultivation of the emotions. Just as the book of Buckle was fortunate in meeting the mood of the public, so the book of Kidd was equally fortunate. It fell in with that general anti-intellectualism which Aliotta has particularly traced in his *Idealistic Reaction against Science.* In Kidd's view we have to approach the study of evolution with the knowledge that it was progressing along lines in which it was the interests of society, not of individuals, that mattered. It is a position which Bagehot assumed when he demonstrated the utter lack of any connection between the interests of the State and those of the individuals who compose it. Herein lies the tragedy of the world which Kidd, in imitation of Bagehot, reveals with grim power.

If Henry Drummond bore witness to the worth of *Social Evolution,* so too did Alfred Marshall. They were moved by the grandeur of Kidd's conception, and the skill with which he unified diverse and seemingly disconnected facts into a support of it. Many of his incidental criticisms were just, penetrating, and original, and it was easy to draw the conclusion that his grand conception possessed all these qualities. By means of his conception he seeks to test the truth of religion by its social functions. Religion has usually been tested by its share in the origin of the constitution of the universe or by its part in the human mind, but Kidd leaves these to the one side for his view of the functions performed by religion in the life of societies. He points out that the inter-racial struggle for existence incidentally conserves these races whose internal social organisation renders them more efficient; and that those races are the most efficient in the external and inter-racial struggle in which the acutest conflict takes place between their own members. This internal struggle for existence, however, though beneficial to the race as a whole, is injurious to the vast majority of the living individuals who take part in it, and benefits only a small aristocratic minority. What prevents the majority, then, from suspending this struggle and rearranging society on a socialistic and non-competitive basis? The majority, remarks Kidd, might do this at any time. Would they not thereby sacrifice the future of their race? Of course they would, but they themselves would be the gainers. What motive induces them to pursue the opposite course? One thing, and one thing alone, can persuade them to behave so irrationally; and this thing is the mysterious influence of religion. Is the sole function of religion, he asks, to induce the masses to submit to conditions of subjection? Nothing, he holds, could be falser than any supposition such as this, for the action of religion is twofold. On the one hand it restrains the masses from accomplishing their desires by force, and on the other it so softens the heart of the classes, the "power-holding classes," that they voluntarily surrender to the masses one privilege after another. But for the influence of religion, they would have reserved these privileges for themselves. It is clear that Kidd impales himself on the horns of a dilemma. In one part of his book he argues that the masses could at any time deprive the classes of their privileges, and that nothing but religion induced them to forbear from so acting.

In another part he argues that the classes could always—if they so desired—keep their privileges to themselves, that the masses could never have taken them from the "power-holding classes," and that nothing but religion persuaded these classes to part with their privileges. Nor is this dilemma the sole criticism we offer. The history invoked by the author is astonishingly deficient in breadth of appeal and inaccurate in substance. With Gibbon, who was misled by Montesquieu, Kidd assumes the decrepitude of the Byzantine Empire, a view which has been exploded by Finlay and Bury among our own scholars, and by Rambaud and Schlumberger, Krumbacher and Stryzgowski among foreign scholars. Nor is this by any means the only blunder in his book.

A scholar to his fingers' tip, C. H. Pearson published in 1893 his forecast of *National Life and Character*. Herbert Spencer has expressed his conviction that "the future has in store forms of social life higher than any we have imagined," holding "a faith transcending that of the Radical, whose aim is some re-organisation admitting of comparison to organisations that exist." In his *Philosophical Dialogues* Renan dreams of an oligarchical solution of the problem of the universe, when the elect of intelligent beings, possessing the most important secrets of reality, shall dominate the world by the potent instruments of destruction of which their science has given them absolute disposal, and shall cause as much reason as possible to reign there. These, however, are dreams, and Pearson is content to base his forecast on facts. His qualifications for undertaking the rôle of the prophet are large knowledge of the past and present of human thought and human action, an unusual power of stating and marshalling facts combined with a lively and luminous diction.

The thought of writing his book, the author tells us, was suggested to him by his conviction that the United States are rapidly filling up, and that the spaces fit for the white races are quickly contracting. Climate and the circumstances of prior populations render China, India, and the greater part of Africa not possible fields for European colonisation. True, Russia may contribute a large immigration to

Western Turkestan. France and Italy may gradually Europeanise Algeria, Tunis, Tripoli, and even Morocco. Yet these small triumphs of the Aryan race are likely, in Pearson's judgment, to be more than balanced by the disproportionate growth of the Chinese in the Malay Archipelago, the spread of the Hindu to Beluchistan and Southern Persia, of the negroes in Africa, Brazil, and even in the United States. If China were to become a great Power, which Pearson believes; if her flag floated on every sea, and her naval officers visited every great port as honoured guests; if her army was an important factor in the peace of the world, and her diplomatists were accordingly respected; if her commerce were world-wide; if her literature was achieving a success for its style and thought, it is inconceivable that these influences should not tell upon the character and conduct of mankind. Years ago Baron Hübner put this fear of the yellow race in a striking form when he declared that Lord Palmerston, in thinking that he had opened out China to Europe, had in reality let out the Chinese. Nor does Pearson overlook the danger that Dean Inge obviously fears. For the expansion of the Chinese may involve another kind of danger, as, working as they do for wages which cannot support a white man, it is conceivable that they may in a not distant future absorb the labour of the world. A Chinese can work for twelve hours a day for a shilling, and can continue this amazing amount of work week after week. In the first part of his book Pearson occupies himself with the increase of the inferior races, and with the diminished opportunities of the white races for expansion.

Pearson proceeds to his second part, and in it he states his reasons for thinking that the white races, under the combined influences of democratic legislation and city life, are becoming fibreless and weak; and are consequently less well equipped than their forefathers for the great struggle which is perpetually going on, and in which the weakest go down and the fittest only survive. Looking back on the thirty-six years since *National Life and Character* was written, we remember the deeds of the World War by our race at home and our sons from the nations overseas, and we certainly are unable to discern a fibreless and weak condition, and if we transfer our gaze from our own side to that of the enemy it was not apparent there. It is by no means easy even for a prophet so well-equipped as our author to forecast the future. Who at the beginning of the thirteenth century would have anticipated that the Black Death would reduce the population of Europe so seriously as to bring the Middle Ages to an end? Who at the beginning of the seventeenth century would have foreseen that the Thirty Years' War would hinder the development of Germany for a hundred and fifty years? Who at the beginning of Queen Victoria's reign would have foreseen that the population of Ireland, which had been increasing more rapidly than that of England, would in the next sixty years be reduced to about one half of its then existing numbers? Calamities, such as the Black Death, the Thirty Years' War, and the Potato famine, may not recur in the future, though we have had the World War from 1914 to 1918 and the dire pestilence of influenza in the winter of 1918 when more died from its effects than died during the four years of war.

Pearson believed that universal military service will become the rule, but the trend of recent events is against it. No one can doubt the enormous influence the League of Nations exercises for good in this respect. Our author also believes in the urbanisation of peoples, and here of course evidence supports him. As a result of this urbanisation he holds before us the prospect that men tend to shift all responsibility upon the State. He imagines the State crèche, the State doctor, the State school, and the child, already drilled by the State, passing from the State school to the State workshop.

Physical science, in our author's opinion, has done its greatest and most suggestive work. This seems to us almost the most questionable generalisation in the whole book. We questioned it before, and we question it again. Every year has apparently fresh scientific revelations in store for us; and though, in the abstract, it may be true that there are limitations to our achievements, every generation finds an answer to problems which previous ages declared to be insoluble. Though Newton discovered the law of gravitation, and though we freely admit that he had one of the most colossal brains ever given to a human being, yet there are more secrets in the universe than what Pearson regards as "the only secret of the universe to be discovered." A hundred years after Newton's time Sir W. Herschel detected the extraordinary fact that the sun was travelling through space and bearing its own planetary system with it towards the constellation Hercules. A hundred years after Herschel's time Einstein discovered the law of relativity which corrects the Newtonian conception in a remarkable fashion. The spectroscope has placed in our hands an instrument by which we can detect the composition of the stars, an idea that might well have seemed incredible to Newton who possessed only a telescope. No one to-day who knows anything about the labours of Sir J. J. Thomson and the Cambridge School of Physicists are revealing of the nature of the atom will dream of imposing a limit on what may be discovered. Our work-a-day world, the world of Pearson in science at any rate, is bounded by three dimensions of the space in which we live and move. The mathematician, like Weyl or Einstein, has long transcended these three dimensions, forming a conception of space of 4 or 5 or n dimensions. A Sir J. J. Thomson or a Sir Ernest Rutherford, engaged on the mass of an electron or the mass of a hydrogen nucleus, piercing the secrets of the smallest entities, brooding over the dance of vortices imagined by a Kelvin, with his magic aid summons elemental forces to reveal the nature of their powers to his scientific gaze. From one aspect we behold the disciplined brain of the man of science. From another we behold the imaginative inspiration of the poet. Newton's transition from a falling apple to a falling moon was, at the outset, a leap of the imagination.

The scientific imagination was lacking in Pearson who sees more of the machines on mother earth than the secrets of the heavens. Like Kaiser and Toller, he is afraid of "*l'homme machine.*" Nor does he recognise, what Alfred Marshall shows, that monotony of toil need not mean, and does not necessarily mean, monotony of existence. Despite the views of Coleridge, Mill, and Ruskin, the machine saves human toil, and leaves human beings more time to devote to their own pleasure and profit. During working hours, no doubt the artizan seems to be a mere automaton, no more responsible than an automaton for his actions, but meet him after his working hours, as we meet him, and he is anything but "*l'homme machine.*" At the beginning of the nineteenth century Richter observed that the tendency of our civilisation was to make men as so many drops of water for the service of a monstrous steam-engine, but at the beginning of the twentieth century this tendency has certainly been checked. According to Heine, "See all the gods are flown away, and there sits an old maid all by herself, with leaden hands and sorrowful heart—Necessity." This was true, but is no longer so. We witnessed what some would have deemed impossible before it happened, the way in which our men flocked to the colours during the war, and this they did freely for a long time. The gods of self-sacrifice and patriotism flew back, and the old maid, Necessity, was left deserted. Among the pleasant portents among ourselves and conspicuously so in the United States is the way in which wealthy men steadily and increasingly recognise that property has duties as well as rights. On both sides of the Atlantic we see employers exhibit a constantly increasing disposition to devote their wealth to public objects of importance, and are building improved dwellings, opening pleasure grounds in cities, and providing libraries and pictures, music and museums for the people. Let anyone turn to the days of the Industrial Revolution and witness, say, the horrors of tailoring as depicted in *Alton Locke,* or let him turn to the bluebooks giving a sober account of what was actually taking place in the factories of the north, and will he not gladly confess the progress that is evident?

Our author may be right in maintaining that "such men as Drake and Frobisher, Clive and Warren Hastings, are likely to become rare and disappear." Each generation has its own type; and the future can never exactly reproduce the past. Yet the nineteenth century may match Drake with Nelson, Frobisher with Livingstone, Warren Hastings with Cecil Rhodes. In India there are Wellesley and the two Lawrences. Pearson says but little here about men of science, but a bead-roll which includes Faraday, Clerk-Maxwell, Kelvin, Darwin, Sir Gabriel Stokes, Cayley, Dalton, FitzGerald, George Green, Sir W. R. Hamilton, Joule, Lister, Lyell, Rayleigh, and Wallace need not be afraid of scrutiny. Nor, in spite of Pearson, do we believe that literature is in any more parlous plight. There may be silence in one part of literature or another, but even a silence of fifty years in any department will not prove that the creative faculty has said its last word. If the nineteenth century opened with Scott and Shelley, Byron and Keats, there came Tennyson and Browning. In fiction Thackeray and Dickens, Charlotte Brontë and George Eliot, produced work of distinction. In history, with the single exception of the great name of Gibbon, the eighteenth century can produce few names fit to be set alongside Bryce, Bury, Carlyle, Creighton, Finlay, Freeman, Froude, Gardiner, Green, Grote, Hallam, Lecky, Macaulay, Maitland, Seeley, Stubbs, and Thirlwall.

If Pearson seems to underrate these men and their labours, he underrates the conservative, the preservative, element provided by Christianity. He assumes that religion will pass into a recognition of ethical precepts and a graceful habit of morality, but what will give people power to practice these ethical precepts and wear this graceful habit of morality? Religion, if there be truth in history, does not pass into morality unless there is a personality behind it. He had admitted in his *History of England during the Early and Middle Ages* that "The mediaeval theory of a people framing their life in accordance with God's law, and regarding eternal truth, not cheap government or success, as the first cause of their existence, is among the grandest conceptions of history." Since he wrote these words much water has flowed under the bridge, and the State assumes the pride of place he formerly conceded to the Church. The closing words of *National Life and Character* tell us of a Stoicism akin to Matthew Arnold's "When the gods of Greece passed away with the great Pan, nature lost its divinity, but society was overshadowed by a holier presence. When Christianity itself began to appear grotesque and incredible, men reconciled themselves to the change by belief in an age of reason, of enlightenment, of progress. It is now more than probable that our science, our civilisation, our great and real advance in the practice of government are only bringing us nearer to the day when the lower races will predominate in the world, when the higher races will lose their noblest elements, when we shall ask nothing from the day but to live, nor from the future but that we may not deteriorate. Even so, there will still remain to us ourselves. Simply to do our work in life, and to abide the issue, if we stand erect before the eternal calm as cheerfully as our fathers faced the eternal unrest, may be nobler training for our souls than the faith in progress."

REFERENCES

ACTON, Lord. *Historical Essays and Studies.* (London, 1907.)

ANET, H. *Christianisme et Évolution sociale.* (Paris, 1900.)

BAGEHOT, W. *In Memoriam.* (London, 1878.)

BAGEHOT, W. *Literary Studies.* Vol. I (for Hutton's Memoir). (London, 1902.)

BARRINGTON, Mrs. R. *Life of Walter Bagehot.* (London, 1924.)

BIRRELL, A. *Miscellanies.* (London, 1902.)

CECIL, H. M. *Pseudo-Philsophy . . . Kidd, etc.* (London, 1897.)

DAVIS, M. M. *Psychological Interpretations of Society.* (New York, 1909.)

DRUMMOND, R. B. *Free Will in relation to Statistics.* (London, 1860.)

ÉTIENNE, L. *Le Positivisme dans l'Histoire.* (Paris, 1868.)

FISCHER, E. L. *Ueber das Gesetz der Entwickelung auf psyschisch ethischem Gebiete . . . mit Rücksicht auf . . T. Buckle.* (Berlin, 1875.)

FRAENKEL, F. *Dr. Buckle u. seine Geschichtsphilosophie.* (Berlin, 1906.)

GRANT DUFF, Sir M. E. *Out of the Past.* Vol. II. (London, 1903.)

HOVRE, F. DE. *La Philosophie sociale de Benjamin Kidd.* (Paris, 1910.)

HUTH, A. H. *Life and Writings of Henry Thomas Buckle.* (London, 1880.)

HUXLEY, L. *Life and Letters of Thomas Henry Huxley.* (London, 1900.)

LORIA, A. *Mistico del materialismo Benjamin Kidd.* (Roma, 1902.)

MACKINTOSH, R. *From Comte to Benjamin Kidd.* (London, 1899.)

MAZEL, H. *L'Évolution sociale de Benjamin Kidd.* (Paris, 1896.)

MORGAN, F. ED. *Works of Walter Bagehot.* Vol. I (for Morgan's preface and Giffen's study of Bagehot as an economist). (Hartford, 1891.)

ROBERTSON, J. M. *Buckle and his Critics.* (London, 1895.)

STEBBING, W. ED. *Charles Henry Pearson.* (London, 1900.)

STEPHEN, Sir L. *Studies of a Biographer.* (London, 1910.)

Chapter VII.

GREEN'S POLITICAL IDEALISM

THOMAS HILL GREEN was a great philosopher and a remarkable personality. A brilliant and accurate scholar, fresh and stimulating in his teaching, he thrust his way at once into the heart of philosophical problems. He was, however, much more than a philosopher: he was in Oxford an influence whose full force is even yet not wholly spent. To know him was to experience the power of a great mind and of a still greater spirit. The simplicity and sterling worth of his character were evident in all he did or said, and left an unforgettable impression. The massiveness of his intellect and the nobility of his character dominated all his students. When they became intimate with him, they discovered that to him scholarship was subordinate to service, service to Oxford and to the State. The note of quiet conviction rang through all his utterances in lectures or in his books. This steadfast conviction is characteristic of his scholarship and of his life, of his scholarship because, though he was patient of inquiry and open to correction, his opinions had not been lightly formed; of his life, because his whole personality reposed on a resolute and unshaken faith in the things that are eternal.

Green (1836–82) was the youngest son of Valentine Green, rector of Birkin, Yorkshire, and on his paternal ancestry he was related to Oliver Cromwell. His mother died when he was a year old, and the two sons and the two daughters were brought up by their father. Birkin was seven miles from any town, and the children grew up with little interference on the part of their father. In the days to come the son regretted that "the union of magnanimity, insolence, and a bad digestion" had prevented his father from making the best of himself, and this union appeared in the son. In the summer of 1850 he went to Rugby, then under the head-mastership of E. M. Goulburn. He had not been a precocious child, and he was an awkward and indolent schoolboy. Masters and boys alike recognised his ability, but it was not the sort of ability that won prizes. Once, to the wonder of everybody, he won the school prize in 1855 for a passage of Milton's *Areopagitica* to be translated into Latin. He was so fired by the passage that he produced a version in which he surpassed himself as much as his competitors. Between him and the headmaster there was little sympathy, though the latter thanked him on his leaving school for the discipline he had maintained. He impressed the boys by his sturdy character and his friends by his independent outlook. His favourite authors in 1854 are F. D. Maurice, Kingsley, and Carlyle.

In October, 1855, he entered Balliol College, Oxford, as a pupil of Jowett. Classical scholarship but faintly appealed to him, and accordingly he won only a second-class in moderations. Stung by the sense of failure, due to his idleness, he worked hard for eighteen months, gaining a first class in the school of *Literae humaniores*, impressing the examiners as the ablest among several able candidates. He then read hurriedly for six months for the school of law and modern history, obtaining a third class and, what was more important, a background for his thought. He owed much to Conington, C. Parker, and Jowett, above all, to the last, who exerted a strong influence in determining the course of his career. With Conington he spent parts of his first four long vacations, indulging his love of the country and his delight in walking. Milton and Wordsworth attracted him, and the *Ode to Duty* of the Lake poet struck him as "the high-water mark of modern poetry." He liked meeting farmers and tradespeople, and he took care, without a trace of condescension, to meet them on their own level. The wrongs and sufferings of the poor he met in his father's parish, and he at all times manifested the deepest sympathy with them. At College he wrote an able essay on national life, and a sentence in it ran thus: "Let the flag of England be dragged through the dirt rather than sixpence be added to the taxes which weigh on the poor." Politically he was a philosophic radical whose views coincided with those of

Bright and Cobden but not for their reasons. An idealist in philosophy, he argued on idealist principles on behalf of the most Utilitarian of schools. He spoke seldom at the Union, though in 1858 he proposed a motion eulogising Bright, and, to his shame, found himself in a minority of two. The attraction he felt for Bright was due to his belief in the moral responsibility of nations, his love of the people, and the noble simplicity and restrained passion of the eloquence of the great Quaker. If Green was a philosophic radical, he was also a religious one. He desired to be a minister of religion, a student of philosophy, and a member of parliament, and he spent time making up his mind what he really was going to be.

He gained the Chancellor's prize for an essay on novels written in 1862. Twice he competed for the Ellerton theological prize, and competed unsuccessfully. For the essays he wrote his old masters, Milton and Wordsworth, Maurice and Carlyle, were still perused. Fichte was among the new, and from Fichte he learnt the nature and vocation of the scholar as well as the man. He speaks of the "tendency to form societies and the reverence for supernatural beings" as affording the twofold evidence of the higher nature of man and the twofold source of loyalty. The impulse which produced and maintained family life, the system of chivalry, and the free constitutions of modern Europe, is the same as that which has produced and maintained true religion. A unifying tendency is characteristic of his thought. Behind all his thought lay the conception of duty which was a clarion call to him.

As an undergraduate Newman and Mill had been among the intellectual forces of the day, but both men moved Green by way of repulsion. He heartily hated the whole Utilitarian school, and Buckle formed a special object of his scorn. Carlyle led him to German thought, and he studied Kant and Hegel, exhibiting a livelier interest in ethical than in metaphysical questions. His central conception is that "the Universe is a single eternal activity or energy, of which it is the essence to be self-conscious, that is, to be itself and not-itself in one." His religious philosophy is a constant reproduction of "the idea that the whole world of human experience is the self-communication or revelation of the eternal and absolute being." He came to these views by a slow process of thought enriched by his experience of life. At Heidelberg he felt the fascination of Baur, and began a translation of his *History of the Christian Church,* but this was never finished.

Through Jowett he returned to his college to lecture on Greek history for the school of *literae humaniores* and on English and early European history for the school of law and modern history. He grasped facts with no secure hold, but he grasped their connection and consequences with a secure hold indeed, evincing as lively a sense of the dramatic aspect of events as Carlyle himself. With his efficiency as a lecturer was combined the magnetism of his personality. He is Mr. Gray in Mrs. Humphry Ward's *Robert Elsmere.* Though he gave up lecturing in history, he retained his interest in it, and in his political writings he never forgets the pedigree of the teaching he is investigating. In 1860 he became a fellow of his college and in 1869 a tutor. In 1861 he lectured on Aristotle. He prepared an edition of the *Ethics,* but this he also abandoned. In 1864 he was a candidate for the chair of philosophy at St. Andrews when Flint was appointed.

In the light of after history it is interesting to note that in 1864 he did not want his countrymen to become excited about the Danish question or even about the Italian one. Green was glad when Garibaldi's visit to our shores in 1864 came to an end. This is the more remarkable, for in 1861 he had vindicated Mazzini at the Union. On the other hand, he was passionately on the side of the North in the American Civil War. He was conspicuous for his whole-hearted devotion to the emancipation of the slave, and was at all times ready to champion the cause of equality and freedom. No abolitionist welcomed the fall of Vicksburg with keener joy. He used to say that the whole future of humanity was involved in the triumph of the Federal arms. "The fabric of European society," he wrote in 1868, "stands apparently square and strong on a basis of decent actual equity, but no adequate rationale of this equity is generally recognised. The hedonism of Hume has been turned into utilitarianism, the jacobinism of Rousseau into a gentle liberalism, but neither ism could save the 'culture' of England, in the great struggle between wilfulness and social right across the Atlantic, from taking sides with the wilfulness. Whatever might be the case practically, it had not learnt speculatively that freedom means something else than doing what one likes. A philosophy based on feeling was still playing the anarch in its thoughts." Like Kant, he set himself to answer David Hume, for he experienced his power still in life.

In December, 1864, he accepted an appointment as assistant-commissioner to the Royal Commission upon middle class schools. Warwickshire and Staffordshire fell to his lot, and subsequently his work extended to three additional counties. He liked his duty, which absorbed his time during the great part of 1865 and the second part of 1866. Just as he desired the opening of the universities, on the ground of justice, to the poorer classes and the dissenters, so he desired the opening of the schools. He defended endowments, as they enabled the teacher to stand out against the tyranny of the parent who took a narrow view of the scope of education. To the increase of first-grade day schools in large towns he looked for the development of higher education in our country, and this hope time has not belied. His strong sympathy lay with the education of the middle classes whom the universities were just beginning to touch. His aim was to efface the demarcation of class, to give freedom of self-elevation in the social scale other than that given by money, and to keep "the career open to the talents."

In 1866 he lectured at Edinburgh on the English Revolution, and, despite the charm of Cromwell, Green is more interested in Vane than in the Protector, in Milton than in Pym, in Harrison than in Monk, and in Lilburne than in Lambert. Ideas moved Green far more than events, and his lectures are still valuable, though Gardiner and Firth spent a lifetime on the history of this Revolution, for the power with which ideas are set forth. Green cared for history, but he was never an historian. At the same time he felt the fascination of an age when men were engrossed with ideas and ideals, for these engrossed him. Much as he admired Carlyle, he felt to the full that his book attaches too little prominence to "the strength of circumstance, the organic growth of custom and institution, which acts on the individual from without and from within, which at once informs his will and places it in limits against which it breaks itself in vain. In modern life, as Napoleon said to Goethe, political necessity represents the destiny of the ancient drama." The tragedy of life lies in "the conflict between the creative will of man and the hidden wisdom of the world, which seems to thwart it," and it is this which gives to Green his interest in the history of the Great Rebellion. This conflict assumed form at the Reformation when mankind found itself face to face with the situation in which there lay a gulf between its aspirations and the shape those aspirations wore in existing customs and institutions. Maine had shown that there is always a gulf between them, and from the legal aspect he had shown how this gulf may be bridged. Green discerns a similar gulf in the seventeenth century. "English puritanism originated in the consciousness of a spiritual life which no outward ordinances could adequately express." Once admit Luther and Calvin, and you at the same time admit Vane and Cromwell. How can the outward correspond to the inward? How can the things temporal correspond to the things eternal? Yet though the rite must always be inadequate to the spirit, the spirit cannot be a power in the world except through the rite. Despite puritanism, the antithesis between the two cannot be pushed to the length of complete separation.

Gardiner realised the antithesis as warmly as Green, though the latter exhibited a more lively sympathy with it. The spirit of independency made a special appeal to our philosopher who discerned in it the power which "more than any other has ennobled the plebeian elements of English life." If he appreciated its spirit, he appreciated its danger. It was the spirit which "anticipates in moments of ecstasy and assurance that which must be to us the ever-retreating end of God's work in the world." It was also the danger of attempting "to construct a religious life which is nothing without external realisation, on an inward and momentary intuition." Cromwell possessed enough insight, and he spent himself in vain efforts to create a body of wide comprehension which would sustain the enthusiasm of the men of the spirit. In fact, his problem essentially was the reconciliation of old interests with new enthusiasms. In the concluding words of his lectures there is an allusion to Hegel, whose philosophy had "for its professed object to find a formulae adequate to the acting of reason as exhibited in nature and human society, in art and religion."

In the spring of 1866 Green thought of standing for a chair at Owens College, Manchester, and the following year he unsuccessfully stood for the Waynflete professorship of moral philosophy in his own university. The death of James Riddell left a vacancy in the teaching staff of Balliol, and Green was appointed to fill it. In 1870 Jowett became Master. Green, as tutor, had now the whole subordinate management of the college. He had an immense respect for practical ability, and was not sorry to have the opportunity of using his own. His power of thought and his earnestness of manner commanded the respect of his pupils, and he was pleased when five of them were in the first class in 1867. He lectured on Aristotle and early Greek philosophy, and especially upon the English and Scots thinkers of the seventeenth and eighteenth centuries. Through his lectures the sun of Mill set in Oxford and the new stars, Kant and Hegel, rose high in the heavens. The man fascinated many who felt difficulty in following his thought, and indeed he expressed himself with but little facility. A story was current how when one day he had been explaining to a small class his theory of the origin of our ideas, the class listened with rapt attention to his forcible rhetoric, admiring each sentence as it fell, and thinking that all their difficulties were fast being removed. When he ended they expressed their gratitude for the pleasure he had given them, and were quitting the room, when one, halting at the door, shyly said, "But, Mr. Green, what did you say was really the origin of our ideas ?"

If hearers found the lectures hard to understand, they

were a model of fairness to the philosophers of the past. It was an education in impartiality to listen to them, and if hearers carried away with them few ideas on their subject-matter, they certainly carried away the impression that truth mattered, and that fairness of mind is not the least of the requirements for discovering it. The work of philosophers was worthy of study for the sake of truth: it was worthy for the sake of life. For Green always had a practical object in his mind. "We best do reverence to their genius, we most truly appropriate their spirit, in so exploring the difficulties to which their enquiry led, as to find in them the suggestion of a theory which may help us to walk firmly where they stumbled and fell." Such was the lecturer's own attitude, and he scarcely ever departed from it. Once he allowed himself to be sarcastic at the expense of Herbert Spencer, and he tendered his apology to his audience. "While I cannot honestly retract anything in the substance of what I then wrote, there are expressions which I very much regret, as far as they might be taken to imply want of personal respect for Mr. Spencer." Unlike Huxley, he realised that the spirit of controversy was by no means conducive to the discovery of truth.

The teaching of philosophy at Oxford centred around Aristotle, to which portions of Plato had recently been added. Pattison and Jowett introduced the writings of German thinkers, and Green strengthened this tendency by his eagerness to view philosophical problems from the historical angle. The historical method is of course but one application of the evolutional principle which was fast transforming many departments of thought. Green lectured on Aristotle because he was the chief writer studied in Oxford, but his own interests led him to the study and the criticism of seventeenth and eighteenth century thought. Nor was it easy to avoid a transition to modern thought, for if he criticised Hume, he, implicitly at any rate, criticised Mill. Feeling intensely the fundamental unity of the human mind in all its manifold activities, in religion and law, in society and science, he could not accept the antithesis which he saw in Hume, as he had seen it in Puritanism. Hume showed conclusively that from the conception of the human mind with which he started none but a self-contradictory explanation could be given of what the mind does and experiences. His successors in England, instead of being led thereby to reconsider his premises, have gone on "digging in the old vein which he had exhausted, and of which his final dilemma had shown the bottom." Reconstruction had not come directly from philosophy but indirectly from such poets as Wordsworth and Shelley. Evangelical religion had also assisted in reconstruction, and so too had Rousseau, for he had popularised the conception of right and freedom.

The main idea in Green's philosophy is that the universe is a single eternal activity. Experience leads us to form the conception of self-consciousness as the ultimate reality. The reality of everything lies in its pointing beyond itself to something else, and it is found to consist in relationships. Complete reality means "a system in which every element, being correlative to every other, at once presupposes and is presupposed by every other." Green takes occasion to point out that "If all interests were identical, there would be no state. On the other hand, the state tends to overcome, and, so far as it approaches perfection, actually overcomes, separation of interests. In other words, just so far as there is a state, interests no longer are really separate. In the state separation of interests may be said to exist as one factor of reality, but as in one sense neutralised by the other factor, which is its opposite, viz. the sense of common interest. Neither would be what it is without the other, but in the state neither retains any separate reality." The idealism he expresses is due, in its manner, to his sympathetic study of Kant and Hegel. It is the common heritage of all true idealism, which is "not the admission of an ideal world of guess and aspiration alongside of the empirical, but the recognition of the empirical itself as ideal," which "trusts, not to a guess about what is beyond experience, but to analysis of what is within it."

Kant and Hegel based their systems on a spiritual idea, though they handled this idea diversely. Kant handled it from the point of view of individual consciousness while

Hegel handled it from the point of view of the world of organised institutions. Kant broke thought into its elements, Hegel into its germs. The former is critical, the latter evolutional. For we must not forget that Lamarck and Goethe had been at work before Darwin.

Kant's *Rechtslehre* appeared in 1797, bearing on it the impress of the French Revolution. Like this Revolution, on one side Kant is destructive and on another constructive. Heine calls him the great iconoclast, and he is so when he assigns rigid limits to human reason, setting up an impassable barrier between the world of appearances and the world of thought. If he is destructive, he is also constructive as the father of idealist philosophy. In the creative energy of the will he found the true self and the God who, in speculation, had almost disappeared. The Revolution was in fact the most signal act of will which had been witnessed in Europe since the Revolution. "Nothing in the world or out of it can be called good without qualification but the good will," was the famous utterance of Kant; and it is zealously enforced by Fichte and Green. Kant no doubt gave the conception of right too fixed a form, but with him, Fichte, and Green the law of right is essentially a moral principle.

Hegel insists that there is nothing in the world of man's experience that is not the creation of growth, and that reason being essentially a principle of growth, no one of its manifestations is intelligible, unless it is studied along the lines of its historical development. As Vico traces "the ideal and eternal laws of that history which runs its course in time," so does Hegel. He traces the efforts made by the will of man to establish its outward and collective as opposed to its inward and individual freedom. It is the antithesis which Green perceived, and Hegel is as determined as Green to blend the two inseparably. To Hegel "freedom, and freedom alone, is the truth of the life of the Spirit." In the classical world the realisation of this freedom is unconscious or conscious in a rudimentary form. It was Christianity that first consciously conceived freedom as an ideal—the ideal to be realised by all men. The early Christians were content with freedom in its most abstract form—the freedom of the spirit in inward communion with God. The formation of the German States on the ruins of Roman Empire allowed the application of the idea to the outward life of man, his social and political requirements, but this application, even yet, is not at all complete.

Hegel plainly envisages progress towards the gradual realisation of the idea of freedom. In spite of obstacles, it is slowly travelling down the ages. This freedom is neither the mere absence of external restraint nor the liberty of the individual to do what he pleases with his own faculties and possessions, though these are among the conditions of true freedom. Freedom is rather the untrammelled development of man's powers, moral, spiritual, and intellectual, according to the fundamental laws of his own nature. Man instinctively acted on these laws of freedom long before the philosophers demonstrated their existence. Progress affords the key to history and to political philosophy, and it affords the key to right. Of course this progress is not continuous, and Hegel appeals to the annals of the past to prove this point. Nevertheless, there is progress, progress from a more to a less imperfect realisation of moral and intellectual truth. He uses all his powers to convince us of the truth of this progress. To him history is the pilgrimage of the spirit of man in search of itself. History is reasonable in showing this, and in showing its reasonableness he appeals to experience and philosophical necessity. He lays weighty stress on the share of reason in moulding history, and it is but one manifestation, coordinate with others, of its creative power in general. Hegel fully allows for the general movement of historical progress, and he no less fully allows for the place of the individual in it. If he exalts the march of the idea, he also exalts the passion of the individual. Not for a moment will he sacrifice the individual to the community. Nevertheless he belongs to a family, and the family belongs to society, which stands between him and the State. The society is to the State as the particular to the universal.

Every individual is a "person," standing before the bar of legal right. In virtue of his personality he is conscious of himself as equal to any other individual. His rank, talent, character, motive—all are left to the one side, and he stands starkly forth as the embodiment of will. The first movement of the will, in the sphere of morality, is to fall back on itself, and its next is to find a resting-place without. There must be a law of moral action, and of course moral consciousness is of gradual growth. A universal element is essential to morality, and Hegel finds it in the inclusion of the happiness of others as well as of one's self. In the sphere of duty the universal element of the happiness of others and the particular of one's own unite, and for Hegel, as for Green, the claim of duty is peremptory. What is true of the individual is true of the State. Each State is to make progress in its own life, and this life is to be duly related to the world of humanity. In this world of humanity each State can find the corrective to its own narrowness and insularity. In very diverse fashions Maine and Arnold, Seeley and Green continued this teaching of Hegel. In "the soul of the wide world" rather than in that of the individual, or even in that of the State, Hegel discerned the true "region of ideas." "*Die Welt Geschichte,*" to use Schiller's well-known words, "*ist das Welt-Gericht.*" If world history is world judgment, nevertheless the test is world history.

Green took the "vital truth which Hegel had to teach" to be "that there is one spiritual self-conscious being, of which all that is real is the activity or expression; that we are related to this being, not merely as parts of the world which is its expression, but as partakers in some inchoate measure of the self-consciousness through which it at once constitutes and distinguishes itself from the world; and that this participation is the source of morality and religion." The belief that "the objective world, in its actual totality, is thought" requires, however, the constant reminder that "the processes of our intelligence are but reflections of that real thought under the conditions of a limited nature." Both points of view are to be kept in mind, and only by keeping them in mind can we appropriate to ourselves the true spirit of Hegelianism. The ideal is the free life of the individual in a free State. Rational faith and reason inspired by emotion were to transform this individual into the good citizen. One of the misfortunes of university life, so Green thought, lies in its tendency to overrate the importance of opinions as compared with the practical principles of the inner life. "Even here, however, in our intercourse with each other, there are opportunities for us 'to bear one another's burdens, and so fulfil the law of Christ'; nor, because much of our intellectual activity is the result of mere curiosity or emulation, should we forget that there is such a thing as a pursuit of truth, in principle identical with the striving after God which animates the moral life. Those of us to whom university life is merely an avenue to the great world, would do well betimes to seek opportunities of co-operation with those simple Christians whose creed, though we may not be able exactly to adopt it, is to them the natural expression of a spirit which at the bottom of our heart we recognise as higher than our own. In the everyday life of Christian citizenship, in its struggle against ignorance and vice, such opportunities are readily forthcoming."

In January, 1871, Green married Charlotte Symonds, sister to John Addington Symonds, one of his oldest friends. His habitual reserve grew less and his life, in spite of ill health, was brighter and more serene. In the society of his wife, he felt hospitality less of an effort, and she helped him to make friends with the poor of Oxford. He was re-elected to a fellowship at Balliol in 1872, and taught with increasing influence and effect. In 1867 he had first appeared on a platform on behalf of the Reform Bill of that year. Nor was he put out when the Conservatives passed it. "The whole nation wins by a measure which makes us for the first time one people." In 1870 he spoke in favour of Forster's Education Bill, and in 1874 he was elected to the Oxford School Board. After social reforms the subject which enlisted his sympathy was temperance. He joined the United Kingdom (Temperance) Alliance in 1872, and set up a coffee tavern in St. Clement's in 1875. Local option met with his approval, and at the end of 1872 he attacked Sir William Harcourt, then one of the Liberal members for Oxford, because he treated the evil of drunkenness too lightly. Green felt keenly disappointed with the use the workmen made of their weekly half-holiday and of their shorter hours. To Disraeli's government from 1874 to 1880 he showed unrelenting hostility.

In 1878 he had at last been elected Whyte professor of moral philosophy at Oxford, and his lectures form the substance of his unfinished *Prolegomena to Ethics*, which Mr. A. C. Bradley edited in 1883. He took part in a translation of Lotze's *Logik* and *Metaphysik*, which was published the following year. Little as he could spare the time from his own work, a strong sense of civic duty urged him to enter the City Council of Oxford. He was the first tutor who ever offered himself to a ward for election. The citizens warmly appreciated his action, and by means of his influence on the Council a grammar school was established. He founded a scholarship in it for boys from elementary schools, a policy which County Councils to-day follow. In 1881 he wrote a short political pamphlet on freedom of contract, which formed a justification of the interference between landlord and tenant which was proposed by Gladstone's Irish Land Bill of 1881. This measure foreign observers regard as one of the advanced Socialist measures of the nineteenth century. Green proceeds upon the principle that true political freedom means "the power on the part of the citizens as a body to make the most and best of themselves." Freedom of contract, freedom in all its forms of doing what one wills with one's own, is only a means to an end. No contract is valid which "defeats the end for which society alone enforces contracts at all," i.e. "that equal development of the faculties of all which is the highest good of all." On this principle he justifies interference in the past with individual freedom in matters of labour, health, and education; and on this principle he justifies interference in the present with the sale of alcohol and the sale of land. Like many Liberals then and to-day as he witnessed some of the results of the policy he advocated in Ireland, he confessed it produced a "certain political depression."

Depression there was in the practical life of the philosopher, but he always clung to the dependence of the will of man in its service on behalf of others, and behind this dependence he always realised the constant presence of a universal spiritual principle. The essence of human life he finds in the deep purpose of the will which lies in the pursuit of an ideal of its own betterment, which in turn involves the betterment of the society of which each individual is a member. Society reaches its end in the State, and in this end the goal before us is the true condition of the life of the individual, the maintenance and development of free personality. To Green "will, not force, is the basis of the State." So he taught in his very important *Principles of Political Obligation,* which Nettleship edited after his death in 1886.

In Platonic spirit Burke tells us that "all persons possessing any portion of power ought to be strongly and awfully impressed with an idea that they act in trust, and that they are to account for their conduct in that trust to the one great Master, Author, and Founder of Society." It was a spirit familiar to Green. Burke believes in progress because he believes in God: "that sense of awe at the workings of Nature, Providence, God, in the government of man—the sense that the house nations build to live in is not all made with hands," the sense that Aristotle and Augustine, Burke and Salisbury all had, this sense is graven on the heart of Conservatism as it is graven on the outlook of Green. To-day we have travelled far from the position of Burke. Yet it is worth while to remember that what the Divine Right of Kings accomplished on a small scale, religious belief accomplishes on a great one. There were revolutionary elements in England as there were in America and France. In England John Wesley travelled through the length and breadth of it, turning men's revolutionary energies to the reform of their souls. Milton's generation is not the only one to serve as if for ever in the Great Task-master's eye. Green felt this powerfully when he wrote that "it is in the form of imagination, the imagination of a supreme, invisible, but all-seeing ruler that, in the case at least of all ordinary good people, the idea of absolute duty is so brought to bear upon the soul as to yield an awe superior to any personal inclination."

The man Green envisages is not the isolated individual

of Rousseau but the social being contemplated by Aristotle. Early history knows nothing of Rousseau's individual, and Green in turn repels the notion. How can society come into existence by contract? For such a notion implies that there were separate individuals, and Green, in the pages of history, finds no such beings. Not only is this so, but this theory implies that these isolated individuals had fundamental natural rights, and Green cannot believe in the existence of such rights. The social contract means that in forming it men were free and equal. Let us see what this implies. "But if freedom is understood in the sense in which most of these writers seemed to understand it as a power of executing, of giving effect to one's will, the amount of freedom possessed in a state of nature, if that state was one of detachment and collision between individuals, must have been very small. Men must have been constantly thwarting each other and thwarted by the powers of nature. In such a state, those only could be free, in the senses supposed, who were not equal to the rest, who in virtue of superior power could use the rest. But whether we suppose an even balance of weakness in subjection to the crushing force of nature, or a domination of a few over many by means of a superior strength, in such a state of nature no general pact is possible." In fact, as well as being unhistorical, the social contract is logically impossible.

In *The Principles of Political Obligation* Green provides his view of natural rights. To him natural means necessary, necessary for a given purpose, "which it is the vocation of human society to realise." Natural rights are a means to an end, and that end the fulfilment of men's vocation as moral beings. It is plain that no one could speak of such rights unless he is a member of a society, and of a society whose members recognise some common good as their ideal. These rights discredit the absolutism that attributes rights to the grace of the sovereign. In the sense of Hegel and Green, a person cannot exist apart from society. Persons and society are mutually dependent. With Kant, he believes that every man, as a being endowed with reason and will, is to receive the respect due to him. He distinguishes the State from society. The State presupposes other associations. It does not, then, create rights so much as it gives fuller reality to rights already existing. These rights "arise out of social relations that may exist where a State is not. . . . They depend for their existence indeed on society but not on society's having assumed the form of a State." These rights are independent of the State, and in a sense are more fundamental than the State.

So far, the teaching of Green is in keeping with the conservatism of Burke and Hegel, yet he himself was a man imbued with the importance of reform. What is the explanation of this? It lies in his conception of political right which flows from his conception of good as perfection of human character. The moral ideal he held before him demands that which is right, "what in the outward intercourse of men corresponds to the inviolability of the essential material conditions of moral humanity, i.e. to the idea of the existence and perfection of personality." A man claims the capacity to conceive a common good as his own and to direct his energies in the light of that common good. Society recognises his claim as necessary for each and for all the members of the society for the purpose of furthering that common good. This claim on the part of the individual and this recognition of it on the part of society are two vital considerations. A right, accordingly, has two sides, a positive and a negative: On the positive side a right is the condition of self-realisation, and on the negative it is that on which others are prohibited from encroaching. If self-realisation is necessary, so is the prohibition against encroachment. For if the individual is aiming at the good of all, any obstacle placed in his path obstructs this realisation of the goal of the community. In his *Principles of Political Obligation* Green is at pains to set forth that "it is on the relation to a society, to other men recognising a common good, that the individual's rights depend, as much as the gravity of a body depends on relations to other bodies." Right is relative to society. In origin, contents, and condition of maintenance, right depends on society. Clearly, if an individual asserts himself against society, he is asserting himself against his very life. As Green emphatically puts it, "a right against society is a contradiction in terms."

With a conception of right such as this, Green was provided with an immense lever towards reform. Not a few members of the body were living a life which was not the Platonic or the Hegelian good life. Obstacle after obstacle stood in its way, and Green set himself steadfastly towards their removal. Reform to James Mill meant the triumph of the middle class, but to Green it meant the union of all classes in their supreme desire to achieve all that the body should achieve.

If Green states *The Principles of Political Obligation*, he is quite ready to apply them, and he applies them to property. The fundamental action involved in the acquisition of property is appropriation, and appropriation according to Green is an expression of will, of the effort of the individual to give reality to a conception of his own good. This act of appropriation reflects a self-consciousness, which says "this shall be mine to do as I like with, to satisfy my wants and express my emotions as they arise." Property, from this angle, is not a mere external material required for bodily sustenance, but has become interwoven with the personality of its owner.

What bestows validity on property? It is a question which Green considers from the historical point of view. Grotius attributes the right of property to a contract, but, as Green shows, does not contract presuppose property? Hobbes attributes this right to the sovereign power of compulsion which grants such a right. Green, who never likes force as the basis of right, objects. He holds that the sovereign power, if it is merely a strong force of compulsion, cannot form the source of rights. The sovereign power, if it is a representative maintainer of rights, implies or presupposes rights. Locke attributes the right of property to the law of nature and the law of reason. Just as a man is entitled to his body, so he is entitled to the results of the work of his body and the labour of his hands. In fact, Locke maintains a labour theory of value which has been much used by the Socialists. Green allows that Locke shows the complex relationship between personal rights and the rights of property, but does he explain the exact grounds upon which these rights can be rights in any sense? He shelves this question by appealing to a law of nature and of reason. The way is now clear for Green to bring forward his own view. He bases the recognition of the claim to property on the same ground as the recognition of the other claims to rights. Just as society recognises the claims of a free life as necessary conditions for moral realisation and for the common good of the whole, so it also recognises the claim to property as necessary for that common good. Just as the foundation of the rights of free life rests in the human will, so also does the foundation of the right of property.

The rational justification of property is one thing: its actual development is another. This Green realises as fully as Mill. Theoretically, all may have property, but practically this is not true. If a man has nothing but his labour for sale, does he possess property? In a sense, he does, but not in that ethical sense on which Green lays such stress. In his view, this is an accident of history, and is not inherent in the right of property. That right is necessary for a moral purpose. The fact that many who have property do not use it for that purpose forms no ground for believing that it cannot be used for that purpose, and therefore ought to be abolished. The abuse of a thing does not prevent its use. It is condemnable when the possession of it by one interferes with possession by another. When one man uses property to prevent the acquisition by another we reach the position of Proudhon that property is theft. With Green the right of property carries with it the positive condition of possessing it, viz. labour, and the negative condition of respect for it as possessed by others. Force is not the essence of property any more than it is the essence of the State. The essence of property is its utilisation for social ends, and herein Green finds the ground of the permanent recognition that constitutes a right to property. "The rationale of property," such is his view, "is that every one should be secured by society in the power of getting and keeping the means of realising a will which in possibility is a will directed to social good."

Our philosopher feels no antagonism towards freedom of trade and freedom of bequest on the ground that they give rise to inequality of wealth. For he argues that wealth, given the purpose for which it alone can be claimed and recognised as a right, will be unequal as men are unequal. As he sees that men are unequal, he also sees that wealth is unequal. He does not believe for a moment that the increased wealth of one man naturally means the diminished wealth of another. For wealth is a flow, not a fixed fund. The wealth of the world is constantly increasing in proportion as the constant production of new wealth by labour exceeds the constant consumption of what is already produced. Production increases, and distribution can be improved. Moreover, though he deplores the condition of a large number of the working men, he points out that many, while working in factories, own shares of stock. He hopes for a wider diffusion of income, a result which economists like Mr. Bowley expect.

Property is founded, so we see, on the "effort of the individual to give reality to a conception of his own good as a whole, or as something permanent in distinction from the mere effort to satisfy a need as it arises." A like reason exists for the foundation of the family. It stands for the well-being of others as well as that of the individual. This well-being is only possible on a monogamous basis involving the suppression of all forms of slavery and that concubinage which practically forms part of slavery. Such was the deep-rooted conviction of Green who held that "the principles (1) that all men and all women are entitled to marry and form households, and (2) that within the household the claims of the husband and wife are thoroughly reciprocal, cannot be realised without carrying with them not merely monogamy, but the removal of those faulty relations between men and women which survive in countries where monogamy is established by law." His object was to strengthen and to fulfil the idea of the family and the home by making it a real possibility for all. The unity of the family was ever dear to him, and he would have liked but little such proposals as those of Mr. H. G. Wells for the "economic independence" of married women.

The attitude of Spinoza, Hobbes, Locke, Rousseau, and Austin to political obligation is considered, and in their consideration view after view of our thinker emerges. It is significant that Hobbes and Spinoza, like Descartes, Pascal and Leibniz, were all mathematicians. In fact, all the great thinkers of the seventeenth century, except Vico, were mathematicians of mark. Both Hobbes and Spinoza believe in a science of politics, and both men construct it by means of psychology, seeking out the facts of human nature that concern them. As Hobbes regards power as the main motive of men, Spinoza regards self-interest. Both entertain the same lofty view of sovereignty, and both regard the State as an organism with a high degree of vitality. In practice Hobbes tends to become the apologist of despotism, whereas Spinoza undertakes the ideal construction of the most stable types of institutions for monarchy, aristocracy and democracy respectively. To both expediency proves the unbounded authority of the sovereign. Both examine the diseases to which the body politic is liable, and both share the same dislike of revolutions which with Hobbes amounted to mania. Both look on religion as aiding the State in imposing imperative restraint on human passion.

The social contract, as presented by Spinoza and Hobbes, makes no appeal to Green who cannot believe in the natural rights of the individual being enjoyed apart from society. These natural rights exist, and can only exist, for man as a member of a society. The isolated individual may have the power Spinoza discerns, but how can he possess any right whatever? Worse still to Green is Spinoza's rejection of final causes. For Spinoza regards man as determined by material and efficient causes and as himself a material and efficient cause, a view abhorrent to Green. He criticises Hobbes's conception of natural rights much as he criticised Spinoza's. Combined with this criticism, there is something specially due to the fact that Hobbes was a materialist and Green an idealist. At the same time Green exhibits sympathy with Hobbes, for Hobbes preserves the idea of will. Our philosopher cannot regard power as the main motive of man any more than he can believe in the absolutism of the sovereign. The real flaw in the theory of contract is not that it is unhistorical, but that it implies a possibility of rights and obligations independently of society, a notion that is fundamentally opposed to Green's whole outlook. Its profound weakness is that it contemplates rights existing apart from society.

Locke is a potent influence with Rousseau. The disciple is never quite like his master, and we are accordingly prepared to find that while Locke regards the social contract as irrevocable, Rousseau regards it as revocable. Both men distinguish sharply between Sovereignty and Government. On the other hand the English thinker allows his compact to be absolutely free; the French thinker allows nothing of the sort. Once men enter upon the contract, Rousseau allows no choice as to its terms. "They are so completely determined by the nature of the case," according to Rousseau, "that the smallest departure from them would make the whole act null and void." Locke conceives of the contract as an instrument of individual freedom with terms varying indefinitely, the individual holding all the powers not granted to the State. His conception of sovereignty is essentially unrestricted within constitutional limits. Rousseau reverses all these conceptions. He insists that the individual makes a "total surrender" through the compact. In fact, it is the "mutilation," the "annihilation" of separate personality, the "collective self" of the community as a whole.

Rousseau's conception of sovereignty is essentially unrestricted with no constitutional limitations. The State holds all the powers of the individual, his goods, his rights, even his very will. In a word, Locke's contract preserves the rights of the individual which it is the very object of Rousseau's to destroy. The moral life of the *individual* imagined by Locke stands outside the State: the moral life of the *citizen* imagined by Rousseau stands within the State. For Rousseau is nothing if he is not Platonic in his outlook. He was a citizen of Geneva: he was also a citizen of Athens, for the City-State had woven her spell of enchantment around him.

Green criticises Locke's social contract, as he had criticised

Spinoza's and Hobbes's. The state of nature and the social contract are a logical contradiction in terms, for these terms imply a transition from a non-political society to a political one. If man in a state of nature regarded man as *homo homini lupus,* then there was but little freedom. A social contract means equality and freedom, yet there is no equality in freedom. Locke in truth asks for the simultaneous existence of opposites. As Green regards the state of nature as implying a recognition of social claims, it must practically be a political state, and in fact there are many such inconsistencies in the Lockeian conception. Much as Green agrees with the Hobbeian stress on the idea of will, he agrees even more with the Lockeian, which is as democratic as the Hobbeian was aristocratic. Strong democrat as he was, Green does not allow himself to be swept off his feet by his feelings. Locke's contract justifies revolution if it is broken by the sovereign, but can our thinker accept this justification? It is tempting for him to do so, yet he realises the strength of his old position that the State stands for will, not force. If the will of the people demands resistance, then resistance there must be. He, however, safeguards this perilous right by suggesting three questions. "A, What prospect is there of resistance to the sovereign power leading to the modification of its character or the improvement in its exercise without its subversion? B, If it is overthrown, is the temper of the people such, are the influences on which the general maintenance of social order and the fabric of recognised rights depend so far separable from it, that its overthrow will not mean anarchy? C, If its overthrow does not lead to anarchy, is the whole system of law and government so perverted by private interests hostile to the public, that there has ceased to be any common interest in maintaining it?" The conservative spirit of the asker of these three questions is manifest. The obvious way out of the difficulty is some sort of national referendum, though Green drily adds that revolutions are never carried out in this fashion.

In Locke, as in Spinoza and Hobbes, our critic finds much that is amiss, and this is in no way surprising, for he is a political idealist in search of will as the basis of the State.

This is the outstanding principle of political obligation. Rousseau comes closer to his conception than the others, for he of course lays stress on general will, carefully distinguishing it from the will of all. General will is not the will of all, according to Rousseau, but the will common to all. This is a distinction that marks a real difference. Rousseau elaborately explains that by the general will he does not mean the sum of the individual wills taken separately; but the corporate will which, from the nature of the case, belongs to a body having a common life, an organised being, of its own. The simple process of counting heads will not necessarily disclose this will. Indeed, we learn that "*la volonté générale est rarement celle de tous.*" It implies a collective consciousness, the complete realisation of the different selves with the State, which gives unity to the mass of the people. The self of the individual is part and parcel of the State, and indeed so much is this the case that the individual is the State. For he exercises no will save in a corporate capacity. The story of the member of the Church of England who was pressed to explain the nature of his beliefs is one of which Rousseau would have approved. "What do you believe?" inquired the questioner. The reply was, "I believe what the Church believes." "And what does the Church believe?" "The Church believes what I believe."

That there is much agreement between Rousseau and Green is evident. That there is to be criticism of the position of the Genevese is equally evident. The test of the dominance of the general will in the assemblies of the people is an approach to unanimity. Rousseau indeed required complete unanimity in the original compact, but was this a true version? Once it has been signed, there are farther difficulties. What rightful claim can there be for the submission of the majority? What is to settle whether anyone is a party to the compact or not? To this question Rousseau suggests residence, but Green destroys this test of residence, which is no indication of consent. Our critic sees quite clearly that it is possible that no State realises the general will, and he also sees that there may be a State without a true sovereign.

The last thinker to be analysed is Austin. According to Green, the conception of sovereignty has come to be more or less Austinian. As the analytical jurist finds sovereignty in a determinate person or persons, and as he considers its essence to lie in power, it is plain how deeply he dissents from the position of Rousseau and of course from that of Green. At the same time our philosopher is willing to admit that if you take the views of Rousseau and Austin as complementary each to the other, you gain the truest view of sovereignty as it actually exists. Rousseau emphasises will at the expense of force, and Austin emphasises force at the expense of will, but if sovereignty is the power to maintain rights, it has the elements of will and force. If the sovereign exercises power, it is not because he is tyrannical or coercive that he receives habitual obedience. He is not for a moment omnipotent, for if the general will does not sustain his command, he ceases to exist.

Incidentally, Green draws attention to the limitations which Maine had pointed out. Green thinks that Austin is right when he regards sovereignty as essentially resident with determinate person or persons; for history, past and present, supports this contention. This is true of all forms of society, of despotic as much as of self-governing communities. Green is careful to distinguish the sovereign from the State. There is a person or persons whose authority knows no legal limitation. This is the sovereign. The king in Parliament is the sovereign of Great Britain. There is no legal limitation to the action of the king together with the House of Lords and of Commons.

The Austinian conception is satisfactory, but it is not surprising to learn that this satisfaction is for Green chastened. Austin lays far too much stress on the element of force. Force there is and force there must be, yet it will not explain the origin of sovereignty for our critic. Here Rousseau furnishes a surer guide. Surely, asks Green, "it then needs to be pointed out that if this sovereign power is to be understood in this fuller, less abstract sense, if we mean by it the real determinant of the habitual obedience of the people, we must look for its sources much more widely and deeply than the 'analytical jurists' do;

that it can no longer be said to reside in a determinate person or persons, but in that impalpable congeries of the hopes and fears of a people, bound together by common interests and sympathy, which we call the general will." Maine saw this, and Green sees it far more deeply. Maine had laid down that "the vast mass of influences which we may call for shortness moral, habitually shapes, limits, or forbids the actual direction of the forces of society by its sovereign." There is a source from which power is derived. "While the American lawyer," according to Mr. Pound, "as a rule, still believes that the principles of law are absolute, eternal, and of universal validity, and the common law teaches that principles of decision must be found, not made, the people believe no less firmly that law may be made. While to the lawyer the state enforces law because it is law, to the people law is law because the State, reflecting their desires, has so willed." Nominally, the sovereign is supreme, but actually his supremacy depends on the good will of his people. In the background lies *vox populi*. When the voice of the people and the voice of the sovereign are agreed, they are irresistible, and their irresistibility comes from the agreement of their will. When their voices disagree, what becomes of sovereign power? A contemporary of Hobbes had said that

> there's on earth a yet auguster thing
> Veiled though it be, than Parliament and King.

For Green this auguster thing is will which forms the real basis of the State. Mr. MacIver makes an important distinction. General will is not so much the will of the State as the will *for* the State, the will to maintain it. Green of course is eager to maintain the State. He has weighed in his judicial balance the claims of the sovereign to his attention, and he has duly considered the conceptions offered to his notice by Spinoza, Hobbes, Locke, Rousseau, and Austin. The last two weigh most with him, for they attach importance to the complementary claims of will and of force as the basis of the State. Nor can anyone forget, at the end of this impressive examination, the place occupied by will in the thought of Green. The moral philosopher is supposed to move in the world of abstraction, and Green was a moral philosopher. He was, however, a moral philosopher with a difference, for he related his abstractions to the concreteness of life. Seeley loved concreteness, and so did Green, and his concreteness lends an air of reality to his *Principles of Political Obligation* which leaves its mark on the reader. He sees, from the point of view of political idealism, the element of value in each thinker, Spinoza, Hobbes, Locke, Rousseau, and Austin, and we see how anxious Green is to present this element with the fairness that characterises all his writing. This is specially true of Austin, a jurist who might seem as if he could but make scanty appeal to Green. Our philosopher is as eager to appreciate the truth of the *Province of Jurisprudence determined* as he is to appreciate the *Contrat Social.*

The claim of the State as based on will stands out as paramount. He discerns the potency of the appeal to a law of nature as conceived by Rousseau or Kant, for he is very well aware that this appeal has been "the moving principle of the modern reconstruction of Europe." Yet he is able to reject this appeal, for it failed to give that wide interpretation to life which his own leading conception duly provided. The State affords the fullest development of the rights of all its members. Indeed "the claim of the State is only absolutely paramount on the supposition that in its commands and prohibitions it takes account of all the claims that arise out of human fellowship." Where it fails to give this complete development, the individual may appeal, if not to a law of nature independent of society, yet to a law of nature presupposed in society. We are coming close to the classical and mediaeval conceptions which regarded law not as something primarily created or made, but as something which already existed as part of local or national life. Green, like Duguit, cannot countenance a right against society, for in and through society we realise the fullness of our life. The State, unlike the king, can do wrong, and he is prepared to admit the rights of a better form of State against a worse. To him right then merged with duty. For he saw no sense in asking what gives individuals a right to resist society, "unless we suppose a wrong done to society in their persons, and then it becomes a question not of right merely, but of duty." Force is a factor in the maintenance of right, but it is only a factor, a factor too subordinate to right. "There is no right 'but thinking makes it so'; none that is not derived from some idea that men have about each other. Nothing is more real than a right, yet its existence is purely ideal, if by 'ideal' is meant that which is not dependent on anything material but has its being solely in consciousness. It is to these ideal realities that force is subordinate in the creation and development of states."

The old conception of liberty is generally the negative one of the absence of restraint, of compulsion and obstruction. Green's conception is positive. It is not the absence of restraint, advocated by Mill and Seeley. It is not to do as one likes, irrespective of what others like. It is the positive power of doing or enjoying something worth doing which we can do or enjoy along with others. It adds something to the common life. Freedom is, then, for Green as for Hegel, the liberation of all the powers of men for the social good. It is a means to an end, and that end the good life of all. On this view of freedom it is easy to justify interference on the part of the State. "When we measure the progress of society by its growth in freedom, we measure it by the increasing development and exercise of those powers of contributing to social good with which we believe the members of the society to be endowed; in short, by the greater power on the part of the citizens as a body to make the most and the best of themselves. Thus, though of course there can be no freedom among men who act not willingly but under compulsion, the mere enabling a man to do as he likes, is in itself no true contribution to true freedom." The Utilitarian ideal had been the greatest happiness of the greatest number. The ideal now set before us is not the greatest happiness of the greatest number but a form of human life, the good life. It is a conception as old as Plato and as new as Green. Perhaps we ought to say as old as Aristotle, for our author is more of an Aristotelian than a Platonist. He is more of a Kantian than a Hegelian, and he corrects Kant by Aristotle and Aristotle by Kant.

Green stamped as forcible an impress of his strong individuality on men as Mazzini. As powerful in argument as Mazzini was passionate, neither man argued for victory. Both cared for truth with all the intensity of their natures. The simplicity of both men, their earnest devotion to an ideal, their sense of duty, their uprightness of mind, and their simplicity of character inevitably gained adherents for their respective political creeds. As Mazzini's ideals developed out of the past of his native country, so Green's developed out of the past of his. Vane and Cromwell meant as much to him as John Bright. In the last resort Mazzini and Green fell back on the visions that Plato and Aristotle set before men. The claim of the good life is insistent with both. "The value of the institutions of civil life," remarks Green in his *Principles of Political Obligation*, "lies in their operation as giving reality to the capacities of will and reason and enabling them to be really exercised. . . . So far as they do in fact operate they are morally justified." The fundamental likeness between the two men lies in the fact that both claim that the theory of rights rests on the doctrine of political duty. Rousseau may talk as he pleases of "natural rights" just as Paine may talk of "the rights of men." Green simply remarks that these men were so taken up with innate rights that they somehow seemed to have forgotten innate duties. Of the two conceptions of right and duty, Green is wholeheartedly convinced that duty is the more fundamental of the two. "True rights," so runs Green's definition, "are powers which it is for the general well-being that the individual (or association) should possess, and that well-being is essentially moral well-being."

Like Mazzini, Green joined the worth and the dignity of the individual man to the institutions he worked. Mystic feeling is present with both. "The enthusiasm of Vane," Green writes in his lectures on the English Commonwealth, "died that it might rise again. It was sown in weakness that it might be raised in the intellectual comprehension which is power. 'The people of England,' he said on the scaffold, 'have been long asleep. I doubt they will be hungry when they awake.' They have slept, we may say, another two hundred years. If they should yet awake and be hungry, they will find their food in the ideas which, with much blindness and weakness, he vainly offered them, cleared and ripened by a philosophy of which he did not dream." This philosophy is of course Hegel's, which influenced Green as consciously as it influenced Mazzini unconsciously. "The professed object of Hegel's philosophy," according to Green, was to find "formulae adequate to the action of reason as exhibited in nature and human life, in art and religion." Hegel's object was Green's and Mazzini's. Green vitalises, humanises and moralises institutions. What life is worth living without institutions? Freedom has to be earned through their working. Carlyle and Mazzini used to say that freedom stood in need of new definitions. Green gives us one. Freedom is "a positive power or capacity of doing or enjoying something worth doing or enjoying, and that too something that we do or enjoy in common with others." The corporate life, realised in institutions, is as present to the English thinker as to the Italian.

Mazzini and Green, unlike Marx and Bebel, proceed from kin to kind. "Everything," according to Green, "that makes life human, the institutions by which

relations dear
And all the charities of husband, son,
And brother first were known;

which create honour and dishonour, loyalty and disloyalty, justice and injustice; which make it possible to die for one's country or be false to it, to sacrifice oneself to a cause or a cause to oneself, to defraud the fatherless and widow or befriend them—all these the animals know not. They are not primary, but derived, not given by nature, but constituted by man." Nor is man their sole author. Making allowance for Hegelian phraseology, Mazzini could have said—if we bear in mind that with Green this "perhaps" introduces a settled conviction: "Perhaps on thinking the matter out, we should find ourselves compelled to regard the idea of social good as a communication to the human consciousness, a consciousness developing itself in time, from an eternally complete consciousness." With the quietism of Dante and of Mazzini, Green holds that there is room in the genius and the reformer for "a wise passiveness to the heavenly influences which are ever about him."

Mazzini and Green feel, though in different ways, that there is purpose in history, and both accordingly view the past conservatively. Evolution, not revolution, was what both desired. The "return to Nature" of Rousseau and the French Revolutionist was in the eyes of both a reversion to barbarism. Both believe in a progressive revelation to which no final limits can be set. "To anyone who understands a process of development," writes Green, "the result being developed is the reality." In this process Mazzini and he manifested a deep sympathy with the wrongs and the sufferings of the poor. Both hated slavery and both rejoiced in the war between north and south that brought slavery in the United States to an end. Both were anxious to raise the condition of the degraded population. How could the proletariat develop the self-respecting life of citizenship which ought to be his under present conditions? Yet much as both sympathised with the masses, they justified private property and private capital. Green regards it as unfair to blame capital for the admitted evils for which Socialism offers itself as a remedy. Equality of wealth is neither the ideal of Mazzini nor of Green. As the latter regards private property as an instrument for the realisation of human capacities, he holds it reasonable to find that the inevitable inequalities of capacity which diversify society should meet their counterparts in inequalities of riches.

Green used to advise his pupils at Oxford to read Burke: he might also have advised them to read Mazzini. For all three recognised in the State no mere secular product. "There is an order that keeps things fast in their place; it is made to us, and we are made to it," so runs the creed of Burke, the creed of Mazzini and Green. The dependence of the finite spirit on God is as fundamental with Green as it is with Burke and Mazzini. The citizen of the State, guided by what Burke calls the "Divine tactic," succeeds to no mean heritage. "In great books and great examples," according to the English idealist, "in the gathering fullness of spiritual utterance which we trace through the history of literature, in the self-denying love which we have known from the cradle, in the moralising influences of civil life, in the sacramental ordinances which represent that fellowship, in common worhip, in the message of the preacher through which, amid diversity of stammering tongues, one spirit still speaks—here God's sunshine is shed abroad without us."

The champions of the idealistic school of thought are Bradley and Bosanquet, who are more Hegelian than Green. Bradley heard Green's lectures though he was a commoner of University College and not a Balliol man. His passion for philosophy was not the reformer's impulse which dominated Green, but it was in part an innate theoretical curiosity, and in part an aspiration towards religion in its deepest meaning. Though he won only a second class in *Literae Humaniores*, he obtained a fellowship at Merton, and if ever the old "idle" fellowship was justified, it was justified in his case. He hardly ever took a pupil; he never gave a lecture. The world knew Kant and Hegel, and it knew Mill and Spencer, but Bradley, philosophic genius as he was, remained unknown to it. In spite of his gift of expression, his logic is more difficult to follow than Mill's to which he administered the *coup de grâce*. He annihilated the atomic association of the Mills and Bain, and he established the principle that association weds only universals. If he attacks Utilitarianism, it is not the Utilitarian theory of conduct but rather the Utilitarian frame of mind. His books were treatises on subjects: the title of his *magnum opus, Appearance and Reality* speaks for itself. He had of course studied previous philosophers, and in his *Ethical Studies* (1876) he cites Hegel more than once at length. Wherever he takes ideas, he manages to stamp on them an individuality of thought as impressive as the hearing of a lecture by Green. His *Ethical Studies* was an analysis of the substance of actual morality, its grades, the nature of its aspiration, and in it he finally insisted on the contrast between the special moral attitude, even at its best, and religion in the full sense of the word. The early part of this volume dealt a death-blow to Hedonism.

In *Ethical Studies* the chapter on "My station and its duties" sets forth Bradley's attitude to the community and the individual, and sets it forth with such power as to suggest the utter dependence of the individual on the community. Hegel had exposed the fallacy of the belief in a sharp cleavage between the State and the individual, showing its inconsistency with itself and its untruth to the facts of history. The conscience of the individual was nothing like the law to itself that Kant had imagined, for it owed its character, its determinate form, to the unconscious working of the practical instinct, the common sense of the community. That these ideas were present to the mind of Bradley is clear from his quotations from Hegel's *Philosophische Abhandlungen*. Bradley traces the influences at work on the mind of the individual, due to the qualities of his parents, heredity, environment, the influence of national feeling, and the like. The forces Hegel discerned at work Bradley also discerns at work. "If I wish to realise my true being, I must therefore realise something beyond my being as a mere this or that; for my true being has in it a life which is not the life of any mere particular, and so must be called a universal life. What is it then I am to realise? We have said it in 'my station and its duties.' To know what a man is . . . you must not take him in isolation. He is one of a people, he was born in a family, he lives in a certain society, in a certain state. What he has to do depends on what his place is, what his function is, and then all comes from his station in the organism." In truth, man is a social being; he is real only because he is social, and can realise himself only because it is as social that he realises himself. The mere individual is a sheer delusion of theory.

If the thought of Hegel is present with Bradley, so too is the thought of Green. Bradley, however, perceived more weakness than Green in the idea of duty for duty's sake. Bradley's fatal objections to this view are (1) the universal was abstract. There was no content which belonged to it and was one with it; and the consequence was, that either nothing could be willed, or what was willed was willed not because of the universal, but capriciously. (2) The universal was "subjective." It gave itself out as "objective," in the sense of being independent of this or that person, but still it was real in the world. It did not come to us what *was* in fact, it came to us as what in itself merely was to be, an inner notion in moral persons, which had not power to carry itself out and transform the world. And self-realisation, if it means will, does mean that we, in fact, do put ourselves forth and see ourselves actual in outer existence. (3) The universal left a part of ourselves outside it. However much we tried to be good, however determined we were to make our will one with the good will, yet we never succeeded. There was always something left in us which was in contradiction with the good. Bradley concludes that the man cannot find self-realisation in the morality of pure duty; because (1) he cannot look on his subjective self as the realised moral law; (2) he cannot look on the objective world as the realisation of the moral law; (3) he cannot realise the moral law at all, because it is defined as that which has no particular content, and therefore no reality. This failure of the content of the universal will is crucial.

Bradley turns from the disadvantage of duty for duty's sake to the advantages of the conception of my station and its duties. (1) It is concrete, and yet not given by caprice. The concreteness comes out in the circumstance that the universal which is to be realised is no abstraction, but an organic whole, a system where many spheres are subordinated to one sphere, and particular actions to spheres. The organs are always at work for the whole, the whole is at work in the organs. And the individual is one of the organs. That our station is not due to caprice is evident that the individual does not choose it according to his own liking, yet he and everyone else must have some station with duties pertaining to it, and those duties do not depend on our opinion or liking. (2) It is "objective"; and this means that it does not stand over against the outer world as a mere "subject" confronted by mere "object." It is a real identity of subject and object, which is the only thing that satisfies our desires. (3) It leaves nothing of us outside it.

Duty, Bradley insists, was an infinite process, an unending "not-yet"; a continual "not" with an everlasting "to be," or an abiding "to be" with a ceaseless "not." "From this last peevish enemy we are again delivered by 'my station and its duties.' There I realise myself morally so that not only what ought to be in the world is, but I am what I ought to be, and find so to my contentment and satisfaction. If this were not the case, when we consider that the ordinary man is self-contented and happy, we should be forced to accuse him of immorality, and we do not do this; we say, he most likely might be better, but we do not say that he is bad, or need consider himself so. Why is this? It is because 'my station and its duties' teaches us to identify others and ourselves with the station we fill; to consider that as good, and by virtue of that to consider others and ourselves good too. It teaches us that a man who does his work in the world is good, notwithstanding his faults, if his faults do not prevent him from fulfilling his station. It tells us that the heart is an idle abstraction; we are not to think of it, nor must we look at our insides, but at our work and our life, and say to ourselves, Am I fulfilling my appointed function or not? Fulfil it if we can, if we will: what we have to do is not so much better than the world that we can not do it; the world is there waiting for it; my duties are my rights." Kant gave us "good will." It was an empty conception, which Bradley fills with "my station and its duties." At the same time the latter provides no test for distinguishing the evil and the good in different systems of stations. To forms of government he is indifferent. The station of the citizen may be under autocracy or aristocracy or democracy. He is to render to Caesar the things that are Caesar's. The question remains, Is Caesar entitled to such obedience?

The community is a real moral organism, which in its members knows and wills itself, and sees the individual to be real just so far as the universal self is in his self, as he in it. The belief in this real moral organism, Bradley urges, breaks down the antithesis of despotism and individualism.

It denies this antithesis, while it preserves the truth of both. The truth of individualism is saved, because, unless we have intense life and self-consciousness in the members of the State, the whole State is ossified. The truth of despotism is saved, because, unless the member realises the whole by and in himself, he fails to reach his own individuality. The individual becomes what he is by including in his being his relationship with society. If morality consists of the realisation of the self, it also consists in the realisation of those relations with society. There is a sort of regimentation in society according to which each has his station and therefore also his duties, the fulfilment of which constitutes the realisation of the self and social relations.

The conception of the moral organism is strong in many directions. It confines the assertion of individuality, the encouraging oneself in having opinions of one's own, in the sense of thinking differently from the world on moral subjects, which may be, in any person other than a heaven-born prophet, sheer self-conceit. It prevents a person throwing off the yoke of custom too lightly. He may become a Philistine, but he may learn that "Philistinism is after all a good thing." The community gives us self-realisation, and at the same time it gives us limitation. For it bids us say farewell to visions of superhuman morality to "ideal societies, and to practical 'ideals' generally. But perhaps the unlimited is not the perfect, nor the true ideal. And leaving 'ideals' out of sight, it is quite clear that if anybody wants to realise himself as a perfect man without trying to be a perfect member of his country and all his smaller communities, he makes what all sane persons would admit to be a great mistake. There is no more fatal enemy than theories which are not also facts." Our philosopher evidently is as practical as Green himself. A caution similar to Bradley's is administered by Marshall in the preface to his *Industry and Trade*. There we read: "The average level of human nature in the western world has risen fast during the last fifty years. But it has seemed to me that those have made most real progress towards the distant goal of ideally perfect social organisation, who have concentrated their energies on some particular difficulties in the way, and not spent strength on endeavouring to rush past them."

Idealism in politics has enlisted such adherents as Green and Bradley, Nettleship and Wallace, the two Cairds and Bosanquet. The last wrote *The Philosophical Theory of the State* in 1899, and its place on our library shelf is close to that of *The Principles of Political Obligation*. He admits that he follows the footsteps of Green, parting company with him occasionally because of the scrupulous caution which Green displays in estimating the value of the State to its members. We meet once more with the familiar conceptions of the general will, of the State as a moral organism, and of institutions as the embodiment of ethical ideas. Nor does the individual as such occupy a high place in Bosanquet's esteem. The individual is an organ of the common good. He belongs to a body and his character as a citizen stands paramount. Home and family, workshop and profession, trades union and guild, Church and State—all these are "nurseries of citizenship" and "symbols of the social will, and must be made more so." In himself the individual is a miniature state, a field of various and conflicting activities, harmonised by the general will of a stably ordered life. At the same time the ideal of the individual is inconceivable if it does not carry the individual to the fulfilment and the enhancement of his life.

Bosanquet has no high opinion of the logical capacity of the English mind, but he has the highest opinion of our practical logic, and it pleased him to adduce in proof of this the great organised institutions which have sprung unaided from the brain of our wage-earning class. This practical logic he jealously desires to safeguard. The State, he argues in the spirit of Green, should remove obstacles or create opportunities for the exercise of the public efforts of the individual. The hindrance of hindrances to such efforts is, in fact, the ideal of the State. At the same time he dreads any weakening of the private initiative by which a man learns by experience the sense or the senselessness of the course he pursues. The criterion he suggests for State-action is its effects on the moral character of the citizen. Such a discernment of effects was for him an *articulus stantis aut cadentis philosophiae.* Two instances will illustrate the fashion in which he applied his criterion. He argued that it was better for a man to be paid wages monthly or quarterly rather than weekly, because it requires more self-control to administer a larger sum. Similarly he criticised old age pensions on the ground that to relieve men and women of the responsibility of planning for their old age weakened their purpose and shortened their views.

If Green was Aristotelian, Bosanquet was Platonist, and accordingly he praises the Greeks for inventing the device of government by discussion and vote, the minority acquiescing in the will of the majority. Naturally he has much to say on the large share taken by the Greek citizen in determining the policy of the City-State. Public opinion at Athens was effective, yet the part to be taken by such opinion in the modern State is ignored by our author, as it was ignored by Mill. Our author is so preoccupied with the august majesty of the State that its machinery occasionally eludes his notice. As Seeley required enthusiasm for the maintenance of Christian society, so Bosanquet requires it for his great society. A lover of the State, he seeks, and seeks strenuously, to exhibit "the greatness and ideality of life in its commonest actual phases." He complains that critics of the State "hardly believe in actual society as a botanist believes in plants, or a biologist in vital processes. . . . Those who cannot be enthusiastic in the study of society as it is, would not be so in the study of a better society if they had it." The influence of Hegel is plain, and at bottom we see that the idealistic philosophy of the State is a philosophy of patriotism, or, as Royce would say, of loyalty. Of the utter devotion of our author to his ideal there cannot be a question. The State becomes to him something awful and mysterious, not to be approached without reverence. It is too sacred to be touched, except upon rare and solemn occasions, and then only with the deepest awe. What Plato and Aristotle offered to the Greek, Bosanquet offers to the English. The State is for him, as for Pearson, a sort of Church, the Church of humanity, and membership of it is nothing else than a great spiritual experience. In short, for Bosanquet as for

Hegel, the State is the ultimate moral authority for the citizen, the keeper of his civic conscience.

Within the State the ideal held up to our admiration is a lofty one. What are the relations between States? What principles ought to bind them? Hegel of course denies that the same principles of conduct apply between States which apply between the citizens of the same State, and substantially this is the view of Bosanquet. With the German thinker, he denies that the citizens can consent to the creation of any super-authority. It is a problem which Sidgwick attacked, and in practice his solution does not differ widely from that of Bosanquet, who pleads not for a super-authority but for a purification of the will of the different States. Here for him lies the security against that hubris which is the abomination of desolation. Neither Bradley nor Marshall was tempted to believe in short cuts to social salvation, and Bosanquet shares their belief in the slowness of international salvation. He hates war just as much as Green, and his reason is similar. A healthy State, he frankly declares, is non-militant in temper. A non-militant State is one in which stability and social justice are dominant, a militant one is one where they are not. He argues that the peaceful State supports such humanising values as knowledge and art, religion and sympathy, and these values can be shared, in part, with other States. In fact, he is as much a believer in the commonwealth of culture as Matthew Arnold himself. We may live nationally as much as we please, yet to this we must add the condition that we must think internationally, a consideration of outstanding worth. The super-State, so he thinks, will inevitably fail for want of that common experience enabling us to understand the ways and works of citizens of other nations. Much water has flowed under the bridge since the appearance of *The Philosophical Theory of the State* in 1899, and the World War has certainly supplied an understanding, a growing understanding, of the ways and works of men we used to regard simply as foreigners. All of us are slowly learning to think internationally, and there is a will to understand other folk seldom witnessed before. If there is this will for the common good, sooner or later, on the principles of Hegel and Bosanquet, it must express itself in an organisation, which may be the League of Nations, the super-State, what you will.

The spiritual experience of the citizen covers the whole of life, and the content of his experience enriches national existence. Royce goes so far as to find in the "beloved community" the core of religion. The welfare of the body is bound up with the welfare of its members. What they create in science and art, in race and religion, suggests to Bosanquet the fruit of the spirit, working together in a common purpose greater than they dream. From the passing we are raised to the permanent, there to witness the sight of our works as chapters in the working of the spirit, appearances of the Absolute. It is a fine conception finely wrought out by our author. If he treats of freedom, it is a freedom which confronts us with a spiritual interpretation. It is, if you like, Rousseau's transformation of the natural man into the moral one. Bosanquet is prepared to endorse the conclusion of the Genevese thinker: "What man acquires in the civil state is moral liberty, which alone makes him master of himself. For the mere impulse of appetite is slavery; while obedience to a law which we prescribe to ourselves is liberty." It is this liberty, this self-government, which Bosanquet expounds with a rare insight. Behind the will of the individual we perceive the will of the community, moulding the will of each into a common purpose of which no single mind is aware. This of course means that the individual can never realise himself so fully as he does when he becomes a member of the community which interprets his will to him, and interprets it to him with a meaning and a value far deeper than any he could possibly give to it. We are indeed greater than we know, and our true greatness depends on the extent to which each of us will render to the community all we owe. Since Green's day such concepts as national spirit, social mind, group consciousness, and the like, enter largely into our life. Bosanquet avails himself of them, and throughout his book we feel how largely these concepts can enrich the life of the whole community. They help towards the realisation of the common good and of the common will

Yet, his conclusion is that the State "is the guardian of our world and not a factor of our organised world."

The idealist position, notably that of Bradley, lends itself to criticism. Did Hegel mistake the kingdom of Prussia for the kingdom of heaven? Did Bosanquet commit a similar mistake? In spite of Green's care, do the idealists in politics not confound the State and society? The term State, in fact, covers the community and the government; it covers spirit and body. Idealists like Bosanquet endeavour to combine the two to such a degree that the body is the spirit. No doubt the spirit embodies itself in the body, the institution, but does it ever embody itself so completely as to become the body? Plato laid down the pattern of such a State, but he knew quite well that it was a pattern. Does the idealist realise this distinction? His enthusiasm blinds his eyes to the circumstance that the ideal is not the real with which he has to concern himself. To him the State is part of himself. Is this so with many? Does the State touch the working man to anything like the same extent as his Trades Union? Does it touch the religious man as his Church does? These are examples of group consciousness which the pluralists naturally emphasise. The State of the idealist is akin to the Leviathan of Hobbes. It is perhaps worth saying that there is no necessary connection between idealism and absolutism. Hegel was of course an idealist who was an absolutist, while Green and Bosanquet were idealists who were democrats.

The transition from the idealists to Professor M'Dougall is natural. He believes in the group mind, which is idealism from another angle. Indeed he himself states that the only difference between his theory and idealism is that the idealists believe in collective consciousness. He is a psychologist with a special leaning to its physiological aspect, and he sets himself the task of tracing out in detail the origin and development of the human mind. His *Introduction to Social Psychology*, 1908, his *Group Mind*, 1920, and his other writings analyse instinctive impulse, tradition, habit, racial prejudice, personal idiosyncracy, sentiment, and the like. The picture of man he draws in no wise resembles the picture of man intelligently seeking his own advantage on a utilitarian basis. Since Bentham's day psychology has been set on a new basis. Increasing knowledge of the physiology of the brain and the application of evolutionary principles to the study of the mind have raised psychology to the dignity of a science. It now claims with ever-increasing right to be the science of conduct and behaviour. It shows conduct as the resultant of the social forces working upon the inherited tendencies and instincts of the race. It is beginning tentatively to offer an explanation of these tendencies, and to show how the simple life-preserving instincts evolved by the struggle for existence, becoming more and more differentiated, form the essential springs of all thought and action, individual or collective, as they are gradually developed under the guidance of the intellectual faculties and the changing environment. In Dr. M'Dougall's view, directly and indirectly the instincts are the prime movers of all human activity. He shows that by the conative or impulsive force of some instinct or of some habit derived from an instinct—every train of thought, however cold and passionless it may seem, is borne along towards its end. In this fashion every bodily activity is initiated and sustained. Past thinkers had laid stress on the sum of activities of individuals moved by enlightened self-interest or by intelligent desire for pleasure and dislike of pain. Our author allows for this, but he also allows for the springs of all the complex activities that make up the life of societies. These springs he finds in the instincts and in the primary tendencies that are common to all men and are deeply rooted in the remote ancestry of the race.

The basis of social relations lies in instincts, and we are led on to consider the place of habit in the individual. The formation of habit as a factor in progress is of marked influence, and is only beginning to be appreciated. The tyranny of bad habits has long been recognised; we now recognise the value of the converse. Knowing that an action once done or a thought once made forms a path in the brain, and thus by providing a line of less resistance tends to be repeated, the advanced teacher of the present day, instead of waiting until the fault has been committed and then attempting by punishment to deter its repetition, tries as far as possible to avoid opportunities for its commission, contriving that the young child should do what is right by what seems his own choice, until a habit begins to be established. To the teacher of the old school this is looked upon as weakening and demoralising, and he turns with approval to the "spare the rod and spoil the child" discipline of his younger days. The same principle runs through medical science: less and less the doctor relies on curing and more and more on providing healthy condition, and so building up strength to resist the onset of disease. Like all principles it is open to abuse, and the process can easily be carried on so long and so far as to weaken character; yet it by no means implies that life is to be made a bed of roses, for this fails to form habits of self-reliance which Bosanquet desiderated. The underlying fact is, however, unassailable—a habit once formed is a lasting influence for good or evil. Certain temptations once formidable hardly exist for the well-brought-up and well-educated classes; they shrink from things, as they would say, "by instinct," which is here really only early inculcated habit. This is a point at which psychology and political science come into close contact in an effort to decide how far the principle can be carried in safety. We now see that one of the serious dangers in unemployment is the breaking of the habit of work and steadiness by months of enforced idleness.

Instinct is, in Dr. M'Dougall's judgment, the basis of all human activity. Mankind is only "a little bit" reasonable, and "to a very great extent unintelligently moved in quite unreasonable ways." The seven principal instincts are flight with the emotion of fear, repulsion with the emotion of disgust, curiosity with the emotion of wonder, pugnacity with the emotion of anger, self-abasement with the emotion of subjection, self-assertion with the emotion of elation, and parental instinct with the emotion of tenderness. No doubt our author is open to criticism on such grounds as his insistence that emotion is the affective aspect of an instinct. This aspect only develops into emotions under certain conditions, viz. when there is a delay or check to the impulse or when there is an excess of excitement which action does not satisfy. That his seven instincts are the prime movers of all human activity is a proposition which requires more qualification than he is apparently prepared to give. They are by no means self-subsistent, and the organism is not a kind of aggregate of them. It is quite in keeping with his criticism of the idealists that Professor Hobhouse should show that within the sphere of instinct intelligence grows up, and that as it develops it decreases the rigidity and fixity of instinctive activity. Besides, instinct exhibits a feeling of satisfaction in the carrying out or fulfilment of an action and dissatisfaction with its non-fulfilment. Professor Hobhouse continues his criticism by showing that it is to this satisfied or dissatisfied element that instinct owes whatever plasticity of adjustment it possesses. In fact, there is very little that is pure instinct. As he remarks, in his *Morals in Evolution*, "Hunger and thirst no doubt are of the nature of instincts, but the methods of satisfying hunger and thirst are acquired by experience or by teaching. Love and the whole family life have an instinctive basis, that is to say, they rest upon tendencies inherited with the brain and nerve structure; but everything that has to do with the satisfaction of these impulses is determined by the experience of the individual, the laws and customs of the society in which he lives, the woman whom he meets, the accidents of their intercourse and so forth."

In his *Group Mind* Dr. M'Dougall applies psychology on an extensive scale to the phenomena of collective life. He employs his former book which explained the fundamental principles of conduct to grasp the behaviour of groups such as the loosely organised crowd, the highly organised army, and the highest form of the group mind yet reached, the State. Instinct and sentiment determine the actions of the crowd, and we learn that an "idea alone as intellectual apprehension cannot exert any influence." His data he gathers from the historian and the biologist, the anthropologist and the statistician. With the idealists we perceive that "Since, then, the social aggregate has a collective mental life, which is not merely the sum of the mental lives of its units, it may be contended that a society not only enjoys a collective mental life but also has a collective mind or, as some prefer to say, a collective soul." When a group exists for some time it possesses a definite organisation, and this in turn means that it possesses a self. The relationship between the groups is mental, and, in spite of his anti-intellectualism, our author allows that a highly developed group can be described only in terms of mind. If we define mind "as an organised system of mental or purposive forces," this group possesses such a mind. The action of the individual as such is one thing: his action in the group is quite another, for the group spirit moves him. Indeed "the structure and organisation of the spirit of the community is in every respect as purely mental or psychical as the structure and organisation of the individual mind." Within this community Professor M'Dougall is as anxious to demonstrate the existence of groups as Bosanquet himself. These groups, to him as to Bosanquet, are no mere mechanical mixtures of men. Each of them links together human beings into an association with a group mind. The question between these groups and the State is the all-important one, Are they completing or competing groups with the State? To men like Bosanquet and Dr. M'Dougall they are completing but to the pluralists they are competing. Nor is it surprising to note that Dr. M'Dougall glorifies public opinion as he glorifies parliament.

Professor M'Dougall was at Oxford before Harvard secured his services for the chair of psychology. Professor Graham Wallas held the chair of political science in London, and his books, like those of Dr. M'Dougall, exercise a widespread influence. His *Life of Francis Place* revealed in 1897 the share that remarkable agitator had in what happened behind the scenes at the passing of the first Reform Bill in 1832. This he followed up with his *Human Nature in Politics*, 1908, *The Great Society*, 1914, and *Our Social Heritage*, 1921. Just as Dr. M'Dougall from his particular point of view marked out the anti-intellectualist character of society, so Professor Graham Wallas marked it out. It is more than a coincidence that the *Introduction to Social Psychology* and *Human Nature in Politics* both appeared in 1908. They attack the same problem, and, attacking it from different angles, are completing, not competing, pieces of work. The share instinct assumes with Dr. M'Dougall is the share assumed by suggestion, imitation, habit, and the unconscious factors generally with Professor Graham Wallas. He asks us to consider in what way our point of view upon political questions is affected by a better realisation of human motive. Dr. M'Dougall employs the laboratory of science while Mr. Graham Wallas employs the laboratory of life as he saw it in politics, in the methods of electioneering, and in the action of public opinion.

Mr. Graham Wallas recognises the unreality of always attributing opinion to an intellectual process. He sees the popular mind at the mercy of the electioneering agent and the syndicated newspaper. He points out the fallacy underlying the assumption of those thinkers who assume not only that political action is the result of inference as to means and ends, but that all inferences are of the same "rational" type. Drawing attention to the way in which psychology has of recent years transformed the science of education and the treatment of criminals, he asks for its application to political science. We require more intellect, he holds, more reason, a philosophy based upon a sound psychological foundation for politics. We must give up simply muddling through and leaving all important posts and work to the cleverest and most unscrupulous manipulator of the popular mind. He attacks and utterly demolishes the whole theoretical foundation upon which democracy rests, yet remains an ardent democrat who does not hold for a single moment that its dangers and drawbacks are inevitable and unavoidable. Mr. H. G. Wells expresses the view of many people in his *Anticipations* when he writes: "I know of no case for the elective democratic government of modern States that cannot be knocked to pieces in five minutes. It is manifest that upon countless important issues there is no collective will and nothing in the mind of the average man except blank indifference; that an electional system simply places power in the hands of the most skilful electioneers." Mr. Wallas sees all this rather more clearly than the novelist. His perception of it lends interest to his protest against those who, following the thinkers and the idealists of the early part of the nineteenth century, treat politics and man, so far as he plays his part in them, upon a basis of simplicity that is, when compared with the complexity of human nature, almost ridiculously unreal. To this unreality is to be attributed the change of opinion which follows when the student of politics leaves his books for contact with practical issues and living men and women. As he finds the reality bears so faint a resemblance to the well-ordered examples of his text-books, he is apt to take his tomes to the second-hand dealer and trust to his common sense and the instinct on which Dr. M'Dougall relies.

The distrust of democracy was not so evident when Mr. Wallas began to write as it is to-day. Nevertheless, he notes its advent in the United States as among ourselves. He realises the unstable action of a crowd and the impossibility of predicting what line it will take. This indeed has always been realised, but Mr. Wallas realises, with a power granted to but few, that the great majority of people live, so far as their mental and intellectual life is concerned, under the conditions of a crowd. Urbanisation allows of the crowd mind to an extent unparalleled before the days of the Industrial Revolution. It is no longer even necessary to be gathered together in one place for suggestion to enjoy full scope. The telegraph and the newsagent, wireless and the cinema—these do their work only too well. Hardly has the catastrophe occurred or the murder committed before everyone is reading about it in the newspaper, hearing it by wireless, or seeing it at the cinema. People remote from each other as John o'Groats and Land's End are practically brought into each other's presence, and this on a steadily increasing scale. Two men speaking of the catastrophe or the murder both unconsciously express the same opinion which neither has formed for himself, but thereby immensely strengthening each other. No better instance of mass suggestion and the arousing of sympathetic excitement under modern conditions exists than the—very intelligible—excitement shown during the World War. On the outbreak of war there was an astonishing revelation of the fashion in which opinion over the whole country could be forced and formed in a few hours. What is true of ourselves is even truer then of Germany.

Mr. Wallas sees that we have to reckon with the more or less simple emotional waves of feeling which are apt to run through the community. He also sees—and this is his signal merit—that we have to reckon with the more subtle, more pervasive, and on the whole far more important formation of opinion by non-rational inference. As he does well to distinguish, the theory upon which so much of our political and economic thought is based contains really two assumptions. One is that men always act on a reasoned opinion on the best means of the attainment of what they desire, and the other is that all inferences are of the same kind and are produced by a more or less uniform process of reasoning. Instead of these assumptions actually functioning, he invites us to contemplate the power of repeated assertion in influencing the mind of the voter. He defines liberty as the "capacity of continuous initiative," and no one has more cogently exposed the incapacity of the elector to take the first reasoned action. Men like Mill believed in education, a belief Mr. Wallas shares but shares imperfectly. And the reason is quite plain. Instead of education minimising the evil, it has maximised it. As it gives the voter little more in many cases than the power to read, it leaves him or her at the mercy of the clever manipulator of public opinion.

Mr. Wallas is a born optimist, an indispensable qualification for all who take part in public life. He has never succumbed to what Lord Bryce calls the pessimism engendered by experience. He looks forward to improvement by education, and he looks forward to guidance rendered effective by a clearer perception of the impulses upon which men and women act. Perhaps an election will become more and more the educational process for which he, like Mill, ardently hopes. Democracy requires teaching; it must betake itself to business methods and scientific enquiry rather than the settling of questions by emotional excitement. In the Civil Service, as he points out, there is a great and well-organised force which will be of increasing utility in obtaining and preparing information for public consumption and in guiding and controlling public action. This last proposal requires careful scrutiny, for we know what such guidance and control meant in Germany where a Bismarck or a Bülow could practically say, I am public opinion, for I manufacture it. Even in the hands of a writer of the calibre of the proposer of it, we frankly shrink from it, and we shrink from it for the reasons adduced by Bosanquet for paying the workman monthly instead of weekly. At present local bodies are apt to throw responsibility on the central body, and this proposal would accentuate this tendency. Nor do English folk take to bureaucracy, be it never so efficient. We are by no means sure that if such a plan were carried out that it would not mean an increase of that careless indifference which constitutes one of the chief dangers of democracy. In his *Great Society* our author argues that thought is itself a true natural disposition and "not merely a subordinate mechanism acting only in obedience to the previous stimulation of one of the simpler instincts." We are somewhat afraid that the guidance of public action would tend to weaken this true natural disposition.

The labours of men like Dr. M'Dougall and Mr. Graham Wallas aid us not only by the knowledge they give us but also by the insight they throw on the influences at work. We have travelled past the stage when we consider the interference of the State good or evil. This simple attitude will not enable us to decide whether, say, greyhound racing ought or ought not to be stopped. We realise increasingly that a knowledge and study of psychology, heredity, and evolution will certainly provide grounds for any decision at which we may arrive. A main consideration in our mind will be the effects of legislation on character. What are the effects, for instance, of old age pensions? To one they are demoralising, tending to improvidence, and, by reducing responsibilities, to a weakening of character. To another they are an inducement to thrift, cementing family ties, and affording an opportunity of a slight rise in the standard of life. Men like Dr. M'Dougall and Mr.

Wallas will enable us to come to a decision on points like these, and they are thereby rendering an incalculable service to politics.

Dr. M'Dougall diagnoses the ills from which the State is suffering, but he has less to say about the remedies than Mr. Graham Wallas. He certainly suggests remedies. Some of these are far-reaching enough, yet he plainly feels the need of that enthusiasm for the State which Seeley felt so strongly. In effect, Mr. Wallas asks the citizen to adopt the attitude of Pearson who substituted the State for the Church. The State will never reach its height till all its members feel that reasonable and calculating emotion for which Mr. Wallas pleads. Emotion, however, is seldom reasonable and less seldom calculating, and we end our chapter on a note of interrogation. Can the State become a Church once more?

REFERENCES

BARKER, E. *Political Thought from Spencer to To-day*. (London, 1915.)

BRYCE, Lord. *Studies in Contemporary Biography*. (London, 1903.)

CHIN, Y. L. *The Political Thought of Thomas Hill Green*. (New York, 1920.)

FAIRBROTHER, W. H. *The Philosophy of Thomas Hill Green*. (London, 1896.)

GINSBERG, M. *The Psychology of Society*. (London, 1921.)

HOBHOUSE, L. T. *The Metaphysical Theory of the State*. (London, 1918.)

JAMES, G. F. *Thomas Hill Green u. der Utilitarianismus*. (Berlin, 1894.)

JOAD, C. E. M. *Essays in Constructive Social Philosophy*. (London, 1919.)

JOHNSON, R. B. C. *The Metaphysics of Knowledge. Being an examination of T. H. Green's Theory of Reality*. (Princeton, 1900.)

MACCUNN, J. *Six Radical Thinkers*. (London, 1910.)

MEINECKE, F. *Die Idee der Staatsräson*. (München, 1924.)

MUIRHEAD. J. H. *The Service of the State*. (London, 1908.)

NETTLESHIP, R. L. *Thomas Hill Green. A Memoir*. (London, 1906.)

RITCHIE, D. G. *Principles of State Interference*. (London, 1891.)

RITCHIE, D. G. *Darwin and Hegel*. (London, 1893.)

ROCKOW, L. *Contemporary Political Thought in England*. (London, 1925.)

ROGERS, A. K. *English and American Philosophy since* 1800. (New York, 1922.)

SIDGWICK, H. *Lectures on the Ethics of T. H. Green, etc*. (London, 1902.)

WATSON, J. *The State in Peace and War*. (Glasgow, 1919.)

Chapter VIII.

BRYCE'S MANY-SIDED OUTLOOK

THE north of Ireland, like the north of England, prides itself on its hard headedness in business and on the quality of its thought. If Green came from Yorkshire, Bryce came from county Antrim. The north-east corner of Ireland has produced men in the front rank out of all proportion to her numbers. In the ranks of judges there stand Lord Cairns, the greatest judge of the Victorian era and probably of the nineteenth century, and Lord Macnaghten. Among soldiers there are such men as John Nicholson, the Bayard of India, and Sir George White. Among ambassadors and statesmen there stand the Cannings of English and Indian fame, Lord Dorchester of Canada, a proconsul of the same rank as Robert Clive and Warren Hastings, Lord Castlereagh, Sir Robert Hart, Lord Bryce, Lord Dufferin and the great figure of Lord Lawrence, who more than any other single man saved India in the crisis of the Mutiny of 1857. Among metaphysicians there are such men as Francis Hutcheson and William James, and among writers the Brontës, William Hazlitt, Sir Samuel Ferguson, the real precursor of the Gaelic Revival, and Henry James. Among scientists there stand Sir Hans Sloane, the founder of the British Museum, Joseph Black, the discoverer of carbon dioxide, and Lord Kelvin, the Napoleon of science in the nineteenth century. Among historians there are such men as Sir Samuel Dill, J. P. Mahaffy, and J. B. Bury.

It is a long bead-roll and might easily have been longer had we not excluded the names of living men. How do we account for this roll of honour? Undoubtedly one reason lies, to borrow a biological term, in the contact and the cross-fertilisation of cultures. When a backward race is in contact with a somewhat more forward one, one fructifies the other and a higher civilisation results. It is, then, possible that the crossing of two cultures in the minds of extremely able people may initiate a superior civilisation. One condition is that the two races, brought into contact, must have ideals capable of approximation, thus securing that open-mindedness which is essential to progress; otherwise there is apt to be prejudice. In the past there are striking examples of this cross-fertilisation in the meeting of East and West giving rise to neo-Platonism, in the meeting of Greek science and Arabic skill influencing the thirteenth century so profoundly, and in the meeting of Christian tradition and classical learning producing the Renaissance. The outstanding instance of our theory in Ireland is the Ulster Plantation of 1608 when the backward Ulstermen met the forward Englishmen.

James Bryce (1838–1922) was born in Belfast. His grandfather, bearing the same name, was a Glasgow man by birth, but had migrated while still a young man to Ulster; he was minister of the Anti-Burgher Secession Church and left his native city under suspicion of too free opinions in theology. His son, also educated at Glasgow University, was born near Coleraine and kept up his connection with Ulster by marrying the daughter of James Young, of Abbeyville, county Antrim; but his life was mainly spent in Glasgow, where he became Headmaster of the High School, achieving a high reputation as a teacher. The third James Bryce spent the first eight years of his impressionable life in Belfast and in a country house belonging to his maternal grandfather, James Young. The house was finely situated on the shores of Belfast Lough, and there he conceived that passion for the sea which remained with him to his eighty-fourth year. Always enjoying good health, he displayed from his earliest years a strongly marked characteristic, a zest for life which, to the joy of all who had the pleasure of meeting him, never remained satisfied. Though his father moved to the High School at Glasgow, the family maintained a close connection with Ulster, which remained a dominant interest.

At the age of sixteen Bryce passed from the High School to Glasgow University in 1854 where he spent three happy years. He found the atmosphere more stimulating than that of Oxford, and the chief subject of discussion among the undergraduates was metaphysics, not politics, though nothing is so difficult as to imagine Bryce refraining from the discussion of politics in after life. His uncle William invited him to stay with him in 1853 or 1854, and implanted in him a taste for botany which always remained with him, constituting one of the chief pleasures of his life. In the year of the appearance of Darwin's *Origin of Species,* James Bryce, then aged twenty-one, published his *Flora of the Island of Arran,* thus winning his spurs in the world of science. In his later works it is evident that he never quite forsook his old love.

In May, 1857, he was elected to a scholarship at Trinity College, Oxford, at the head of the list. His academic career was one of unusual brilliance. He obtained a first class in Classical Moderations in 1859 and the Gaisford Prize for Prose with an essay on the Plague of London. 1861 was an *annus mirabilis* for him. In that year he was "distinctly the best" of the two First Classes in Greats and publicly complimented by the examiners, "a very signal and unusual honour"; he won the Gaisford Greek Verse Prize with a graceful Theocritean exercise on the May Queen, and he also won a First Class in the School of Law and Modern History, and the Vinerian Scholarship in Law. Nor did he at any time neglect his scientific pursuits.

Naturally he worked hard at college, yet in spite of his hard work he had a large circle of friends. With Dicey, in spite of political differences, he was always on terms of affectionate intimacy. Other friends and contemporaries were T. H. Green, Henry Nettleship, Kenelm Digby, Arthur Butler, T. E. Holland, George Brodrick, Aeneas Mackay, and slightly junior in University standing Courtenay Ilbert and Walter Pater. Among his seniors Jowett, Mark Pattison, Edwin Palmer, E. A. Freeman, Goldwin Smith, and Matthew Arnold were friendly, but indeed it was always easy for Bryce to attract people to him. His interests were wide, his enthusiasm contagious, and his zest in experiences of all kinds insatiable. Never a bore himself, others never bored him. He became President of the Oxford Union, and was a member of the Old Mortality Society, which filled in Oxford life the place filled in Cambridge life by the Apostles, another society which discussed the leading subjects of the day. Even then Bryce discussed history and Greek letters, scenery and education, four subjects which always engrossed him, but what subject did not engross him? His friend Dicey marked off the secret of the real strength of Bryce's character, which he found not so much in his extraordinary talents as in his admirably balanced ones. It was a sound diagnosis, for balance is a quality of his writings, if not of the man. Many men are balanced with a pen in their hand who are not quite so much so when they speak, and to this class belonged Bryce

In 1862 he was elected a fellow of Oriel. The following year he spent a semester at Heidelberg, learning law under von Vangerow and perfecting himself in the knowledge of German. This he did with little difficulty, for he had a natural taste for languages, a taste he sedulously cultivated. In jurisprudence and constitutional law he had always manifested a lively interest, and the fruit of his reading and thought was seen in the remarkable essay on *The Holy Roman Empire* which won the Arnold Prize in 1862. In subsequent editions the slender volume of a hundred and seventy pages grew into the one we all know so well. It went through many editions, and deserved to do so, for it is still one of the finest introductions to an idea which meant so much to the Middle Ages. In the United States it was read as eagerly as among ourselves, and it was soon translated into German, French, and Italian. His labours on *The Holy Roman Empire* gave him a wide knowledge of the literature and history of Germany, and his affection and admiration for the great qualities of the Germans remained firm till August 4, 1914. His book was fortunate in the time of its appearance. The importance of his analysis of the inner meaning and significance of *The Holy Roman Empire* came into prominence by the momentous chapter of events through which Bismarck raised Prussia to a position of paramount place in Europe. A new Imperialism was established in Germany, and men turned to Bryce's book for light and leading on this portentous phenomenon.

He was a born traveller, went everywhere, saw everything and everybody worth seeing, always seized on the most characteristic features of a landscape, or a building or a person, and described them with a freshness which made one feel as if they had never been described before. In 1864 he travelled in Italy with an inborn love for the Italians accompanied by an inborn loathing for the Austrians. The historian of *The Holy Roman Empire* saw Rome, and felt to the full its deep fascination for all who care for the past as he did. On his return home he, like Green, was employed as assistant commissioner to the royal commission on middle class schools in 1865, and for the next two years much of his time was devoted to his work which lay mainly in Lancashire. He noted the poverty of the education which professed to be commercial and he also noted the meagre opportunities provided for the education of girls. He, however, remained a stout opponent of votes for women. Bryce pleaded for that national educational organisation which he was destined to see accomplished.

The movement for the reform of Parliament was attracting attention, and in 1867 a group of Liberals issued their *Essays on Reform*. In it Bryce set forth the historical aspect of democracy, Dicey the balance of classes, Leslie Stephen the choice of representatives by popular constituencies, Goldwin Smith the experience of the American Commonwealth, and C. H. Pearson the working of Australian institutions. The opponents of reform had made much use of the evils of democracy in the past, and Bryce set out to refute their historical examples. The differences between Greece and England are too many to render any comparison between them effective. They are different in size; the Greek republics were all slave States; Greek foreign policy was far more vital than ours, a typical Liberal attitude; and the brotherhood of mankind was unknown in Greece. The analogy between Rome and England is truer, but Rome was never a democracy. Will not the condition of France serve as a warning against democracy? Not at all, for the moral which France teaches, as Tocqueville convincingly proves, is not the evils of democracy, but the evils of a democratic state of society without a democratic government. The examples of America, Switzerland or perhaps Norway are nearer the mark. History, then, we are assured, does not bear witness to the drawbacks of democracy. It possesses many merits. It has a stimulating power such as belongs to no other form of government; experience shows that the less a State mingles in international politics, and, in particular, the less she involves herself in foreign wars, so much the more pressing do questions respecting the internal distribution of privileges become; the experience of all times and countries condemns class government as inherently bad, because inherently selfish; the tendency of the last seven centuries of European history has been to an equalisation of the conditions of men, an equalisation not so much (in England at least) of wealth as of physical force, of manners, and of intelligence; and democracy in its true sense is the product of Christianity, whose principle, asserted from the first and asserted until now, has been the spiritual equality of all men before God. The last statement is of course sheer assertion. God loves mankind, and all men have a value in His eyes. Still, the parables of the Sower and the Talents teach that all men have not the same value in His eyes. There is a native inequality of spiritual status. There is neither equality of grace nor of response to grace. In a word, Jesus teaches that there is no equality of souls in the sight of His Father. The claim that every human soul has an absolutely equal value practically makes the demand that the principles of modern democracy shall be imposed upon that absolute monarchy, the Kingdom of God. Throughout this essay the author has that bold and absolute confidence in the inevitable triumph of democracy which every Liberal felt in the nineteenth century. From 1867 to May, 1926, is not a long interval, yet in the former year Bryce wrote: "The real danger of England now is not from the working class, for no working class in any country was ever more peaceably disposed than ours is, but from the isolation of classes."

At Oxford, where he continued to reside, he examined in the school of law and history. In 1867 he was called to the Bar by Lincoln's Inn, and in 1870 he was appointed Regius Professor of Civil Law at Oxford, a chair he was destined to hold to 1893. Meanwhile he won distinction as an intrepid and intelligent mountain climber. In 1872 he paid a visit to Iceland, and, in spite of much discomfort, thoroughly enjoyed it. In 1876 he climbed Mount Ararat, and of course the next year he published his book on *Transcaucasia and Ararat,* giving an account of an exploit which few had ever undertaken. It was fitting that from 1899 to 1901 he should be President of the Alpine Club. In the meantime in 1870 in the society of Dicey he paid his first visit to the United States, the land on which he wrote his most important book and in which he did his most important work as ambassador. He was an ardent democrat and the United States furnished an admirable opportunity of studying the working of a great democracy. At first sight he fell in love with the United States, and, better still, remained in love with it, and his love was heartily returned.

The Ulster ancestry of Bryce stood him in good stead in the United States. As an historian he knew that there was a nemesis for the emigration of the Ulster Scots thither. George III could have cursed the laws which deprived him of the services of so many Presbyterians fighting so gallantly against him in the American War of Independence. "We guard it (i.e. the Declaration of Independence)," declared Whitelaw Reid, "sacredly preserved in the handwriting of the Ulster Scot who was the secretary of the Congress; it was first publicly read to the people by an Ulster Scot, and first printed by a third Ulster Scot." Twice the Dutch saved the liberties of the world. The first time they defeated Philip II of Spain in their heroic struggle for independence. The second time they produced that European statesman, William III, who devoted the whole of his life to the resistance of the despotism of Louis XIV. Twice too the men of Ulster helped to save the liberties of the world. The first time they defeated James II at the battle of the Boyne, and through his defeat the far-reaching ambitions of Louis XIV. The second time was when they fought in the American War of Independence and took part in ruining the efforts of George III to play the part of a tyrant.

The Ulster Scot enjoys a roll of honour at home; he also

enjoys one abroad. President Roosevelt used to remind us that the dominant strain in the early migrants to the American colonies was that of the Ulster Scot. Men of this race supplied some of the finest soldiers of Washington. Northern Generals in his army were Knox and Montgomery, great-grandsons of the men who had defied Tyrconnel. Stonewall Jackson was the son of an Ulster Scot. "As American citizens," stated President McKinley, the men of this breed "have ample reason for pride. They were the first to proclaim for freedom in these United States; even before Lexington, Scoto-Irish blood had been shed in behalf of American freedom. . . . Next to their intense patriotism the distinguishing characteristics of the Scoto-Irish are their love of learning and of religion. The Scoto-Irishman is the ideal educator, and he is a natural theologian. It would be difficult to find a college or university without a Scoto-American upon its Faculty." Robert Fulton, the inventor of steam navigation, and Morse, the inventor of the telegraph, were Ulster Scots. To this race belongs John Marshall, a judge of as high rank as Lord Cairns. The number of Presidents the northern province can claim is astonishing. Presidents Andrew Jackson, James K. Polk, James Buchanan, Andrew Johnson, Ulysses S. Grant, Chester A. Arthur, Stephen G. Cleveland, William McKinley, and Woodrow Wilson all hail from the race of the Ulster Scots. Out of thirty Presidents no less than nine are of Ulster descent. In the past its numbers have never exceeded a million. Is there any other race on earth which can produce a record like this? So Bryce felt, and his feeling gave him a natural kinship with the United States which proved of inestimable value.

Americans have so many interests outside politics and the men in politics are so debased that they find it hard to understand the force which imperiously impels men to enter Westminster. As a Liberal, Bryce passionately longed to serve under the leadership of Gladstone who was fighting his lifelong duel with Disraeli. At the general election of 1874 Bryce stood for Wick, and was beaten. It was a general election disastrous for the Liberals, and Disraeli became Prime Minister. The pro-Turkish schemes attributed to the Prime Minister encountered the fierce opposition of Bryce, who was an active member of the Eastern Questions Association. As a journalist he criticised the Conservative Cabinet, especially on foreign policy. His best work in this department was done not in our newspapers but in the New York *Nation,* then vigorously edited by E. L. Godkin, an Irishman bent on arousing the American conscience. Bryce felt that Godkin's passion for truth, his hatred of wrong and injustice, his clear vision, and his indomitable spirit were all contributing to the improvement of American life, a matter dear to our publicist.

At the General Election of 1880 he was elected the Liberal member for Tower Hamlets by a large majority. It was said at the time that his success was largely due to the fluency with which he could address the German sugar-bakers in their own language. Valuable as his services were, he never succeeded in capturing the favour of the House of Commons. He was no more a House of Commons man than his biographer, Mr. Fisher, who wrote an admirable biography. The truth was that he was partly academic, and partly he had far too many interests in life to give himself up wholly to parliamentary work, and this work suffers no divided allegiance. His travels abroad convinced him that, in spite of Disraeli, Russia was not the eternal enemy. They also convinced him of the hopelessness of the Turk and the hopefulness of the Armenian. No truer friend to the unhappy Armenians ever lived, and he affirmed that there was no nobler race in the world. He was an Irish Home Ruler, admitting to Archbishop Davidson that he was so *in despair.* He adopted this policy as the least of a choice of evils and was far from hopeful of the results of it. Ulster was for him the formidable obstacle, for he knew Ulster from the inside, and remembered that the Ulster Plantation was older than the voyage of the *Mayflower.* He records his view that the assassination of Lord Frederick Cavendish by the Irish Invincibles produced a greater impression than that of any event he could recall, "perhaps even greater than the news of Abraham Lincoln's assassination in 1865, and the news of the entry of the Germans into Belgium on August 4, 1914."

In the parliament of 1880–85 he often took part in debate on foreign and domestic subjects with which he was concerned. These were the condition of the Eastern Christians under the Treaty of Berlin, suffering of course at the hands of the Turk, Egypt and the Suez Canal, reform and redistribution of seats, education, international copyright and the codification of the law. As his interests in politics increased, his interests at the Bar decreased, and he ceased to practice soon after entering the House of Commons. At the general election of 1885 he did not stand again for Tower Hamlets, but was elected for South Aberdeen, holding this seat till 1907. When Lord Salisbury's Government fell at the beginning of 1886, he was one of the new recruits to be taken in to fill gaps in the short-lived Administration which followed, becoming Under-Secretary for Foreign Affairs. His opportunities for distinguishing himself were, however, small, for the controversy on the Irish Home Rule Bill overshadowed all others. The future historian, he thought, if he honours the memory of the Ministry of 1886 by saying that it fell valiantly for a cause which the subsequent course of events has approved, may also say that it was the beginning of the end of the historic Whig and Liberal party which dated from the Civil Wars. It began with the Civil War of England of the seventeenth century, and it ended with the Civil War of Ireland of the twentieth.

From 1886 to 1897 the Liberals were in opposition, and Bryce employed not a little of his time in the preparation of his *magnum opus, The American Commonwealth.* He visited the United States for the second time in the autumn of 1881, and threw half his bold generalisation of 1870 overboard. A third visit followed in 1883. "Though the two later journeys gave birth to some new views, these views were fewer and more discreetly cautious than their departed sisters of 1870." On the third journey, fifty years after the appearance of Tocqueville's *Démocratie en Amérique,* his big book loomed before his mind, and he set to work to collect material for it. The man who was not "a good mixer" in the House of Commons proved himself so in the United States, and one reason of this undoubtedly lay in his Ulster birth. How much this quality of "a good mixer" meant to the matter in his three volumes is clear from the author's confession to Mr. J. F. Rhodes that five-sixths of them was derived from conversations and only one-sixth from books. Not only was he of Ulster stock but he was also familiar, as Tocqueville never was, with English history and the working of English institutions. He had been behind the scenes as a member, no doubt a junior member, of the Government, and if ever a man possessed what Bagehot called an experiencing nature, it was he. His object is not to draw lessons from the United States for our benefit, but to set down a view of them as a Government and as a nation. If he paints the lights in the picture, he also paints the shades. There are deficiencies in the Government, but they are more than atoned for by the virtues of the citizen. His conclusion is that "America marks the highest level, not only of material well-being but of intelligence and happiness, which the race has yet attained."

At home men like Lord Acton and Frederic Harrison praised *The American Commonwealth,* and in the United States men like E. L. Godkin, Woodrow Wilson, Hadley of Yale, O. W. Holmes, and Roosevelt did the same. In Hadley's judgment, "the most salient feature of his work, as I saw it, was his thirst for truth and fearless pursuit of it. The fact that he so obviously wanted to know the truth as other people saw it, made them ready to tell him the truth as they saw it without reserve. His thirst for information was the best possible credential with all men who had real information to give. They told him the truth because they saw that he would use the truth in the way they desired—would try to understand their point of view and not to distort it." At the same time the author remembered the outcry raised by Americans on the publication of Mrs. Trollope's *Domestic Manners of the Americans* in 1831, and he certainly did not commit her offence of utter frankness. Godkin indeed would have liked more boldness and less caution.

With characteristic generosity Roosevelt wrote to him on January 6, 1889: "You must by this time be tired of hearing your book compared to De Tocqueville's; yet you must allow me one brief allusion to the two together. When I looked over the proofs you sent me I ranked your book and his together; now I see your book as a whole I feel that the comparison did it great injustice. It has all of Tocqueville's great merits; and has not got, as his book has, two or three serious and damaging faults. No one can help admiring the depth of your insight into our peculiar conditions, and the absolute fairness of your criticism. Of course there are one or two minor points on which I disagree with you; but I think the fact that you give a good view of all sides is rather funnily shown by the way in which each man who refuses to see any but one side quotes your book as supporting his. I was rather amused to see that the *Spectator* considered that the facts you gave told heavily against Home Rule—because our State Legislatures were not ideal bodies—and that similarly *The Saturday Review* had its worst suspicions of democracy amply confirmed.

"I was especially pleased at the way in which you pricked certain hoary bubbles; notably the 'tyranny of the majority' theory. You have also thoroughly understood that instead of the old American stock being 'swamped' by immigration, it has absorbed the immigrants, and remained nearly unchanged. Carl Schurz, even, hasn't imported a German idea into our politics; Albert Gallatin had nothing of the Swiss in his theories; our present Mayor Grant, of Irish blood, will rule New York, whether well or ill, solely by American precedents.

"But I do not think that the Irishman loses his active hatred of England till the third generation; and I fear that a good deal of feeling against England—mind you, none whatever against an Englishman—still foolishly exists in certain quarters of our purely American communities. But they are perfectly ready to elect Englishmen to office; relatively to the total number of immigrants, many more English than Irish are sent to Congress for instance.

"Did you notice this fall we, for the first time in five years, beat the Irish candidate for Mayor in Boston, because the

Irish were suspected of hostility to the public schools? Though they warmly protested that the accusation was untrue."

By the time these eulogies arrived the recipient of them was again travelling, this time in Egypt and India. Before he had finished one matter his thoughts were hurrying to their next task. When some men finish one book they are busied with its successor. As Bryce was actually writing or working, he discerned all sorts of tasks which already engrossed his attention. He was not one who was sometimes in a hurry: he was always in this condition, even in in his eighty-fourth year. There was, so he felt, so much to be done and so little time in which to do it. He found time to be a lawyer and was a professor of law, an historian, a political philosopher, a geologist, a botanist, a mountaineer, a parliamentarian, an ambassador of outstanding distinction, and a traveller whose range his biographer finds it simplest to sum up by the remark that he did *not* visit the Malay Peninsula, Borneo, or Java.

Shortly after his return from India in 1889 he had the good fortune to marry Miss Marion Ashton, daughter of Thomas Ashton, a leading Liberal of Lancashire. As vigorous as her husband in mind and body, she shared his taste for travel and his views in politics. For the future the days of solitary travel for Bryce were at an end. He continued to oppose votes for women, and in 1892 he argued against this policy. Countries more democratic than ourselves, Switzerland, France, our colonies, the forty-four States of America, for instance had not tried it. Why? he demands. "We are asked to make this change on abstract theory. There is nothing more pernicious in politics than abstract doctrine." In 1892 Gladstone, then eighty-three, formed his fourth and last administration. Bryce became Chancellor of the Duchy of Lancaster with a seat in the Cabinet, and in 1894 he became President of the Board of Trade, holding this post to the defeat of Lord Rosebery in 1895. Home Rule for Ireland still dwarfed the importance of all other measures. Was there nothing abstract in Bryce's advocacy of a measure based on despair? In 1893 he resigned his Oxford chair, and in

1901 he published much of his teaching in the two volumes of *Studies in History and Jurisprudence.*

The rise of the Independent Labour Party filled him with misgivings and in 1895 he delivered a speech in which, while he conceded that the doctrines of Collectivism deserved to be examined and tested with reference to their applicability to each problem as it arose, a vigorous protest was uttered against the creation of a political party based on class. Nor did he ever in this respect change his attitude. He was plainly surprised to find that the World War increased the spread of Socialism, though men much less well-informed than he saw that this was one of its effects. With apprehension he saw in 1920 that Socialism and Communism have gone much further here than they have in the United States. He had pleaded for the extension of the franchise in 1867, yet in 1920 he writes: "The most significant change at present is the wild rush of a large part of the well-educated but sentimental and unthinking youth of both sexes towards socialism; the results of the wide extension of the suffrage have begun to be felt. Organised workers are intoxicated with the sense of their power and are prepared to overthrow the foundations of society. The middle classes are suffering heavily in income, and are being squeezed out between the new rich and organised labour. Nothing is too absurd to find adherents among the working class and the large section of our youth to which I have referred. My alarm was first started not only by the Feminist movement, but by the extraordinary tolerance, to say the least of it, with which the outrages perpetrated by the suffragettes (1907–12) were received by the respectable classes, who did not seem to feel that when one class of persons, whatever sympathy might be felt for their aspirations, were openly violating the law in every direction, the spirit of lawlessness would grow. It has grown. Those who ought to lead the middle class by their intelligence have mostly gone over to what is called Labour, but is really revolution."

The Liberal defeat in 1895 gave Bryce time to visit South Africa. His stay there resulted in another book, his *Impressions of South Africa,* which came out in 1897. In it he frankly recognised the difficulties between the

Boers and the Uitlanders. On the outbreak of the Boer War in 1899 he constituted himself a stern critic of the war, the terms of the peace, and the resettlement. He also exhibited lively opposition to the fiscal views of Joseph Chamberlain, for he was a convinced Free Trader. He had been educated in Glasgow. the home of Adam Smith, and he had come under the personal influence of John Bright and Richard Cobden. He found time in 1903 to issue his *Studies in Contemporary Biography*, a series of sketches of twenty men all of whom, except Disraeli, he had known. It counted with him that Cairns was an Ulsterman, and accordingly one of the finest estimates of the great judge, who was also a pillar of Conservatism, comes from a Liberal opponent.

From 1905 to 1907 he acted as Chief Secretary for Ireland, and discharged that office with less than his usual ability. For one thing he was instrumental in the repeal of the Small Arms Act, in 1906, and this repeal allowed the free importation of arms into Ireland, leading in the end to the use of the revolver which contributed so enormously to the deadly and despotic power wielded by Sinn Fein. His main reason for this calamitous repeal was that arms could be imported into England, and he saw no reason why they should not be imported into Ireland, a reason which certainly savours of those abstract politics that he denounced in the case of women suffrage.

In 1907, at the age of seventy, came the great opportunity of his life. He was appointed Ambassador to the United States, a position which he held till 1913. He came to his new duties with all the prestige of the author of *The American Commonwealth*, supported by his ease of manner and freedom from class feeling. Mr. Fisher notes that it was no small part of his equipment that he was of the Scoto-Irish race. "It is true that Ulstermen form a very small proportion of the American population, but the number of leading figures in American public life who have family affiliation with the North of Ireland is surprising, and Bryce found in America that many of the influential men with whom he was brought into contact came of the stock from which he himself was sprung and shared the simple puritanical outlook upon life which he had inherited from his forbears."

He came at a difficult season in our relations with the United States. Their people remembered how the Irish Admiral Chichester had come to the help of Dewey when threatened by the German fleet at Manila Bay. In the meantime the Boer War, envenomed by Irish hostility, had altered the temper prevailing between the two nations. Nor can it be doubted that the language and views of Bryce himself, during his many visits to the United States, had encouraged hostility to our monarchical and aristocratic institutions. There were difficulties in his way, and it is entirely to his credit that he overcame so many of them. On the conclusion of his period of office as Ambassador Mr. Asquith in 1913 spoke no less than the truth when he declared that "No one in our time has contributed more largely to create and foster this temper between the two great kindred peoples than our distinguished Ambassador, now once more home among us."

The residence of our Ambassador is Washington, but it would be true to say of Bryce from 1907 to 1913 that his residence was the United States. He set himself the onerous task of meeting the citizen as he is scattered all over the territory of the Union, and no one ever spent himself more strenuously than he did. He succeeded in removing obstacle after obstacle to goodwill, for he created the atmosphere in which they could be discussed and perhaps removed. Nor was he afraid to speak out his opinions. He plainly thought that the rupture between Britain and her colonies was a grave misfortune for the human race, a view in which such an American historian as Beer concurs. He no less plainly thought that the grant of equal franchise to the slaves had been a serious blunder, leading to the debasement of political life in the Southern States.

There were successes during his Ambassadorship though these successes were mingled with failures. He let it be known that he considered himself a friendly intermediary on behalf of Canada no less than on behalf of Great Britain. In accordance with this view of his functions he was mainly instrumental in bringing about the negotiations for reciprocity between Canada and the United States in 1911. The Canadian elections showed that he had misinterpreted the temper of the Canadian people. The failure of these negotiations and of the General Arbitration Treaty between Great Britain and the United States, with the complications due to the Panama Canal tolls, cast a shadow over the close of his tenure of office. Of the many tributes to the manner in which he had discharged his duties, he must have specially valued that paid by Sir Robert Borden, who spoke of "the valuable service you have rendered Canada in respect of many important and difficult questions with which you have had to deal since we assumed office in October, 1911." He had made it his aim to wipe out the impression bluntly noted by Earl Grey, the Governor-General of Canada, that the Dominion had been "sacrificed again and again by John Bull in his desire to cultivate the friendship of Uncle Sam." At the same time he cultivated the friendship of Uncle Sam, and the years spent at Washington must be counted the most successful episode in a singularly successful career. On his retirement in 1913 his departure called forth remarkable and almost universal expressions of the affections and esteem in which he was held in the United States. If he experienced disappointments in his own special work—and what man has not?—he also experienced them as he witnessed the progress of politics in the United States. He discerned formidable dangers in the selfish power of the party machine, in the weakness of the State judiciary, and in the recklessness of the press. Yet with his invincible optimism, in his revised editions of *The American Commonwealth,* he let the following stand. "The Americans have fortunately the power of recognising, trusting and following a strong and honest man. In this quality coupled with that instinct for order, that sense of justice, that freedom from class bitterness which belong to the native American, we may perhaps find the best ground for hope for the future of the nation."

His own addresses from 1907 to 1913 are filled with hopefulness. In them he repeatedly bids his hearers reflect on the glorious heritage to which they are heirs. He lays stress on the common bond of free institutions which belongs to every branch of the English-speaking race, just as he lays stress on the continuity of English and American history. Nor do his disappointments prevent him holding fast to his ideals. In a private letter from Roosevelt written in 1912 he reads words which fill him with joy. "I am a dreamer of dreams. I venture to hope that ultimately there may be some kind of intimate association between Great Britain and Ireland, Canada, Australia, South Africa, New Zealand, and our own country which will put us upon some such footing that we can literally have every question that may arise within our own limits settled exactly as similar difficulties within the British Empire, or within the United States, are now settled."

It was entirely in keeping with the energy of Bryce that during the term of his office he should pay a visit to South America by taking double leave from September, 1910, to January 1, 1911, and this resulted in the production of his *South America* in which he shows the wide range of his sympathy and the depth of his insight. As a warm believer in democracy, he wanted to see for himself what truth there was in the attack Maine made in 1885 on South American governments. His observation led him to the conclusion that Maine's reasonings were valid against those who held that the name of a republic is enough to ensure good government, but valid against them only. In his *Modern Democracies* he returns to this charge, holding that whatever one might call the Spanish-American republics now, they were certainly not democracies thirty-five or forty years ago, and only two or three of them could be called by that name now. Plato and Aristotle would have described them as forms of tyranny, i.e. illegal despotisms resting on military force, and this is in truth what they are.

On his return home he was created in 1914 Viscount Bryce of Dechmont in county Lanark, in the peerage of the United Kingdom. He valued his new honour not for the sake of the title of Viscount but because it gave him an opportunity of expressing his mind in the House of Lords on public affairs. One of his first public speeches as a peer was an address which he delivered at Manchester on the constitution of the Second Chamber. In 1917 Mr. Lloyd

George appointed him the chairman of the Second Chamber Conference. He reported in the spring of 1918 at a time least favourable to the reception of proposals for reform of the House of Lords.

Bryce had been opposed to the Boer War, but the invasion of Belgium brought him into the World War. During the war he naturally kept in close touch with opinion in America, and he delivered address after address on the historical and philosophical aspects of the conflict, and these were published after the Armistice. They were moderate in tone, and all the more influential on that account. The war had been fought only a few months when Mr. Asquith appointed him chairman of a Committee on "Alleged German Outrages"; and the report was the first judicial presentment of the atrocious conduct of the German Army in Belgium. It concluded with the belief that the disclosures which it revealed would not be in vain if they touched the conscience of mankind, and the hope that "the nations of the world in council" might in future devise sanctions to prevent the recurrence of war. This report was translated into twenty-seven languages, and exercised far-reaching effects on public opinion, notably in America, where Bryce's name carried immense weight. To the cause of international peace and to the League of Nations he naturally gave the full support of his authority. He might be an Ulster Scot, but he was as fine an internationalist as Mazzini himself. If Roosevelt entertained visions of a union of the English-speaking races, he entertained visions of a union of mankind. The League of Nations was an earnest of the realisation of his vision

He was eighty-three when his *Modern Democracies* was published in 1921. From 1864 when his *Holy Roman Empire* appeared two generations had been instructed and delighted by the penetrating studies in political philosophy he had given to the world. His two volumes on the course of modern democracy are marked by all the judicial qualities so long associated with his pen. There is no sign that the author's intellectual eye has even begun to grow dim or that his pen has lost any of its strength. His record almost equals that of Sir Adolphus Ward or Leopold von Ranke.

At the age of eighty-five the great German historian informed his publisher that he proposed to write a new work on universal history; when he died six years later seven volumes of his *Weltgeschichte* had been dictated. Ranke, however, remained a professor his life long. Bryce served his country not only as a teacher but also as a statesman. He won distinction for himself and did good work for the world as a member of parliament, as a minister of the Crown and, above all, as ambassador at Washington. And his experience in the realm of action has given additional value to his work in the realm of thought.

In 1921 he paid his last visit to the land he dearly loved, the United States. He gave a course of lectures at the Institute of Politics in Williams College, and he was glad of the opportunity of delivering his mind on the congenial topic of international relations. His faith in the future was unshakeable, and all the more unshakeable because of his deeply religious nature. The last lecture of his course was on possible methods of averting war, and he spoke to an audience penetrated by heartfelt emotion of the part the United States could assume in the salvation of humanity. As a citizen of the world—and this was ever his true character—he appealed to the American public "to take their share in the great task of raising international relations on to a higher plane, he would not venture to prescribe the mode in which this should be done, for that must be left to themselves, but to take their share, each and all taking responsibility as citizens of a great state contributing to the formation of public opinion."

Natural as it is to compare Bryce's *American Commonwealth* with Tocqueville's *Démocratie en Amérique*, it is even more natural to compare the authors rather than their books. Both are men of letters with attractive styles. Both possess a sound practical knowledge of law, always useful but indispensable to any real grasp of American institutions, which are essentially the work of lawyers. In addition to their qualities as legists, both are statesmen, statesmen, too, preoccupied with the philosophy of government rather than with its details. Their books betray a knowledge of the world of affairs which lends reality to their pages, and they also betray the intense desire of their authors to investigate the true inwardness of democracy. They are absorbed with the share it must take in the deepest interests of mankind. Behind the passing they are eager to discern the permanent. Each author has of course a bias of his own, and Tocqueville is as biased against democracy as Bryce is biased in favour of it. In spite of this bias—after all, both men are human beings—each analyses the institutions of the United States free from sympathies with Democrat or Republican. The proof of this is that just as Tocqueville's treatise perplexed the reactionary Conservatism of France no less than the Benthamite Radicalism of England in 1835, so Bryce's book perplexed the Democrats and the Republicans of the United States no less than the Conservative and the Liberals of England in 1888. The English prophet, like the French, declined either to curse or to bless, and consequently was as little liked as Balaam of old. Tocqueville bases his work on the deductive method which Bryce wisely discards. There are other differences. Tocqueville's object is to analyse not American democracy, which is Bryce's, but a far different thing—democracy in America. Democracy is to him a condition of society whereas it is to Bryce a form of government.

Like many another author, though Tocqueville writes consciously about democracy in America, he writes subconsciously about democracy in France. "*J'avoue,*" he admits, "*que dans l'Amérique, j'ai vu plus que l'Amérique; j'y ai cherché une image de la démocratie elle-même, de ses penchants, de son caractère, de ses préjugés, de ses passions.*" Like Plato in the *Republic,* he sets out by imagining that there exists somewhere a type or pattern of democracy, and as the American republic comes nearest to this pattern, he accordingly selects it for examination. Tocqueville is impressed in the United States by the thoroughness with which the principle of the sovereignty of the people is carried out. He is no less impressed by the greater importance to ordinary citizens of State government than of Federal government, and their warmer attachment to the former. The basis of all American government he finds to be in local government, the ultimate unit of which is in New England the township, in the Southern and Middle States the county. Curiously enough, the President appears to our author as a comparatively weak official. The Federal Supreme Court forms the noblest product of the wisdom of those who framed the Federal Constitution, a view heartily re-echoed by Maine and Bryce. We learn that next to the people, the greatest power in the country is the press; yet it is less powerful than it is in France, because the number of journals is so prodigious. Tocqueville perceives the striking inferiority of the House of Representatives to the Senate, a view also re-echoed by Maine and Bryce. He also notes the instability in administration, and, above all, in legislation. Laws are being constantly changed; nothing remains fixed or certain. Nor is it correct to think that democratic governments are specially economical.

There is another side to the picture Tocqueville draws of American democracy, and here we employ the summary Bryce gives of views entertained in 1835. In democracies, the majority is omnipotent, and in America the evils flowing hence are aggravated by the shortness of the term for which a legislature is chosen, by the weakness of the Executive, by the incipient disposition to choose even the judges by popular vote, by the notion universally accepted that the majority must be right. The majority in a legislature being unchecked, laws are hastily framed and altered, administration possesses no permanence, and officials are allowed a dangerously wide range of arbitrary authority. There is no escape from the tyranny of the majority. It dominates even thought, forbidding, not indeed by law, but through social penalties no less effective than legal ones, the expression of any opinion displeasing to the ordinary citizen. In theology, even in philosophy, one must beware of any divergence from the path of orthodoxy. No one dare tell an unwelcome truth to the people, for the people will receive nothing but incense. Such repression sufficiently explains the absence of great writers and of great characters in public life. It is not therefore of weakness that free government in America will ever perish, but through excess of strength, the majority driving the minority to despair and to arms.

Tocqueville's range was nominally American, but it was also European. Maine's range is the whole world. Making use of the comparative method, he ransacks the field of history. He holds, like Tocqueville, that the opinions of the party reflect less the mind of its leader than that of the mind most likely to win favour with the greatest number of supporters. Tocqueville is as afraid as Maine of the wide electoral basis with its tendency to a dead level of cosmopolitan opinion, which rulers are compelled to adopt as the standard of legislation and policy, the "common sense of the most," as it was glorified by Tennyson in his earlier days.

"You may fool all the people some of the time," owned Abraham Lincoln, "and some of the people all of the time; but you cannot fool all the people all the time." This was a profound belief with Bryce, and it inspires his *American Commonwealth*, a book we now proceed to examine. In it he insists that the whole American fabric is founded, in the first instance, upon English constitutional principles, English institutions, and English law. All that is new is the extension of them, in details and political machinery. No doubt the scale on which the democratic experiment is being tried is unprecedented. For it is being tried in a continent new to civilisation, extending from the Atlantic to the Pacific, and from Canada to the Gulf of Mexico; infinite in the variety, and practically inexhaustible in the amount, of its physical resources, natural wealth, and fertility; with an atmosphere at once healthful and invigorating, and a scenery so striking and noble as to be in itself an inspiration. He knows that the character of political institutions depends on the circumstances which have given them birth, the influences under which they exist, and the customs of the people among whom they flourish. His third volume, which is nearest in aim with Tocqueville's, analyses social life, as far as it bears on politics. Under the three heads of Public Opinion, Illustrations and Reflections, and Social Institutions, he considers a host of questions which are full of interest.

The chapters on Public Opinion are no mere account of American feeling, but are also an acute analysis of the nature of public opinion. Under the head of Illustrations and Reflections we have the tale of such corruption as the Tweed Ring in New York, the Gas Ring in Philadelphia, and Kearneyism in California, an account of the agitation for women's suffrage, and a balanced estimate, in the light of American experience, of the faults imputed and imputable to democracy. Under the head of Social Institutions Bryce ably handles such topics as the bench, the bar, the position of women, the pleasantness of American life, and the like.

The distinction between rigid and flexible constitutions he had worked out in an Oxford lecture in 1884, and he employs it to contrast the difference between the rigid constitution of the United States and the flexible constitution of England. The former is a fundamental law, to which all exercise of governmental authority in any department and for every purpose, State or Federal, is subordinate, and must conform. Neither the President, nor the Congress, nor any State government, possesses power to disobey or dispense with the requirements or the limitations of the written instrument, from which all their authority is necessarily derived. All governmental acts, legislative, executive, or judicial, must consist with it, or they are absolutely void. The Supreme Court, which sits at Washington, acts as the interpreter of the constitution. It is, in effect, the arbiter of all constitutional rights between the States and the National Government, and between the citizen and either. Nor does Bryce omit to point out that the position and action of the Federal Courts are in fact determined by the ideas of laws and of judicial duty which have long governed the conduct of the English bench. The formation of the Constitution of the United States, during the period in which it took its decisive shape in the early nineteenth century, was principally the work, as Bryce particularly points out, of John Marshall, an Ulster Scot by descent, a very great judge, and beyond doubt the greatest constitutional lawyer who has left his impress upon jurisprudence.

With all his favourable impressions of American institutions our author is compelled by candour to allow that in the contest for the Presidency a man of the highest order will not often be a candidate, and can hardly ever be elected. The office is great, now one of the greatest in the world, but can rarely be filled by a great man. To have a chance of success, a candidate must not only be acceptable to the workers of the political machine, interested not to give the country an outstanding President, but to obtain one they themselves can control, but he must also appeal successfully to all the ignorant prejudices of the lower classes, and to a considerable extent foreign classes of voters. Once in four years there is a Presidential election. It means a tremendous strain, interruption, and excitement all over the Union: it also means a pandemonium of clamour and uproar, of vituperation and corruption. The result is, as our author sees, that the better class of men generally withdraw from public life, leaving political affairs to those who make a trade of them; that the quality of the national as well as of the State legislatures has accordingly very much deteriorated in character, ability, and dignity; and the corruptions, robberies, and scandals of municipal government have reached a point seldom seen before in the history of civilised government.

Uniformity in essentials, combined with variety in particulars, appears to be the law of State constitutions. State governments follow the lines of the Federal Government. In each State there is found a constitution which cannot be changed by the ordinary legislative body, and constitutes the supreme law of the State as truly as the Constitution of the United States is the supreme law of the Union. Guarded as Bryce is in his statements, he does not conceal the fact that in some State legislatures corruption has become intolerable, and controls all the important features of legislation. The highest place belongs to the legislative bodies of New England States, the lowest to the States with large cities, which have consequently received the largest influx of European immigrants, and have fallen most completely under the management of unscrupulous party bosses. New York, Philadelphia, and other large cities have poisoned the legislatures of the States to which they respectively belong. Bryce reveals the extent to which parochialism moulds politics. It pervades Congress and the State legislatures. A senator must reside in his own State: a member of Congress must reside in the electoral district which he represents.

The degradation of politics is evident, and yet it is in defiance of public opinion, and not in consequence of it; and is at once the cause and the consequence of the practical exclusion of the better class of the people from politics. Bryce deals very fully with the subject of national character and social institutions, and his high estimate of both is sustained by all who have had the good fortune to visit the United States. The whole tone of his pages bears witness to his belief that the American people are high-spirited, noble, generous, brimming over with energy, life and hope. He shared to the full "the intense faith which the Americans have in the soundness of their institutions and in the future of their country." He examines every charge which philosophers and censors have brought against popular government, notably as it exists in the United States, and he pronounces each charge unfounded. He disbelieves in the tyranny of the majority, he disbelieves in the fickleness of the people, and he disbelieves in democratic incapacity for energetic action. He sees no connection between popular government and anarchy, and inclines to the belief prevalent among Americans that, on large matters of policy, the multitude of ordinary men will, in the long run, come to a right decision; while he drops more than one hint of a tendency towards the optimism which suggests that the sentiment of the masses is a safer guide than the knowledge or the thoughtfulness of an educated class.

In 1921 he returns to the problem of *Modern Democracies*, and he sets out by discussing considerations applicable to democratic government in general. Since 1888 he has been gradually impressed by the decline in the reputation of representative assemblies. Mill hailed their coming as the dawn of the millennium, and so did the Liberals he influenced. The two defects charged against them Bryce finds to be that they were too little representative of the best knowledge, wisdom, and experience of the country, and that they were liable to fall under the control of one political party disposed to press through class measures in a hasty and tyrannical spirit. What is the remedy or remedies? With all his faith in the value of representation, Bryce sees the remedy in a properly constituted Second Chamber.

He uses the word democracy in its old and strict sense, "as denoting a government in which the will of the majority of qualified citizens rule, taking the qualified citizens to constitute the great bulk of the inhabitants, say, roughly, at least three-fourths, so that the physical force of the citizens coincided (broadly speaking) with their voting power." This is, in effect, the view adopted by Sir Henry Maine, Edmond Schérer, and by J. R. Lowell. Of course it is possible to argue that democracy is as much a form of State or a form of society, as Tocqueville argues, as a form of government. We simply note the restriction Bryce imposes on himself in considering the problem to which he devotes himself. He proceeds to trace the historical evolution of democracy, its theoretical foundations, its relations with liberty, equality, education, religion, and the power exercised by tradition, and by the press in controlling the action of the voter. There is an illuminating account of the share taken by public opinion in this process.

Dealing next with the republics of classical times, Bryce points out, as he did in his 1867 essay, that the democracies of Athens, Syracuse, and Mitylene differ in respect after respect from the democracies of our own day. We hear again that the classical State was a City-State, built on the foundation of slavery. Besides, its business was simple when compared with the complexities of a modern State. There was then no moral or spiritual bond to link men of different races together. Men then invariably regarded a stranger as an enemy. The feeling of human brotherhood, transcending race and colour, estate and privilege, was entirely unknown. From Athens Bryce turns to the republics of Spanish-America, and he only allows two or three of them any title to be called a democracy.

The rest of the first volume of *Modern Democracies* is

devoted to France, Switzerland—a land receiving a meed of warm praise—and Canada. The working of the referendum and the initiative, i.e. the right of a prescribed number of citizens to propose the passing of any enactment by popular vote, in Switzerland is examined. He analyses the qualities of the Swiss mind revealed in the working of the referendum and finds them to be independence, parsimony, dislike of officials, jealousy of the Cantonal government and suspicion of novelty. His cautious conclusion is that the referendum is specially suited to "small areas and to small populations not dominated by party spirit." Yet blessed are the Swiss, for they have no party bosses, no corrupt party machine, few cranks, and a splendid tradition of honest politics. There is an able survey of French political institutions, which is truer in insight and deeper in discernment than the tincture of Taine and of the prejudices of the Quartier St. German which Bodley gave to an admiring world in his volume on *France*.

Able as is the survey of French political institutions, we could have spared some of it for ampler consideration of Canada, especially of its attitude to the United States and of its relationship to the Mother Country. The second volume deals with the United States, Australia, and New Zealand, and concludes with a masterly criticism of the democratic institutions in these six democratic countries. That it was impossible for Bryce to cover the whole of the ground of all countries which to-day are the subjects of democratic experiment is obvious; nevertheless we feel unfeignedly sorry that he omits all consideration of our own islands. This, he explains, he did of set purpose on the ground that he did not feel confident of his own impartiality in discussing controversies in the British Islands where the ashes of many hot disputes are not yet cold. Yet few of his readers will share his lack of confidence in his own impartiality. A man is truly impartial when, though convinced that one side is right, he sees the arguments for the other side, sets them down fully, and then refutes them to the best of his ability. In this sense Bryce shows that he is impartial. He is convinced that the democratic side is right, but he sees the arguments employed by its opponents and gives full weight to them in his own conclusions. He himself, in his *Studies in Contemporary Biography*, quotes the example of Bishop Fraser, who was so anxious not to overstate his own case that when he came to speak at a public meeting on behalf of some enterprise, he was not content, like most men, to set forth its claims, but went on to dwell upon the possible drawbacks or dangers, with the result that the more ardent friends of the scheme thought that he was pouring cold water on them, and called him a Balaam reversed. In the same spirit Bryce is so honourably anxious to say nothing more than he thinks true in favour of democracy, that his defence of this form of government is sometimes embarrassing to its friends. His "generation busied itself with institutions; this generation is bent rather upon the purposes which institutions may be made to serve." That they may serve the purpose of any one class seems to him nothing short of disastrous. Progress there has been, but will there be progress in the future? Is there any certainty of its assurance? The Bryce of 1867 is ready with an affirmative to all these questions, but the Bryce of 1921 is more doubtful. He now by no means excludes the possibility that "an ice age might await the mind of man."

To take one example—the extent to which bribery and democracy go hand in hand in the United States—Bryce writes: "Bribery is, or recently was, common in some districts, such as parts of Ohio and South-Eastern New York, as well as in some cities, where a section of the less intelligent voters, especially the negroes in the Middle States, have been corruptible. Though prosecutions are sometimes instituted, the offence more often goes unpunished, the two parties agreeing not to rip up one another's misdeeds. The commonest method of corruption has been to give an agent a lump sum for all the votes he can deliver, and many of these he got without payment, perhaps by persuasion, perhaps, until Prohibition began to conquer State after State, by drinks and cigars."

He adds that in Congress "there is plenty of jobbery and log-rolling, the latter not necessarily corrupt, but mischievous and wasteful even when no bad motive is present."

Nor are the States a whit behind Congress. "The carnival of jobbery and corruption which private Bills have induced in State legislatures has done more than anything else to discredit those bodies. Secret arrangements are made between the lobbyists who act for the promoters of the Bill, the members whom these lobbyists approach, and other members who usually have similar jobs of their own, and thus by the system called 'log-rolling' support is obtained sufficient to put the Bills through. Unscrupulous members use their powers in another way, introducing Bills designed to injure some railway company or other wealthy corporation, and then demanding to be bought off. This form of blackmail is called a strike, and has been frequent in almost every State where there are large corporations to be squeezed. The threatened interests, obliged to defend themselves, justify their methods by the plea that their shareholders must be protected, and when legitimate means fail, because the composition and rules of the legislatures afford no protection, illegitimate means must be employed."

The judges of the Supreme Court and those of six or seven States are above reproach. In most of the other States—there are close on fifty altogether—"The justices of the highest court are tolerably competent, even if inferior in learning and acumen to the ablest counsel who practise before them. Almost all are above suspicion of pecuniary corruption, though some are liable to be swayed by personal or political influences, for the judge cannot forget his re-election, and is tempted to be complaisant to those who can afford it. In these States the justices of the lower courts are of only mediocre capacity, but hardly ever venal."

Of the remaining States Bryce speaks out vigorously: "All that can safely be said is that in a certain small number of States the bench as a whole is not trusted. In every court, be it of higher or lower rank, there are some good men, probably more good than bad. But no plaintiff or defendant knows what to expect. If he goes before one of the upright judges his case may be tried as fairly as it would be in Massachusetts or in Middlesex. On the other hand, fate may send him to a court where the rill of legal knowledge runs very thin, or to one where the stream of justice is polluted at its source. The use of mandatory or prohibitory powers of the court to issue injunctions, and of the power to commit for some alleged contempt of court, is a fertile source of mischief. Injunctions obtained from a pliable judge are sometimes moves in a stock-gambling or in a political game, especially if the lawsuit has a party colour."

Apart entirely from the question of corruption, there is the fact that even yet Judge Lynch has not abdicated his functions, and widespread lawlessness prevails in the Southern States. In all the States ex-President Taft, who enjoyed both exceptional experience and exceptional judgment, holds that "'the lax enforcement of the criminal law" is one of the greatest evils from which the people of the United States suffer. It is indeed obvious that the *advocatus diaboli* will experience no trouble in penning a grave indictment against not only democracy in the United States but against democracy in general. For it would be as unfair as it would be untrue to prefer the charge of lawlessness against the people of the United States in particular. We have only to look at our own country to see how, concurrently with the increase in legislation, there has been a decline in the spirit of obedience to law. The Reform Bills of 1832, 1867, and 1885 ushered in the new idea that there must be many measures passed in every session of Parliament. We tremble to think of the ultimate effects of the 1918 and the 1928 Reform Bills in this respect. It is true to say that more Acts are passed to-day in a single session than were passed during almost the whole of the eighteenth century. Has the habit of obedience grown to the same degree? During the Great Civil War of the seventeenth century the judges held their assizes as if not a single Cavalier or Roundhead were in arms. Contrast this striking fact with our recent records. The Nonconformists, headed by Dr. John Clifford, refused to pay rates on the ground of conscience. The suffragettes refused to pay them on similar grounds. The refusal spread to the doctors who threatened their refusal to administer a Public Health Act. There was no need for Ireland to follow the example of England: she was able—and willing

—to set her own precedent. The Sinn Fein movement began in 1906, and turned to drilling as early as 1909. The Ulster Covenanters, to meet the contemplated assaults on their lives, armed themselves in 1912. The Munitions of War Act prohibited strikes, but, in spite of it, the Welsh miners struck. Yet these miners received complete indemnity for their breaches of contract, which had imperilled thousands of lives at the battle front. Inevitably the condonation of these breaches of contract led to threats of "direct action" by large organised bodies, like the Triple Alliance of miners, railwaymen, and transport workers in Great Britain, culminating in the General Strike of May, 1926. The workings of democracy elsewhere are calculated to stagger the confidence of its advocates a generation ago. In Russia the Bolsheviks have violently abolished universal suffrage. And what are we to say of the doings of the Fascisti under Mussolini and of the Sinn Feiners under Collins?

It is the fashion of foolish people to laugh at the idea of the divine right of kings, though J. N. Figgis ought to have taught them better. If they laughed at the divine right of Parliaments we might understand them much better. For the divine right of kings taught people that the duty of obedience was a sacred one. It is easy to belittle this theory, but it is far more important to understand it. It may be laughed at as a sentiment or a prejudice. Still, that sentiment or prejudice bound the allegiance of the people to its government. "It is most true," taught Thomas Carlyle, "that all available authority is mystic in its conditions." The divine right of kings has passed away for ever, and in its place all we can teach is seemingly the utilitarian theory of obedience. If we pursue this theory to its logical conclusion, however, it means that whenever calculation shows that there is a pecuniary gain in disobedience, then the law ought to be defied.

In the past we believed in freedom slowly broadening down from precedent to precedent. We believed that there was a continuity in our history. Yet if the habit of disobedience to law grows, how long will this continuity last? All over the world democracies are enacting laws.

Is there a habit of obedience to them also being enacted? Some indeed seem to imagine that liberty is licence. On the contrary, liberty increasingly involves self-restraint. As one peruses the pages of *Modern Democracies*, one perceives, not only among ourselves but also in the United States and in our daughter nations beyond the seas, the same impatience of restraint and the same impatience of discipline. A law has been broken. What does it matter if it is broken with impunity? So some fancy, yet let us here record the measured judgment of Sir Henry Maine: "If any Government should be tempted to neglect, even for a moment, its functions of compelling obedience to law—if a democracy, for example, were to allow a portion of the multitude of which it consists to set at defiance some law which it happens to dislike—it would be guilty of a crime which hardly any other virtue could redeem, and which century after century might fail to repair."

Tocqueville taught us that it is never the down-trodden who make revolutions; on the contrary, it is rather those who have been downtrodden and are no longer so, who organise rebellion. To-day we are witnessing this phenomenon all over the civilised world. The poor, so far as we are able to learn, are almost as patient of their conditions of life as their fathers were. On the other hand, the men in well-paid positions in the industrial world are passionately in revolt against the existing social order. The conflict to be dreaded is not the conflict between capital and labour, grave as that undoubtedly is; it is the conflict provoked by the writings of men who plead for what is in essence anarchy. There is a day coming on which we shall find ranged on one side law, liberty and true democracy, and on the other side anarchy, licence and true oligarchy.

It is plain that Bryce entertains fears akin to those here outlined, for he holds that: "Democracy has become, all over Europe, and to some extent even in North America also, desired merely as a means, not as an end, precious in itself because it was the embodiment of liberty. It is now valued, not for what it is, but for what it may be used to win for the masses. When the exercise of their civic rights has brought them that which they desire, and when they feel sure that what they have won will remain with them, may they not cease to care for the further use of those rights? . . . If the spiritual oxygen which has kept alive attachment to liberty and self-government in the minds of the people becomes exhausted, will not the flame burn low and perhaps flicker out? The older school of Liberals dwelt on the educative worth of self-government which Mazzini represented on its idealistic, and Mill in its utilitarian aspects; but who would keep up the paraphernalia of public meetings and of elections and legislative debates merely for the sake of this bye-product? Much will depend on what the issue of the near future is likely to be. If that which the masses really desire should turn out to be the extinction of private property or some sort of communistic system, and if in some countries such a system should ever be established, the whole character of government would be changed, and that which is now called democracy would (as indicated in a previous chapter) become a different thing altogether, perhaps an industrial bureaucratic oligarchy."

There was a day when some of us used to read our Mill and our Mazzini for the sake of the ideals of freedom that both thinkers dreamed. Now part of their dream is simply dismissed as a bye-product, and we are invited to contemplate a time when we shall be confronted with Sidney Webbism or Leninism. The danger is not so remote as many people may imagine. To realise the dreams of a large section of the artisans of Great Britain we must have a despotism akin to that now flourishing in Leningrad. Even now we are being drilled and disciplined in a way our fathers never would have tolerated, and the outcome of this drill and discipline is an oligarchy of industrial bureaucrats. Needless to say this is not a prospect which appeals to Bryce. Put into blunt English, present tendencies mean that the mass of mankind will be content with the modern equivalent for *panem et circenses*; they will be satisfied with subsidised wages and cheap cinemas, and will take but little interest in public affairs. The Australian demand, for instance, is, "More wages for shorter hours; less work, and more amusement."

For the moment Carlyle is out of favour, and the Carlyle that wrote after 1850 deserves to remain out of favour. Yet there were two Carlyles, and the man who wrote before 1850 belongs to a very different class from his successor. It is not a little curious to find that the earlier Carlyle and the later Bryce attain a substantial measure of agreement in their outlook on the future. Carlyle unquestionably taught that democracy could not in the nature of things be permanent, that it was in fact merely an expedient ensuring the transition from an old order which is dying to a new which is coming to birth. All present indications show that Carlyle was quite right in his forecast; and Bryce does not substantially disagree, though he is reluctant to admit the painfulness of the labour pangs through which the world will have to pass.

It is quite obvious that the ideal of the new *régime* will be equality, not liberty. "*L'essence de la démocratie,*" points out E. Schérer, "*c'est l'égalité.*" In his *Démocratie en Amérique,* Tocqueville emphasises the fact that equality is the leading conception involved in the very principle of democracy. Of course there is difficulty in showing, as Treitschke does, that human beings are fundamentally unequal in capacity. Some of our middle and working class advocates of anarchy turn this very argument of Treitschke to their purpose of pressing home the truth that under their enlightened guidance they must tyrannise over the majority. There is, however, a real sense in which in a democratic society there is a general equality of rights and a similarity of conditions. Indeed in 1867 Bryce was at pains to lay stress on the view that democracy in its true sense is the product of Christianity, whose principle has always been the spiritual equality of all men before God. It is natural to expect that Mazzini should emphasise this aspect. "If anything ever profoundly surprised me," he confessed, "it is that many persons have hitherto been blind to the eminently religious character of the (democratic) movement." Equality, then, is an ideal. There is a spiritual dignity attaching to each member of the human race. But liberty is also an ideal, and it is not at all certain that it is possible to combine these two ideals of equality and liberty. As Lord Acton remarked, the underlying cause which rendered the French Revolution so inimical to liberty was its theory of equality.

Madame de Stael used to say that her countrymen were a vain race, and therefore they demanded equality, whereas the English, being a proud race, demanded liberty. Behind this *obiter dictum* there is much matter for reflection. What is the ideal of the working man in the six countries surveyed by Bryce? Is it liberty or is it equality? It is perfectly plain that the artisan can have either liberty or equality. What is no less certain is that he cannot have both at the same time. He can have liberty to develop his capacities to the utmost. He can work by the piece, he can become a foreman or a manager, as he regularly does in the United States. On the other hand, he can have equality. He can earn the same wages as the rest of the artisans, but he can earn no more and no less. It is manifestly impossible to combine liberty and equality in this sense. Unquestionably the chief desire of the organised working man all the world over is the securing of equality. Liberty spells efficiency, but is equality at all likely to spell this magic word?

The special advantage of Bryce's last book is that it enables us to compare and to contrast conditions over a wide range of experience. Of course it is difficult to compare French and Swiss experience with our own. It is less difficult to compare the experience of our overseas dominions with our own, and we learn much from the comparison. In all lands under the British flag there are Labour parties, and the experience of Australia and New Zealand probably forecasts much of the future that lies before ourselves. On the other hand in the United States with its population of some one hundred and ten millions there is not a single Labour member in the House of Representatives. In a singularly informing chapter in the 1920 edition of *The American Commonwealth* Bryce reckons that no less than thirty million people have left the shores of Europe for those of the United States. Even for the lands and cities of the far West this constitutes an enormous addition to the number of labourers. Does this immigration account for the fact that in all but a few occupations the trade unions exercise comparatively slight influence? This no doubt is a part reason, but another lies in the fact that in no country perhaps in the world does the capable working man realise so keenly the possibilities of the industrial world. He knows that he can certainly become a foreman, and that, provided he has ability, he can rise to the rank of manager on a small scale. Nor is managerial work on a large scale in any wise outside the scope of his ambition. The millionaire capitalists of America have been for the most part men who once were members of low rank in the industrial scale. Some of these capitalists, it is rumoured, give an able working man promotion when he deserves it. But with this promotion comes the question, If there is a strike, where do you stand? If the artisan stands with the employer, there is an extra sum added to his wages. The outcome is that the working man with brains is tempted away from the trade union ranks in America, and this furnishes another reason for the notable lack of success of these unions in the United States. True, the longshoremen of the Great Lakes possess a trade union which has a vigorous life of its own, but this case is exceptional.

The quality of a democracy largely depends on the quality of its leaders. In the past France could point to Gambetta, Jules Ferry and that fine character, Waldeck Rousseau; Switzerland to Welti, Ruchonnet and Numa Droz. We have had such men as Peel and Palmerston, Gladstone and Disraeli. Canada produced two striking men in Sir John Macdonald and Sir Wilfred Laurier, and the United States produced one of the great men of all time, Abraham Lincoln, not to mention such men as Calhoun, Clay, and Webster. Australia possessed such strong personalities as Robert Lowe, who there contracted his fierce dislike of democracy, Sir Henry Parkes, Sir Graham Berry, William Bede Dalley, C. C. Kingston, G. H. Reid, and Alfred Deakin. In New Zealand there is the noble figure of Sir George Grey and there is the figure of J. Seddon. As we survey a roll like this, we are driven to ask the question, Have these statesmen successors of equal rank? When we answer the question in the negative, as we are bound to do, we come to the conclusion that though our age has been an age of great events, it has not been an age of great men. Bryce regretfully admits that, in spite of the case of Abraham Lincoln, universal suffrage and the growth of equality in opportunity have not enlisted men of the highest ability in the service of the State. This is specially true of the United States, where not only able men but also decent men stand aside from political life. Our cousins possess men of outstanding qualities in business, and these qualities they devote to the accumulation of wealth. In a land where there are no rank and no eminence to be achieved in politics, the possession of the dollar seems to make a man almighty. There is some point still in the gibe of J. S. Mill that America has produced nothing but dollars and dollar hunters. In his *Etude d'Histoire Réligieuse,* Renan enquired: "If it were necessary that Italy with her past, or America with her future, should be blotted out of existence, which would leave the greater void in the heart of humanity? What has all America produced that can compare with a ray of that infinite glory that adorns an Italian town, even of the second or third order—Florence, Pisa, Siena, Perugia? Before New York and Boston reach in the scale of human greatness a rank that is comparable to these towns, how many steps have they still to take?"

It is seventy years since Renan penned his indictment; forty years later J. R. Lowell stated that: "Democracy must show a capacity for producing, not an higher average man, but the highest possible types of manhood in all its manifold varieties, or it is a failure. No matter what it does for the body, if it does not in some sort satisfy that inextinguishable passion of the soul for something that lifts life away from prose, it is a failure. Unless it knows how to make itself gracious and winning, it is a failure. Has it done this? Is it doing this, or trying to do it?"

It is characteristic of the fairness of Bryce that he does not hesitate to reproduce this quotation, though he clearly thinks that this is asking more from democracy than any form of government can be expected to give. Still, the political godfathers of democracy used to claim that it possessed a stimulating power such indeed as belongs to no other form of government. Were they right in preferring this claim? Monarchy in the sixteenth century gave that passion of the soul Lowell longed for. Mary, Queen of Scots, gave it, and her rival, Queen Elizabeth, gave it. Monarchy in the seventeenth century gave it. At its beginning Henry of Navarre evoked that passion, and at its close Louis XIV evoked it. No one can read the history of the eighteenth century without seeing how splendidly our aristocracy also evoked it. Examples like these attest how lofty is the standard to which democracy has to attain. Yet it has attained that standard both in a past and in the present generation. In the great struggle between north and south during the sixties when Abraham Lincoln dominated the United States, democracy showed its capacity for high endeavour; it showed similar capacity in the World War which engrossed all our energies from 1914 to 1918. The past attainment belonged to one nation: the recent attainment belonged to all the nations who were fighting to defeat German ambitions. It was as manifest in Belgium as it was in Britain.

Among the good points which Bryce puts to the credit of democracy are its maintenance of public order, its efficiency in civil administration, its legislative enactments for the welfare of the poorer classes, its patriotism or courage, and its freedom from the charge of inconstancy or ingratitude. On this last point E. A. Freeman used to insist with all his wonted vehemence that the Swiss were loyal to a degree to their leaders. R. Michels dwells on the presence of the same quality in the ranks of the German Socialists. Nor does this quality belong only to the Old World. Canada displays it as strikingly as either Australia or New Zealand. The charge of ingratitude might be far more fairly preferred against monarchy than against democracy. Let anyone compare the treatment Francis Joseph accorded to Benedek after the war of 1866 with that accorded, also after 1866, by the men of the Confederacy to the general whom Lord Acton almost ranked with Napoleon, Robert E. Lee.

If democracy is not to be a failure men must exercise restraint and discipline. They require to note what they can and what they cannot do in order that their leaders may supply what they lack. It used to be an argument against the enfranchisement of women that the bloom might fade from the flower. Is it not a point to be borne in mind in considering the leadership of democracy? In the effort for a leader from the ranks to arrive, is there not a tendency in his case for the bloom to fade from the flower? He is tempted to offer higher wages or shorter hours of work, even when he thinks them distinctly disadvantageous. Must he not outbid his rivals? The people are on the look-out for a man with initiative, with the power of grasping their wants, with the force of eloquence. Yet his initiative may prove to be simply that of getting ahead of his rivals, his power of grasping may be the quality of grab, and his eloquence may be so much claptrap. The leader requires insight into the past and foresight into the future. Will the democratic leader possess this insight and this foresight?

> The echoes of the past within his brain
> The sunrise of the future on his face.

These are among the qualities of the great statesman. Do the echoes of the past resound in the minds of the leaders of democracy? Does the sunrise of the future irradiate their faces? On the answers to these questions depends the future of modern democracies.

Bryce was a lawyer, and it is plain that on the attitude of democracy to law and order will depend its future as much as on its attitude to leadership. In truth, law and leadership go hand in hand. In 1885 A. V. Dicey worked out *The Law of the Constitution* in a book which was as successful in one field as *The Holy Roman Empire* was in another. He carefully discriminated between rules which are true laws, the law of the constitution, and rules which are not laws, conventions of the constitution. An example of the first is that the King can do no wrong, for some Minister is legally responsible for every act done by the Crown. An example of the second is the convention that the King must assent to any bill passed by the two Houses of Parliament. In fact, Parliament is sovereign, and Dicey emphasises its unlimited legislative authority, and the absence of any other competing or completing authority. He rapidly disposes of such alleged limitations of the legislative supremacy of Parliament as those due to the moral law, its incapacity to touch the Prerogative, or preceding measures. Unlike the United States, our constitution is flexible, and this means that we do not acknowledge the American distinction of fundamental laws. Dicey is well aware of the practical difficulties standing in the way of parliamentary sovereignty. A lawyer like him or Bryce maintains that Parliament is the legal sovereign, yet he is of course clear that the power of Parliament is not unlimited. There are enactments which Parliament never would and never could pass. Austin recognised this when he admits that the sovereign power is vested in the King, the House of Lords, the House of Commons or the electors. The last forms the political, as distinguished from the legal, sovereign. Dicey, remarkably enough, is willing to recognise this dualism. He also recognises the external limit imposed on the real power of the sovereign by the likelihood that a number of his subjects will disobey or resist his unwise law, and by the internal limit similarly imposed by the nature of sovereignty itself. Public opinion, in effect, indicates the external and the internal limits.

With cogent argument Dicey shows that there is no law Parliament cannot change, that there is no distinction between constitutional and ordinary laws, and that no person is entitled to pronounce any measure void. Non-sovereign bodies possess none of these three signs of sovereignty. Our author excels in the use he makes of illustrations in order to drive his points home. You may agree or you may disagree—it is seldom possible to disagree—but it is quite impossible to forget his points. As examples of subordinate law-making bodies he adduces corporations like a railway company, the Legislative Council of India, and the Courts in India or anywhere else, and he successfully shows that they are all under the authority of Parliament. He admits that our daughter nations overseas occupy a somewhat peculiar position, and indeed it is by no means easy to fit them into their proper place as under the sovereignty of Parliament, and developments during the World War and since then suggest that the peculiarity of their position, from Dicey's point of view, has decidedly increased.

Like Bryce, he demonstrates the distinction between a flexible and a rigid constitution. This rigidity will check innovation, but may it not provoke a revolution? If there is a rigid constitution, its real safeguard is a court like that of the Supreme Court at Washington.

The discussion of the two types of constitution leads on naturally to a survey of federalism, and Dicey's account of it is every whit as acute as Bryce's. There are two conditions of federalism, the countries concerned must desire union, and they must not desire unity. Its three essential characteristics are the supremacy of the constitution, the distribution among bodies with limited and co-ordinate authority of the different powers of government, and the authority of the Courts to act as interpreters of the constitution. The working of these characteristics is rendered plain by a consideration of the forms of federalism in the United States, Canada, and Switzerland. Nor does our author omit to draw attention to the results of federalism. It means weak government, it means conservatism, and it means the prevalence of the legal spirit.

The first part of *The Law of the Constitution* discusses with the insight and the thoroughness that mark all Dicey's writings the sovereignty of Parliament, and in the second part he discusses in similar fashion the applications of the rule of law to such matters as the right to personal freedom, the right to freedom of discussion, the right of public meeting, and the like. The rule of law involves the absence of arbitrary power on the part of the Government, it involves the assumption that every man is subject to the ordinary law administered by ordinary tribunals, and it involves the assumption that general rules of the constitutional law are the result of the ordinary law of the land. Our Courts are independent of the Executive, and the Executive in fact respects this independence. Lord Hailsham, the Lord Chancellor, pronounced in 1928 that the Judiciary regard this independence as "the palladium of the liberty of the subject." Such a pronouncement will certainly check the progressive inroads upon this fundamental principle which have been successfully made by the Executive, whatever party was in power, during recent years, not all of them war years. In many cases the substitution of departmental decrees for legislation, and of the decisions of unknown departmental clerks for judgments in open Court, have been exposed, and their pernicious tendency has been condemned, by judges of the highest authority. Administrative tribunals no doubt are necessary for the efficient dispatch of the mass of business entrusted to the Departments by recent legislation. Their powers and procedure, however, ought to be determined by enactment as a well-considered and consistent whole.

In France there are the *droit administratif* and in Germany the *Verwaltungsrecht.* Dicey examines the former, and explains that by it the French Government, and every servant of the Government, possesses, as representatives of the nation, a whole body of special rights, privileges, or prerogatives as against private citizens. By it there is the separation of the powers of the executive, the legislature, and the judiciary. *Droit administratif* is marked by four characteristics. The rights of State are determined by special rules; the Law Courts are without jurisdiction in matters concerning the State; questions concerning the State are determined by administrative bodies; and conflicts of jurisdiction are determined by the *Tribunal des Conflits* All this does not exist in England, though it is quite plain that the officials of the departments of the Tudors and Stuarts, like the officials of the departments of George V, endeavoured to introduce the *droit administratif.* To Tocqueville, or French Liberal politicians of a much later date, such as Prévost-Paradol, it was synonymous with tyranny; and they were wont to contrast the reign of law in England. In the early days of the Second Empire there were grounds for complaint. The *Conseil d'état* was sometimes a shield to the high-handed official who set himself above the law, Whatever may be the case in the past, M. Hauriou, in his masterly *Précis du droit Administratif,* shows that its action for many years past has been in favour of extending the rights of private persons.

The consideration of the right to personal freedom and all other rights leads Dicey to the conclusion that at bottom these are not acknowledged by our constitution. They are all simply the working out of the rule of law. Is freedom of discussion, for instance, recognised by our law? It is not. Our law simply secures that no one shall be punished for what he says except for statements proved to be a breach of law. Is there a right of public meeting? There is none. If A can meet B and C, he can also meet D, E, F, and as many more as he pleases. A meeting is not unlawful because it will excite unlawful opposition, nor is it made unlawful by official proclamation of its illegality. A meeting may be quite lawful though its holding be contrary to public interest. In similar fashion Dicey explains the different ways in which the rule of law holds good, and no reader can ever forget its *modus operandi*.

Tributes to *The Law of the Constitution* were paid by Professor A. Pillet, a distinguished member of the Faculty of Law in Paris, by Sir Paul Vinogradoff, and by Professor Geldart, Dicey's successor as Vinerian Professor of English Law at Oxford. The public paid its tribute by its steady demand for edition after edition, recognising in it the standard work for those on the threshold of their study of constitutional law.

Dicey was a Fellow of All Souls' College, and its Warden, Sir William Anson, published in 1886 Part I of his *Law and Custom of the Constitution*, and in 1892 Part II. It possesses the same merits of orderly arrangement and lucid expression as Dicey's well-known volume. Anson's work is not for the beginner, yet his book, like Dicey's, is not written in any spirit of narrow specialism. He surveys the actual machinery of the existing constitution, and he surveys it with no desire to speculate on the merits or the demerits of parliamentary government. A glance at his table of contents shows that he touches upon and explains every part of its machinery, and he explains it from the angle of his title. He skilfully traces the connexion between the growth of party government and the development of the constitution, and no one can lay down his two volumes without recognising the paramount place occupied by party.

That our institutions are all the growth of history is clear throughout *The Law and Custom of the Constitution*.

If you wish to understand the position of the Crown or the Church, the Cabinet or the Houses of Parliament, Anson reminds you that the beginning of legal memory is the reign of Richard I, and that a statute of his day is still in force, unless repealed or modified. The continuity of the constitution is perfectly plain. If yow wish to understand the position of the Church and the Enabling Act, of 1919, you cannot stop at the reign of George V, for, sooner or later, your labours will compel you to grasp the inwardness of the legislation of Henry VIII and of Elizabeth. Nor does Anson commit the lawyer's mistake of assuming that the constitution is not continually growing. He realises not only that it has grown, but that it is still growing, and we glean from his book that it has undergone more serious alterations since the death of Queen Victoria than it underwent through the long reign of sixty years of George III. Now and then he indulges in comment on the course of events. Take, for instance, his short summary of the actual effect of the Reform Bill on the character of Parliament. "The result," in his judgment, "as it worked out between 1832 and 1886 was to give the House (of Commons) a greater share of political power than it possessed before that date, or possesses now (1907)." Nor does he fail to perceive other changes. "In truth the Redistribution of 1885 has done much to destroy the independence of the members of the House of Commons. The power and influence which it has lost has gone partly to the Cabinet, partly to the constituencies, or rather in many cases, to the (party) organisations by which the constituencies are worked." He was a Unionist, as Dicey was a Unionist, and yet there is not a trace of party politics in the whole of his two massive volumes.

The strength of the Oxford Law School is clear when we recall the fact that Bryce, Dicey and Anson all belonged to it. Bryce, of course, could not restrict himself even to the wide range allowed him by the study of jurisprudence, but strayed off to *The American Commonwealth.* The debt the Americans owe him for his analysis of their constitution and the forces working it has been amply repaid by the great study of *The Government of England,* which Mr.

Lawrence Lowell, President of Harvard, gave us in 1908.[1] He has nothing to learn in constitutional theory from Bagehot or Bryce or in constitutional law from Dicey or Anson. The friendliness of his tone is due no doubt to his own character, and is also due to Bryce's services as our ambassador at Washington. Nor is his criticism untempered by that hearty optimism which characterises so many American authors.

The Government of England is an exhaustive treatise on the central government, the party system, local government, education, the Church, the Empire, the Courts of Law, and reflections of the mature mind of its distinguished author. Now we cannot range over all these topics, and accordingly we prefer to concentrate on the one on which Mr. Lowell lays so much stress, the party system. He glorifies party as no one since Burke has glorified it, and he glorifies it as the fundamental condition of the existence of the Cabinet. As Burke regarded Church and State as but two aspects of the same institution, so Mr. Lowell regards party government and the Cabinet as but two aspects of the same constitutional factor. With Bagehot he admirably brings out the fact that the Cabinet is our executive, and with Bagehot he no less admirably brings out the privacy of its debates, the absence of any written record of their result, the knowledge that a Ministry, however powerful, is exposed to the criticism of formidable opponents, the flexibility of Cabinet government, the gain of its being constantly in touch with the House of Parliament, and the right of a Ministry, when defeated in Parliament, to appeal by means of a dissolution to the nation. These are all old points, though the author contrives to shed new light upon all of them.

He maintains, with a wealth of concealed learning, that the Cabinet is at once the creation and the instrument of party government. The latter we all acknowledge; the former is explained as it never has been explained before. Instead of seeing in party our weakness, he sees in it the condition of the strength of our government. The Cabinet arises out of party conflicts. "Little by little," so he shows,

[1] No doubt Mr. Lawrence Lowell is an American, but his book is too important to be ignored.

"with halting steps, the rivalry of parties built up the responsibility of Ministers, and this in turn helped to perpetuate the party divisions; for the parliamentary system, like every other rational system of government, reacts upon and strengthens the conditions of its own existence. It is based upon party, and by the law of its nature tends to accentuate party." Between the conventions of the constitution, as Dicey explains them, and the party system there is absolute harmony, and this harmony arises, so Lowell insists, because these conventions were created by the warfare of parties, and were in fact evolved out of party life. The result is that ours is the only large country in which the political institutions and the party system are thoroughly in harmony.

It is sufficiently obvious that Mr. Lowell identifies our party system with the existence and the character of a parliamentary Cabinet, and he draws three conclusions from this identification. One is that our constitutionalism can hardly work successfully unless the state contains two parties, and not more than two. There were four parties at the time when Mr. Lowell wrote, the Unionists, the Liberals, the Labour Party, and the Irish Nationalists. The Free State absorbs the last, and it seems as if the Liberals were destined to absorption. Practically, in 1929 we have two parties once more. The second conclusion is that every party which exerts influence in Parliament must be loyal to the constitution. One of the causes of the downfall of Mr. Ramsay MacDonald's first Government was the knowledge that an outside committee endeavoured to control the course of the Cabinet. A third conclusion is the closeness of the connexion between the administrative successes of the Cabinet and the characteristics of our permanent Civil Service. Mr. Lowell's volumes enable us to realise the share taken by accident in the growth of our constitution. A regiment mutinies, and we pass a measure to deal with this crisis. We make this Mutiny Bill annual, and so without design regulate the relations between the army and the Government. In similar fashion we secure the exemption of our Civil Service, one of our great glories, from the spoils system by which one party, on accession to power, turns out the nominees of its rival. In 1782 Lord North sent word to the revenue officers that it would go hard with them if they did not support his party. His opponents sent them a similar warning with the result that they begged to be excluded from the franchise, and excluded they were till 1868. Then they were re-enfranchised but on the clear understanding that no civil servant should take an active share in politics. Carlyle suggested to Lord Wolseley that a day might come when he should turn the key in the House of Commons, locking out the members. If this course were pursued, the ordinary government of our country would be carried on quite well by the Civil Service. The lack of special knowledge on the part of a Cabinet Minister is more than atoned for by the skill of this splendid Service.

That the power of the Cabinet has increased, and is increasing for more than half a century is obvious, and, so far, no one seriously asks for its diminution. As it reposes on the party system, and as party discipline has steadily increased, the position of the Cabinet inevitably has increased with it. Members of Parliament are more obedient to the party whip in 1929 than they were in 1859. The identification of the party system with the Cabinet also explains the gradual decline of the caucus. In his *Democracy and the Organization of Political Parties* Dr. Ostrogorski sees in the machinery and the influence of the caucus a greater—and sinister—danger to the proper development of our institutions than Mr. Lowell does. On the side of the Liberals Chamberlain tried it, and on the side of the Conservatives Lord Randolph Churchill tried it. The result has been that the National Liberal Federation of the one and the National Union of Conservative Associations of the other have been kept in due subjection by the Cabinet of either party.

There is no Cabinet in the United States in our sense of the term, and accordingly Mr. Lowell thinks that our system has preserved us from the presence of the boss, the machine, the party platform, and the caucus. Yet a review of our party history chastens us more than it does the President of Harvard. Take the case of Peel. We see him in Ireland refusing concession after concession till all grace in their gift was lost. For many years he delayed concessions to the Roman Catholics which a Tory like Sir Walter Scott would have given in 1825 or even perhaps in 1819. True, he passed the Roman Catholic Relief Bill, but he passed it in a way which irritated O'Connell. For instance, he granted the rank of King's Counsel to his follower Sheil, and refused it to the leader. The tithe war could have been settled long before it was. Reforms were granted, but Peel taught the Irish that they were granted by the employment of force. Nor can we acquit him of needless delay in law reform. We simply take him as an instance of the evils of party, and we suggest that these evils are chargeable to the Conservatives just as much as the Liberals. Party government wears new merits at the hands of Mr. Lowell, merits unknown even to Burke, yet the facts of history never allow us to forget that party government means the government of partisans. The caucus has not triumphed to anything like the same extent as in the United States, yet it is beyond question that the party managers behind the scenes influence policy. Nor can one overlook the circumstance that there is a decided tendency on the part of the party leader to outbid his rival in the hope of gaining popular support. We no longer corrupt persons but do we not corrupt classes? Here Lord Bramwell's dictum is very much to the point: "A candidate used to gain a seat by paying £5 to each elector; the practice was said to be illegal, it certainly was expensive. A candidate now gains a seat by promising the electors part of their neighbours' property; the practice is said to be legal, it is certainly expensive."

REFERENCES

FISHER, H. A. L. *James Bryce*. (London, 1927.)
HENSON, H. H., *Ed. Sir William Anson*, 1834–1914. (Oxford, 1920.)
MARCEL, R. P. *Essai Politique sur Alexis de Tocqueville*. (Paris, 1910)
RAIT, R. S. *Memorials of Albert Venn Dicey*. (London, 1925.)
ROCKOW, L. *Contemporary Political Thought in England*. (London, 1925.)

Chapter IX.

MAITLAND AND PLURALISM

Bryce and Dicey, Anson and Lowell are all lawyers inclined to look on the State as the fountain of law. Maitland is also a lawyer as brilliant as any of them and with one of the most original minds of the nineteenth century. While they are monists, he is a pluralist characterised by the most astonishing insight. "*Beati qui verum quaerunt*" is a blessing they all earn and none of them more richly than Maitland.

Frederic William Maitland (1850–1906) came of an ancestry which beqeathed to him an aptitude for historical investigation. He was at Eton from 1863 to 1869 where he failed to become prominent in work or play. Classical scholarship did not attract him, and history, in spite of Arnold's efforts, was not then usually taught at public schools. In 1869 he entered Trinty College, Cambridge, as a Commoner. Athletics, music and mathematics divided his attentions at first till he had the good fortune to fall under the influence of Henry Sidgwick, who fostered in himself and in others that pure love of truth which is so rare an intellectual virtue. Abandoning mathematics—and music—for philosophy, Maitland won a scholarship, and came out in the Moral and Mental Tripos of 1872 at the head of the First Class, bracketed with his friend W. Cunningham, afterwards the distinguished economic historian. It is noteworthy that Westlake, the father of private international law, won a double First Class in Classics and Mathematics. It is a striking fact that neither he nor Maitland read law as undergraduates. He competed for a fellowship at his own college, and the other candidates were such outstanding men as Arthur Lyttelton, W. Cunningham, and James Ward, and Ward won. Maitland's fellowship dissertation was *A Historical Sketch of Liberty and Equality as Ideals of English Political Philosophy from the time of Hobbes to the time of Coleridge.* While the estimates of the thinkers betray the inimitable style which even then characterised his work, the survey of Coleridge's thought is still adequate to its great subject. If Coleridge remarks that the right to property was "abstractedly deducible from the free agency of man," Maitland remarks that "We may doubt whether a kind of property, the *esse* of which is *abstrahi*, can be of much value to its owner." A charming conversationalist and a witty speaker, he achieved a considerable reputation at the Union, becoming Secretary and then President. He belonged to the famous Cambridge society commonly called the Apostles, where he was no less beloved than admired.

He entered at Lincoln's Inn in 1872 and was called to the Bar in 1876. For the next eight years he practised as conveyancer and equity craftsman, devilling mainly for B. B. Rogers, the Aristophanic scholar. The art of conveyancing requires insight in order to extract from a document all that its words and phrases mean. Gifted with insight by nature, Maitland acquired more by his practice as a conveyancer. Naturally such a document taught him to look backward, and at the same time he possessed that rare mind which insists on looking forward. His bent, accordingly, was towards the study, not towards the court. Though he enjoyed a thorough training in practical law, his interests led him to theoretical, scientific, and historical law. He read Stubbs's *Constitutional History*, and fell under its fascination all the more because he had not to study it for any examination. He also read Savigny's *Geschichte des Römischen Rechts* and Brunner's *Das anglo-normannische Erbfolgesystem*, and fell under the fascination of Savigny as much as he had fallen under the spell of Stubbs. Of the German historian of Roman law he used to say that Savigny first opened his eyes as to the way in which law should be regarded. Law was a product of human history, the expression of human needs, the declaration of the social will. With Browning he felt:

> Justinian's Pandects only made precise
> What simply sparkled in men's eyes before,
> Twitched in their brow or quivered in their lip.
> Waited the speech that called but would not come.

What Savigny might do, surely he might at least try to do.

He could gather the undigested and scattered materials of our law. When this preliminary task had been duly accomplished, he could turn his attention to what was a crying need, a scientific and philosophical history of our law from the earliest times considered in all its manifold bearings upon the economic, political, constitutional, social and religious life of our people. While he was meditating on this vast scheme, he met Sir Frederick Pollock and Sir Paul Vinogradoff, and they offered him every encouragement. On May 11th, 1884, he met the latter at Oxford, and Mr. Fisher records the significance of this meeting. Maitland first received from the lips of a foreigner, as Mr. Fisher records, a full consciousness of that matchless collection of documents for the legal and social history of the Middle Ages, which England had continuously preserved and consistently neglected, of an unbroken stream of authentic testimony flowing for seven hundred years, of tons of plea-rolls from which it would be possible to restore an image of long-vanished life with a degree of fidelity which could never be won from chronicles and professed histories. Maitland was so impressed by this conversation that he returned the very next day to London, drove to the Record Office, and at once inspected the plea-roll for the year 1221 of Gloucestershire, his own country. He had found his life's work. The firstfruits of his legal labour was the *Pleas of the Crown for the County of Gloucester*, which appeared in 1884 with a dedication to Vinogradoff. In 1885 he wrote a handbook on *Justice and Police*, which deals with the superior courts.

In the meantime in 1884 he was elected to the newly found readership in English law in the university of Cambridge, and there he resided to his lamentably premature death. A rapid worker always, in 1887 he published in three volumes *Bracton's Note-book*, edited with the lavish learning of our enthusiast. The next year he was elected Downing professor of English law, and his inaugural lecture was entitled, *Why the History of Law is not Written*. He spent the rest of his short life in writing it, appealing for those fellow workers sorely needed in an uncultivated field. In 1887 he had succeeded in founding the Selden Society "to encourage the study and advance the knowledge of the history of English law." Before his death it had issued twenty-one volumes on the history of different branches of law, edited by himself or by editors under his supervision. Of these no less than eight volumes are his, and they are sufficient to confer distinction on the whole series. Perhaps the best of the eight is the *Bracton and Azo* in which its editor settled the true relations of the treatise we know as Bracton to Roman law and Italian learning. We try them by a lofty standard if we suggest that his introductions and editions are worthy of a place beside the famous ones Stubbs wrote for the Rolls Series, and right worthy of such a place they undoubtedly are. Nor can we overlook Maitland's introduction to the *Memoranda de Parliamento,* which he edited for the Rolls Series in 1893, and is, in the judgment of Professor Pollard, the most original and suggestive essay ever written on our mediaeval parliament. In fact, there is nothing our editor touched that he did not adorn.

With Sir Frederick Pollock he planned his *History of the English Law before Edward I.* Both names appear on the title page, but no one is more anxious than Sir Frederick to acknowledge that the labour was substantially that of his colleague. On its appearance in 1895 it at once took that standard rank which belongs to all Maitland's writings. As he looked backward he also looked forward, and the close of the second volume marks his attitude to the past. "Those few men who were gathered at Westminster round Pateshull and Raleigh and Bracton were penning writs that would run in the name of kingless commonwealths on the other side of the Atlantic Ocean; they were making right and wrong for us and for our Children." His *magus opus* has left its mark on the course of the legal historian ever since, and has been the source of volume after volume.

His great history suggested many questions which he answered in his *Domesday Book and Beyond* and in his *Township and Borough* in 1897, and in his *Roman Canon Law in the Church of England* in 1898. He came to the conclusion that the hide of Domesday Book contains 120 arable acres, and of course this means that the manorial system could not be normal in early Saxon times. The origin of the town he finds in its work as a unit in the scheme of national defence. In face of the opposition due to Stubbs's views, he proved that the pre-Reformation Canon Law enforced in England was purely Roman, and he succeeded in convincing Stubbs that this position was the only tenable one. At the request of Lord Acton he wrote his brilliant chapter upon the Anglican Settlement and the Scots Reformation, and it certainly relieved the dullness of the *Cambridge Modern History*.

He found himself increasingly attracted to the realistic theory of corporate personality, and for the purpose of introducing it to the notice of English scholars he wrote in 1900 his short and suggestive introduction to the *Political Theories of the Middle Age*, a portion of the third volume of Gierke's great work, *Das deutsche Genossenschaftsrecht*,[1] the greatest book, he declared, he had ever read. He worked at the growth and definition of the corporate idea for its own sake and also because it dug deep into the foundations of law and of politics, especially the politics of a composite empire. He also expounded this idea in the third volume of his *Collected Papers* in the highly important survey of trust and corporation. We have been taught by Gierke, speaking through Maitland, to look for our philosophy of the State not only to Aristotle but also to Marsiglio and Ockham.

The question to which Maitland addressed himself was, What is the nature, legal and other, of groups among themselves? Long ages since the law divided groups into two classes, and to one of the classes it added the gift of perpetual life. On them it bestowed the title of corporations, and, according to the legal maxim, a corporation never dies. The citizens of London may die, and others spring up in their stead, the shareholders of the Bank of England may die or sell their scrip to others; but from generation to generation, and century to century, the City Corporation and the Bank of England live on, whatever may befall citizens or shareholders. Further than that, for practical purposes the law treats these corporate bodies as persons, just as if they were living men. If your bank dishonours your cheque, or a municipal tramcar knocks you down and breaks your leg, you cannot claim damages against the individual shareholders

[1] It was published in 1868.

or ratepayers—you must sue the Bank or the "Mayor, Alderman and Burgesses" (such is the official title) of your borough, and these corporations are alone answerable to you.

We have no space to discuss the various legal theories of the corporation—the "fiction" theory, the "concession" theory, and the like, and the consequences that flow from their adoption. There is, however, one particular theory that Maitland expounds, and himself maintains, viz., that the corporation is a "real" person, though a group person, with a real will, though a group will. Such a body has a common life, and then from the very nature of the thing it has added to it the general will (*volonté générale*), which is manifestly of the mental life of the new body, and a thing quite different from the sum total of the individual wills (*volonté de tous*). Plainly the influence of Rousseau in politics is by no means dead, and this distinction of his is a most useful one. No one who has ever sat on a committee or a board of directors can have failed to notice that every permanent organisation has a feeling, a tradition, an atmosphere, an opinion of its own—in fact, a group-mind which differs from that of any individual member, and is certainly not the same as the sum total of the minds of the individual members. The conception of the corporation is present to the minds of men like M. Duguit in France and Mr. Laski in England. M. Duguit assumes the solidarity of men living in a given social group. Since man lives in society, and since society can subsist only by the solidarity which unites the individuals who compose it, it follows that upon man as a social being a rule of conduct is imposed which obliged him to do only that which tends to promote the social solidarity. Such a rule of conduct is a veritable rule of law. Now, according to Duguit, there are no natural rights inhering in a person irrespective of the law. Law is in fact worked out independently of the State, and is claimed to be true of societies not yet *étatisées*. Law is a spontaneous formation, a natural product of social evolution. If the natural right conception disappears in one form, it disappears only to appear in another, a trick it frequently adopts. For with M. Duguit we hear of the existence of law and of rights anterior and superior to law emanating from the State and indeed higher than the rights conferred by the State. Behind the word State he finds only the individual wills of the governors and of the governed. The sovereignty of the State vanishes. From Bodin to Duguit the wheel has turned full circle. Yet can we substitute for the sovereignty of the State such conceptions as Preuss's *Herrschaft* or Mr. Cole's democratic court of functional equity," or M. Duguit's *solidarité sociale*?

At the back of the mind of men like M. Duguit we have to face the fact that there is now a school of political philosophy which advocates the substitution of the direct representation of economic and professional interests in political parties and parliamentary institutions for representation on the basis of territory and population. It is the view of Gumplowicz and Ratzenhofer in Austria, of Gierke and Krabbe in Germany, of Duguit, Durkheim and Benoist in France, of De Greef and Prins in Belgium, of Maitland, Figgis and Laski in England, and of Bentley and Small in America. These thinkers all alike tend to strengthen the occupational group at the expense of the economic functions of the State. This conception boasts of a long pedigree. Plato and Aristotle grasped the idea of the representation of interested groups. Such a type of representation prevailed to some degree in the mediaeval estates and the mediaeval municipal organisations, and it received a theoretical formulation in the doctrines of the Conciliar Movement. This movement was the first to raise the problems of the State in their present form, e.g. consent is of the essence of law; all power is a trust; government is therefore limited in authority by its purposes; the need of representation limits the validity of absolutism; need is always a valid cause of change against historic prescription. The catastrophe of the Council of Constance lay in the fact that nascent national sentiment proved too strong for joint European action. No doubt Europe did not grasp the significance of this fact. The conciliar system stood for an inchoate federalism and the rights of national groups. The Pope stood for a centralising bureaucracy and absolutism in the Church. The Pope triumphed, and his triumph witnessed not merely absolutism in the Church, but it was one day to witness absolutism in the State. The nature of post-Renaissance Catholicism was determined at Basle. The question, however, was wider, and concerned the character not only of ecclesiastical, but also of the civil, State. Absolutism, which was to be the rule throughout Europe, with the outstanding exception of England, triumphed first of all in the Church. The conflict between the friends and the enemies of the conciliar movement was the same as that which—in France, Spain, Germany, and within an ace in England as well—eventually decided in favour of a strong monarchy, a ubiquitous administration, and the removal of all constitutional restraints on the activities of governments and the removal of the groups in conflict with the governments.

In theory Althusius in the seventeenth century and Mirabeau in the eighteenth century revived the idea of a similar arrangement of the different groups that go to the formation of the State. Part of the argument seems to be that the *volonté générale* of the group constrains the individual mind, and accordingly it maintains social control effected mainly by its own solidarity or cohesion. The family is far too small for this purpose and the State far too great. As beyond the visible red and violet rays on either hand of the solar spectrum the play of the waves of ether produces rays undiscerned by sight, so in the political spectrum beyond the band of clear vision in State action extend vital activities of associations. As a proof of the friction at present existing, we hear of the growing prevalence of suicide, crime, the antagonism of capital and labour, social anarchy and general economic *malaise*. Is not the occupational group well adapted to enforce an adequate type of social control? Is not its control likely to be more agreeable to the individual than the authority now inadequately exercised by the State? Will not the individual always be more conscious of his own interests in the group? Modern life, so we learn, is in reality what Hobbes imagined the state of nature to be, namely, a condition of economic warfare. Will not the group put an end to such a condition? The historian will advance the plea that exclusiveness and corruption characterised the Roman sodalities, the mediaeval guilds and the mediaeval estates. Such a plea must be taken into account, for it is by the experience of the past that we measure the worth of proposals in the present. Mr. Laski declares that the mediaeval suspicion of pluralism as anarchic has never deserted the modern world, yet the guilds and other corporations of the Middle Ages were never anarchic. They had their own organisation, which was subordinate to that of the community as a whole. The Reformation undoubtedly strengthened the claims of the whole at the expense of the parts.

The spirit of Calvinism is influential in the uninspiring yet original mind of the German jurist, Johannes Althusius (1557–1638) who is at least as important because Gierke wrote his masterpiece of mediaeval learning about him in 1913, as he is for his own sake. A Calvinist elder in the church at Emden, a courageous magistrate in that town for thirty-six years, and a professor of laws at Herborn, there is inevitably a legal spirit in his *Politica methodice Digesta, Exemplis sacris et profanis illustrata,* which he published in 1603. Jewish law in general and the Decalogue in particular, which is really natural law, are admiringly put before us. The code of Discipline of Calvin counts for everything. As in Geneva, the State is to supervise morals and conduct on a truly paternal scale. What attracted Gierke and Maitland to him was his attitude to group life. Gierke held that the German Genossenschaft or Fellowship was not the fiction theory which Sinibald Fieschi, who became Innocent IV in 1243, laid down and which Savigny had adopted and developed. He held that the German Fellowship was neither fictitious nor a State-creation. It was in fact "a living organism, and a real person with body and members and will of its own," a group person with a group will. "Behind the screen of trustees and concealed from the direct scrutiny of legal theories, all manner of groups can flourish: Lincoln's Inn, or Lloyds, or the Stock Exchange, or the Jockey Club, a whole presbyterian system or even the Church of Rome with the Pope at its head"—all, in Maitland's judgment, fell under the trust-concept. Each was, in fact, a group.

It is inevitable that Gierke should take pride in showing

that Althusius holds every species of associated life finds its foundation in an agreement or contract to which the individuals are parties. These associations link themselves together into small groups, and these small groups into larger. The union of these groups arises through necessity, and is based on contract. From the family we proceed to the corporation, from the corporation to the commune, from the commune to the province, and from the province to the State. Naturally Althusius defines the State as "a general public association in which a number of cities and provinces, combining their possessions and their activities, contract to establish, maintain and defend a sovereign power." It is the *communitas communitatum*. Clearly these associations are anterior to the State, which derives its life from them. In fact, we reach the position, revolutionary in the seventeenth century and even to-day, that the groups are essential and the State non-essential. As in the republics of antiquity, the members of such a State are not all the individuals who reside within its limits. Indeed it was not till after the French Revolution of 1789 that this idea of residence was really entertained. Plainly, the *Politica* forms the bridge to span the gulf between the rudimentary governmental contract of Mornay's *Vindiciae contra tyrannos* and the highly developed social contract of Rousseau.

Sovereignty is the supreme and supereminent power of doing what pertains to the spiritual and bodily welfare of the members of the State. By the nature of the associated life (*consociato*) this power inheres in the people. Althusius, unlike the Monarchomachi of the sixteenth century, makes the advance of basing his social contract upon the conception of the people as a societas rather than as a universitas. His sovereignty belongs to the corporation as a whole, not to its members. He endorses the dictum of the Digest that "what is owed to a corporation is not owed to individual members," a position that sufficiently checks the vagaries of the will of the individual. It is the view held by Mornay, clothed in legal form. Obviously the duties of the State devolve on officials, and hence he bestows this delegated authority on kings and magistrates. By basing the State on associations, Althusius effects the disappearance of the distinction between private and public rights. Sovereignty is therefore vested in the whole body of the people, and as it is out of the question for the part to claim to be the whole, neither monarch nor his official can genuinely claim to be sovereign. Twenty-six years before, Bodin for the first time had developed a theory of sovereignty, which was novel and held the field practically down to our own day, and this Althusius proceeds to criticise and to reject. For Bodin left no room for the group. His sovereign was as much a Leviathan as Hobbes's.

The officials of this Calvinist State fall into two classes: first, what Althusius calls the "ephors" and second the "chief magistrate" (*summus magistratus*). Under the first head he includes in his pluralist conception all the various orders and estates in the provinces and cities whose function it is to act as a restraint upon the chief magistrate. As these various bodies are representative of the whole people, the real sovereign, they act as a check upon the head of the State. Like Hotman and Mornay, he conceives that if they do not take action against the tyrant, then their authority falls to the assembly of the whole people. The king does more than reign, for he governs. He is the executive of the people, carrying out the details of administration and executing the laws. He stands towards his people as an agent (*mandatorius*), and the kingly office, in the opinion of Althusius, shares the nature of agency. There are two contracts, the contract of society and the contract of government. The contract between king and people is perfected through his choice and coronation. He undertakes to govern in conformity with the fundamental laws of the realm, and on this condition his subjects agree—are they his subjects really?—to obey him. With Hotman he maintains that the obligation of the monarch is absolute, while that of the people is merely conditional. They are practically in the position of "Heads I win, tails you lose." Did Althusius ask himself the question similar to that Napoleon asked the Abbé Siéyes when offered the nominal First Directorship, Am I a hog simply to fatten at the expense of the people?

The task of Althusius in drawing the usual deductions on

the question of tyranny is readily anticipated. Unmistakably when the chief magistrate transforms himself into a tyrant, he releases his people from their allegiance, and he sets in motion their right of resistance and of deposition. Woe betide the individual, however oppressed, who dare act on his own initiative! Clearly such action is not to be tolerated. The corporation must act as a whole. Its will is to be manifest through the ephors to which Calvin had almost seventy years before called attention. The assembly of the ephors, representing the sovereign people, possesses the right and the duty of resisting, of expelling and of putting to death the tyrannical chief magistrate. To each member of the confederacy, acting through its particular ephors, belong the right and the duty, as an ultimate means of security against tyranny, of renouncing its connection with the rest and of associating itself with some other realm. So wrote Althusius in 1603, as if foreseeing that remarkable reaction against royalty that characterised the second quarter of the seventeenth century.

Savigny had fallen back on the Innocentine conception as if joint-stock companies had never arisen since the thirteenth century. Yet there had been, as Maitland emphasised, village communities and townships, merchants guilds and crafts, in the Middle Ages, and in our own time there was all manner of groups, and our thinker endeavoured to "distinguish and reconcile the manyness of the members and the oneness of the body." It was a new inquiry in England, for our lawyers had accepted the Innocentine conception that the corporation was a fiction of the law created by the State. It was a mindless thing, "incapable of knowing, intending, willing, acting, distinct from the living corporators who are called its members." The corporation is the creature of the State. "Into its nostrils the State must breathe the breath of fictitious life, for otherwise it would be no animated body but individualistic dust." Such a theory repelled Maitland, who felt far more at home with the conception of Althusius than with that of Savigny. With Gierke our jurist passionately maintained that a group was a living organism, a real person with a body and a will of its own. He wrote: "By those who have neither leisure nor inclination to understand competing theories of German partnerships, German companies and German communes, it may none the less be allowed that theories of the State and theories of the Corporation must be closely connected. The individualism which dissolves the company into its component shareholders is not likely to stop at that exploit, and the State's possession of a real will is insecure if no other groups may have wills of their own." Thus the conceptions of Green as well as those of Gierke are pressed into service. As the former realised that the State can apply coercion only to outward conduct, he writes, "the only acts which it ought to enjoin or forbid are those of which the doing or not doing, *from whatever motive,* is necessary to the moral end of society."

Short as Maitland's life was, the life of his pupil, John Neville Figgis, was even shorter, for he never really recovered the torpedoing of his ship in 1918, dying the following year. Maitland had applied the pluralistic theory to the State, and in his *Churches in the Modern State,* which appeared in 1913, Figgis applied it to the Church. For him the sun of Austin has set and his luminaries were Maitland and Gierke, which of course meant Gierke's interpretation of Althusius. This seventeenth century thinker never came into his own in his day whereas now he is in the heyday of his power in the pluralistic world. Gierke was deeply influenced by him. The views of Gierke appear in his *Das Genossenschaftsrecht* (1868) and in his *Die Genossenschaftstheorie* (1887), notably in the former. He strongly protests against the mediaeval theories of the State, which, under the guidance of Roman law, tended to put all forms of group life into the category of the *persona ficta* of a corporation. These social groupings come into existence naturally and possess the power of development. To Gierke they possess natural rights which the State is bound to respect. Not only do they come into existence apart from the State but they exist before the State. Similarly, Maitland insists that such a body possesses the "real personality, the spontaneous origin, the inherent rights of corporate bodies within the State." It is well worth while to contrast Ihering's view: "These new purposes being foreign to the State, led a separate and independent existence in the form of associations until they had attained the necessary degree of maturity; and then they burst the covering in which they had existed hitherto and emptied their entire content into that form which it would seem was intended to take up everything within itself, viz., the State. What was instruction formerly? *A private affair.* What was it next? *The business of association.* What is it now? *The business of the State.* What was the care of the poor formerly? *A private matter.* What was it next? *The business of association.* What is it now? *The business of the State.* Individual, Association, State—such is the historical step-ladder of social purposes." The attitude of Ihering is also that of C. H. Pearson.

Figgis, like Pearson, knows his history far too well not to recognise that Althusius never came into his own. Bodin in the sixteenth century, Hobbes in the seventeenth, Blackstone in the eighteenth, and Austin in the nineteenth were too powerful for him The reaction against this traditional doctrine of sovereignty is plain in the idealists who regard the State as the chief agency for the moral development of mankind. Figgis stoutly opposes this traditional doctrine which he sees entrenched in popular thought and still more in the opinion of the lawyers. He points out how much it owes to the survival of the State idea of the classical world and to the majesty of Imperial Rome, inherent in the Canon no less than in the Civil Law. Such an attitude is not congruous with the facts of life. It ignores what Green, Bradley, and Bosanquet proclaim when they lay down that the force of State action is a synthesis of living wills. Still, in a significant paragraph, Figgis writes: "The theory of sovereignty, whether proclaimed by John Austin or Justinian, or shouted in conflict by Pope Innocent, is in reality no more than a venerable superstition. It is true only in a cosy, small and compact State, although by a certain amount of strained language and the use of the maxim, 'whatever the sovereign permits he commands,' it can be made not logically untenable for any conditions of stable civilisation. As a fact it is as a series of groups that our social life presents itself, all having some of the qualities of public law and most of them showing clear signs of a life of their own, inherent and not derived from the State. The State may recognise and guarantee (and demands marks for so doing) the life of these societies—the family, the club, the union, the college, the Church; but it no more creates that life than it creates the individual, though it orders his birth to be registered." Clearly, the group exists, yet Figgis is prepared to allow the existence of the State as well. The State still stands as well as "an ascending hierarchy of groups, family, school, town, county, union, Church, etc., etc."

The doctrine of Althusius is not fundamentally pluralistic any more than the doctrines of Gierke, Maitland, and Figgis. They do not look upon the State as *unus inter pares* but *primus inter pares*. The State is for them, as for Althusius, the *communitas communitatum*, possessing a distinctive function and a superior authority over any group. In the opinion of Figgis one of the main elements in the worth of the smaller groups is that they foster not only that individual development which he emphasises but also "loyalty to the great 'society of societies' which we call the State." Each group requires State restraint not to indulge in acts of injustice to one another or towards individuals. The State exists, in fact, for the regulation of group life. Such a conception is in truth rather federalistic than pluralistic, though it can lead to pluralism. Nor are the views of Durkheim, Hauriou, or even Miss Follett essentially different from those of Gierke, Maitland, and Figgis. They all acknowledge the existence of a series of groups, and they acknowledge this fact with the utmost eagerness. They recognise that the principle of the group fulfils functions which the State neither can nor does. No doubt they are far more preoccupied than the advocates of the traditional view of sovereignty with questions of representation and government. Nor do they for the most part forget the distinction between the State and the government. For failures charged against the State are in reality failures chargeable against the government which occasionally misinterprets the will of the people.

Psychologically, as Figgis emphasises, the State is limited by its own nature. Externally there are certain things which no government could do without provoking resistance.

It is quite certain, for instance, that though Voltaire put into the mouth of Louis XIV the remark, *L'état, c'est moi*, yet even the French King could not have ordered his subjects to become Mohammedans. Use and wont, custom and tradition limit the political power of even the absolute State. Mr. Laski, who is one of the foremost exponents of pluralism, seizes hold of limitations due to the psychological nature of the Leviathan and the external limits imposed on it. Let us quote two clear statements of views like his. One is, "In almost every independent political society, there are principles or maxims expressly adopted or tacitly accepted by the sovereign, and which the sovereign habitually observes. The cause of this observance commonly lies in the regard which is entertained for those principles or maxims by the bulk or most influential part of the community; or it may be that those principles or maxims have been adopted from a perception of utility or from a belief of their conformity to the Divine will." The second is, "Like the sovereign body of which it is a member, it is obliged or restrained morally by opinions and sentiments current in the given community." This is a pluralistic view, yet these two quotations embodying it come from the pages of Austin's *Province of Jurisprudence Determined*. Blackstone and perhaps Cornewall Lewis in England, Sybel and Treitschke in Germany may have pushed the doctrine of the sovereignty of the State to an extreme, but for the most part its advocates have been as temperate as John Austin. In his definition of sovereignty Austin is careful to define him as receiving "habitual"—not necessarily invariable—obedience, and he is no less careful to say that this obedience comes from the bulk—not necessarily from every individual—of a given society. Nor are Bentham and Bodin a whit behind Austin in recognising the limits set by morality to State action. Hobbes knows—he lived in the days of the Great Rebellion—that there are some demands sprung upon the subject which no legal, political, and rational sovereign would dream of making. The reason is the obvious one that the subject cannot be supposed to have surrendered rights of self-determination in such matters. What Austin and Hobbes say, Grotius and Bodin also say. Grotius defines the State as "a perfect association of free men united for the sake of enjoying the benefits of law and for their common advantage," thus reflecting the views of Althusius. Such a definition does not identify the State with absolute power. Bodin, who of course is the father of the doctrine of sovereignty, is particular to allow that "what we have said as to the freedom of sovereignty from the binding force of law does not have reference to divine or natural law." There are fundamental laws (*imperii leges*) of the realm, and Bodin is sure that "the prince cannot abrogate or modify them, since they are attached to the very sovereignty with which he is clothed; such is the Salic law, which is the foundation of our monarchy." Reason governs the State, according to Bodin, and divine or natural law and fundamental law set due limits to the power of the prince. Bodin is not far removed from the view of Troeltsch, whose death we still deplore: "Now, therefore, there abide these three, individual morality, state morality, and cosmopolitan morality, but the greatest and most important of these at the present time is state morality."

Figgis realises limit after limit imposed on the doctrine of sovereignty by those who upheld this doctrine. He passes on to the question of trusts, and, following Maitland, he shows that part of the practical difficulty due to our non-recognition of the real personality of the corporation has been overcome by the institution of trusts. Behind the doctrine of trusteeship action has taken place which is essentially that of corporate personality without the society being subject to the disabilities incident to the "concession theory." Maitland points out that the Inns of Courts, being bodies of lawyers, may be supposed to know what is their interest, yet they have always refused incorporation. For the lawyers find that they can do under the doctrine of trusteeship what they want, and enjoy most of the advantage without the disadvantages of corporate life. Under the name of a trust many of the qualities of true personality, which attach to a real corporation, have been thus able to develop unhindered. Figgis recognises this as amply as Maitland, yet he cannot help thinking that the trust has prevented the growth of the true conception of a real corporation. It has allowed us to "muddle through," since we did not experience the sense of our utter destitution.

The hope of the future, according to Figgis, lies in our attitude to corporate societies. Are they to be conceived as real personalities or as fictitious ones? Is their union to be throughout of such a nature that it enjoys a life greater than the sum of the individuals composing the body? He willingly admits that the State must require such marks of the society as proofs of registration, permanence, constitution, and the like. He urges that corporate personality, this unity of life and action, is a thing which grows up naturally and inevitably in bodies of men united for a permanent end. Can it be denied, in ostrich fashion, merely by the process of saying that it is not there? The State sets itself over the competing claims of groups, and Figgis does not ask it to set all sorts of groups over the State. He does ask that the real corporation should enjoy a life of its own.

Of the group life Figgis speaks eloquently. His school or his college, his parish or his county, his union or his regiment, his wife and his family—these are the most vitally formative parts in the lives of most men; "and in so far as England has anything worthy in civic life to show to the world, it is the spectacle of individuals bred up or living within these small associations which mould the life of men more intimately than does the great collectivity we call the State." Men turn to fellowship as the needle turns to the pole, for they eagerly admit that fellowship is life and lack of it is death. Monists like Bodin and Grotius, Hobbes and Austin note the existence of the group life, though of course they do not note it with the emphasis placed upon it by Gierke, Maitland, Figgis, and pluralists like Duguit and Laski. Monistic thought considers questions of sovereignty as more far-reaching than questions of representation and government, while pluralistic emphasises the latter at the expense of the former. Groups exist, and they of course claim the allegiances of their members, but if their claim is paramount what becomes amid these competing groups of any completing authority? Is there not a danger in this competition of the loss of law and order, or liberty and right? Figgis perceives this drawback to social groupings, and acknowledges that "to prevent injustice between them and to secure their rights, a strong power above them is needed. It is largely to regulate such groups and to ensure that they do not outstep the bounds of justice that the coercive power of the State exists. It does not create them; nor is it in many matters in direct and immediate contact with the individual."

The group feeling is strong and we do not wish for a moment to deny its strength. No one can read Mr. MacIver's book on *Community* without realising the power of this feeling. At the same time anyone in contact with the world of industry will candidly tell you that business claims greater talents and more time than it has ever done before. In her passionate pleading for *The New State* Miss Follett does not seem to allow much potency to the world of the business man. She advocates a policy which accepts and wholeheartedly encourages the active political functioning of various groups, such as professional associations and neighbourhood societies, yet leaves the sovereignty of the State undisturbed. Her separate groupings do not, however, live in isolation. In their interdependence and in their interpenetration she discerns the unifying elements of the one supreme sovereignty of the new democratic State of the future. It is significant that in spite of the keener pressure of business claims in England the Whitley scheme of joint standing councils in the Civil Service has come into being. The plan of the Sankey Commission for the participation of the miners in the administration of the coal-mining industry with national ownership of the coal royalties has been before the public. The French government too is willing to allow a greater recognition of, and co-operation with, the syndicates in the public service. This feeling is also spreading in the United States. Guild Socialism is a reflection of it.

Eloquent advocates of pluralism like Miss Follett speak of the interdependence and the interpenetration of the groups, but we earnestly wish we were as certain as she of this happy consummation. She believes that every law *could* be made to express a complete interest within which differences are "integrated." We wish we could share her belief. No doubt as she lives in the United States, she notes the failings due to the division of powers in her federal State. For our part we feel that where there are co-ordinate authorities there may be conflicts akin to those in German *Verwaltungsrecht* or the French *droit administratif*. Unity and order must emerge if there is to be any life worthy of the group or the State. If fellowship is a condition of life, order stands close to it. For a loss of order normally means a loss of liberty. Perhaps indeed if the pluralist State were established this would not be so serious as it sounds. For it is clear that similar questions between the groups would arise, producing similar answers. These would tend to stablise State life because of their very similarity.

The pluralists occupy a strong position when they draw attention to instance after instance where State or rather Government authority has broken down. Mr. Laski urges that "government does not range over the whole area of human life," and of course the group conception lends powerful assistance to his contention. Does not the omnicompetence of the State mean its incompetence in aspect after aspect of private life? Figgis, like him, recognises that the final allegiance of the individual is to conscience. Nothing, not even the group, can estop the claim of conscience. He also adduces the case of the South African Parliament which passed an immigration law which the Imperial Parliament did not like, and yet did not feel sufficiently strong to override it. As a proof of the impotence of the State Mr. Laski invites us to consider the inability of Parliament to coerce Ulster in 1914, the ability of the suffragists to defy the law for a long period before the War, and its inability to force the subjection of the conscientious objectors to the Military Service Act of 1916. He also mentions the impotence of Bismarck to coerce the Roman Catholic Church and the impotence of Gladstone to coerce Wiseman. In both these cases, however, it was obvious that the Roman Catholic Church was not politically a source of danger. Certainly this was the case in England, which means that the Government blundered, not that the State suffered. For Governmental impotence is not invariably State impotence. The "Direct Action" of the Trade Unions, so far at least, has failed, and the General Strike of 1926 failed the moment the public realised that a revolution in government was at stake. The question of miners' wages left the people calm, but the General Strike roused their general will, and this general will broke the strike. A *political* General Strike can claim some success, as the Belgian one in 1893 for universal suffrage and the German Kapp Putsch. Has an *economic* General Strike ever succeeded? The General Strike of 1903 in Holland, of 1909 in Sweden, and the semi-general strike of 1913 in New Zealand proclaim its failure. It is significant that Mr. Ramsay MacDonald and Mr. Sidney Webb recognise the permanence of the State and the necessity of its sovereign authority.

The pages of history throw light on the past and the present of pluralism. With the downfall of Rome the "State" disappeared in Western Europe. In the past the Holy Roman Empire wore a pluralistic form, and its success was not so unqualified as to force us to long for its revival. Was there a "State" in the Middle Ages? There is no State where there is anarchy. The absence of a central authority then encouraged strife between the mediaeval guilds. Nor does the present history of pluralism in the nineteenth century in the United States prove more encouraging. There was no true monistic State there for two generations, for it was the creation of more than fifty years of political development and experience. The question of slavery proved that North and South possessed competing wills with the outcome of the bloodiest war in the annals of history before 1914. Even an idealist like Bosanquet reluctantly allows that "the state, as the operative criticism of all institutions, is necessarily force."

Figgis faces facts fairly, and he sees that the Government has broken down where the State has not. Primarily he cares for the group theory because he is a Churchman anxious that she should live and grow. She is a *societas perfecta* with her own internal liberty. It is a claim with which we feel the deepest sympathy. The difficulties arising from divorce, education, and Establishment are tolerably obvious when we assume that the Church is a group. When the State recognises divorce and the Church does not, when the State insists on secular education and the Church insists on religious education—these are among the problems raised. A conflict between the things of Caesar and the things of God is always possible. If the Church Assembly pass a Deposited Prayer Book measure and if the House of Commons reject it, what is to be the outcome? Nor can we confine such a question within narrow English limits. Was the government of India right, from a Hindu angle, to abolish suttee? Is this government right in propagating Western learning which is slowly undermining the Hindu faith? Was the United States similarly right in forbidding polygamy among the Mormons? To questions like these Figgis provides no answer.

He is quite clear that so long as the Church assumes no real personality, it matters but little, so far as her freedom is concerned, whether she is established or not. Here he speaks with no uncertain voice. "Mere disestablishment would not of itself ensure liberty." The Free Church of Scotland in 1905, was not an established Church, yet her affairs fell within the purview of the State. Formally, the Lord Chancellor, Lord Halsbury, disclaimed all intention of meddling with church doctrine, but practically he was forced to do so, though of course he was forced with the utmost reluctance.

So long as the present view of the relations between Church and State prevails in England, so long will it be impossible to forbid the Judical Committee of the Privy Council from uttering what in practice are doctrinal judgments. Take a case. Suppose that a bishop entertains reason for believing that a rector teaches what is contrary to the Prayer Book. The case no doubt will be tried by a regular hierarchy of ecclesiastical Courts. First, there is the Bishop's Court, then the Archbishop's. Then there is the Court of the Sovereign, represented by the Judicial Committee of the Privy Council, whose members are lay judges as well as ecclesiastical. On hearing the appeal of the rector, these lay and ecclesiastical judges are bound to treat the Prayer Book as a legal document—not as a book of devotion,—and their business with this legal document is to see if the rector's doctrine is in any wise compatible with the Prayer Book. They of course will not pronounce whether, doctrinally speaking, the rector is right or wrong, but they must pronounce that his teaching is or is not compatible with the contents of the Prayer Book. In some respects this case is not unlike an appeal on a measure passed by the Congress of the United States which a citizen considers *ultra vires*. Such a citizen can sue out a writ to have the case tried before the Supreme Court at Washington. That Court will not pronounce that the measure is *ultra vires*, but if it infringes the federal constitution it will simply declare that the new legislation is not one on which the judges can act.

In his interesting book on *Christianity and the State*, which Archbishop Temple obviously wrote before the first rejection of the Deposited Prayer Book by the House of Commons, he considers in his second appendix this question. He of course admits that by the Enabling Act of 1919 the Church Assembly was empowered by Parliament to frame measures which Parliament can accept or reject by a single resolution of each of the two Houses. From the point of view of a lawyer like Dicey this Church Assembly is a strictly subordinate body. Its measures possess no legal binding force till Parliament passes them. This of course is due to theory of sovereignty which now prevails, but of course would not longer be true if the Church were a real corporation in the sense of Figgis or Maitland or Gierke. The group theory is slowly making its way, but it *has* not made its way with the result that the legal view of sovereignty still holds the field. Nor is it a case where Parliament has refused to exercise its right of veto. The Church Assembly has been in existence eight years, and during that period Parliament has rejected four measures, the Shrewsbury Bishopric Bill, a measure dealing with the parishes and churches in the city of London, and the Deposited Prayer Book twice. Dr. Temple urges that "it is most emphatically not the business of the State to determine what is, and what is not, compatible with theological truth." Directly of course we all agree that this is not the work of the State, and we may feel quite sure that the State will never undertake such a duty. At the same time if a York ecclesiastical court decides that a rector teaches heresy, and if the rector appeals to the Judicial Committee of the Privy Council, and if that Court decides that the rector's teaching is compatible with the recognised standard of doctrine, it seems to us that practically the State is forced to settle whether a dogma is or is not a possible view for a rector to take. Dr. Temple pleads that Parliament has "a complete legal right, but not (I hold) a moral right, to determine what the Prayer Book of the Established Church shall be." Questions of morality are proverbially difficult to decide, and Archbishop Temple is a distinguished moralist. If the group theory held the field, the moral argument would weigh heavily, but as the State is still unitary, what is the value of it? If Parliament in the end passes the Deposited Prayer Book, the question of the relations between Church and State is simply postponed —to a more convenient day or, what we fear far more, to the time when an even more critical question arises.

Two of our leading political philosophers, Mr. Barker and Mr. Lindsay, in *The Political Quarterly* of February, 1915, and of February, 1914, discuss the discredited State and the State in recent political theory respectively. The former in his article and in his illuminating little book on *Political Thought from Spencer to To-day* does not accept the doctrine of the real personality of the group persuasively urged by Gierke and Maitland. At the same time he holds that these groups exist prior to any act of creation on the part of the State, and, as he so holds, he believes that the theory of the nature of the State and its relations to other associations stands in need of revision. In fact, "We see the State less as an association of individuals in a common life; we see it more as an association of individuals, already united in various groups for a further and more embracing common purpose." The State has become a fetish whose worship brought on the World War, and we must decidedly abate the worship of what amounts to superstition. "The State," in Mr. Barker's judgment, "as a general and embracing scheme of life, must necessarily adjust the relations of associations to itself, to other associations, and to their own members—to itself, in order to maintain the integrity of its own scheme; to other associations, in order to preserve the equality of associations before the law; and to their own members, in order to preserve the individual from the possible tyranny of the group." The situation is slowly altering, and "We see the State invited to retreat before the advance of the guild, the national group, the Church. Yet whatever rights such groups may claim or gain, the State will still remain a necessary adjusting force; and it is even possible that if groups are destined to gain new ground, the State will also gain, perhaps even more than it loses, because it will be forced to deal with ever graver and ever weightier problems of adjustment."

Mr. Lindsay believes that the old theories of individualism and Socialism split on the rock of considering politics as concerned entirely with the relations between the State and the individual. Naturally any theory which ignores man's need of fellowship ignores the chief problem of politics. So Mr. Lindsay considers. Like Mr. Barker, he deems it absurd to think of associations within a State as the creation of the State. "They and the State are equally the expressions of man's social nature and the outcome of their common interests. The State may be necessary to control them; it does not follow that the citizens would give it power to destroy them." He holds, however, that the coercive power of the State is not an ultimate fact in politics, and he also holds that the doctrine of sovereignty assumes the distinct and separate nature of different sovereign States, and in point of fact the members of these States are not so independent as is commonly supposed. It is quite clear that the rapid development of world-wide economic organisation, of rapid and easy travel, and still more rapid correspondence, has, as Mr. Lindsay urges, substituted for the old and relatively isolated-nation States of the eighteenth and nineteenth centuries a world of societies all equally affected by the new economic organisations but at the most different stages of political organisation.

So far the political philosophers, no doubt in different degrees, accept the authority of the State. This authority Mr. Laski sweeps to the one side, and the strength of his argument for his action lies in the instances he adduces of the failure of the State to assert its alleged power over those unwilling to admit it. He has been influenced by William James, for he is a pragmatist in politics, and he has been influenced by Duguit who limits the sovereign power by the conception of the *solidarité sociale,* interpreting law in terms of social force. The State, according to Duguit, is subject to more than moral limitations. Law, we learn from him, is not the creation of the State any more than the group: it is superior to and anterior to the State, a position akin to the old view of the binding power of the law of nature. There is no such thing as a national will, and of course there is no organ to express it. In France law comes from other sources than Parliament, and he instances the power of the President of the Republic to issue ordinances, and similar powers possessed by communal and other local administrative authorities. Yet on examination it seems as if these examples relate to what Dicey would regard as subordinate law making bodies.

Mr. Laski's extremely able contributions to political thought are mainly to be found in his *Studies in the Problem of Sovereignty*, 1917, and his *Authority in the Modern State*, 1919. In the former work he promised a volume on pluralistic political theory which, so far, has not appeared. His *Foundations of Sovereignty*, 1921, is certainly not the promised volume which we await with the utmost eagerness. His important *Grammar of Politics*, 1925, supplies much, but we want more. Mr. Laski asks questions, and his questions are always well worth answering. Is the power of the State over the individual or over the group actually absolute? Is the State morally entitled to its present pre-eminent position in society? To both questions he replies with an unhesitating negative. At the same time in the answer to his first question he scarcely allows sufficiently for the limitations on the power of the State acknowledged by Bodin and Grotius, Hobbes and Austin. They are very far indeed from believing in the absolute authority of the Leviathan. To Mr. Laski it is "only one among many forms of human association," competing with other associations in its claim upon obedience. Is there any ultimate authority? Apparently there is none. The State is but the government which is but an association contributing to the social good. Many other associations contribute to this good, and we cannot say that the State is "necessarily more in harmony with the end of society than a church or a trade union or a freemason's lodge." As a matter of fact he admits that the State absorbs much—too much—social power, but this absorption is a matter of real regret. To a working man his Trade Union means more than the State, and to a Churchman his Church means more. The group life grips the individual in a closer tie than the Leviathan. Mr. Laski contemplates with equanimity competing groups in which the State is but one among many. Take wealth, for instance. There will be an association to represent the production aspect, and of course labour will control it. There will also be an association to represent the consumption aspect, and the national legislature will control it. "Nor is the central authority within either division to be envisaged as uniquely sovereign." The judiciary is to settle any dispute between these two sets of association. If the past reveals a knowledge of human nature in, say Trade Unions it is safe to prophesy, in spite of George Eliot's dictum, that a court of appeal will certainly not suffer from lack of business.

The individual, according to Mr. Laski, is no longer subordinate to the State: he is simply subordinate to the group, and of course he holds with Maitland that such groups possess real personality. His view denies "the rightness of force." At the same time he points out that "It dissolves—what the facts themselves dissolve—the inherent claim of the state to obedience. It insists that the state like every other association shall prove itself by what it achieves. It sets group competing against group in a ceaseless striving of progressive expansion." It is, in truth, a case of the survival of the fittest. If the State is the fittest—but plainly this is impossible. Yet surely if there is this ceaseless striving there is force. If nature is not red in tooth and claw, there is, to vary Hobbes's famous phrase, *associatio associationi lupus*. There is the inevitable tendency at work for the larger group to swallow up the smaller. It surely will be not a little difficult for any court to afford satisfaction to the claimants from different groups coming before it. No one who knows Trade Unions will deny that not the least onerous part of their work lies in the adjustment of the claims of the different classes of men whose labours lead them to perform functions well-nigh identical. We may broaden the issue. A small determined association possessed of political initiative can effect by mass suggestion efforts out of all proportion to their numbers. There is no more effective method of manufacturing a revolution. The English Revolution of 1688 and 1832, the French Revolution of 1789, and the Russian Revolution of 1917 are due to the action of a resolute group. The revolutions of the mass of the people are failures. This is as true of the revolt of the slaves in the ancient world as of the peasants in the sixteenth century.

Mr. Laski asks us to consider his associations as assuming federalist forms, but it is a federalism without an unifying principle. Dicey insists that federalism means legalism, yet Mr. Laski attacks that supremacy of law on which federalism rests. At the same time he has rendered service by his insistence that the State, in spite of its legal omnipotence, is still subject to the moral law. He thereby safeguards us against those who work out the views of Kant and Hegel to their logical conclusion. He certainly compels us to realise that we live in a world which is far more dynamic than such supporters of statics as Bodin and Grotius, Hobbes and Austin realised. This is another way of stating that Austin published his *Province of Jurisprudence Determined* in 1832 whereas Mr. Laski published his *Foundations of Sovereignty* in 1921. If ever he had written the former book, its title surely would have been *The Province of Jurisprudence Indeterminate*. One feels the flux, the fever, of life pulsing in all that Mr. Laski writes. Nor is it possible to glance around modern civilisation without perceiving everywhere the increasing part that the principle of association is playing, and is increasingly destined to play. The pluralist school has made us their debtors by revealing the Many in the One.

The pluralists have rendered undoubted service. They can ask such questions as the following: Do the words "Be it enacted" really make law? Is not society superior to law? Are not the monists committing the mediaeval mistake of confounding society with the State? Is not society distinct from the State? Does not the pluralist idea protect us from the horrors of the Treitschkean conception of the State? Does it not recognise the influence of the complex of opinions, prejudices and desires of social groups? Will not spontaneous action, self-expressive and initiative action, enjoy free play in the groups?

It is open to the opponents of pluralism also to ask, in their turn, questions. Is the State no more than a liaison officer between different but equal groups? Is it only one in a long series of groups? Does it possess no special significance in comparison with other groups? Does it possess no special authority in comparison with the others? Is each group, such as a church, a trade union, or a masonic lodge, in its own sphere independent of the State? Is it only when the groups overstep the boundaries of their sphere that the sovereignty of the State emerges? Does not the State enlarge the domain of sympathy and solidarity? Does not the group system contract both? Have we come to hold *tot sententiae, quot societates*? Is the ecclesiastical group, the industrial group, the masonic group, really as significant as the State? Is the doctrine not fundamentally anarchic? Does it settle such questions as compulsory taxation and citizenship? Is not the unitary State a great timesaver for its members? Does it not set them free for constructive tasks? Mr. Graham Wallas, in *Our Social Heritage*, argues that sectionalism produces group selfishness, conservatism, the rule of mediocrity, inefficiency in the accumulation of social necessary capital, and the loss of patriotism and co-operative activity.

Mr. Laski contends that the State does not take its pre-eminence by force, but wins it by consent, a position we can heartily adopt. It is among the limits tacitly recognised by Bodin, the father of unitary sovereignty. In 1672 Sir William Temple, with Hobbes's *Leviathan* in his mind, penned the words that "all government is a restraint upon liberty; and under all, the dominion is equally absolute, where it is in the last resort. So that when men seem to contend for liberty, it is, indeed, but for the change of those that rule. . . . Nor, when vast numbers of men submit their lives and fortunes absolutely to the will of one, it should be want of heart, but must be force of custom, or opinion, the true ground and foundation of all government, and that which subjects power to authority. For power arising from strength is always in those that are governed, who are many; but authority arising from opinion is in those that govern, who are few." Sir William proceeds to urge that "the ground upon which all government stands is the consent of the people, or the greatest and strongest part of it." Nor is the doctrine of Hume one whit different. "As force," he acknowledges, "is always on the side of the governed, the governors have nothing to support them but opinion. It is, therefore, on opinion only that government is founded; and this maxim extends to the most despotic and most military governments, as well as to the most free and most popular. The Soldan of Egypt, or the Emperor of Rome, might drive his harmless subjects, like brute beasts, against their sentiments and inclination; but he must, at least, have led his mamelukes, or praetorian bands, like men, by their opinion." David Hume and Sir William Temple will agree with Mr. Laski that the State wins its position by consent.

Mr. Laski occupies strong ground when he emphasises the difficulties standing in the way of the practical application of the Austinian doctrine of sovereignty, though we wonder if he is right in believing that it breeds servility when men obey it. No doubt in a crisis there is a danger of its authority breaking down, but will not the power of the group in this instance also break down? Does this occasional breakdown justify us in holding that the State is no more than a corporation among other corporations? Must there not be some ultimate authority in the last resort? Is it possible to federalise the State on the basis of functions? If there are differences among the groups, must not the State, whatever form it takes, possess power to enforce its decisions? If this is so, is it not sovereignty in another form?

The pluralists emphasise the circumstance that there are many groups with many members within the State. Mr. Norman Angell, who is not necessarily a pluralist, attacks the authority of the State from the angle that co-operation of members of any State and their common dependence extend far beyond the bounds of the State. The Manchester cotton merchant recognises many ties with the cotton growers in the United States or in Egypt, and this recognition is by no means due to the fact that Egypt is within our Empire and the United States without it. The economic prosperity of Western Europe and America depends, as Mr. Angell acknowledges, on an elaborate organisation of credit and commercial enterprise between individuals belonging to different States. As facilities for travel and correspondence grow this co-operation between citizens of different countries for all kinds of purposes, business and other, becomes increasingly frequent. In 1910 Mr. Angell, in his *Great Illusion,* takes trouble to emphasise this interdependence and interpenetration of States, and his inevitable deduction is that war does not and cannot pay. While the historical instances he adduces are not at all impeccable, yet he makes out a strong case for his view that war is economically futile between modern civilised nations. He has no difficulty in proving that military security is not synonymous with commercial security. But he slurs over the fact that while both may lose, the vanquished may lose the most, and may in fact lose everything. Nor is it true to argue that the cause of modern war is economical. Chief among the influences which brought about not a few of these wars were a desire not for wealth but domination, racial antipathies, racial affinities and aspirations, dislike of alien rule, longing for political unity, and the desire to destroy an uncongenial political system. He approaches the State not in the manner of the pluralists. They are anxious to show that the group is a real corporation while Mr. Angell is no less anxious to show that the State is nothing of the kind. From this point of view it cannot head the groups, for this view would compel us to attribute personality to the Leviathan. He argues that the spread of modern communications, and notably of international credit and the banking system, has produced an entirely new situation in the world, and in face of this situation the Austinian notion of independent sovereign States is meaningless. The forces of modern exchange are "so much a part of the warp and woof of the ordinary life of the world that they are rapidly and surely weaving society into an indissoluble whole." He sees as little future for the State as Mr. Laski. "It has become impossible for the army of a State to embody the fight for an ideal, for the simple reason that the great moral questions of our time can no longer be postulated in national terms." Is nationality the spent force he chooses to imagine? It is the irony of history that his book appeared in 1910, for the World War demonstrated that the men postulated great moral questions in terms of their respective nationalities. Socialism was supposed to be international, but in August, 1914, socialists at once found their national character. Jean Jaurès discovered he was a Frenchman, and his discovery was shared by many. They became a party to the view of my country, right or wrong. Nor is it possible for us to forget the ideal enshrined by Treitschke in the attitude: "The moment the State calls: 'Myself and my existence are now at stake,' social self-seeking must fall back, and every party hate to be silent. The individual must forget his own ego, and feel himself a member of the whole; he must recognise what a nothing his life is in comparison with the general welfare. In that very point lies the loftiness of war, that the small man disappears entirely before the great thought of the State; the sacrifice of fellow-countrymen for one another is nowhere so splendidly exhibited as in war. In such days the chaff is separated from the wheat."

That force is no remedy is a cardinal proposition with Mr. Norman Angell, and yet the existence of the policeman in ordinary life bears testimony to the fact that force is a remedy against the wilful breakers of the law. The half truth is always dangerous, and Mr. Angell usually deals in half truths. There is of course the distinction between latent and patent force. Formerly force was patent whereas now it is latent. The latent force of the Roman Empire kept it in existence till it forgot to employ its patent force, falling before the invasion of the barbarians. Similarly the latent force of the British Empire constitutes a striking testimony to the fact that she has been so seldom involved in war since Waterloo Her patent force has shrunk into the background, but foreign observers, more acute than Mr. Angell, never doubt of its existence. Apologists of the

United States sometimes point to the fact that she has infrequently waged war, but the countries like Mexico to which she sent an ultimatum so keenly recognised the presence of her latent force that they did not dare go to war. The circumstance that you hold a pistol to a man's head but do not fire when he yields does not prove for a moment that your force has disappeared. You did not employ it simply because there was no occasion to do so, but it is there, a truth that Mr. Angell persistently ignores. At the same time we admit with Joubert, "*C'est la force et le droit qui règlent toutes choses dans le monde ; la force en attendant le droit.*"

With Mr. Angell we freely grant that the Argentine merchant and the British trader alike regard the Trade Union as a possible enemy, and that the Hamburg docker and the London one share many feelings. This means that in not a few respects we are returning to the conception of the Middle Ages when the divisions of society were horizontal not vertical as they were till lately. If our author cares to peruse the history of the Middle Ages he will discover that they were not altogether free from war, and that in fact it is as easy to fight for horizontal interests as it is for vertical. Nor is the prospect he envisages at all attractive. For if the horizontal interests grow in importance, we may live to see a war of cosmopolitan classes extending over the civilised world. A War of this type between the capitalists of Europe and America against the Trade Unions of these continents might readily be more appalling than the World War. Our fear, in fact, is that the growth of economic relations at the expense of political is fraught with the gravest danger to the future peace of mankind.

Chapter X.

SOCIALISM

THERE is a striking resemblance between the period after 1815 and the period after 1918. In this country after the battle of Waterloo all those efforts and aspirations which are more and more claiming political and public attention—whether in the name of Socialism, Syndicalism, Trade Unionism, or any allied ism—had their real beginnings. There is no phase of the Labour movement to-day that we cannot trace, at least in embryo, to this period. It was a time of as extraordinary ferment as our own day; it produced a welter of ideas, theories, projects, agitation, experiments and efforts, economic, social, and political, which anticipated everything since advocated or attempted. And since neither doctrines nor events can be properly understood except in the light of their development, a knowledge of this period is essential to a right comprehension and valuation of modern movements. The current notion—invented by Marx and Engels—that up to their time Socialism consisted of a few absurd Utopian schemes and that it has since become something entirely different is quite false. Our consideration of the thought of Godwin, Thompson, Hall, Gray, Hodgskin, and Bray has, we hope, shown how utterly erroneous is this idea. The Belgian Socialists engineered in 1893 a general strike in favour of general suffrage, and the public were informed that this was a new and unprecedented departure; but in 1839 the Chartists did precisely the same thing. They voted a general strike for universal suffrage; only it fell through. William Benbow was the originator in 1831 of the general strike as an industrial and political weapon. Syndicalism is as old a weapon as the general strike. The extraordinary outburst of Trade Unionism in 1833 had a true Syndicalist side. Its promoter was not Owen, but James Morison, a member of the Builders' Union and editor of their paper, the *Pioneer*. It is clear that genuine Syndicalism is essentially a Trade Union policy, which came at once into conflict with Owen's superficially similar but radically different aims. Another point is also clear. There is an inherent antagonism between direct and political action which showed itself then, as now, directly organised Labour took hold of the doctrine taught by the Socialists.

The pursuit of happiness is natural to man, and, in some form or other, has always employed his activities. The builders of Utopias may roughly be divided into these two categories; those who seek to subtract, and those who seek to add and multiply. The worst of any general scheme of the sort is that—in no other matter is the adage so true—one man's meat is another man's poison. Fourier, for instance, considered variety, constant employment, and promiscuity as elements of happiness; but there are those who love nothing so well as monotony, solitude, and leisure—divine trio, out of which issue great thoughts, combined ideas, deep and instinctive memories, even as bees issue forth and hover above their quiet hives. The man in the street is wise who has summed up rightly that it is impossible to make a man happy by Act of Parliament. The same shoe will never fit Thomas Arnold and Matthew Arnold, Goethe and Gambetta, Maitland and Marx.

If the physics and the metaphysics of Fourier provoke a smile, there is something of prophecy in his sociological outlook. True his Phalanstery came to hopeless grief, and Elizabeth Browning divined the reason:—

> It takes the ideal, to blow a hair's-breadth off
> The dust of the actual.—Ah, your Fouriers failed,
> Because not poets enough to understand
> That life develops from within.

But, if the vain phalanstery dissolved itself, and the programmes and systems proved ineffectual, let us remember that Fourier himself admitted that his social nurseries *might* possibly prove premature. In four or five thousand years, said he, they will reappear of their own accord, by a natural process of evolution; but several periods must elapse ere we enter on this reign of harmony. The next age, which will immediately succeed the abject depths of so-called civilisation, is the Age of Guarantees, *le Garantisme, "ère caracterisée par les garanties mutuelles que se donneront les hommes contre les fléaux économiques: on y instituera un* minimum *de bienêtre, les assurances de toutes sortes contre la maladie, le chêmage, la viellesse, les accidents* . . . ." And as we read, we wonder whether the Age of Garantisme has not come upon us like a thief in the night, unawares. In that case, Fourier was among the prophets.

The Utopias of the future, as they are before the eyes of Mr. Sidney Webb, Mr. Ramsay MacDonald or Mr. Bernard Shaw, appear as the product of Socialism combined with mechanical science. But there are other reformers who hold with Elizabeth Browning that "life develops from within," and in whose eyes the City of our Dreams owes its chance of existence less to a change of government, or a development of industry, than to a general change of heart. After all, our feelings no less than our sciences are conquests and acquirements; they enlarge and modify not only our private life but our conception of society and our ideal of happiness.

He who attacks the present economic order has before him something palpable; he can fasten upon and make the most of its imperfections, and hold it answerable for every existing evil. In fact, the controversy between Individualism and Socialism is not conducted on equal terms. The assailant or critic of Socialism does not enjoy the advantages of the critic of Individualism. He demonstrates the untenableness or absurdity of some system. He proves that it has failed wherever it has been tried. He is told that his refutation counts for nothing: "that is not our Socialism; we agree with your criticisms, which do not touch our scheme." When, turning to some other schemes, he exposes their weakness, again comes the rejoinder, "It is not ours; we admit your criticisms, only they do not happen to affect our plan." The controversy is between those who defend an existing state of things and those who as a rule have all the advantages of maintaining invisible positions. Many of those who profess to be scientific Socialists draw no small part of their strength from the fact that they do not say, except vaguely and illusively, what they mean to substitute for that which they would destroy. Their system, like bachelors' children, possesses no faults, because it never existed. It is invisible and therefore unassailable; at all events, what is palpable and open to attack can always be declared to be non-essential.

Since the Russian Revolution of 1917 there have been many Socialistic experiments, and the defence of the scheme, accordingly, is not quite so easy as formerly. Socialism has been tried in Russia, Germany, and Austria on a pretty large scale, and the outcome can scarcely be regarded as satisfactory. Lenin, the genius of the Russian Revolution of 1917, belonged to the bourgeoisie, for his father was director of the high school in the city of Simbirsk. When seventeen, his elder brother was hanged for his share in a student revolutionary movement. When Nicholas Lenin entered the university he was promptly excluded. Still, after four years of private study he succeeded in passing the examinations for the bar. Shortly afterwards he was arrested in Leningrad for organising a group of workers. After serving a long period in jail, he was exiled to Siberia in the later nineties, where he wrote two books, *The Aim of Social Democratic Party* and *The Growth of Capitalism in Russia.* As the outcome of their publication, he was forced to fly from his native land, joining the revolutionary group of Russians in Switzerland. In 1903, at a conference of the Social Democratic party, Lenin led a faction which pledged itself to "pure revolutionary action" without any compromise with the bourgeois parties. His faction secured the majority of the delegates, and ever since has been nicknamed the majority, or Bolshevik. "In any and every serious revolution," Lenin acknowledges, "a long, obstinate, desperate resistance of the exploiters, who for many years will yet enjoy great advantages over the exploited, constitutes the rule. Never . . . will the exploiters submit to the decision of the exploited majority without making use of their advantages in a last desperate battle or in a series of battles." Thus "the transition from Capitalism to Communism forms a whole historical epoch."

If the works of Marx and Lenin may be described as the

Communist Bible, the *Course of Political Instruction* (*Politgramota*), edited by Bukharin, holds the place of the Communist Catechism. Without some knowledge of the *Politgramota* it is extremely difficult to exist in Soviet Russia and impossible to obtain any Government stipend or post. Rudiments of it are taught in elementary schools and in the "round the fire" talks in the "pioneer" camps. The soldier in the barracks has his "hour of political instruction," and the student's diploma often depends on his progress in that particular branch of learning. No school teacher, from the elementary schools upwards, can obtain a post without a preliminary examination in the *Politgramota,* and it forms one of the principal subjects in the "Soviet Party Schools," where special Communist agitators and responsible workers are trained.

The main point of all Bolshevik propaganda abroad is the inevitability of civil war for the achievement of Communism. When power is won, Bukharin affirms that "the false and treacherous demands of democracy" must be "ruthlessly" swept aside. Freedom of the press, freedom of public meeting, "and so forth"—every medium for the free expression of individual opinion—must be abolished. Bukharin proceeds to show that "the very idea of the possibility of a peaceful subordination of capitalism to the will of the majority of the toilers, through Parliament or a constitutional assembly, or a peaceful transition to Socialism cannot be tolerated." It must be regarded as "a dangerous fraud."

In Russia the Bolsheviks created a very effective secret service organisation. It is called the All-Russian Extraordinary Commission for Fighting Counter-Revolution, Speculation and Sabotage. In the course of two years' work, according to its own record, it suppressed three hundred and forty-four revolts and shot over eight thousand people. None but the faithful belong to it. Among the unfaithful are all who belonged to the capitalist class who are debarred from voting or holding office. Among the disfranchised are the following classes: persons employing hired labour for profit, those living on unearned income, private merchants, the clergy, and ex-police agents.

In spite of an unprecedented Reign of Terror the Bolsheviks have been compelled to abandon their early positions. At first they paid a uniform wage. To-day they pay workers according to an output test. At first they planned the confiscation of all factories and their management by the workers. To-day experts, no doubt under the direction of a Supreme Council of National Economy, run the factories. At first Communism was to work miracles. To-day the capitalists of Europe are begged to come and run the industries. At first there was to be paper money. To-day there is a silver currency. At first all bank accounts above a very small amount were confiscated. To-day unlimited deposits are permissible. The most outstanding abandonment of Bolshevism is to be witnessed in agriculture. At first Lenin nationalised it, compelling the peasants to yield all their produce to the Soviets. Nationalisation failed so completely that he was forced to grant private ownership. Individualism has won a complete triumph. Amazingly enough, the final result of the Russian Revolution in land has been that the mass of the people are more firmly wedded to the idea of private property than ever. The violent adjusters of economic inequality have as a rule been much more successful in injuring their victims than in helping those whom they intend to benefit. One of the exceptions to this rule is the moujik. On the other hand, the townsmen illustrate the working of this rule, for they have suffered —and are suffering—cruelly. Does not science—as well as history—increasingly declare that the worship of the goddess Equality is, as Burke affirmed from the first, a delusion, and its idol an impostor whom Nature knows not?

There are spurious as well as scientific Socialists. We put among the former those who rely upon some analogies, remote and uncertain, derived from biologists; analogies which real biologists such as Huxley and Zittel do not accept. To the latter class belong those who base their creed upon some economic principle. A generation ago they were, with scarcely an exception, followers of Marx. They believed with him that wealth was produced by labour only; that an iron law of wages was in operation with the result that the capitalist class acquired more and more of the total produce, the workman less, and that wages must fall. The more intelligent Socialists have long ago abandoned the Marx theory of value, which indeed is as good as given up in the posthumous volume of *Das Kapital*. Facts have impressively refuted Marx's conclusion; wages have everywhere, broadly speaking, risen. The thoroughgoing Marxist is now rare; he will in a few years be extinct; at any moment we may hear that the last Marxist has been interred. But it is common to repudiate Marx's theory that labour alone creates wealth, and yet, before less intelligent audiences, Marxism in its crudest form is still stated as if it were true. In the modern literature of Socialism a whole world of fallacies revolves round the word "labour"; the chief argument for the wholesale appropriation of the means of production, which is the programme of a large class, goes if the various meanings allotted to labour are examined. If it is extended so as to include the skill and forethought of a Vanderbilt, the exercise of the inventive genius of Watt, Bessemer, or Edison, the organising skill of the captains of industry, it is little better than a truism. The tactics of one class—the baser—of Socialists is to use this word with this comprehensive signification when they are engaged in theoretical discussion, and in another and much narrower sense, equivalent to physical or manual labour, when they address popular audiences and there is demand for action. Of course Mr. Sidney Webb and Mr. Ramsay MacDonald do not belong to this class.

There is another class of scientific Socialists who, seeing the weakness of the Marxian doctrine in theory and facts, throw it over, and rest their case on the tendency for wealth to accumulate in enormous masses, and to the creation of monopolies not the less powerful because without legal sanction. This tendency is specially notable in the United States where trusts are dominant in business. Here indeed are corporations, but they are corporations at which a Maitland would shudder. When we ask the Socialist what he would substitute for the "trust" or the "pool" or the "ring," he generally answers that he would create a monopoly even more powerful than Rockefeller's; he would hand us all over for meat and drink, for raiment and housing, for the wants of the body and the mind to the State. He lays stress, just stress, on the growth of monopolies and the need of a corrective to them. Yet does he not place the State in a position in which it would be the greatest of monopolists? Can it be impartial? Will it not abdicate its functions as administrator of justice to become a trader and manufacturer with all sorts of special interests? The question too of motive is a serious one. No one can deny the drawbacks to self-interest, but what motive will take its place with the non-elect as well as the elect? With the latter it is fair to say that the mere pleasure of excelling and the joy in creative work will provide a motive; but will this induce the non-elect to labour as self-interest did? Is not the postulate of all forms of Socialism a condition of things in which the ordinary motives to activity will be weakened or suspended? In the absence of a high—and new—sense of duty, will not the majority "ca' canny"? In fact, has Socialism found its working ethical creed? That it has lost its economic Marxian basis is undoubted. Mr. Sidney Webb insisted at the 1923 conference of the Labour Party that the father of British Socialism is not Karl Marx with his economic determinism, but Robert Owen with his gospel of human brotherhood. Be it so, but does the brotherhood embrace all the inhabitants of our country? Or, does it simply embrace the world of Labour?

That the world of Labour enjoys considerable prosperity is obvious to all. The rise in wages means the diffusion of wealth which we can notice in many directions. If we take railways in 1925 there were 308,028 shareholders in the London, Midland and Scottish Railway; if we take banks in 1925 there were 69,882 shareholders in the Westminster Bank; and if we take business there were 43,826 shareholders in Courtaulds and 33,253 in Harrods. Of course it is fairly likely that the investors in these concerns belonged to the well-to-do classes. Those with smaller means resort to the Post Office and other Savings Banks, National Savings Certificates and other Government securities. Sixteen millions have £204,000,000 deposited in the Post Office, and they also hold stock of the value of £29,000,000 National Savings certificates amount to £171,100,000. Mr. Runciman calculates that in 1925 investments of this kind amounting to £770,000,000 were held by 15,000,000 people. When he reckoned provident societies and insurance funds, he came to the conclusion that small investors were the main owners of no less a total than £400,000,000. These are results that even so far-sighted a man as Robert Owen could scarcely credit. Nor are such results confined to our people. In the United States the number of shareholders has increased since the beginning of the century from 4,000,000 to 14,000,000 at the present day, and many of them are workmen employed in the concerns in which they own shares. In fact, we are witnessing the diffusion of wealth among all classes, whereby workmen are increasingly becoming capitalists.

Between 1914 and 1924 Professor Bowley and Sir Josiah Stamp estimate that the average earnings for a full week increased 94 per cent., compared with an increase in the cost of living index of 75 per cent. The advance in real wages, accordingly, has been resumed in spite of the great increase in free and subsidised social services. The balance, for instance, of the National Health Insurance Fund is £83,000,000. No doubt the prevalence of unemployment reduced earnings, and unemployment was undoubtedly greater in 1924 than in 1914, but these earnings were received for a working week that was on an average 10 per cent. less in length. In spite of the great war and in spite of the most serious and prolonged industrial depression we have ever experienced, the standard of life of the working classes has been maintained unimpaired. The best measure of the change is given by Professor Bowley and Miss Hogg's repetition in 1924 of the inquiry into poverty in five towns made in 1913. Adapting the same standard of poverty, they found that in spite of the excessive unemployment of 1924 the proportion of families in poverty was little more than one-half what it had been in 1913. Fewer persons go short of food in a post-war depression than in pre-war. Medical officers of health report that in public health, and particularly the physical condition of school children, is better in the worst spell of unemployment that the country has known than at any time in their recollection.

Mr. Sidney Webb freely acknowledges that the spirit of Owen abides with him. In his *Towards Social Democracy* in 1916 Mr. Webb reviews the tendencies of the past seventy-five years which have been, in his opinion, gradually substituting the collective action of the State for the private organisation of producers and consumers. Between 1840 and 1914 he discerns a growth of popular liberty probably unparalleled in any previous century. This liberty has been steadily marching towards Socialism by a "Fourfold Path." He perceives this path in the gradual extension of collective ownership and management, whether national or local, of land and industrial capital; the expansion of collective supervision over land and industrial capital still left in private hands; the gradual removal of existing inequalities by heavy taxation of rent and interest; and the provision of a national minimum for all classes that cannot obtain it for themselves.

A Constitution for the Socialist Commonwealth of Great Britain offered in 1920 the plan that Mr. and Mrs. Webb approved. In her fascinating account of *My Apprenticeship*, Mrs. Webb notes that "The 'Webb speciality' has been a study, at once historical and analytic, of the life-history of particular forms of social organisation within the United Kingdom." It is appropriate, accordingly, that they should remove the reproach of vagueness from Socialism. The old centralisation is replaced by a decentralising policy, and in place of the State we are invited to consider the group. Green and his followers have accomplished their work. Man is no longer the political animal contemplated by Aristotle. The Webbs clearly perceive that he has a bundle of relationships other than political. No doubt man is a citizen with a political interest in defence, police, and justice. This legal view of the State is far from sufficient. The State is much more than a mere police-State: it is in fact a culture-State as well. For we are asked to survey man with a care for cultural civilisation, as well as a care for his work as a producer and as a consumer. The Webbs cater for this fourfold view of man.

There are to be two equal and co-ordinate Parliaments, one political and one social. The members of both may be equal in number, are to be properly paid, expected to devote their full time to their work, and are elected from geographical constituencies. These two parliaments may differ in procedure, in terms of office for their members, and in day of election. for the authors of this scheme are anxious that the issues may be kept still further distinct. Each of these Parliaments consists of a single chamber. The executive ministers of the Political Parliament conform to the present Cabinet type, but this is not so with the Social Parliament. Its executive ministers are committees of its own members without the collective responsibility of the Cabinet. There will be committees of finance, of health, of education, of transport and communication, of mining, of economic and social research, of general purposes, and of any other national industry taken over from private owners. Plainly this Socialism will avoid the tyranny of an omnipotent State with universal control over all business. As long as there is an alternative, the tyranny of one Master—be he who he may—is avoided, and one Master inevitably means despotism. So long as there is any form of private business collectivism can acquire something from private ownership, and no doubt private ownership from collectivism. The Russian Commissary for Home Trade, Lezhava, acknowledged in 1924 that "the most remarkable phenomenon of recent times is the expansion of private trade, which now dominates the home market, especially in articles of current consumption and textile products. It is also gaining a monopoly of the wholesale supply of commodities to private retailers, who transact practically the whole retail business of the Soviet Union." Dzerzhinsky, head of the Supreme Economic Council, at the Conference of Industry and Transport, bore witness to the superior efficiency of the private trades, and confessed that the State textile trust transacted more than 56 per cent. of its sales through private traders. Rykoff, president of the Council of People's Commissaries, quoted figures to show that private traders demanded only from 5 to 15 per cent. for their services as the medium between producer and consumer whereas the State organs demanded no less than from 50 to 100 per cent.

It is clear that the Social Parliament will not have to seek for difficulties in the smooth working of its various committees. The members of this parliament are to be elected for a fixed term of office, and are not subject to dissolution except by a majority vote of its own members. The powers of each parliament are to be defined by statute, which of course means a written constitution. With Mr. Laski our authors place the final interpretation of any statute in the hands of the judges. They may declare any measure not authorised by the written constitution to be constitutional, though, unlike the procedure in the United States, the Webbs allow a joint session of the two parliaments to overrule the decision of the court. There will also be joint decisions when the decisions of one parliament may affect the other. For instance, a commercial treaty with a foreign State will affect both Parliaments. So too will the Budget. A knowledge of human nature suggests that agreement at these joint sessions will be by no means easy. In case of a deadlock, there is to be a double dissolution of the two Parliaments, and a reference to the electorate by referendum. Here, again, the referendum presents difficulties of its own. For if more than one issue is submitted, it is next to impossible to interpret what the wishes of the voters really means.

The Social Parliament is to devote special attention to the fourfold aspect of man's character. We suspect, however, that this Parliament—if ever it comes into existence—will pay more time and thought to man as a consumer than man as a producer. The appropriate committee will look after each industry, but decisions relating to the administration of the industry will lie with the industry itself. The group conception comes out in the administration of each industry by a tripartite National Board, composed of representatives of the management, of the consumers, and of the manual and clerical vocations. In turn each industry will be divided into districts, each in charge of tripartite District Boards, to which the National Board may grant a certain degree of autonomy. Each establishment will also have Works Committees composed perhaps exclusively of the representatives of the employed, and it will be the business of these Committees to make suggestions and discuss grievances. Special Boards will make appointments, and in appointing and promoting superior officials these Boards will consult the workmen.

This constitution for the British Socialist Commonwealth presupposes expert knowledge, and it is with reason that its authors say that "the deliberate intensification of this searchlight of published knowledge we regard as the corner-stone of successful Democracy." With this conclusion we find ourselves in thorough agreement. A doubt, however, steals over our mind. Socialism is no longer an ideal, but it is an ideal which has been translated into practice. No doubt the plan of the Webbs differs by worlds from that now being tried in Russia. The working of Communism in Russia suggests many matters to which all the committees of the Webbs lend themselves. Among these matters we certainly place the lavish employment of decrees. In the issue of these the Soviet Government is more prolific than the Tsar's Ministers. At the end of 1925 they occupied 2000 pages of print, and these decrees are far from being self-consistent. According to the *Voprosy Trood* it seems that "neither the officials of the Commissariat of Labour nor the trade unions can keep pace with the continuous flood of decrees and instructions." It is the weakness of all bureaucracy, and, decentralise it as much as we will, it remains the weakness of the committee. The ideal is not the real in Russia even to-day. The truth is that Socialists overrate human nature as much as Bentham ever did. The authors of these schemes are always public-spirited folk. If the men and women who executed them were also public-spirited, we should usher in the millennium, but are they? Where is the working ethical creed of Socialism? Where are all the experts to be found? How are we to safeguard them against the innate conservatism of a bureaucracy? How are two Parliaments to remain co-ordinate? Is not the lesson of history that one gains at the expense of the other? Till this result is achieved, will there not be deadlock after deadlock, working to the detriment of the public weal? Will not the multitude of the authorities in local government result in confusion and delay? The evils of our present Parliamentary government are manifest, but surely the evils of this scheme are more manifest.

If Mr. and Mrs. Sidney Webb think for themselves, it is obvious that in his *Socialism and Government,* which appeared in 1909, Mr. Ramsay MacDonald thinks for himself. His Socialism is, in his opinion, the true Socialism; but it is not that of other Socialists who are in prior possession of the field—at least ostensibly. It is too subtle and confusing. Take this definition, for instance: "The fundamental definition of Socialism is that, in work in which persons co-operate there should be organisation, and that when circumstances exist which allow a person or a class to take undue advantage of another person or class, these circumstances should be the subject of the control of all collectively in the interests of all individually." This takes us but a very little way, if indeed it takes us any way. The right and the duty of making any laws rest on that conception; they are restraints imposed by the collective will —whether exercised through a single head, a small or a large number of representatives, of a general assembly— to safeguard all individual members from oppression, and certain laws establishing the rights of property afford a conspicuous example. Their object is to guarantee possession of anything acquired by the individual against forcible dispossession by some one who happens to be strong enough to take it by force or cunning enough to take it by theft. Without such laws the strongest and most cunning dominate the rest. Mr. MacDonald would admit that; his Socialism permits and even encourages individual ownership of accumulated and inherited property. This is what he writes: "Certain is it that the organisation of the economic state which Socialists desire will not suppress but strengthen individual initiative and individual effort; and, so far from preventing property in those things which personality requires for its nourishment, it will in reality make it possible for the first time for every service-giver to own them. None of the inducements which accumulation now offers—from personal enjoyment to willing one's property to heirs—will be taken away under Socialism." What, then, will be taken away? "The opportunity of monopolising and using for his own purposes forms of property which when privately owned limit the liberty of great classes of persons."

Enough has been said to show how Mr. MacDonald's Socialism differs from more familiar brands. That difference extends to his views about government and the State, with which his book is mainly concerned. He thinks that the ordinary conceptions of Socialists are not truly Socialistic at all, but taken over from the individualistic traditions of the Radical party and rather anarchist than collectivist. He repudiates that conception of democracy which implies the right of the individual, or of a section of individuals, to rule, and the assumption that every individual is, for political purposes, the same as every other individual. He calls this the anti-Socialist spirit which "too often rears its head in our Socialism"; and one reason for writing this book is his desire to combat "influences inside the Socialist movement which are making for Anarchism rather than for Socialism, and for political ineptitude rather than for administrative efficiency." He denounces in strong terms the degradation of Parliament due to conduct thus inspired, and says that is how Socialism is to be retarded, not advanced.

His own view of government and the State springs from the conception of society which he has previously put forward. He goes to biology for his inspiration, and takes his ideas from an analogy which is not new, but has not been pushed so far before. He regards society as a living organism, composed of different organs differentiated in function but all working together for the Whole and the Each—to use the language in vogue among the intellectuals of Socialism. At the same time we desire to note that while metaphors or analogies are very useful aids to exposition, they become traps for fallacy unless applied with great discretion, especially for those who have no technical knowledge of the subject from which they are drawn. The broad idea of a living organism composed of mutually interdependent parts which have grown together is illuminating because it involves the truth that change must be gradual and no large disruption can take place with safety, but when extended into details it becomes misleading. Mr. MacDonald, following up his idea, regards industry as the nutritive process and the State as the nervous system or organ of control. The central authority is therefore indispensable, marking thereby his disagreement with the Marxian view that the State eventually becomes unnecessary and dies out. He condemns that view, which is based on Hegelian metaphysics, whereas the true view—his own—is based on Darwinian science. In truth, the "scientific" basis laid by Marx, before which we have been bidden to bow, now turns out to be not scientific at all.

That the State is an organ of society and the embodiment of the general will is clearly accepted by Mr. MacDonald. It is not a coercive authority nor a majority ruling by force, but "something of the nature of an organic body in which the various organs find a place in a unified personality and discover their liberty in that personality." It follows that the Radical idea of majority rule is wrong; the member of Parliament is not a delegate, but the representative of society which Burke conceived him to be. From this Mr. MacDonald proceeds to discuss a number of political problems in the light of these notions. He condemns the referendum as based on the same wrong idea, and does not think much better of proportional representation, which would weaken the representative character of legislation. Its fundamental error lies in regarding Parliament as a mirror of opinion, whereas it is the "active will of the State." With regard to parties he upholds them as stoutly as Mr. Lawrence Lowell, for he upholds programmes, which imply parties, and thinks two the right number; but the writer of 1909, not the statesman of 1924 or 1929, thinks that a Socialist party is quite wrong. "The Socialist assumptions are like the light and air," and what is wanted is a party that will "journey towards Socialism." Group government is bad, but party government is also faulty, mainly on account of excess of Cabinet and party control. He advocates shorter Parliaments. The Monarchy may be let alone as possessing some utilitarian value, but a second Chamber is a mistake, and should be replaced by a technical Revision Committee, composed of Law Lords. These naturally lead on to a consideration of the Empire, and Mr. MacDonald leans to Imperialism, thinking that large federations are in certain respects beneficial. He does not bestow much space upon finance, but what he writes is very significant. He derives revenue mainly from money arising from natural monopolies like land, politically created monopolies like liquor licences and profits on such communal services as the post, gas, and trams. Mr. MacDonald gives us his solution of our economic difficulties. The champion of a solution believes that his key fits every door and no other key fits any; but there are many doors and many keys.

The Socialism of Mr. Ramsay MacDonald is not the type in favour in Leningrad. He recognises what Socialism can and cannot undertake to perform, and miracles he does not reckon among the possibilities. The ape and the tiger in man have been controlled, but there remains that singularly intractable animal, the donkey in man. The stupidity as well as the self-interestedness of humanity is to be reckoned with. Socialism, in the Marxian sense, is to our author a frank impossibility. But what about social reform? That is another matter altogether, and of course it is well within the bounds of possibility. So we see in his 1921 survey of *Socialism, Critical and Constructive*. Social democracy and social reform, we learn, are pretty well synonymous terms, a conception which would give a shock to an older school of Socialists. There will be communal control of finance without which society can never escape from exploitation. The colossal blunders of Whitehall will cease—or begin on a larger scale. In a speech at Dundee in September, 1924, when he was Prime Minister Mr. MacDonald confessed that he could not fulfil Socialist pledges, and this non-fulfilment was not due to the hostile majority present in the House of Commons. The time was not ripe: "it would be cutting green corn," so he announced. Even were he to remain Prime Minister for fifty years, "the pledges I have given you from my heart would still be unfulfilled—not because I fainted or failed, but because the corn was still green." In September, 1924, he had been eight months in office, and difficulties not keenly perceived in the cool shades of opposition contrive to present themselves in a fashion impossible to be ignored by the Prime Minister faced with the task of putting a scheme into operation. These difficulties are even more keenly perceived in June, 1929. Lenin overlooked these difficulties to be confronted with an increase of individualism on a scale unprecedented in the annals of the world, and to receive the reports of his officials that the whole of agricultural Russia had turned individualist, and that in the retail trade the private owner had beaten the State. Confronted with facts like these, Mr. Ramsay MacDonald was forced to acquiesce in the verdict of the individualist thinkers who demonstrate that the establishment of Socialism, in his day at any rate, is an utter impossibility. Once upon a time Socialism was to be realised in a remarkably short period, but that was before the Socialists assumed office. "Capture the County Councils," cried Mrs. Besant in 1889 to the Fabian Society and Socialism will come. The astute men who bestowed that name upon this Society were wiser, far wiser, than they ever dreamt. The Fabian policy beat Carthage, and it may beat individualism—some day. Capture the Cabinet, and Socialism will come. Now the Prime Minister postpones the date of the victory to the Greek Kalends. In the eighties Mr. Bernard Shaw was asked how long it would take to set up Socialism. He cheerfully answered, "about a fortnight." Mr. and Mrs. Sidney Webb surveyed the fourfold aspect of man's character, but, needless to say, their survey is far from exhaustive. No doubt man is a citizen, a consumer, a producer, and a culturist, but he is many things besides. He has a family with all that a family means. He has his amusements with all that they mean. Above all, he has to earn his living with all that it means. The outcome of all his interests, as well as his fourfold aspect, is that he is not in the least degree class conscious. Agitators may say that he is, but the occasions when the general will makes its presence felt demonstrate his lack of class consciousness.

organised on a vocational basis. The syndicate is the cell of the new order. The local workers in a trade, organised into this unit, will exercise complete control over all matters concerning that trade, but all capital used by the workers will be owned in common by all the syndicates. Pelloutier, one of the Syndicalist leaders, affirms that "the task of the revolution is to free mankind not only from all authority, but also from every institution which has not for its essential purpose the development of production."

Biassed with all their strength against the State, the Syndicalists abhor all manner of political action. How can the State, they argue, built on force and obedience, in which the initiative comes from politicians, rulers and demagogues, agree with a philosophy demanding a minimum of restraint and the initiation of all movements for social improvement by the workers themselves? Whatever is to be preserved, the State must be destroyed. Its gradual disintegration is inevitable. Its inherent defects will cause a series of violent explosions, each of which will tend to weaken its power. What natural explosions will not effect, artificial ones in the shape of direct action will effect. The employed must wage a never-ceasing warfare with the employers. The weapons are the strike and sabotage. The strike is of course the main weapon. Ultimately there will be a general strike of all the workers. In Sorel's language this general strike is to be a "myth" to the workers, a myth being an idea which fills men with ardour, as the expectation of Christ's second coming inspired the early Christians. The purpose of the general strike can be fulfilled by lesser ones. For, according to Sorel, sporadic strikes "have engendered in the proletariat the noblest, deepest, and most moving sentiments they possess; the general strike groups them all in a co-ordinated picture, and by bringing them all together, gives to each one of them its maximum intensity. . . . We thus obtain that intuition of socialism which language cannot give with perfect clearness, and we obtain it as a whole, perceived instantaneously."

There are many forms of sabotage. You can break machinery, you can blow up workshops, and you can blow up recalcitrant workmen along with them. You can persistently turn out bad work, you can spoil work already done, you can obey the letter of all rules exactly and literally in such a way as to prevent industry being carried on, you can use the policy of the label and the boycott, and you can invariably pursue the plan of "ca' canny." Knowledge is decried, for it is always a false ethical guide. It is much better to trust intuition, sentiment, enthusiasm, passion, or even religious fervour, than any form of human wisdom. As there is to be no State, naturally there cannot be any general will: it is a mere "fiction." Majority rule is of course inert, clumsy, conservative, and hence always stands in the way of progress. In the United States ten per cent. of the Syndicalists control the action of the workers.

Among the arguments for the new order is the consideration that it stands as a protection against the corruption of modern politics. Does it not allow of the development of original dispositions now thwarted? Will not the inferiority complex dissappear? Will it not allay the sense of discontent which threatens the very existence of the State? Does it not substitute an organised and voluntary sovereignty for an external and involuntary one?

On the other hand, its opponents observe that we cannot over-emphasise the unity and the solidarity of the group. If the porter of a college and the professor belong to the education group, what homogeneity of interest is there between them? May we not obscure the individuality of the units composing it? Will not Syndicalism give rise to competing guild selfishness? Will not such key-industries as the railroads, the mines and the light and power services employ their economic position to increase wages and decrease the hours in these industries? Will not some industries limit the numbers engaged in them and become monopolistic? Will the best business man or the best talker rise to the top? Mr. Wallas defines liberty as the "capacity for continuous initiative." Will syndicalism allow full room for the development of this capacity? Does it not substitute the chaos of particular wills for the cosmos of the general will? Is not a human being a complex of relationships? Do not these diverse relationships require diverse treatment? Will not the separate bodies give rise to confusion, especially in the domain of finance? Does not syndicalism over-emphasise the economic aspects of society? If it encourages local variation, will it not also encourage local anarchy? Did not the absence of a central authority in the Middle Ages encourage strife between the guilds?

Long ago Burke discerned sectionalism as the enemy. Writing to the Sheriffs of Bristol concerning his membership of the House of Commons, he informed them that "Parliament is not a congress of ambassadors from different and hostile interests, which interests each must maintain as an agent and advocate against other agents and advocates; but parliament is a deliberative assembly of *one* nation with *one* interest, that of the whole; where not local purposes, not local prejudices ought to guide, but the general good resulting from the general interest of the whole. You choose a member indeed, but when you have chosen him he is not the member of Bristol, but he is a member of parliament," the doctrine to which Mr. Ramsay MacDonald subscribes.

The objections to Syndicalism do not press with quite the same weight against Guild Socialism. Its aim is to reduce the activities of the State, notably in the field of economic control. Its advocates assume that the gravest evil of the moment is the complete ordering of the working life of man by the capitalists. Mr. Cole holds that "the state should own the means of production, the guild should control the work of production." So the worker will be emancipated from what Mr. Hobson terms slavery or "wagery" which is far worse than poverty, for "poverty is the symptom—slavery the disease. The many are not enslaved because they are poor; they are poor because they are enslaved." The remedy is that each industry should organise itself into a guild. No novelist save Mr. Butler, and no guildsman save Mr. Penty, proposes that machinery should, in imitation of the mediaeval guild, be discarded for handicraft, and that society should return to small self-sufficing units. The co-ordinating centre of the guild society will be the commune, composed of representatives of the consumers' councils and of the guilds. Mr. Cole's guild state will practically be a federation of groups. We learn that it is by industrial action, not by political, that the guild society will owe its creation. Mr. Cole believes that "apart from capitalistic blunders, a catastrophe will be necessary to end the wage-system." The historian, however, notes that the records of the old guilds are not very encouraging. They soon developed the tendency to change into close oligarchies, which Professor Michels predicates of all democratic groups; and for the most part they ended as close and oppressive corporations. In the heyday of their power their internecine quarrels proved a fruitful source of civic war. Nor is the possibility of similar development under the *régime* of Guild Socialism altogether remote.

Communism is defined in the *Manifesto*, the work of Marx and Engels, issued in 1848. It is Socialism accompanied by means of the class war and the revolutionary power of the proletariat. As Engels points out, "The party which has triumphed in the revolution is necessarily compelled to maintain its rule by means of the fear with which its arms inspire the reactionaries. If the Commune of Paris had not based itself on the authority of the armed people against the bourgeoisie, would it have maintained itself more than four-and-twenty hours?" According to Marx, "in order to break down the resistance of the bourgeoisie the workers invest the State with a revolutionary and temporary form."

Marx remained whole-hearted in his convictions to the end of his life. In this respect the master is above his disciples, for the leakage of leaders from the ranks of Socialism is not a little remarkable. In England we have John Burns, George N. Barnes, G. H. Roberts and Sir David Shackleton; in France we have Clemenceau, Millerand, Briand, and Viviani; and in Germany we have David, Noske and Scheidemann. Once upon a time these were advanced men, yet gradually they assumed a relatively conservative position. To-day we are apt to forget the fact that Clemenceau, for instance, began his long career as a communist. No doubt these men have become disillusioned through the pessimism engendered by the experience of life. Some have come to dislike the argument of force advocated by Marx and Lenin, and have come to like the force of argument.

The motive of social service ought to be the common weal, yet somehow in the working of the corporation self-interest seems to prevail. The classical economists assumed the existence of an economic man, but no one actually ever found such a man. The Socialists assume the existence of an "ethical" man, but have they actually found many such men? If the economic man is a monster from the nether world, the ethical man, portrayed by the Socialists, is an angel who will not walk on mother earth. That Fabian Socialist, Mr. Bernard Shaw, believes that democracy is merely the substitution of the incompetent many for the corrupt few. Civic enlightenment is conspicuous by its absence and the existence of this circumstance occasions Mr. Wallas grave concern. Professor M'Dougall holds that "mankind is only a little bit reasonable, and to a great extent unintelligently moved in quite unreasonable ways." According to Mr. Bernard Shaw, "we must eliminate the Yahoo, or his vote will wreck the commonwealth." Is there truth in his pungent criticism that "there is no sincere public opinion that a man should work for his daily bread, if he can get it for nothing"? An English Guild Socialist like Mr. Cole announces that "in this country at least it is useless to invoke public opinion, because it is selfish, unenlightened and Vindictive"; and the marks of our people are "narrowness, egoism, and intellectual indolence." When he has demonstrated how little thought actually enters into the political life of the individual, Mr. Wallas urges the social organisation of thought as a method of attaining a more rational basis of behaviour. The truth is that Socialists assume that human nature is malleable, yet trained observers like Mr. M'Dougall and Mr. Wallas are rather sceptical of its malleability.

Mankind cannot be changed in a day any more than schemes can become successful in a day. Lord Randolph Churchill accused Mr. Gladstone of being an old man in a hurry, and it seems to us that some Socialists are young men in a hurry. It is, as Burke reminds us, by the slow "discipline of nature" that plans at last come to fruition. The Irish philosopher exclaimed with penetrating reason, "Alas! they little know how many a weary step is to be taken before they can form themselves into a mass which has a truly politic personality."

People require knowledge for the guidance of their political life just as much as their leaders require enlightenment. A brilliant American, Mr. Lippmann, postulates the theory that the new ideal can be found in the idea of Mastery—an ever-increasing mastery founded on an ever-increasing knowledge of man over nature and equally—this is very important—over himself. Let us imagine the vision that it would imply. On the material side we might see disease and suffering reduced to narrower and narrower limits; the soil rendered productive to the utmost limits of its capacity; the amenities of life in town and country made as sweet and wholesome, and therefore, as beautiful as art and science can together accomplish, the *joie de vivre* made as real in work as in recreation. On the moral side we might see the full and fearless mastery of man over himself; the principle of religion recognised and acted upon; the study of the human intellect, emotions and instincts undertaken in order that their limitations might be guarded against, and their potentialities developed, and institutions adapted to the known needs of human nature, and not constructed to *a priori* principle. Science—that is exact and ordered knowledge in all departments, and not merely the subjects discussed at meetings of the Royal Society—would be enthroned as the arbiter of affairs, and every problem would be approached upon a foundation of the best knowledge available. One had only to look at any aspect of life to realise how far such an ideal is from being conceived, much less realised; in fact, in many of the most important departments of life exact knowledge is regarded as an impertinence rather than as an essential.

Ordered knowledge forms an ideal, a worthy ideal; so too does liberty. The belief of our fathers in liberty seems to have deserted the present generation. Yet its virtues inspired Byron and Shelley and Wordsworth in his loftiest moods as they inspired Godwin and Hazlitt. In Shelley's *Ode to Liberty*, and in a thousand effusions breathing the same spirit, we feel the sense of mankind prematurely entombed shaking off its grave clothes and emerging vigorous and confident to enjoy that life of which authority would cheat it. Passionate utterances for liberty as a blessing in itself are now rare. Do we hear, ask men, in their place loftier strains? Where and what are the poets of authority? Critics observe that Fabian Socialism has been for a quarter of a century the creed of many men of letters, but their lips have not been touched with the sacred fire. The Russian no doubt hesitates to be openly rapturous over the bonds and shackles, the multitude of punishments, small and great, which are necessary if men are to be drilled into conformity with his system. The rage for controlling everything and everybody, men note, along with the presence of the anarchical spirit forms a characteristic of our age. Yet those who are most active in promoting the incessant interference of the bureaucrat are the very first to disregard these restrictions when in conflict with their own interests. It is the soil upon which flourishes the irreconcilable, the impracticable enthusiast who must have his own way, even if society be wrecked. It is also the soil that seems to refuse to nourish the feeling for liberty. The deepest and most enduring matters always find fit poetic utterance. What the poet does not sing does not last.

Mazzini felt impressed by the inestimable spiritual dignity and incalculable moral worth of each individual member of the human race. With the same sense of ethical value Kant contended that each man was an end in himself, and not a mere means to some other end, however exalted. "In conception at least," Professor Dewey powerfully maintains, "democracy approaches most nearly to the ideal of all social organisation, viz. that in which the individual and society are organic to each other. . . . The individual embodies and realises within himself the spirit and will of the whole organism. . . . The individual is society concentrated; he is the local manifestation of its life. . . . Thus every citizen is a sovereign; a doctrine which in grandeur has but one equal in history, viz. that every man is a priest of God."

Idealism in politics has enlisted such splendid adherents as T. H. Green and his school. Whatever we may think of its purely philosophical position, we can cordially assent to the proposition of Bosanquet that what we are to work for is a purification of the will of the State. States in which the supreme, non-competitive, humanising values—knowledge, art, religion, human sympathy between classes—are dominant in the lives of their citizens will live in peace with one another. According to Bosanquet "the Kingdom of God has come on earth in every civilised society where men live and work together, doing their best for the whole society and for mankind. When two or three are gathered together, co-operating for a social good, there is the Divine Spirit in the midst of them." In short, the State for man can become a spiritual phenomenon, and citizenship can form a great spiritual experience. For, as Horace Bushnell put it, the soul of all improvement is the improvement of the soul.

It may be surprising but is certainly true that the virtues which are continuously preached to each generation are precisely those which it already possesses in the greatest abundance. The ages of faith, like the Middle Ages, preach the need of faith; the ages of reason, like the eighteenth century, preach the need of reason; and the ages of Socialism, the twentieth century, preach the need of Socialism. There was probably never a time when the thought of God, the consciousness of His presence, and the claims of His service were so common among the people of England, whether Puritan or Anglican, as in the seventeenth century; and these were the very subjects with which all the pulpits rang. So to-day because the "service of man" is the preoccupation, almost the passion of our day, that is the one virtue to the exclusion of all others which is incessantly urged upon us by our preachers, both clerical and lay. What is new in our social situation is not its evils but our consciousness of them and our determination to remove them. Even in many of the churches the calls for faith and reverence and the love of God, for truth and honesty, and humility and meekness—nay, even for Pauline charity—are almost silent before the insistent claims of social service. Yet it is quite certain that neither faith nor hope nor charity has increased in at all the same proportion. Herein lies the strength—as well as the weakness—of Socialism.

Index

PRINTED BY
W. HEFFER & SONS LTD
CAMBRIDGE